China in 2008

China in 2008

A Year of Great Significance

EDITED BY KATE MERKEL-HESS,
KENNETH L. POMERANZ, AND
JEFFREY N. WASSERSTROM

with Miri Kim

Foreword by Jonathan D. Spence

ROWMAN & LITTLEFIELD PUBLISHERS, INC.
Lanham • Boulder • New York • Toronto • Plymouth, UK

ROWMAN & LITTLEFIELD PUBLISHERS, INC.

Published in the United States of America
by Rowman & Littlefield Publishers, Inc.
A wholly owned subsidiary of The Rowman & Littlefield Publishing Group, Inc.
4501 Forbes Boulevard, Suite 200, Lanham, Maryland 20706
www.rowmanlittlefield.com

Estover Road, Plymouth PL6 7PY, United Kingdom

British Library Cataloguing in Publication Information Available

Library of Congress Cataloging-in-Publication Data

China in 2008 : a year of great significance / edited by Kate Merkel-Hess, Kenneth L.
Pomeranz, and Jeffrey N. Wasserstrom.
p.   cm.
ISBN-13: 978-0-7425-6659-0 (cloth : alk. paper)
ISBN-10: 0-7425-6659-5 (cloth : alk. paper)
ISBN-13: 978-0-7425-6660-6 (pbk. : alk. paper)
ISBN-10: 0-7425-6660-9 (pbk. : alk. paper)
1. China—History—2002– I. Merkel-Hess, Kate, 1976–   II. Pomeranz, Kenneth.
III. Wasserstrom, Jeffrey N.
DS779.4.C45   2009
951.06—dc22   2008047536

Printed in the United States of America

∞ ™ The paper used in this publication meets the minimum requirements of American
National Standard for Information Sciences—Permanence of Paper for Printed Library
Materials, ANSI/NISO Z39.48-1992.

Contents

CHAPTER 15: CHINA AND THE UNITED STATES, 275

Foreword

Jonathan D. Spence

Despite the endless ways in which humans have chosen to express themselves, the genre of history-writing has proven to be fairly uniform. In countless cultures, over the centuries, the writing of history has been seen as a multilayered discipline, drawing from the experiences and ideas that gave definition to a particular span of time. The sorting and arranging of this legacy into patterns or structures could be seen to give definition to the past, and also to help us interpret and even understand past actions and their possible impact on the future. History-writing was believed to have achieved its goal if it could orchestrate those multilayered moments and images into a coherent structure, one that followed certain rather simple rules so as to convey a sense of order that lay at the heart of human hopes and actions.

Bias was accepted, as was ideological conformity, but a work of history could be conceived of as "finished" only when it had been organized into a structure that allowed for consistency, proportion, and accessibility. In this it was perhaps not totally unlike the discipline of architecture, in which great effort also went into concealing the component units that made the structure workable, in order for the façade and the function to form a unity that would be both practical and aesthetically powerful. Once the history had been shaped into its coherent form the historian (like the architect) could withdraw to the sidelines.

At various times over the last century, however, architects have chafed under these restrictions, and seen it as a fundamental aspect of their discipline to reveal every layer of their labor in terms of materials used and texture. Historians, though open to aesthetic experimentation, emerging technologies for research and retrieval, new inclusiveness in terms of subject and interpretation, and even expressed desires for reaching a more comprehensive readership, were usually more guarded and less prone to expose the sinews of their labors; they still believed their work could be completed in a definitive form, with some variation of a "beginning, middle, and end" and some confidence that such a procedure remained comfortably accessible to the society in which they lived and for which they wrote. But Internet search engines, instant messaging, blogging, and the culture of total accessibility and unconditional sharing have cumulatively projected the discipline out into new terrain, where old rules no longer apply and new ones have not yet been formed—and maybe never will be.

These ruminations were prompted by reading *China in 2008: A Year of Great Significance*, for this is not a conventional book but more a collection of materials waiting to be a book. On the surface, some of the old rules may still be relevant here: we have, after all, a central subject, the year 2008, and a location, China. And we have several themes of considerable power and resonance that assure us that this was indeed a "year of great significance," both for the Chinese and for those non-Chinese interested in tracking events and trends in that country. 2008 was the year that saw the global drama of the Olympics unfold in Beijing, along with the often-angry contestations over the routing and the symbolism of the Olympic flame. The same year saw rioting and death in Tibet and its borders, the vibrant elections and leadership change in Taiwan, murders of Chinese and Uighurs in Xinjiang, checks to the spread of democratic institutions in Hong Kong, mining disasters in Shanxi, Politburo debates concerning the nature and duration of rural contracts in the countryside, disastrous cold-weather patterns in southern China that paralyzed the lunar new year celebrations for many millions, a bewildering assemblage of often-fatal product tampering that had worldwide impact, in Sichuan Province a terrible earthquake rendered all the more agonizing by the fact that collapsing school buildings led to the deaths of many thousands of Chinese children, and at the year's end the economic crisis affecting the United States was clearly also having a powerful negative effect on China's economy.

But unlike earlier generations of histories, *China in 2008* is not in the business of explaining all this to us, or linking the various factors into a conceptual pattern. It hints at explanations for some of the juxtapositions, certainly, and draws on the knowledge of a wide roster of journalists, scholars, bloggers, historians, eye witnesses, and participants, fifty-three in all by my count, many of whom have original insights to share. They write in many modes, at widely varied lengths, with many motives, and their cumulative contributions build up a montage of sources from which a coherent narrative might at some future time be drawn. There is more than enough here to keep any reader intrigued and instructed. There is also an implicit challenge to all of us concealed within this volume's particular shape and discursiveness. In this new world of communication, the guts of the entire structure stand revealed, and all of us are free—one could even say induced—to make our own links and pass our own judgment. Probably few of us, after reading this collection, will challenge the basic statement that 2008 was a year of great significance. But whether 2008 was of unusually great significance is a different question altogether. To answer it, we will have to compare 2008 with previous years in this often riven and damaged society, and attempt to make an informed comparative judgment on China's past. And at the same time we will have to don the prophet's mantle, as we strive to conjure out of cryptic utterances some sense of what China's future holds in store for all of us.

Introduction

China in 2008

Reflections on a Year of Great Significance

The subtitle of this volume is a play on Ray Huang's groundbreaking Ming history, *1587: A Year of No Significance*. In that book, Huang examined a year of no particular importance when the emperor Wanli was in power. The irony of Huang's title is that Wanli's disastrous reign was the beginning of the end for the Ming dynasty (1368–1644), which fell to internal rebellions and then the Manchu invasions that led to the establishment of the Qing dynasty (1644–1911), China's last. Fifteen eighty-seven matters a great deal because, while it was not a year of important events, it was apparent in its day-to-day affairs that the Ming was headed toward ruin.

The year 2008, in contrast, was a year of important event after important event for China. In fact, the year was enormously important globally, both for stories that pointed the way toward a new world order (geopolitically and financially) and for stories that seemed resurrected from news cycles past. In the early panicked days of the fall's economic woes, coming amidst the U.S. presidential campaign as well as several other big domestic and international stories, David Folkenflik commented on National Public Radio that "the breakneck pace of developments means a lot of news worth knowing receives the briefest burst of attention before being dropped for something hotter." The riots in Tibet and the contentious U.S. Democratic primaries pushed rising international food prices off the front pages. Russia's invasion of Georgia coincided with the highly anticipated Olympic opening ceremony. China's tainted milk story was overshadowed by the U.S. presidential election and the escalating credit crisis.

China's presence in many international stories, from the banking crisis to the genocide in Darfur, was further evidence of its role as an emerging superpower. Just as Russia did for previous generations, China raises the specter for Americans of a functioning superpower with a markedly different economic system as well as a divergent set of political assumptions (several contributors explore the results of these fears in chapter 15). In July, *New York Times* columnist Thomas Friedman wrote about the Chinese (and Russian) vetoes of UN attempts to impose sanctions on Robert Mugabe, president of Zimbabwe. The votes, Friedman asserted, show us where the world is headed: "a world of too much Russian and Chinese power." Some China fearmongers went further than the moderate Friedman, talking about "the coming China wars." But the fact was that the China stories of 2008, taken together, sketch a picture of a China not on the verge of destruction, as in 1587, or a nation spoiling for a fight with the international community but instead a relatively stable country, focused above all else on trying to maintain its phenomenal annual 10 percent economic growth rate.

This may seem an incongruous assertion, as other than the relatively smooth two weeks of China's triumphant Beijing Olympics, when China was in the international news in 2008, it was at moments of crisis: crippling winter storms hit the country in late January, riots occurred throughout Tibet and other parts of southwest China in March, international protests accompanied the spring's Olympic torch relay, a devastating earthquake rocked Sichuan in May, a massive food safety scandal broke in September, in October a plummeting stock market hit the Shanghai and Hong Kong stock exchanges as well as the New York, London, and Tokyo exchanges, and in November widespread labor protests broke out as the economy slowed. Instead of a year of Olympic celebration, for the Chinese people 2008 was the most tumultuous and traumatic year of the post-1978 economic reform era. Unlike 1587, however, we cannot discern in China's day-to-day life signs of impending doom. Business as usual looked pretty good: the economy continued to grow and consumers continued to spend, China continued to increase international engagements, and all signs pointed to continued (if incremental) increases in citizen participation in government affairs.

Despite the overall impression that China is generally doing well but had a tough 2008, it is still too early to predict how the year will be remembered in the decades and centuries to come. That didn't stop a group of China scholars and journalists from trying to figure it out. In January 2008, this group, founded by two faculty members in the history department at the University of California, Irvine (UCI), launched a blog called *China Beat* in order to chronicle what we felt certain would be a newsworthy year for China and one in which international interest in all things China would run high. As a result, *China Beat* (for which I've served as the first editor) recorded 2008's events as they happened, bringing to bear a deep collective knowledge of context and history to the analysis of these events. The goal was in part to engage cutting-edge scholarship with contemporary events and to contextualize China and Chinese history in world events, both particular emphases of the history program at UCI. But founders Kenneth Pomeranz and Jeffrey Wasserstrom also wanted to bring together China watchers from diverse backgrounds, including college faculty from a variety of disciplines, graduate students, and journalists. In this sense, *China Beat* fostered not only a community of readers but also a community of writers.

Over the past twelve months, this community has struggled to contextualize the events of 2008 and try to figure out what their future importance might be. These efforts reflected a larger project among international commentators and China watchers to sort out the meaning of 2008's events. For instance, some commentators wondered if hosting the Olympics would change China and, if so, in what ways (though one founding contributor to the blog, anthropologist Susan Brownell, stressed throughout the lead-up to the Games that we also consider the ways that China might change the Olympics). Just as some observers feel the 1988 Seoul Games signaled the beginning of Korea's emergence as an economic powerhouse and democratic nation, so too did some members of the international community hope that in anticipation of the coming Games, the Chinese people would be granted greater freedoms. Others feared a coming human rights crackdown as Beijing geared up for its international unveiling. Some hoped China would fall into line on environmental and safety regulations, but others predicted greater degradation as Beijing and other Olympic venues around the country underwent a massive facelift and restructuring. Some hoped China would express its support for international norms, others feared the competitive games would provoke violent nationalist demonstrations. (For examples of these Olympic reflections, see chapters 8, 9, and 10.)

None of those hopes or fears were realized during the largely subdued August days of the Games. In the end, one of the few tangible results of the Olympics as of this writing is that Beijing has permanently adopted (to the overwhelming disapproval of local residents) an altered version of the vehicle restrictions that were in place prior to and during the Olympics in an effort to reduce pollution and street traffic. But there were other glimmers—in the Olympic planning and execution but mostly elsewhere—of important shifts in China in 2008.

Starting at the top, it appears that Chinese national leaders are redefining their relationship to Chinese citizens; 2008 saw some of the highest-ranking Chinese Communist Party (CCP) figures communicating in incredibly casual ways with the Chinese people, and the Chinese people responding warmly. As several *China Beat* writers noted (and we've published some of these essays in chapter 11), this is not a new phenomenon. Mao Zedong was famously photographed at several points "among the people," particularly during the early days of the Cultural Revolution, as when he swam across the Yangtze River in July 1966 or when he reviewed the Red Guards in Tiananmen Square a month later. And Jiang Zemin, who was president of the People's Republic of China (PRC) from 1993 to 2003, was known for impromptu piano recitals. When visiting the United States in 1997, newspapers heralded him as China's "folksy" leader after he attempted to play the steel guitar on a Hawaiian beach. But the Chinese people didn't warm to Jiang the way they reached out to "Grandpa Wen," or Premier Wen Jiabao, in 2008.

This is what made 2008 different—the increasing affection and familiarity for China's national leaders, facilitated by technologies like the Internet that brought Premier Wen Jiabao and President Hu Jintao right into China's homes. Though Wen has always had a populist's touch, in 2008 he began to be available and personable with the news media in a way that, while familiar for a politician in the United States, seems strange for a man who has never stood for popularly elected office. When Wen showed up in Sichuan after the earthquake, he was photographed holding hands with parents grieving for their dead children, tears in his eyes. Through a bullhorn, he exhorted still-buried children to hang on until rescuers could unearth them. And in September, when thousands of babies were sickened by melamine-tainted milk powder, Wen Jiabao ordered inspections and called for increased regulation. President Hu Jintao is a leader in the older style, but even he reached out in 2008, sitting in for the first-ever Web chat between a Chinese leader and Chinese "netizens."

It is possible to cynically read both Hu and Wen's steps as belated attempts at public relations by a Chinese government that was being battered by the media abroad. At home, however, Chinese people broadly express satisfaction with the national government (it is the local corrupt officials at whom they directed their ire). So why bother? Given Wen's political background—in the late 1980s he was chief of staff for Zhao Ziyang, who so famously pleaded with the students protesting in Tiananmen in 1989 to leave the square and voted against the martial law regulation that led to the June 4 massacre—it is quite possible that he believes the government should be more responsive to the people. But the fact that national leaders' expressions of solidarity resonated with the Chinese people also indicates a shifting relationship between citizens and government—one in which the Chinese people feel that some government leaders are working on their behalf and one in which government leaders are eager to convince Chinese people that they feel concern and empathy for regular people's lives.

This may strike many Westerners as odd, as China is so often portrayed in Western media as a totalitarian state, and the two things—concern for the people and one-party rule—don't seem compatible. But the Chinese state, even in imperial times, was particularly concerned with the stability and contentment of its population, which it maintained by storing massive amounts of grain in case of famine and shoring up river banks, among many other large-scale public works. These efforts to safeguard the population from harm have continued under the Communists—as evidenced by rapid evacuations, often multiple times per year, of tens of thousands of coastal residents in advance of deadly typhoons making landfall.

In 2008, this kind of responsiveness was evident in the quick and effective response to May's earthquake in Sichuan. Watching the prompt care offered to survivors, many Americans compared it favorably to the bumbling management and partisan bickering that characterized the U.S. government's response to the flooding and death in New Orleans following 2005's Hurricane Katrina. Important as this kind of effective response to disaster is to a government's legitimacy, in 2008 Chinese officials renewed their efforts to salve the national soul in addition to proffering material assistance.

The second notable trend in 2008 was less about dramatic change than the continued efforts by the government to uphold its end of a crumbling social welfare bargain. Ever since the 1978 reform and opening policies were adopted, state social services have decreased for the majority of Chinese people. The state once took care of health care, education, job placement, housing, and any number of other daily life issues. In the 1980s and 1990s, many of these services were privatized (or, in the case of public education, school fees for individual families increased dramatically). As the economic burdens for families grew, the gap between the haves and the have-nots has widened, a gap even more pronounced when comparing increasingly affluent urban areas to neglected rural ones. But what is rarely discussed are the government's continued efforts to meet the needs of its citizens in both the city and the countryside. In recent years, this has included establishing pilot projects at the county level to provide pensions to the elderly and eliminating all agricultural taxes (for the first time ever in Chinese history).

Responses to the government's mostly inadequate measures vary from country to city and among classes of people. In 2008, Western media paid a lot of attention to a jump in the prominence of middle-class protests in China as one response to the Chinese government (a topic covered in detail in chapter 1). The middle class makes up an increasing component of the Chinese population, particularly in the cities, where estimates indicate that the middle class will soon constitute over 40 percent of the urban population (though, since it is a relatively new term, debates continue in China about what makes one "middle class"). The protests of these urban, professional, educated Chinese are part of a trend toward small-scale, local-centered demonstrations in China. Even though commentators made much a few years ago of the rapidly rising numbers of small-scale protests in China—in 2005, for instance, numerous Western media outlets noted a rise in reported protests, giving numbers ranging from 60,000 to 150,000 separate incidents—these numbers alone tell us very little, as they include protests involving only a handful of people to those that involved thousands and were over issues as varied as land seizures, environmental degradation, or protests of local policies. What we *do* know about these protests is that most were *local* in nature and that their issues (such as land seizures by the township government to build a new shopping center) were decidedly local as well—we are not talking about a web of organized protests aimed at undermining the central government.

Among these thousands of protests, China watchers picked out the emerging number of middle-class protests centered around environmental and lifestyle issues as particularly important. In 2008, a new form of urban protest emerged. The handful of well-covered demonstrations took the form of organized "strolls" in which groups of protesters, notified by text message of location and time, walked leisurely down the same street at the same time. Since organizers of demonstrations must apply for permits in China (and the permits are almost universally denied), the "stroll" circumvents those regulations. This is not a new tactic—after street protests were outlawed in Belgrade in late 1996, Yugoslavians protesting Slobodan Milosevic's rule all brought their dogs out for walks at the same time—yet it is a novel addition to the Chinese urban protest repertoire.

But expressions of dissatisfaction were equally (if not more) likely to come out online, where, despite government efforts to control the discourse, Chinese "netizens" were constantly contriving new ways to circumvent filters and censors (for more on the Chinese Internet and censorship, see the essays in chapter 12). Sometimes online demands for increased government response were quite straightforward—as in the calls for increased government regulation of the food system after thousands of babies were sickened by tainted milk powder or the grumbling, early in 2008, over the rapidly rising price of food staples. Often, though, dissatisfaction was expressed in clever puns and online memes.

One such example occurred after a violent riot in the town of Weng'an in June 2008. Thousands of residents rioted in the Guizhou city after a girl was found drowned in a local river. It was perceived that the main suspects in her death had ties to local government officials and that officials had ruled the death a suicide to protect her murderers. Hundreds of middle school students were then beaten during a protest at the local public security bureau office, and in response tens of thousands took to the street, burning police vehicles and apparently buildings as well.

News of the riots was tamped down and censored online (though videos purported to be of the demonstrations are still posted on YouTube at this writing), so to discuss it, netizens played on what they felt was a ridiculous phrase uttered by one of the suspects. When asked what he was doing when the girl jumped into the river (so the official report went) where her body was eventually found, the suspect told them he was "doing push-ups." In the face of government efforts to wipe out every online report on the incident, netizens twittered that they were "doing push-ups," Internet groups for "doing push-ups" skyrocketed, and one local television host was even photographed doing push-ups, naked, in front of Beijing tourist attractions (including the recently unveiled Bird's Nest stadium).

Similarly, after the melamine scandal broke in September, black humor over the thousands of babies sickened and dozens killed permeated the Internet, as Anna Greenspan describes in detail in her essay in chapter 1. Suspicions grew of a conspiracy to keep the tainted milk story under wraps until after the Olympics, with outraged citizens accusing Chinese Internet search engine Baidu of having collaborated with the milk company Sanlu to suppress and block information about the contamination (this rumor was confirmed in late September). Internet censorship, though widespread in China, seemed largely irrelevant to most people's daily lives when the government was blocking photos from the 1989 massacre, news stories about Tibetan independence, and foreign websites that many Chinese would never bother to visit anyway (or for which there were convenient mainland substitutes), like Blogspot and Flickr. But when Internet censorship contravened parents' and grandparents' abilities to protect their children, it gave the lie to officials' repeated claims that they blocked "sensitive" material for "security" reasons.

On the Internet and off, China watchers postulated that what we saw in 2008 was the formation of a new middle-class consciousness focused on quality-of-life issues. As 2008 closes, all signs point to a continued economic slowdown, a situation that will likely increase the Chinese people's demands on the state, as we saw in November 2008 when taxi drivers protested in southern China. The sprouts of future demonstrations, if they occur, emerged in 2008 in leisurely protest walks and online jokes.

Either way, the "middle class" is massively outnumbered by poor farmers—about 727.5 million people live in rural areas, and in 2005, the government classed 869 million of its citizens as "agricultural." So, given these staggering numbers, why do middle-class protests, more than the thousands of local protests over, say, land seizures, matter?

Partly, they matter because demographic trends tell us that the middle class will continue to grow in the coming years. In the 1930s, China was 85 percent rural, and the transition to a largely urban society has taken longer in China that in other countries, in large part because of strict residency regulations that prevented rural people from moving to the cities. But as those restrictions loosen, China is on the verge of shifting to a majority urban population (despite the fact that urban parents stick to the one-child rule with greater regularity that rural parents), with recent censuses reporting that the percentage of the population living in rural districts has dropped to around 60 percent—and these numbers are likely inaccurate, as millions of Chinese continue to be registered in rural districts but live and work as migrants in urban areas. Moreover, incomes have outpaced inflation for both rural and urban people in recent years, meaning that for the average person, there is more money to go around. The government has attempted to adopt policies that will allow rural areas to match the increasing prosperity in the cities, such as the decision in the fall of 2008 to allow rural people to buy and sell land use rights (Mao—who spent decades both before and after the establishment of the PRC working on land reform—is likely rolling over in his mausoleum at the prospect; and the policy itself marks an important turn away from Chinese state efforts dating back to the Han dynasty to maintain stability by keeping peasants on the land). Thus, it seems probable that many Chinese people will have the time in the coming decade to turn their attention away from pocketbook issues and toward the sorts of lifestyle concerns that drove middle-class protests in 2008.

In canvasing the trends of 2008, the Olympic Games are also at the top of the list, but perhaps not in the way China hoped: while the Olympics did raise

China's international profile, the international community was not always paying positive attention. China wants to be a superpower—and increasingly is viewed that way internationally, protestations from Chinese leaders about the country's continued poverty aside—but the Chinese people still think of themselves as underdogs. The cognitive dissonance of the increasingly powerful continuing to view themselves as the persecuted led to a number of clashes in 2008.

Early in the year, for instance, the government's response to the riots in Tibet, for whose independence movement there is broad sympathy in the West, provoked protests around the world. The most newsworthy of these happened along the Olympic torch relay route, a route that Beijing planned as the longest Olympic torch route ever (about 85,000 miles total). Protests disrupted what was supposed to be a triumphal procession of rising China. In Paris, for instance, torchbearers were attacked by activists; in San Francisco, the torch was never seen along the planned parade route because organizers feared a repeat of the Paris disaster; in Korea, fights broke out between Chinese students and Korean protesters. (For more on the torch relay, see chapter 4.)

China's international affairs plagued the country all year: a food crisis following a tsunami in Myanmar raised questions about why China propped up the military government there (which refused to allow entry to foreign aid workers even while its citizens starved); well-organized activist groups pushed China on its laissez-faire attitude toward the Sudanese government, which was in the midst of perpetrating a genocide in its Darfur region; and consumers from the United States to Japan to France continued to be jittery about the safety of Chinese food products and toys. As China ramped up its militarization, including massive investments in development of a modern deep-water navy and aerospace technology (2008 saw the first spacewalk by a Chinese astronaut) and increased military aid to countries like Lebanon and Myanmar, some analysts warned that China might increasingly raise its global presence by extending military assistance to other nations.

There was much consternation about these negative attentions in China that manifested itself as boycotts of CNN and occasional demonstrations against Western media or Western businesses. Regardless, there were no signs that the international community would let up in its criticisms—in early October, oddsmakers were betting that the Nobel Peace Prize would go to either human rights activists Hu Jia (currently in prison in China for subversion) or Gao Zhisheng (currently believed to be in police custody). In the end, neither was awarded the prize (though Hu Jia was awarded the Sakharov Prize for Freedom of Thought by the European Parliament in October 2008), but the strong belief that the Nobel would go to a Chinese indicated the broad perception of the Chinese government as unjust and worthy of criticism.

It is possible, many China commentators have argued, that nationalism will continue to grow in China and that Chinese will perceive the international fear and consternation at "China's rise" as a continuation of the "national humiliation" at the hands of imperial powers that has plagued China since the Opium War of the mid-nineteenth century. But as Chinese governments of the past have discovered and as Jeffrey Wasserstrom discusses in his piece on the history of Chinese protests in chapter 8, nationalist rhetoric can quickly turn against the state. We saw a mild case of this phenomenon in the spring of 2008 when Chinese students, angered by the Olympic torch's Parisian reception, tried to organize a boycott of French superstore Carrefour (a fixture in many Chinese cities). Scattered reports surfaced of public security officers crashing the students' boycott organizing meetings and firmly putting the kibosh on future plans. Students who reported these sorts of interactions were frustrated and confused, though their anger didn't in this case turn into antigovernment demonstrations. But the public security bureau's close watch of young nationalist activities is an indication that the Chinese government is—rightly—concerned that nationalists who one day protest the defamation of their country could the next day be calling for a new government that would more strongly, even belligerently, represent their views. Cultivating a close relationship between Chinese leaders and the Chinese people and ensuring a relatively equal distribution of wealth are two ways the government is trying to keep its population sated. The danger of true and widespread unrest does not come from middle-class Shanghainese unhappy about a new rail line in their neighborhood or from nationalistic youth who feel that the CCP no longer represents "Chinese" interests but rather from a coalition of these two groups, coming together in a moment when they feel they have nothing left to lose.

Turning a blog into a book is still rare in the United States, but in China, where online writing has opened up a new realm of publishing alternatives to the limited, regulated print media, blog-based books have made regular appearances on the best-seller lists for several years. And while it may seem that the two publishing forms are not compatible—the blog being the medium of up-to-the-minute, published-as-it-happens commentary and a book being a more leisurely retrospective of current events—we have tried to imbue this volume with both the timeliness of our blog and the reflections that our contributors have gained through years of study and writing. We have collected in this volume some of the best pieces published at the blog, pieces that were published at sites we regularly read and link to, as well as new content (over one-third of the book is composed of new, previously unpublished material) that expands on and reflects the events of the year.

Much has been written in recent years about the tendency of bloggers to rehash other media, but we were interested not just in commenting on other media (though we did some of that) but also in bringing the research and analysis of the academy and the investigative journalist to a China-interested public. Particularly in the United States and other parts of the West, where public familiarity with the broad strokes of Chinese history is limited, historical research on

China is often viewed as esoteric. Attacks on public funding of research frequently trivialize just the kind of illuminating work conducted by *China Beat* contributors in fields ranging from history and anthropology to literary and film studies.

What would you say, for instance, about a scholar who tells you that she examines late Qing elite charity organizations. Irrelevant? Arcane? But two such scholars have made important contributions to *China Beat*, framing the enormous outpouring of charity to Sichuan earthquake survivors by discussing their research on late Qing charity work. While popular media talked about how the earthquake charity was a "new" phenomenon for China and signaled the growth of China's civil society, these scholars were able to point out the familiar patterns in what was happening today, deepening our readers' understandings of the events in southwest China. You can check out their work for yourself in chapter 5.

Similarly, newspaper readership around the United States has plummeted as readers increasingly turn to the Internet for their news, resulting in the gutting of newspaper editorial staffs. It's a dangerous trend, as much of what we know about what happens on the ground in China depends on good reporting by foreign and Chinese journalists. So we highly valued the contributions at *China Beat*—in the form of essays as well as regular comments—from many thoughtful reporters working in China. We think it is vital that there is a good and deep understanding of China among the general public and took every opportunity we could in 2008 to point our readers to the best reporting on China available. Some of these writers have contributed to this volume, or you can find their writings at the *China Beat* website.

Our contributors' research and writing highlights the critical importance of international engagement. Most of our contributors speak Chinese, have spent extensive periods living in Asia, and have devoted their lives (or, at least, big chunks of them) to understanding China and its people. Through fifteen sets of short pieces, we have tried to give you snapshots of lots of different writers' views on lots of different subjects. Contemporary China is an enormously diverse, complex, and ever-changing place, but through these pieces, we hope you will get a sense of where China was during the unprecedented year of 2008.

The year 2008 marked the end of the second major era of the PRC. Scholars of China frequently speak of the period from 1949 to 1978 as "Maoist China," but when Deng Xiaoping kicked off massive economic reforms in the early months of 1979, he turned the collectivizing goal of Mao's China on its head. The period from 1979 to 2008 was one of unprecedented growth for China but also one marked by increasing inequality and insecurity. Privatization, as much as concerns for free speech issues and increased political participation, set the stage for the student demonstrations of 1989, an event that still frames Western interactions with China. And today, a younger generation scoffs at the idealism of the

1989 leaders, seeing economic growth and influence as the only way for each of them—and for China—to get ahead.

We have now lived with "reform China" for as long as we lived with "Mao's China." Which will have the greater legacy? Almost certainly, as China snatches up real estate and mineral futures in Africa, buys up American debt, and continues to act as the factory for the world, it will be today's China. Mao's shadow wasn't even long enough to make it into Zhang Yimou's Olympic opening ceremony (though it did make it into this volume—see chapter 9 to see one take on what Mao would have thought of the Games). The past thirty years have seen a complete remaking of China, and that transformative power shows no signs of slowing. That constant change can make it difficult to make predictions about China's future, but it also makes it enormously exciting to live in China's present, a present we've tried to capture for you in this book.

Kate Merkel-Hess

Chapter 1

Anxieties of a Prosperous Age

COAL MINER'S DAUGHTER

Kate Merkel-Hess

In early September, a video of, supposedly, a comely young woman whose father owns a coal mine issued a proclamation that cuts to the heart of Chinese anxieties over increasing economic inequality and rampant consumerism:

> Recently spreading on the Internet have been a lot of domestic Chinese girls showing off their wealth. . . . This kind of nouveau riche showing off, I completely do not take seriously, and to compete with them would be lowering myself to their level. I post these pictures not to show off anything, but only to let those girls see clearly that the most important thing is having high tastes.[1]

The response from netizens was immediate. Commentators made comparisons between the coal mine boss's daughter's lifestyle and that of the coal miners. The glossy pictures and self-satisfied tone confirmed fears that a new generation of wealthy twenty-something Chinese, pampered by their hardworking parents, would take their money and run from the poverty and environmental degradation that are the cornerstones of their wealth.

The video, which supposedly showed images of the woman's Seattle house, cars, designer handbag collection, stacks of U.S. currency, and even her sneaker collection, was ripped apart by searchers who sensed the video was a fake. One Net detective proved that the photos of her Seattle mansion were actually pictures of Yao Ming's pad. Another found the stills of "her" BMW on another website.

Eventually, searchers traced the video to its original source. Shanxi News Net reported that "Huanweichen" was a twenty-two year old Beijing student: "Concerning the many condemnations, she said indifferently: 'How much is real on the Internet? . . . If you believe it, then it is real!'"[2]

In his book on the moral conundrums of another moment of unprecedented wealth, *Confusions of Pleasure: Commerce and Culture in Ming China*, Timothy Brook wrote that "as the prospect of wealth fueled avarice, the moral order that had held society together gave way" (2). Internet searchers insist that they will hold the line against the avarice they perceive has resulted from today's massive social transformation and dislocation; Huanweichen, on the other hand, asks why we should bother at all since in the Internet fantasy world we can all be the coal mine boss's daughter.

Posted 9/28/2008 at 02:56:00 PM

---

1. Translation from chinaSMACK at http://www.chinasmack.com/pictures/daughter-of-shanxi-coal-mine-boss-shows-off-her-us-lifestyle.
2. The original story was published at http://www.6park.com/news/messages/95509.html.

China's increasing wealth garners regular attention in the Western media. Where twenty years ago Americans hoped that Levi's and Coca-Cola would cause an overthrow of Chinese autocracy (as it supposedly did in the Soviet Union), today a shared passion for designer handbags and luxury vehicles is taken as evidence that Chinese values increasingly mirror Western ones.

In China itself, however, there is enormous debate about whether Chinese economic growth should look like that of the West. "New Leftists," for instance, have forcefully argued for a return to the communal farms of Mao's China. More practically, the social safety net that was the promise of Communist China—the guaranteed job providing an "iron rice bowl" that would care for Chinese citizens from birth to grave—has disintegrated in the thirty-year posteconomic reform rush to get rich quickly. The lives of middle-aged and elderly Chinese look increasingly precipitous, particularly balanced on their future dependence on a shrinking workforce made up of only children.

In media coverage of these new insecurities, much attention has been focused on the newest of China's economic classes, those in the middle. At once eager to maintain a status quo that has allowed them moderate wealth and promises affluent futures for their children, China's middle class has also become more demanding, increasingly perceiving their own interests as separate from those of the incredibly wealthy and the impoverished. As Jeff Wasserstrom describes in this chapter, in 2008, concern about pollution and threats to housing values generated NIMBY (not in my backyard) protests in various urban settings, while outrage over unsafe food (see Anna Greenspan's piece on the 2008 melamine scare), dissatisfaction with rising prices on staple goods, and concern over the escalating expectations for teenage academic achievement (as Leslie T. Chang describes in this chapter) were among the bread-and-butter issues that worried China's new middle class.

Their concerns point to the particular anxieties that plague China today— concerns over increasing wealth disparities, anger over the government's shrinking role as social guarantor (even while restrictions on speech and politics remain), and the fear that life may not be as good for their children as it has been for them. The increasingly political response to these concerns may mark a new phase for the traditionally narrow civil society of the People's Republic of China.

NIMBY Comes to China ☆ Jeffrey N. Wasserstrom

Shanghai is famous for many things, from its eye-catching architecture to its historic role linking China to the world. But within the People's Republic of China, the city also is revered for its central role in twentieth-century protests.

In the early 1900s, Shanghai workers staged some of China's first strikes. The Cultural Revolution began in Beijing in 1966 with the Red Guards but peaked in the Shanghai uprising of 1967, when revolutionary groups, modeling themselves after the Paris Commune, took over the city government and the Communist Party Committee. And though the great upheaval of 1989's Beijing Spring is rightly associated with Tiananmen Square, the student-led protests that paved the way for that epochal struggle took place two and a half years earlier in People's Square, Shanghai's counterpart to that plaza.

This is worth remembering in light of what's been happening lately in China's largest city. In 2008, protesters opposed to plans to extend the city's fastest-on-earth magnetic levitation train—the maglev—took to the streets in marches that organizers dubbed "collective walks," to avoid seeming too controversial when confronting a regime that often deals harshly with acts of dissent.

The maglev, which can rocket passengers at record-breaking speeds well over 200 miles per hour, currently connects the Pudong airport at the eastern edge of the metropolis to a nearby subway station. The authorities want it to do much more. The first extension in the works would link Pudong's new airport to the old Hongqiao airport west of the city.

This has angered residents of some largely middle-class neighborhoods through which the new rail line would run. They claim that proximity to the path of noisy maglev trains would make their property values plummet, disturb the tranquility of their homes, and perhaps even pose health hazards to their children.

This is not the first time a novel mode of transportation has triggered a Shanghai protest. A century ago, rickshaw pullers smashed trams that threatened their livelihood. But as a longtime student of Shanghai protests, I can say with conviction that the antimaglev protests aren't quite like anything seen in the early 1900s or even Tiananmen times. Describing mass actions as "collective walks" is new, as is coordinating actions via text messages and having videos of marches uploaded onto YouTube.

This decidedly twenty-first-century form of protest in Shanghai resonates with recent demonstrations in other Chinese cities—notably the 2007 protests in Xiamen, again mostly led by members of a burgeoning new middle class, which successfully blocked the opening of a chemical plant. Both protests involved specific goals being pursued by people who do not challenge the government's legitimacy but simply call on it to do a better job of listening to those in whose name it claims to rule—and make good on its own stated goals, such as working to improve the material well-being and quality of life of the Chinese population.

It would be a mistake to ignore parallels between the current Shanghai protests and earlier events in the city's history that began with daily-life concerns and calls simply for greater government responsiveness yet ultimately swelled into broader movements that challenged the legitimacy of an authoritarian ruling party. Protests of this sort took place in the 1940s against the Nationalist government of Chiang Kai-Shek, triggered by hyperinflation. When students of the Tiananmen generation first took to the streets in Shanghai in the mid-1980s, their grievances were largely about the living conditions on campuses but mushroomed into a much more radical set of demands that caught the world's attention in the Beijing Spring of 1989.

One enduring tendency in events of this sort, which is again seen in the antimaglev agitation, is for protesters to play upon official slogans. The Communist Party has made a fetish of late of valuing "harmony" and "stability" and introducing reforms that improve the quality of life of ordinary people, in part by allowing them to own their own property. The antimaglev protesters play on these stated goals, insisting that the new rail line will undermine the "harmony" and "stability" of their neighborhoods and make their living conditions worse.

Protesters insist that what matters most to them is something very basic, which the regime has also promised to deliver—a government that will listen to the concerns of citizens and make a meaningful response.

The slogans of the Nationalists in the 1940s and the Communists in the 1980s were not identical, but the tendency of protesters to call on these regimes to live up to their stated ideals was the same. So, too, was the cry for officials to demonstrate a greater readiness to listen.

There are parallels here even with the Tiananmen protests, which Westerners often misremember as involving the same kind of demand for regime change that was heard that year in places like Poland. By contrast, in China even then the core demand of protesters was simply that the Communist Party make good on its promises—especially its promise to fight corruption—and engage in a true dialogue. Chinese students were willing to have Communist Party rule continue but insisted that the country needed that organization to be run by people who would be more transparent, avoid nepotism (the most galling incidents of corruption often involve the family members of high-ranking officials), allow a greater degree of individual freedom, and show concern for the people's welfare.

If the current protests call to mind a single historical moment, it is not 1989 but 1986. And this is not just because protesters are again gathering in the same part of People's Square where I saw students congregate a generation ago.

Then, as now, protesters were largely members of a highly articulate group with reason to feel good about the overall direction in which the country was heading. But this didn't stop them from desiring a government less arbitrary and more willing to listen to their concerns.

The students of 1986 talked more about abstract ideals—including democracy—than the antimaglev protesters have. But they also had specific grievances linked to daily life. Some complained about mandatory morning calisthenics. Others were angered that security guards had roughed up youths for dancing in the aisles at a recent concert by Jan and Dean, one of the first foreign pop groups to perform in China.

Chinese authorities today should keep in mind how things that happened in 1987 and 1988 worked to radicalize and alienate China's university students. Shanghai's students left the streets readily in 1986, once officials signaled that their patience was wearing thin and expressed concern that the demonstrations could end up harming the very reform process that the protesters wanted to speed up.

The youths felt pretty good, initially, about how things had gone. They had not accomplished anything specific but had been allowed to express their opinions without major reprisals.

But the situation soon deteriorated. The regime launched a campaign against "bourgeois liberalization," viewed by the students as a step backward in terms of personal freedom. And Party General Secretary Hu Yaobang was demoted for having treated the protests too lightly—something that transformed him into a hero in the students' eyes.

Even by 1989, many students viewed the party as something that needed to be transformed, not toppled. But their regard for it had been damaged. This made it easy for protests to escalate quickly once the unexpected death of Hu Yaobang brought them back out into the streets.

Things are different now. Middle-class protesters in Xiamen and Shanghai have been more insistently focused on local issues with a NIMBY (not in my backyard) dimension, such as the damaging effects that development can have on air quality and the danger of noise pollution, than were the students of two decades ago.

Still, China's rulers should remember how easily authoritarian regimes can lose the goodwill of even those who like some things the government is doing. This happened when Deng Xiaoping and company alienated a generation of students in the 1980s and four decades before when the Nationalist Party lost the respect of many members of that era's urban middle class with brutal crackdowns by failing to curb official corruption and caring for little other than maintaining their control of the reins of government.

The history of Shanghai protest is filled with reminders of how dangerous it can be for a regime to appear unwilling to listen. While there may be risks to an authoritarian regime in allowing protests to continue unchecked, it may end up more damaged by leaping too quickly to treating any form of criticism as an unacceptable affront to authority.

In the lead-up to the Olympics, commentators in the West and in China have tended to focus on big issues. Some foreign critics have called for a boycott of the Games because of Beijing's links to horrific actions taking place in Darfur and Burma. And Chinese Communist Party spokesmen assert that the Olympics will be a proud moment for all citizens of the People's Republic of China since they will demonstrate that China is a major player on the global stage.

Thinking in international terms is certainly appropriate right now, given China's large global footprint. Still, it is important not to lose sight of the importance of local issues. While some outsiders anticipate that 2008 will be a year when protests with an international dimension break out in China, it may be that the biggest challenge the government faces this year will turn out to be the one posed by a rapidly growing, highly articulate new social group with decidedly local concerns.

Homeowners' Protests in Shanghai: An Interview with Benjamin Read ☆ Angilee Shah

M uch has been written about a rise in the number of protests in China—particularly mass demonstrations and those by farmers and villagers who face government land seizures. But protests from the middle class in China are also garnering increased attention from the American press. The latest, a January "stroll" by homeowners in Shanghai who disagreed with an extension of the city's famous maglev train into their neighborhood, have been described as "the strongest sign yet of rising resentment among China's fast-growing middle class" (*New York Times*) and "a quiet middle-class battle against government officials" (*Washington Post*).

Benjamin L. Read, from the Department of Politics at the University of California, Santa Cruz, has been researching grassroots organizing with a particular focus since 1999 on homeowners' movements in China. In an e-mail interview with *China Beat*, Read put the Shanghai protests into context:

SHAH: How strong do you think organizations that are not run by the state are in China? What kinds of things can they accomplish and whom do they serve most often?

READ: The homeowner groups in China's new private housing estates (*xiaoqu*) are a complicated mosaic. Some of them can be seen as a manifestation of civil society, while others are something else. For instance, a lot of them are not actually controlled by the homeowners themselves but instead are dominated by the property developers and their management companies. Sometimes the homeowners themselves become factionalized and get bogged down in internal conflict, so that there's no functioning organization. In some places the government has blocked the formation of a formal *yeweihui* (homeowner organization), although there can be informal activity regardless. In other neighborhoods, the homeowner group functions well, holding regular meetings and elections and representing the residents' interests much as, say, a healthy condo association might in the United States.

SHAH: In reporting on the January protests against extending the maglev train in Shanghai, the *Washington Post* highlighted the role of a residential organization. The *Post* did not explicitly call these residents a housing association, but is this kind of civil society organization you are referring to?

READ: It's clear that homeowners in the new, private neighborhoods I talked about above played a central role in these demonstrations. One thing that's not immediately obvious from Chinese or Western sources is to what extent the homeowner organizations themselves or their leaders encouraged members to participate in the protests. Concerns about noise and harmful radiation from the maglev trains seem to have galvanized large numbers of people who might not previously have been involved in the homeowner movement.

Regardless, it is clear that the protests drew on infrastructure that is very much a part of that movement, notably the new neighborhoods' Web-based bulletin boards. Some of the posts from the first weeks of January have now been removed from these forums, some are still there. But they carried a flurry of posts and discussion, and this was a key part of how information about the maglev line extension plan came to the attention of homeowners who stood to be affected by it and how they encouraged each other to turn out for the rally in downtown Shanghai on January 12. Moreover, residents in some neighborhoods hung large protest banners from their windows, which is a tactic you often see in the homeowners' struggles against exploitative property developers and management companies. And according to reports in the livelier parts of the Chinese media like *Southern Metropolis* (*Nanfang dushibao*) and *Beijing News* (*Xin jing bao*), residents of some of the neighborhoods organized representatives to talk to government officials about the plans.

SHAH: What kinds of trends do you see among property owners in China?

READ: To the extent that these Shanghai protests were fueled by homeowners, it constitutes a new departure in that the great majority of the time when homeowners undertake collective action it is one neighborhood at a time and inward focused, not about public policy. Usually the spur to action will be something like high management fees, control over neighborhood assets, or shoddy construction. To the extent that homeowners contact and lobby the government in these cases, they are trying to win support from the authorities against the developers, not protesting against something the government is doing. The maglev extension plan is unusual in that it's something the government is directly responsible for, affecting a large number of neighborhoods (one report said nearly forty) in the same way all at once.

So I think we should guard against reading too much into this event. Howard W. French, in his January 27 *New York Times* story makes a rather bold claim that the protests are "the strongest sign yet of rising resentment among China's fast-growing middle class over a lack of say in decision making." Social classes rarely act in unified ways politically, and it's questionable at best whether the middle class in China is generally characterized by resentment.

Still, I agree that we're looking at an important form of political action that deserves our attention. It was undertaken by people who now have resources (money, education, communication tools like cell phones, the Internet, and video cameras) that were missing or less prevalent in earlier parts of the history of the People's Republic of China. When they buy expensive homes in these new housing developments it gives them a strong interest in protecting that investment—British Thatcherites and U.S. "ownership society" advocates would nod their heads at this.

But I think homeowners are also motivated by a sense that when they acquire their piece of what we might call the "Chinese dream," there's an implicit social contract going with it. The system in China now encourages people to devote their energy to getting ahead in the new economy, and once they "make it" by acquiring a nice, modern home, once of the ultimate markers of success, they feel entitled to certain things: fair treatment in matters concerning their home, veto power over unreasonable arrangements, some control over the neighborhood environment, peace and quiet, privacy, and freedom from certain kinds of impositions. This sense of being entitled to things beyond what's specified on the property deed is a big part of what underlies the homeowner movement more generally.

Gilded Age, Gilded Cage ☆ Leslie T. Chang

China's sudden prosperity brings undreamed-of freedoms and new anxieties. At the age of four, Zhou Jiaying was enrolled in two classes—Spoken American English and English Conversation—and given the English name Bella. Her parents hoped she might go abroad for college. The next year they signed her up for acting class. When she turned eight, she started on the piano, which taught discipline and developed the cerebrum. In the summers she went to the pool for lessons; swimming, her parents said, would make her taller. Bella wanted to be a lawyer, and to be a lawyer you had to be tall. By the time she was ten, Bella lived a life that was rich with possibility and as regimented as a drill sergeant's. After school she did homework unsupervised until her parents got home. Then came dinner, bath, and piano practice. Sometimes she was permitted television, but only the news. On Saturdays she took a private essay class followed by Math Olympics and on Sundays a piano lesson and a prep class for her entrance exam to a Shanghai middle school. The best moment of the week was Friday afternoon, when school let out early. Bella might take a deep breath and look around, like a man who discovers a glimpse of blue sky from the confines of the prison yard.

For China's emerging middle class, this is an age of aspiration—but also a time of anxiety. Opportunities have multiplied, but each one brings pressure to take part and not lose out, and every acquisition seems to come ready-wrapped in disappointment that it isn't something newer and better. An apartment that was renovated a few years ago looks dated; a mobile phone without a video camera and color screen is an embarrassment. Classes in colloquial English are fashionable among Shanghai schoolchildren, but everything costs money.

Freedom is not always liberating for people who grew up in a stable socialist society; sometimes it feels more like a never ending struggle not to fall behind. A study has shown that 45 percent of Chinese urban residents are at health risk due to stress, with the highest rates among high school students.

Fifth grade was Bella's toughest year yet. At its end she would take entrance exams for middle school. Every student knew where he or she ranked: when teachers handed back tests, they had the students stand in groups according to their scores. Bella ranked in the middle—twelfth or thirteenth in a class of twenty-five, lower if she lost focus. She hated Japan, as her textbooks had taught her to: the Japanese army had killed 300,000 Chinese in the 1937 Nanjing massacre. She hated America too because it always meddled in the affairs of other countries. She spoke a fair amount of English: "Men like to smoke and drink beer, wine, and whiskey." Her favorite restaurant was Pizza Hut, and she liked the spicy wings at KFC. Her record on the hula hoop was 2,000 spins.

The best place in the world was the Baodaxiang Children's Department Store on Nanjing Road. In its vast stationery department, Bella would carefully select additions to her eraser collection. She owned thirty erasers—stored in a cookie tin at home—that were shaped like flip-flops and hamburgers and cartoon characters; each was not much bigger than a thumbnail, and all remained in their original plastic packaging. When her grandparents took her to the same store, Bella headed for the toy section, but not when she was with her parents. They said she was too old for toys.

If Bella scored well on a test, her parents bought her presents; a bad grade brought a clampdown at home. Her best subject was Chinese, where she had mastered the art of the composition: she could describe a household object in a morally uplifting way.

Last winter Grandmother left her spider plant outdoors and forgot about it. . . . This spring it actually lived. Some people say this plant is lowly, but the spider plant does not listen to arbitrary orders, it does not fear hardship, and in the face of adversity it continues to struggle. This spirit is worthy of praise.

She did poorly in math. Extra math tutoring was a constant and would remain so until the college entrance examination, which was seven years away. You were only as good as your worst subject. If you didn't get into one of Shanghai's top middle schools, your fate would be mediocre classmates and teachers who taught only what was in the textbook. Your chances of getting into a good high school, not to mention a good college, would diminish.

You had to keep moving because staying in place meant falling behind. That was how the world worked even if you were only ten years old.

The past decade has seen the rise of something Mao sought to stamp out forever: a Chinese middle class, now estimated to number between 100 million and 150 million people. Though definitions vary—household income of at least $10,000 a year is one standard—middle-class families tend to own an apartment and a car, to eat out and take vacations, and to be familiar with foreign brands and ideas. They owe their well-being to the government's economic policies, but in private they can be very critical of the society they live in.

The state's retreat from private life has left people free to choose where to live, work, and travel, and material opportunities expand year by year. A decade ago most cars belonged to state enterprises; now many families own one. In 1998, when the government launched reforms to commercialize the housing market, it was the rare person who owned an apartment. Today home ownership is common, and prices have risen beyond what many young couples can afford—as if everything that happened in America over fifty years were collapsed into a single decade.

But pick up a Chinese newspaper, and what comes through is a sense of unease at the pace of social change. Over several months in 2006, these were some of the trends covered in the *Xinmin Evening News*, a popular Shanghai daily: High school girls were suffering from eating disorders. Parents were struggling to choose a suitable English name for their child. Teenage boys were reading novels with homosexual themes. Job seekers were besieging Buddhist temples because the word for "reclining Buddha," *wofo*, sounds like the English word "offer." Unwed college students were living together.

Parents struggle to teach their children but feel that their own knowledge is obsolete; children, more attuned to social trends, guide their parents through the maze of modern life. "Society has completely turned around," says Zhou Xiaohong, a sociologist at Nanjing University who first noticed this phenomenon when his own father, a retired military officer, asked him how to knot a Western tie. "Fathers used to give orders, but now fathers listen to their sons."

Because their parents have such high hopes for them, children are among the most pressured, inhabiting a world that combines old and new and features the most punishing elements of both. The traditional examination system that selects a favored few for higher education remains intact: the number of students entering college in a given year is equal to 11 percent of the college freshman–age population, compared with 64 percent in the United States. Yet the desire to foster well-rounded students has fed an explosion of activities—music lessons, English, drawing, and martial arts classes—and turned each into an arena of competition.

Such pursuits bring little pleasure. English ability is graded on five levels stretching through college, and parents push children to pass tests years ahead of schedule. Cities assess children's piano playing on a ten-level scale. More than half of preteens take outside classes, a survey found, with the top reason being "to raise the child's future competitiveness."

Parents tend to follow trends blindly and to believe most of what they hear. The past is a foreign country and the present too. "We are a traditional family" was how Bella's mother, Qi Xiayun, introduced herself when I first met her in 2003. She was thirty-three years old with the small, pale face of a girl, and she spoke in a nonstop torrent about the difficulty of raising a child. She teaches computer classes at a vocational college; her husband works in quality control at Baosteel, a state-owned company. They were appointed to those jobs after college as part of the last generation to join the socialist workforce before it started to break apart.

Bella's parents met the old-fashioned way: introduced by their parents. But after they had Bella in 1993, they turned their backs on tradition. They chose not to eat dinner with their in-laws every night and rejected old-fashioned child-rearing methods that tend to coddle children.

When Bella was not yet two, her grandmother offered to care for the baby, but her mother worried that the grandparents would spoil her. Bella went to day care instead. When she entered third grade, her mother stopped picking her up after school, forcing her to change buses and cross streets alone. "Sooner or later she must learn independence," her mother said.

So Bella grew up, a chatty girl with Pippi Longstocking pigtails and many opinions—too many for the Chinese schoolroom. In second grade she and several classmates marched to the principal's office to demand more time to play; the protest failed. Her teachers criticized her temper and her tendency to bully other children. "Your ability is strong," read a first-grade report card, "but a person must learn from the strengths of others in order to improve." In second grade: "Hope you can listen to other people's opinions more."

The effort to shape Bella is full of contradictions. Her parents encourage her independence but worry that school and the workplace will punish her for it. They fret over her homework load, then pile more assignments on top of her regular schoolwork. "We don't want to be brutal to her," says Bella's father, Zhou Jiliang. "But in China, the environment doesn't let you do anything else."

Bella teaches her parents the latest slang and shows them cool Internet sites. When they bought a new television, Bella chose the brand. When they go out to eat, Bella picks Pizza Hut. One day soon, her parents worry, her schoolwork will move beyond their ability to help her. When Bella was younger, her parents began unplugging the computer keyboard and mouse so that she wouldn't go online when she was home alone, but they knew this wouldn't last.

Recently, Bella's father and his sister and cousins put their grandfather in a nursing home. It was a painful decision; in traditional China, caring for aged parents was an ironclad responsibility, and Bella's parents have extra room in their apartment for their parents to move in some day. But Bella announced that she would one day put her parents in the best nursing home.

"The minute she said that, I thought: It's true, we don't want to be a burden on her," Bella's father says. "When we are old, we'll sell the house, take a trip and see the world, and enter the nursing home and live a quiet life there. This is the education my daughter gives me."

I went to school with Bella one Friday in her fifth-grade year. She sat up in bed at 6:25, pulled on pants and an orange sweatshirt, and tied a Young Pioneers kerchief around her neck. Her parents rushed through the cramped apartment getting ready for work, and breakfast was lost in the shuffle. Bella's mother walked her to the corner, then Bella sighed and headed to the bus stop alone. "This is the most free I am the whole day."

Today there would be elections for class cadres, positions that mirror those in the Communist Party. "My mother says to be a cadre in fifth grade is very important," Bella said.

The bus dropped us off at the elite Yangpu Primary School, which cost $1,200 a year in tuition and fees and rejected 80 percent of its applicants. Her classroom was sunny and loud with the roar of children kept indoors. It had several computers and a bulletin board with student-written movie reviews: *The Birth of New China* and *Finding Nemo*.

By 8:30 the students were seated at their desks for elections. Their pretty young teacher asked for candidates. Everyone wanted to run.

"This semester I want to change my bad nail-biting habits, so people don't call me the Nail-Biting King," said a boy running for propaganda officer.

"I will not interrupt in class," said a girl in a striped sweater running for children's officer. "Please everyone vote for me."

The speeches followed a set pattern: name a personal flaw, pledge to fix it, and ask for votes. It was self-criticism as campaign strategy.

Those who strayed from the script were singled out. "My grades are not very good because I write a lot of words wrong," said one girl running for academic officer. "Please everyone vote for me."

"You write words wrong, please vote for me?" the teacher mimicked. "What have you left out?"

The girl tried again. "I want to work to fix this bad habit. Please everyone vote for me."

Bella delivered her pitch for sports officer. "I am very responsible, and my management abilities are pretty good," she said breathlessly. "Sometimes I have conflicts with other students. If you vote for me, it will help me change my bad habits. Please everyone give me your vote."

In a three-way race, Bella squeaked to victory by a single ballot. Election day, like everything in school, ended with a moral. "Don't feel bad if you lost this time," the teacher said. "It just means you must work even harder. You shouldn't let yourself relax just because you lost."

The language of child education is Darwinian grim. "The elections teach students to toughen themselves," Bella's teacher, Lu Yan, said over lunch in the teachers' cafeteria. "In the future they will face pressure and competition. They need to know how to face defeat."

Some schools link teacher pay to student test performance, and the pressure on teachers is intense. Bella's class had recently seen a drop in grades, and the teacher begged parents to help identify the cause. Lu Yan had just gotten her four-year college degree at night school and planned to study English next. All her colleagues were enrolled in outside classes; even the vice principal took a weekend class on educational technology. A math teacher was fired three weeks into the school year because parents complained she covered too little material in class.

Life will not always feel like this. The next generation of parents, having grown up with choice and competition, may feel less driven to place all their hopes on their children. "Right now is the hardest time," says Wang Jie, a sociologist who is herself the mother of an only child. "In my generation we have both traditional and new ideas. Inside us the two worlds are at war."

In math class later that day, the fifth graders whipped through dividing decimals using Math Olympics methods, which train kids to use mental shortcuts. They raced across a field in gym class, with the slowest person in each group punished with an extra lap around the track. School ended at 1:30 on Fridays. The bus let Bella off outside her building, where she bought a Popsicle and headed inside. Her weekend was packed with private tutoring, so Friday was the best time to finish her homework.

I told her that no American ten-year-old did homework on a Friday afternoon.

"They must be very happy," Bella said.

In the five years since I met Bella and her family, their lives have been transformed. They moved into a new three-bedroom apartment—it is almost twice the size of their old one, which they now rent out—and furnished it with foreign brand-name appliances. They bought their first car, a Volkswagen Bora, and from taking the bus they went straight to driving everywhere. They eat out a couple of times a week now, and the air conditioner stays on all summer. At age twelve, Bella got her first mobile phone—a $250 Panasonic clamshell in Barbie pink. Her parents' annual income reached $18,000, up 40 percent from when we first met.

As the material circumstances of Bella's family improved, the world became to them a more perilous place. Their cleaning lady stole from them and disappeared. Several friends were in near-fatal car accidents. One day Bella's father saw her holding a letter from a man she'd met online. Bella's parents changed the locks and the phone number of the apartment. Her father drove her to and from school now because he thought the neighborhood around it was unsafe.

Bella's mother took on more administrative responsibilities at work and enrolled in a weekend class to qualify to study for a master's degree. Bella's father talked about trading in their car for a newer model with better acceleration and more legroom. They frequently spoke of themselves as if they were mobile phones on the verge of obsolescence. "If you don't continue to upgrade and recharge," Bella's father said, "you'll be eliminated."

Social mobility ran in both directions. A friend of Bella's mother stopped attending class reunions because he was embarrassed to be a security guard. A company run by a family friend went bankrupt, and his daughter, who was Bella's age, started buying clothes at discount stalls. Society was splintering based on small differences. Family members only a decade younger than Bella's parents inhabited another world. One cousin ate out every night and left her baby in the care of her grandparents so she could focus on her career. Bella's father's younger sister, who was childless, thought nothing of buying a full-fare plane ticket to go somewhere for a weekend. Friends who were private entrepreneurs were having a second child and paying a fine; Bella's parents would probably be fired by their state-owned employers if they did that.

Bella tested into one of Shanghai's top middle schools, where teachers often keep students past 5:00 in the evening while their parents wait in cars outside. She is level 3 in English and level 8 in piano. She still ranks in the middle of her class, but she no longer has faith in the world of adults.

She disdains class elections now. "It's a lot of work," she says, "and the teacher is always pointing to you as a role model. If you get in trouble and get demoted, it's a big embarrassment." She loves Hollywood films—especially *Star Wars* and disaster movies—and spends hours online with friends discussing Detective Conan, a character from Japanese comic books. She intends to marry a foreigner because they are richer and more reliable.

Her parents no longer help with her homework; in spoken English she has surpassed them. They lecture her to be less wasteful. "When she was little, she agreed with all my opinions. Now she sits there without saying anything, but I know she doesn't agree with me," her mother said one afternoon in the living room of their new apartment, as Bella glared without speaking. "Our child raising has been a failure." In China, there is no concept of the rebellious teenager.

Across Chinese society, parents appear completely at sea when it comes to raising their children. Newspapers run advice columns, their often rudimentary counsel—"Don't Forcibly Plan Your Child's Life" is a typical headline—suggesting what many parents are up against. Some schools have set up parent schools where mothers and the occasional father can share frustrations and child-raising tips.

At times educators go to extremes: at the Zhongguancun No. 2 Primary School in Beijing, vice principal Lu Suqin recently took two fifth-grade boys into her home. "Their parents couldn't get them to behave, so they asked me to take them," she explains. "After they learn disciplined living, I will send them back."

Bella had one free day during the 2006 weeklong National Day holiday. Some of her extended family—seven adults and two children—took a trip to Tongli, a town of imperial mansions an hour's drive from Shanghai. Bella's father hired a minibus and driver for the trip: a friend had just been in a car accident and broken all the bones on one side of his body. Bella sat alone reading a book.

Developing China zipped past the window, city sprawl giving way to a booming countryside of fish ponds and factories and the three-story houses of prosperous farmers. Bella's mother indulged in the quintessential urban dream of a house in the country. "You have your own little yard in front," she said. "I'd love to live in a place like that when we retire."

She was thinking seriously about Bella's future. If she tested into a good college, she should stay in China; otherwise, she would go abroad, and they would sell the old apartment to pay for it. She had decided that Bella could date in college. "If she finds someone suitable in the third or fourth year of college, that's fine. But not in the first or second year."

"And not in high school?" I asked.

"No. Study should be most important."

Tongli was mobbed with holiday visitors. Bella's family walked through its courtyards and gardens like sleepwalkers, admiring whatever the tour guides pointed out. They touched the trunk of the Health and Long Life Tree. They circled a stone mosaic said to bring career success. They could not stop walking for an instant because crowds pressed in from behind. It was the biggest tourist day of the year.

Bella politely translated for a great-aunt visiting from Australia who didn't speak Chinese, but it was just an act. "This is boring," she told me. "Once you've seen one old building, you've seen them all."

I sat with her on the ride home. She was deep into a Korean romance novel.

"It's about high school students," she said. "Three boys chasing a girl."

"Do people have boyfriends and girlfriends in high school?" I asked.

"Yes."

"What about middle school?"

"Yes. Some."

"Do you have a boyfriend?"

She wrinkled her nose. "There's a boy who likes me. But all the boys in my grade are very low class."

She wanted to go to Australia for graduate school and to work there afterward. She could make more money there and bring her parents to live with her. "On the surface China looks luxurious, but underneath it is chaos," Bella said. "Everything is so corrupt."

Some observers of Chinese society look at children like Bella and see political change: her generation of individualists, they predict, will one day demand a say in how they are governed. But the reality is complicated. Raised and educated within the system, they are just as likely to find ways to accommodate themselves to it, as they have done all along.

"Just because they're curious to see something doesn't mean they want it for themselves," says Zhang Kai, Bella's middle school teacher. "Maybe they will try something—dye their hair, or pierce an ear—but in their bones, they are very traditional. In her heart Zhou Jiaying is very traditional," he says, and he uses Bella's Chinese name.

Bella is fifteen now, in the ninth grade. She has good friends among her classmates, and she has learned how to get along with others. School is a complicated place. One classmate bullied another boy, and the victim's parents came to school to complain. Because they were politically influential, they forced the teacher to transfer the bully out of the class.

The incident divided Bella's class, and now her friends in the Tire Clique won't speak to her friends in the Pirate Clique. A friend got into school without taking the entrance exam because her mother's colleague had a cousin in the education bureau.

Bella's teacher nominated some students for membership in the Communist Youth League. Bella thought it meaningless, but she fell into line and pulled an application essay off the Internet. She couldn't afford to get on her teacher's bad side, she told me, citing a proverb: "A person who stands under someone else's roof must bow his head."

The high school entrance exam is a month away. In the evenings Bella's father watches television on mute so he won't disturb her studies. A good friend is also an enemy because they vie for the same class rank. Her compositions describe what the pressure feels like:

I sit in my middle-school classroom, and the teacher wants us to say good-bye to childhood. I feel at a loss. Happiness is like the twinkling stars suffusing the night sky of childhood. I want only more and more stars. I don't want to see the dawn.

Melamine and Milk in Modern China ☆ Anna Greenspan

A few years ago a televised singing competition sponsored by Mengniu, the country's largest dairy producer, became one of the most popular events in China, setting off an intense cultural craze. The *American Idol*–like Mengniu Yoghurt Supergirl Contest drew, in the final show of the second series, a staggering 400 million viewers. During the show's third series, "voters" sent over 800 million text messages prompting cultural critics to laud Supergirls as China's biggest-ever experiment in grassroots democracy. In a country where branding is still in its infancy, the show was an unprecedented marketing coup and helped secure Mengniu's position at the cutting edge of advertising.

This might seem a surprising role for a dairy company. In China, however, milk has become inextricably linked to modernity.

Chinese cuisine is notoriously wide ranging. "We eat everything with four legs that isn't a table," goes the familiar saying, "anything that flies that isn't a plane." Yet, while it has succeeded in incorporating all manner of bugs and beasts, there are still no cheese fillings or cream sauces in Chinese food.

Traditionally, this disdain for dairy has been a source of cultural pride as the tea-drinking Han sought to distinguish themselves from the milk-drinking barbarians. Foreigners, it was believed, could be easily identified by their buttery, cheesy, or milky smell.

As China's doors were opened to the outside, however, and the country began to wonder why it was weak when so many others were strong, the wisdom of the nondairy diet came under fire. The argument was increasingly heard: if China was to match the vitality of the imperial powers, it was essential that its people start drinking milk. This assertion first surfaced decades before 1949 among urban reformers based in cosmopolitan treaty ports such as Shanghai, as Susan Glosser notes in her 2003 book *Chinese Visions of Family and State, 1915–1953*, which describes an early advocate for dairies claiming that not drinking enough milk was, along with illiteracy, one of the main obstacles to making China a "modern" country. Not everyone went as far as seeing drinking milk and learning to read as comparably important, but the dairy products' contribution to the strength and modernity of the nation was widely accepted.

Despite this new cultural imperative, for decades consumption was curtailed by poverty. During the Mao era, milk was heavily rationed, a luxury that only few could afford. Once the country began its policies of openness and reform, however, the milk-drinking campaign exploded.

Since many Chinese adults are lactose intolerant, the dairy industry focused predominantly on children since they were not only the prime consumers of milk but also had yet to build up intolerance.

The goal was to encourage an early shift in diet that would, ultimately, alter the biology of the population. In China it is widely believed that the Japanese are taller and stronger because they drink more milk. Strengthen the child, and you will strengthen the nation.

The dairy companies pushed this idea by making use of their Mongolian roots. In their ads and packaging they sought to contrast the rugged health of life on the steppes with the decadent softness of the industrialized urban core (where most of their customers, of course, reside).

The widespread receptivity to this cultural message is evident in the astonishing popularity of *Wolf Totem*, a novel that opposes the weakness of the Han with the vigor of the Mongolian nomads. *Wolf Totem*, as noted elsewhere in this volume, is said to have been the second most widely read book in the history of China, beaten only by Mao's "little red book."

Throughout the past decade, public health campaigns have celebrated the virtues of milk. "I have a dream," said Premier Wen Jiabao on a visit to a dairy farm in 2006, "that all Chinese, especially children, will have sufficient milk each day." Consumption has been encouraged in schools. When China was gripped by the SARS scare, the health properties of milk were especially strongly promoted. In recent years, prompted by these health campaigns, as well as by convenience and cosmetic factors, many middle-class mothers have shifted away from breast-feeding to formula.

In an effort to capitalize on this promotion of both individual and national vitality, dairy ads regularly feature star athletes and patriotic heroes. Mengniu, for example, has a famous product tie-in with the astronauts of the *Shenzhou* space rocket. Yili, another large dairy producer, sponsors the celebrity hurdler Liu Xiang.

This potent mixture of health and patriotism has helped make China home to the fastest-growing dairy market in the world. It was thus especially ironic that in the afterglow of the Olympics (and a record number of Chinese gold medal wins), the country was suddenly shattered by a crisis in its dairy industry.

The production and distribution of milk in China involves a large number of small and highly distributed players. In September 2008 it came to light that somewhere in this complex business chain, melamine, a chemical commonly used in plastics and fertilizers, had been added to the milk supply.

At the center of the crises was one company, Sanlu, whose baby formula was found to contain high levels of melamine. As the investigation spread, however, traces of the chemical were discovered in formula, liquid milk, and milk candy from almost every dairy producer in the country.

Melamine boosts the protein count in milk, allowing unscrupulous traders to disguise a watered-down supply. When ingested in high doses, it also causes crystals to form in the kidneys and eventually leads to kidney stones. A week after the crisis broke four children were dead, and over 50,000 had been sickened by the country's contaminated milk.

As the crisis unfolded, it followed an all-too-familiar pattern. The numbers of those affected jumped suddenly, from 6,000 to over 50,000, within a couple of days. There were widespread recalls in China and boycotts of Chinese-made goods throughout the rest of the world. Stories of a cover-up soon emerged. An investigation uncovered health complaints over Sanlu milk powder dating back at least eight months. Parents' concerns had been ignored. Company employees delayed telling local officials who themselves waited to tell their superiors. The public was kept in the dark until well after the Olympics had finished.

A New Zealand company, Fonterra, which owned a 43 percent stake in Sanlu, was implicated in the cover-up, but in the end it was the New Zealand government that finally told officials in Beijing of the suspected contamination. Once the story broke, there was mass public outcry, and heads began to roll. First the boss of Sanlu and several local officials were fired and detained. A few days later Li Changjiang, the head of China's food and product quality agency, was forced to resign. While this was no doubt a necessary measure, it did little to reassure an outraged public, especially since only a year earlier the former head of China's food and drug agency had been executed for corruption in a similar scandal that also involved the chemical melamine.

The milk crisis is still unfolding at the time I'm writing in late September 2008. There are daily reports of the widespread use of melamine in China and further boycotts worldwide. It is still unclear what the long-term effects will be. Nevertheless, it is already apparent that the 2008 milk crisis touches on precisely those issues that a post-Olympic China must face in order to grow.

First, it involves, in a very intimate fashion, the disparate populations—rural and urban, rich and poor—that the government is so desperate to "harmonize." Official reports veer between sympathy for the dairy farmers and concern for urban middle-class consumers. Any long-term solution will have to placate one group without unduly harming the other.

Second, crises of quality control have a crucial impact on China's role in the global economy. Since China's export-driven rise rests on its position as a manufacturing hub, continuing reports of toxic products are particularly damaging through their impact on the made-in-China brand.

Responding to the crisis, an official in the agriculture ministry has admitted that "the milk procurement sector is basically uncontrolled" and vowed more stringent regulation. Yet this promise has been made before. The dairy industry, like much else in China, is rife with corruption. It is claimed that the silence of both inspectors at Sanlu and parents of affected children was bought with bribes.

Only weeks after the leadership in Beijing was being praised for the spectacular success of the Olympic Games, the milk crisis revealed the shortcomings of a political system that is grappling with reform. Critics have been quick to suggest that until the government allows more openness, transparency, and media oversight, new crises of this type are inevitable.

Here, the story so far is mixed. While reports of tainted milk were published in the local press, all news from inside China came from only a few trusted agencies. The content of these reports was strictly regulated by communiqués issued by the propaganda department (some of which circulated on the Internet). Less than two weeks after the story first came to light, an initial wave of aggressive coverage gave way to comforting reports about forceful government intervention as well as articles that focused on the health benefits of milk.

In cyberspace, however, things have unfolded quite differently. From the moment the story appeared the Chinese blogosphere was flooded with black humor. Images of grotesque monsters promoting baby formula appeared alongside a host of photoshopped spoof versions of Sanlu ads. A satirical diary was widely circulated that horrifically detailed the daily dose of toxins that everyday life in China entails. Fu Janfeng, an editor at *Southern Weekend*—one of the most respected papers in the country—blogged about his frustrations in trying to report the case, his inability to access information, and the impossibility of investigating Sanlu during the pre-Olympic crackdown. Meanwhile, netizens heatedly debated rumors that Sanlu had paid Baidu, China's biggest search engine, to filter information on the crisis. Paradoxically, this uproar over the lack of information is an encouraging sign of the country's increasing openness.

In developed markets brand image and share prices also play an important part in the protection of public safety. Quality matters to manufacturers since, when products are found to be defective or toxic, companies collapse. In China too, it seems, rising brand consciousness will have a growing effect of this kind. Few think the Sanlu brand will ever recover. Sanyuan, however, which is the one major Chinese dairy producer to have consistently tested clean, has seen its milk sales triple and share prices soar. (It is now in talks to buy out Sanlu.) Mengniu, which was implicated in the scandal, held a publicity stunt aimed at restoring consumer confidence. Soon after traces of melamine were found in its products, the chief executive officer appeared in public drinking a box of milk and promising extensive compensation for anyone harmed by the company's products.

Increased openness and transparency, a regulatory system that is free of corruption, and companies that are forced by both the market and the government to act responsibly are all fundamental to China's continued growth. Yet, as the references to Confucius, calligraphy, and kung fu in the opening ceremony of the Olympics made clear, modernity in contemporary China also involves a return to tradition. Here too, it seems the milk crisis is playing an important role.

Scrambling for alternatives to local milk, customers turned to the burgeoning organic market, and many switched back to soy milk, a traditional Chinese drink. In the days following the crisis, stocks in Vitasoy jumped over 9 percent.

There are also reports of a sudden and booming industry in wet nurses. One entrepreneurial breast-feeding mother has offered to sell her surplus milk and feed an infant for 300 RMB a day. Her ad was posted online.

Little Emperors or Frail Pragmatists?
China's '80ers Generation ☆ Yunxiang Yan

Unlike other pieces in this book, the following was not written in 2008 but rather is excerpted from a 2006 contribution to Current History. *It captures so well enduring issues related to other pieces in this section, though, that we thought it valuable to include it here as a supplement to more recent commentaries.*

Using a broader notion of youth that includes both adolescents and young adults, China's youth amounted to 560 million in 2005, with more than 200 million of them between the ages of fifteen and twenty-four. In the Chinese media, these youth have been referred to as the post-1980 generation, or "the '80ers," although some were born in the early 1990s. This is China's most dynamic demographic group; each year more than 20 million children enter adolescence.

The '80ers represent the first generation of Chinese youth who have no life experience of Maoist socialism, who in childhood have heard adults saying that "to be rich is glorious" and talking about "jumping into the sea (of business)," who were showered by increasing supplies of commodities as they grew up, who witnessed the ups and downs of their parents' pursuit of wealth, and, since their first day of schooling, who also experienced unprecedented pressure to score high on various exams. They also constitute the first generation of youth who are either singletons in cities or have fewer siblings in the countryside, thanks to the strictly enforced policy of population control in the 1980s. While receiving more parental attention, love, and investments (hence their nickname, "little emperors"), they also are expected to realize the unfulfilled dreams of their parents and make it big in an incredibly competitive society.

Individualistic, free-spirited, materialistic, competitive, rebellious, westernized, and modern—these are among the adjectives the Western media have used most frequently to describe and define the new generation of Chinese youth. They grew up drinking Coke and eating hamburgers, quickly developing a taste for hip-hop, and watching NBA games. Defying parental advice, they dye their hair, pierce their ears, and wear trendy clothes in a restless pursuit of being cool. The '80ers are well informed, too: a quarter of them have learned a foreign language (mostly English), more than 40 percent have had fourteen or more years of education, and they make up about 40 percent of China's 100 million Internet users. We also know that the current generation of youth, urban and rural alike, has grown up without much influence from Communist ideology. This generation is open to new ideas, is uninterested in party politics, and yearns for freedom and individuality. On these grounds, it is plausible to say the '80ers in China share much in common with Generation Y in America.

Like Generation Y, for example, they are sexually active. The '80ers have continued the sexual revolution that began in China among the 1970s generation. They have moved back their dating experience to secondary school (some even earlier), have been widely exposed to pornography and Internet dating, and have begun to separate sex in dating from a commitment to marriage—hence the emergence of recreational dating. According to a recent survey among urban Chinese youth, only 25 percent thought that premarital sex was improper, and more than 30 percent considered Internet romance cool. A 2005 investigative report by a northeast Chinese newspaper found that twenty-two of fifty high school students interviewed had had sex, while forty-two of the group had dating experiences. Those who have not had sexual encounters by the last year in high school are called "pandas," referring to their underdeveloped sexual desires. And the sexual revolution is by no means confined to urban youth. A 2001 marriage counseling survey in Guangdong province showed that more than 80 percent of young people in the rural areas had engaged in premarital sex, roughly the same as for urbanites. . . .

Unlike their carefree and sometimes drifting counterparts in the United States, most Chinese teenagers and young adults are clearheaded about what they must do for a good life: earn high scores on exams, gain admission to a prestigious university, and secure a high-income job. China scholar Stanley Rosen calls this the victory of materialism and pragmatism. After combing through rich survey data, he concluded that Chinese youth "have become less reluctant to acknowledge openly that instrumental, success-oriented values take precedence." In a survey conducted by Hill and Knowlton in 2004, 76 percent of Chinese college students described themselves as entrepreneurial. In 2000, the Communist Youth League and the National Student Federation conducted a survey on youth aspiration among 1,800 students in southern cities. The number one choice of these students was to be a billionaire; the second was to become a chief executive officer of a multinational company. The students' third most popular ideal was to be a high-ranking cadre. In short, China's students today are preoccupied with money and power—a sharp contrast with the youth of the 1980s, many of whom wanted to be China's Einstein or Mother Teresa. It is no wonder that, according to numerous surveys, Bill Gates has emerged as the most popular role model for Chinese youth. They all know he is the most successful entrepreneur and the richest man in the world. Few talk about the work of the Gates Foundation. . . .

The majority of China's youth find themselves constantly under pressure and anxious. In the 2005 nationwide survey, for example, 67 percent of the teenagers said they always worried about exams, and 41 percent feared they might not be able to enter a prestigious university. Surveys among college students show that some 40 to 45 percent of youth worry about their prospects of finding good jobs, and a small crowd begin to worry about car loans and mortgage payments even before they graduate. Most intriguingly, some of the older '80ers, who are still in their twenties, have shown concerns about being outdated and replaced by the '90ers.

These worries, fears, and anxiety about their future—along with the daily calculated efforts to move oneself ahead—take a serious toll on the health of China's youth, making many of them fragile physically. In a 2002 survey conducted among 1,000 teenagers in Shanghai's Pudong district, 21 percent of the youth said they always felt exhausted because of the pressure of study and the shortage of playtime; 61 percent reported not having enough sleep. The previously mentioned 2005 nationwide survey echoed the findings in Shanghai, showing that 66 percent of primary school students and 77 percent of middle school students did not have enough sleep. When answering the question "What would you like to do if you have free time?" 53 percent of the teenagers chose "to have a long and good sleep." One doctor reflected that some of his young patients were sick from sleep deprivation because they spent only about five hours in bed per night. Yet they asked the doctor to help them find a way to sleep even less so they could spend more time studying and preparing for exams. . . .

Putting all the pieces together, Chinese youth in the current generation come across as both individualistic fun seekers and frail pragmatists, and I would argue that these are the two sides of the same coin. A coin, however, cannot separate its two sides, yet China's youth do to a great degree. In the private sphere, especially when they are dealing with their parents and loved ones, they are individualistic, self-centered, conscious of rights, and bold in their pursuit of fun, the cool, and the fashionable. In the sphere of public life, on the other hand, they are bluntly pragmatic, choosing the safest way to maximize their exam scores, educational returns, income, power, and prestige.

Chapter 2

Tibet

MEDIA COVERAGE OF TIBET

James Miles

James Miles of *The Economist* was in Tibet when the riots and protests started on March 14. China's strict limitations on foreign journalists entering Tibet in the following days made Miles one of the few journalists who saw the riots firsthand. Over e-mail, Miles shared how he felt about the questions he got on returning from the field.

CHINA BEAT: Is there any question that you've been asked a lot since returning to Beijing that you think is off the mark or plays into simplistic or misleading thinking about a complex issue?

MILES: No. The question I get asked most is what happened, and then why. What happened in Lhasa from midday on the 14th to late on the 15th did not fit the normal pattern of unrest in Tibet. It was not monk-led, it displayed little explicitly-stated political purpose, and it was violent. Reporters who interviewed me during the unrest and afterwards seemed to readily understand this. If I were a media studies specialist I'd have a very good look at this case. The foreign media were almost entirely absent from Lhasa (a couple may have sneaked in under cover after the riots broke out but would have had limited access). Yet I have seen some very good reporting on what happened, notwithstanding the Chinese media's nitpicking. Reporting in the official press, by contrast, while reasonably on the mark as far as the violence goes, has been highly misleading by failing to look at the bigger picture of unrest in Tibet and beyond, by not asking what might have caused this anger and by portraying this as the actions of a handful of people organised by the Dalai Lama's "clique." It wasn't a handful, and I saw no evidence to suggest anything other than spontaneity. . . .

Posted 3/29/2008 at 11:51:00 AM

In the lead-up to the Olympics, China worried about potential explosions—both the literal and the figurative kind. There were two domestic ethnic powder kegs the government kept a particular eye on—Tibetan and Uyghur separatists. In the event, both groups were reported to have mounted violent protests, though to differing international effect.

Just days before the start of the Olympic Games, Muslim separatists supposedly attacked a police station in Xinjiang, killing sixteen policemen. This attack came on the heels of several small-scale bombings in the western region. Recent reports by eyewitnesses cast doubt on the story that it was Muslim separatists who committed the attack (these reports make it less clear who the attackers might have been, as the witnesses claim they were dressed like police). Regardless, amidst the War on Terror, Muslim separatists gained little international sympathy for their ongoing attempts to harry the Chinese government.

Not so the Tibetan protests. In March, protests broke out in Lhasa after the anniversary of the aborted 1959 Tibetan uprising. Though we now know that there were important protests as early as late February, the crisis in Tibet took a dramatic turn on March 14, four days after the 1959 anniversary was marked, when footage of Tibetan rioters attacking Han and Hui (Muslim) Chinese began circulating on the Internet. As protests spread throughout the heavily Tibetan Chinese southwest, lines of Chinese tanks poured into the area, and journalists were prevented from visiting and reporting on the increasingly volatile situation. In China, the footage of the violent riots meant that a largely Han nation sympathized with the Han Chinese who had been attacked by Tibetan mobs. Abroad, international sympathies fell with the Tibetans as both celebrities and heads of state stood by the Dalai Lama. For his part, the Dalai Lama, a figure of peace abroad but vilified in China as the head of a separatist clique, called for restraint and an end to violence.

In a year when China hoped to show its best face to the world, the heavy-handed response to what were initially localized riots was the largest misstep. Not only did the Chinese domestic response spawn further, largely peaceful domestic protests from Beijing to Sichuan, but netizen response to international critiques, such as bombarding CNN's Beijing office and its reporters with harassing phone calls and e-mails, made China look petulant and thuggish. Trouble on the borders is one of historical China's tropes—but border trouble has also often been the actual downfall of Chinese political regimes. As they showed in the spring of 2008, the country's current leaders are determined not to let things get out of hand, regardless of how their response plays internationally.

The pieces in this section offer a variety of perspectives on the Tibet crisis. Among them is anthropologist Charlene Markley's eyewitness account, specially written for this volume, of an early conflict between Tibetan residents of Qinghai province and local law enforcement agents. Also included are two commentaries by prominent writers on Buddhism: the religious studies scholar and Prisoners of Shangri-la: Tibetan Buddhism and the West *(1998) author Donald Lopez and the novelist and public intellectual Pankaj Mishra, whose books include* Temptations of the West: How to Be Modern in India, Pakistan, Tibet, and Beyond *(2006).*

At War with the Utopia of Modernity ☆ Pankaj Mishra

Many Western commentators scrambling to interpret the protests in Lhasa found that they did not need to work especially hard. Surely the Tibetans are the latest of many brave peoples to rebel against communist totalitarianism? The rhetorical templates of the Cold War are still close at hand, shaping Western discussions of Islam or Asia. Dusting off the hoary oppositions between the free and unfree worlds, the *Wall Street Journal* declared that religious freedom was the main issue. "On the streets of Lhasa, China has again had a vivid demonstration of the power of conscience to move people to action against a soulless, and brittle, state."

This is stirring stuff. Never mind that the rioters in Lhasa were attacking Han Chinese immigrants rather than the Chinese state or that the Chinese authorities have been relatively restrained so far, one cautious step behind middle-class public opinion—which I sensed in China last week to be overwhelmingly against the Tibetan ethnic minority.

As for religious freedom, the Tibetans have had more of it in recent years than at any time since the Cultural Revolution. Eager to draw tourists to Tibet, Chinese authorities have helped to rebuild many of the monasteries destroyed by Red Guards in the 1960s and 1970s, turning them into Disneylands of Buddhism. Tibet and Tibetan Buddhism have even inspired a counterculture among Chinese jaded by their new affluence.

Indeed, Tibet's economy has surpassed China's average growth rate, helped by generous subsidies from Beijing and more than a million tourists a year. The vast rural hinterland shows few signs of this growth, but Lhasa, with its shopping malls, glass-and-steel office buildings, massage parlors, and hair salons, resembles a Chinese provincial city on the make. Beijing hopes that the new rail link to Lhasa, which makes possible the cheap extraction of Tibet's uranium and copper, will bring about *kuayueshi fazhan* ("leapfrog development")—economic, social, and cultural.

Tibet has been enlisted into what is the biggest and swiftest modernization in history: China's development on the model of consumer capitalism, which has been cheer-led by the *Wall Street Journal* and other Western financial media that found in China the corporate holy grail of low-priced goods and high profits. Tibetans—whose biggest problem, according to Rupert Murdoch, is believing that the Dalai Lama "is the son of God"—have the chance to be on the right side of history; they could discard their superstitions and embrace, like Murdoch, China's brave new world. So why do they want independence? How is it that, as *The Economist* put it, "years of rapid economic growth, which China had hoped would dampen separatist demands, have achieved the opposite"?

For one, the Chinese failed to consult Tibetans about the kind of economic growth they wanted. In this sense, at least, Tibetans are not much more politically impotent than the hundreds of millions of hapless Chinese uprooted by China's Faustian pact with consumer capitalism. The Tibetans share their frustration with farmers and tribal peoples in the Indian states of West Bengal and Orissa, who, though apparently inhabiting the world's largest democracy, confront a murderous axis of politicians, businessmen, and militias determined to corral their ancestral lands into a global network of profit.

However, Tibet's ordeal has been in the making for some time. Before the railway line speeded up Han Chinese immigration, China's floating population of migrant workers, criminals, carpetbaggers, and prostitutes conspicuously dominated Tibetan cities such as Lhasa, Gyantse, and Shigatse. Half of Lhasa's population is Han Chinese, who own most of the city's shops and businesses.

Chinese-style development, which heavily favors urban areas over rural ones, could only exacerbate economic inequality and threaten traditions, such as nomadic lifestyles. Not surprisingly, Deng Xiaoping's post-Tiananmen gamble—that people intoxicated with prosperity will not demand political change—failed in Tibet. Like predominantly rural ethnic minorities elsewhere, Tibetans lack the temperament or training needed for a fervent belief in the utopia of modernity—a consumer lifestyle in urban centers—promised by China.

Far from losing his aura during his long exile, the Dalai Lama has come to symbolize more urgently than ever to Tibetans their cherished and threatened identity. It has also become clear to Tibetans that they pay a high price for other people's enhanced lifestyles. Global warming has caused the glaciers of the Tibetan plateau, which regulate the water supply to the Ganges, Indus, Brahmaputra, Mekong, Thanlwin, Yangtze, and Yellow rivers, to melt at an alarming rate, threatening the livelihoods of hundreds of millions in Asia.

Woeser, a Tibetan poet and essayist, told me that not even the Cultural Revolution undermined Tibet as much as the feckless modernization of recent years. The rail link to Lhasa has further deepened the Tibetan sense of siege. No Tibetan I met last year in Lhasa had any doubt that the railway was devised by and for the Han Chinese, thousands of whom had already begun to pour into the city every day, monopolizing jobs and causing severe inflation.

In the past two decades, new railways have economically integrated China's remote provinces of Qinghai and Xinjiang, making them available for large-scale resettlement by the surplus population. China, its leaders insist, will rise "peacefully," and they may be right insofar as China refrains from the invasions and occupations that Japan resorted to in its attempt to modernize and catch up with Western imperial powers. But it is not hard to see that China has employed in Xinjiang and now Tibet some of the same means of internal colonialism that the United States used during its own westward expansion.

Propelled by an insatiable global thirst for consumer markets and natural resources, China has done little to allay the fear that Tibetans could soon resemble the Native Americans languishing in reservations—reduced, in the words of the Tibetan novelist Jamyang Norbu, to a "sort of broken third-rate people," who in some years from now will be reduced to "begging from tourists."

The most surprising thing about the eruption of Tibetan rage is that it didn't occur sooner. Televised images of Tibetans assaulting Han Chinese immigrants now stoke a middle-class nationalism in the rich cities on the Chinese coast. Well-off Chinese supporting harsh suppression of the "ingrate" Tibetans echo the middle-class media commentators in Delhi and Mumbai who egg on the police to "crush" those daring to resist their dispossession. But then corporate globalization has rarely been more successful in inculcating a culture of greed and brutality among its most educated beneficiaries. Western commentators may continue to tilt at the straw man of communism in China. Tibetans, however, seem to have sensed that they confront a capitalist modernity more destructive of tradition and more ruthlessly exploitative of the sacred land they walk on than any adversary they have known in their tormented history.

How to Think about Tibet ☆ Donald S. Lopez Jr.

Think about Tibet as Latvia, with very tall mountains. Latvia was once the westernmost Soviet republic, although it had little in common with Russia. The language, the religion, the literature, the food, and the society were all quite different. Latvia had been oriented to the West and to Europe over much of its long history. Yet the region that we today call Latvia came under Russian control during the eighteenth century. With the Russian Revolution, it gained independence in 1920, only to fall to Stalin in 1940. After fifty years of Soviet domination, the Soviet Union collapsed and Latvia regained its independence in 1991.

Most Tibetans have never heard of Latvia. But the parallels are striking. Today, the "Tibet Autonomous Region" is the southwestern province of the People's Republic of China (PRC); the Chinese word for "Tibet" is *Xizang*, "Western Treasury." Although linguists today speak of "Sino-Tibetan linguistics," the relation of Chinese to Tibetan is tenuous. Tibet received its Buddhism from India long after the establishment of Buddhism in China; indeed, beginning in the late eighth century, Tibet looked to India rather than China for its literary and religious culture, even modeling its alphabet on an Indian script. Tibetans eat roasted barley moistened with the infamous "yak butter tea," something the Chinese palate finds unappetizing. Yet, during the eighteenth century, much of Tibet's foreign affairs was overseen by the Chinese court. With the fall of the Qing, Tibet became an independent state (although unlike Latvia, it never joined the League of Nations), a status it maintained from 1913 to 1951. Since 1951, Tibet has been part of the PRC. What is today called the "Tibet Autonomous Region" (TAR) represents only a portion of the Tibetan cultural domain. The remaining areas were incorporated into Sichuan, Yunnan, Gansu, and Qinghai provinces of the PRC.

On March 10, 1959, a rumor circulated in the Tibetan capital of Lhasa that the Chinese troops occupying the city intended to do harm to the Dalai Lama. A large mob gathered and surrounded his summer palace in order to prevent the Chinese from coming in or the Dalai Lama from going out. On the night of March 17, the day the Chinese shelled the palace, the Dalai Lama escaped, disguised as a Tibetan soldier, and made his way to exile in India. He has not returned.

March 10 is celebrated as "Tibetan National Uprising Day" by the Tibetan exile community and supporters of the Tibetan cause around the world. It is not publicly observed in Tibet. However, on March 10, 2008, about one hundred monks from Drepung monastery (prior to the Chinese invasion the largest monastery in the world with over 10,000 monks) began walking the five miles into Lhasa to protest the detention of monks that had occurred after the Dalai Lama received the Congressional Gold Medal the previous October. They were stopped by Chinese security forces, and some of the monks were beaten. Monks have always been accorded respect in Tibetan society; since the Chinese takeover of Tibet, to be a monk is to be a patriot, the red robes and shaved head marking a certain defiance of the avowedly atheist Chinese state. Tibetan laypeople are protective of Tibetan monks; it was when Chinese cadres tried to collectivize the lands of Buddhist monasteries in Eastern Tibet in 1950 that the first bloodshed occurred between Chinese Communists and Tibetans. The People's Liberation Army followed soon thereafter.

March 10, 2009, will be the fiftieth anniversary of the uprising. But the monks of Drepung knew that March 10, 2008, would be the last March 10 before the Beijing Olympics. They dared to use the occasion to draw attention to the plight of Tibet, where since 2006 a high-altitude railroad has brought thousands of Chinese workers and Chinese tourists into Lhasa, where last year the Chinese government declared that henceforth it would control the recognition of all incarnate lamas (which would include the Dalai Lama). The monks knew what was at stake. Monks and nuns had been on the front lines of riots in 1987 and 1989, which resulted in the arrest, torture, and long prison sentences for hundreds. Among the Chinese security forces last week were cameramen, capturing for future use the faces of all those who marched in protest.

And so Tibet has erupted in violence. News reports have announced, "Tibetan Protests Spread to Chinese Provinces." But to Tibetans, the regions of Sichuan and Yunnan and Gansu and Qinghai, where protests and violence have occurred, are not Chinese provinces; they are Tibetan. Chinese policies in those areas have generally been more liberal than in the TAR, making the rapid spread of the protests beyond the TAR all the more significant, indicating the level of frustration that has seethed for ethnic Tibetans across a vast region that was once called "Tibet."

Tibet has a violent history; Tibetan soldiers defeated the armies of the Chinese emperor and captured his capital in 763. The fifth Dalai Lama took the throne of Tibet in 1642 with the assistance of Mongol troops. When the current Dalai Lama instructed the Tibetan guerrillas, who had long hounded the Chinese, to give up the fight, some committed suicide. Today (March 18, 2008), the Dalai Lama urged Tibetans not to resort to violence against the Chinese, explaining that a deer cannot fight a tiger. He knows the suffering that has resulted from resistance in the past.

Is there anything to do but wait? Latvia regained its independence with the collapse of the Soviet Union. It would seem that Tibet could only regain its independence with the collapse of the PRC. In Buddhism, time is measured not in centuries but in cycles of creation, abiding, destruction, and vacuity and then creation again.

Ballooning Unrest: Tibet, State Violence, and the Incredible Lightness of Knowledge ☆ Charlene Makley

I was there."

That's the claim that backs the authority of journalists and anthropologists as analysts of world events. In the competitive display of knowledge unleashed on the heels of crisis, being an eyewitness (an "I witness") supposedly gives the pundit a leg up, though how complicated this role can be has only recently become clear to me.

At the end of August 2008, I returned to the United States from a year in China, where I was living in a town in the southeastern part of Qinghai province. It's known as "Tongren" in Chinese, as "Rebgong" in Tibetan. It's located in a valley that local Tibetans proudly consider a center of their cultural and religious heritage since it contains a centuries-old Geluk sect monastery. But it is not a place that most citizens of the People's Republic of China (PRC) think about much, even though in the past few years it has become an increasingly popular tourist destination, and it rarely makes headlines in the West. Like many other Tibetan communities inside and outside of the official borders of the Tibetan Autonomous Region (TAR), though, it grew dramatically in interest quite suddenly in 2008. This is because, like a large number of communities with significant Tibetan populations, it was the site of unprecedented unrest. Though most media attention focused on Lhasa, some reports circulated about what happened elsewhere, including in Tongren/Rebgong, where protests broke out and violent clashes occurred between ordinary Tibetans and civilian members of other ethnic groups and/or state security forces.

Now that I'm back in the States, though I can claim "eyewitness" status, I don't feel like the Intrepid Pundit, ready to describe what *really* happened back there. For one thing, I find myself totally out of step with the global media, which have rushed on to cover other world crises (in May 2008 the Sichuan earthquake and now, as I write in late September, the collapse of Wall Street). For another, far from feeling the certainty that should come with being an eye-witness, I find myself instead grappling with the inherently elusive nature of knowledge in the face of what felt like powerful Chinese state repression.

Since returning to the United States, I've immersed myself in the foreign media coverage of the Tibetan unrest that was unavailable to me while I was in China. I'm left exhausted, shocked by news and images I couldn't get while there, reliving the very trying spring months in Rebgong, and in awe of the efficacy of central Chinese authorities' efforts to control the access to information I had while in the PRC. As I piece together my own chronologies of events, I can't help noticing great differences between the English-language media representations of that time and my recollections of it. Despite the copious notes I kept, I find that any absolute truth about what happened right under my eyes in what was then my own town continues to elude my grasp. And I have come to realize the true nature of the power of the autocratic state in crisis: as citizens curtail their movements and interactions under constant threat of state violence and the steady drumbeat of state-controlled media, personal knowledge of one's world becomes increasingly fragmented, relegated to rumor circulated among trauma-tized locals. Tibetans in Lhasa and the foreign researchers who try to work there perhaps know this all too well. But it was a relatively new thing for those of us who work in those Tibetan regions such as Rebgong, known by local Tibetans as "Amdo" areas, which are located in provinces such as Qinghai that stand east of the TAR. The military crackdown of 2008 was the first residents had experienced in these places since the Maoist years.

Under such conditions, it is easy to understand why there are gaps and points of confusion in the chronologies and narratives of the Tibetan unrest carried in foreign media. And yet, it seems to me that there are relative truths to be found, patterns and trends in narratives in and outside of China that point to larger issues of significance for thinking through the impact of such pivotal times. A particular event in Rebgong's county town of Tongren, relatively obscure in foreign media coverage of the unrest, stands out for me as an impor-tant case to consider in this light since it illuminates some general things worth keeping in mind when trying to make sense of the upheavals of early 2008 involving Tibetans. This event took place on February 21, the fifteenth day of the lunar New Year, fully three weeks before the first major clashes in Lhasa. On that day hundreds of Tibetan laymen and monks fought in the streets with local security forces. Tibetan residents were stunned at the unprecedented scale of the incident. And many Tibetans I spoke to throughout the region came to see that event and not March 10 (the starting point favored in most foreign chronologies) or March 14 (the starting point favored in Chinese state chronologies) as the moment when the unrest that spread across four provinces began.

The circumstances and international media coverage of that incident speak to the deep schism among Tibet watchers, exploited handily by Chinese state media, over attributing motives to Tibetan participants in the unrest. At the poles of the debates, Tibetans who take action end up seeming to be either senseless rioters needing state control or peaceful (Buddhist) demonstrators seeking independence. Chinese state media framed the unrest as beginning on March 14 in Lhasa (it was labeled "the 3-1-4 incident"), when footage of Tibetan men and monks attacking Chinese businesses and some passersby was aired in continuous loops to fan the righteous anger of Chinese citizens gearing up for the August Olympics. Meanwhile, foreign media most often had the unrest beginning on the historic date of March 10, when Buddhist monks at a major monastery chose to commemorate the 1959 uprising in Lhasa by demonstrating in support of detained peers, only to be stopped by Chinese armed police. And yet the unprecedented footage from a few days later of Tibetans' street violence directed at random Chinese passersby, captured by state surveillance cameras, for the first time called into radical question the image of peaceful Buddhists that has so endeared Tibetans to foreigners.

So what about February 21 in Tongren? It was an event for which I was an eyewitness—though like eyewitnesses of acts of conflict so often are, I was one who only saw part of what happened and have had to piece together my sense of events from a mixture of things I saw, things I heard, and things that I learned about from what others said. Locally, the conflict was typically said to have been sparked by a Hui (Muslim Chinese) merchant's helium balloon eluding the grasp of its Tibetan buyer. This seems to me to be highly resonant of the significance of the event. To me, it stands for the hair-trigger nature of local resentments, building up over years of "market reforms" in China's frontier regions; the elusiveness of state development promises since the "Great Develop the West" campaign was launched in 2000; and the incredible lightness of knowledge in the face of state repression, the elusive capacity to know what really happened when a powerful state apparatus would rather you not.

This is what I saw: February 21 was the fifteenth day of the lunar New Year and the second-to-last day of the Great Prayer Festival at Rongbo monastery. That afternoon, as a few local Public Security Bureau and People's Armed Police (PAP) officers kept watch outside, thousands of Tibetan villagers and nomads participated good-naturedly in the traditional scrum around the future Buddha Maitreya as monks carried his small statue on a circuit of the monastery and laity tried to touch it to receive its blessings. Later, I received a mass text message on my cell phone from the county government inviting residents to the annual fireworks display that night to celebrate the New Year. Some Tibetan friends and I joined the festive crowds of townspeople and walked downtown around 8:00 P.M. to watch. The display in the dark streets was stunning, lasting for a whole hour, and I took pictures of happy, upturned faces of spectators, including the three or four Tibetan policemen standing nearby. At 9:00 P.M., it was over and the crowd began to head home. We joined the crowd heading back up the main street, so packed it was shoulder to shoulder, and we could move only very slowly. That was when the young Tibetan guys' whooping began, that high-pitched, exuberant cry one hears at rituals to propitiate the warlike mountain deities. It started behind us and spread forward, as high-spirited young men, including the teenager I was with, joined in while they continued to walk and casually chat amongst themselves.

We were halfway up the street when, from behind us, the crowd suddenly parted. Out of the gap sped a local police paddy wagon, back doors wildly ajar. It tore up the street and away. Behind it, vainly trying to catch up, sprinted about twenty local Tibetan policemen, still in the two-line formation they had been using to patrol the town during the festival season. I took one blurry picture of them before my Tibetan friends called me away to watch more safely from the intersection at the top of the street. We watched as the people at the front of the crowd were overtaken by a crowd of mostly young Tibetan laymen plus a few monks. They caught up with the fleeing policemen and surrounded them. I caught a glimpse, just before they were engulfed, of the policemen's terrified faces as they turned back-to-back, completely outnumbered, and faced the yelling crowd, using their billy clubs to beat them back. Women and children, male cadres, and older folks pulled away to the peripheries as the crowd of young men, heading up the street to chase the policemen, now turned back down it. I took a photo of their backs as men on the outside craned to see what was happening, and a few young monks, just arriving, whooped and ran to join the crowd. We heard a crescendo of whoops and yelling as the crowd pushed back down the street, away from us. By then, my friends had decided this was no ordinary street scuffle, and we sought the safety and anonymity of their home. There we sat, tensely, people clicking their tongues in disbelief, as we listened to news of the ongoing skirmish come in on cell phones and from family members.

This is what I heard: that night, as calls came in, my friends repeated incredulously that the clash seemed to be escalating, that security reinforcements had been sent in, and that young men and monks were throwing ice chunks and rocks at them (a huge gravel pile for bridge construction stood at the end of the street, ready ammunition). No one knew what had sparked the fighting. Hours passed. Around midnight, just before I finally slept, a breathless male relative came in with wide eyes to say he had heard gunshots and had been told security forces had resorted to firing guns over the crowd's heads. Now they were chasing them down and arresting them. The next day, February 22, when the monastic dance ending the Great Prayer Festival was supposed to take place, rumors flew about the night before. People's consternation grew when for the first time since the 1980s reforms allowed the Great Prayer Festival to take place again, the final monastic dance had to be canceled because several monk performers were in prison for participating in the brawl. A young Tibetan man I knew told me of how the night before he had seen some monks raising their fists and yelling "rise up!" but he said he and his lay male friend had been too terrified, and they fled to the mountains. I told my ex-pat friend that from now on everything would change in the valley; she told me later she hadn't believed me until the events of March unfolded.

We learned that day that since morning other monks had been quietly sitting in the street outside the county government offices. They sat, surrounded by the male relatives of the laymen and monks arrested the night before, silently challenging the police to release the prisoners. Around 4:00 p.m., I passed the demonstration in a taxi and saw them there, by then not more than a few hundred people. Later I saw the photos a Tibetan friend took there at the same time, including the blackened remains of the motorcycle a Hui man had tried to drive through the demonstration. My friend was told that the Hui man had insisted that the monks move out of the street for him to pass, but Tibetan laymen had beaten him, chased him away, and then burned his motorcycle. I saw pictures of young monks, heads down, sitting in the street; of grim lay elders waiting; and of the injured faces of the prisoners released to their custody that day. That night for the first time ever, the monastic dance actually took place at night to ensure that it occur on its proper lunar date. I heard that that was made possible after negotiations between monastic and government officials. In the ensuing days, more rumors flew, and Tibetan male taxi drivers would ask any Tibetan man I was with whether they had "fought" that night.

The contours of a consensus narrative emerged in the valley: Tibetans across the community were convinced that the fighting broke out when a Tibetan youth tried to buy a balloon from a Hui merchant after the fireworks. But the balloon got away and drifted into the sky. The Hui merchant insisted he pay for it, and when their argument escalated, local police stepped in. Despite some evidence to the contrary, Tibetans I spoke to insisted the police had favored the Hui merchant and had tried to arrest and manhandle the Tibetan youth, whose friends jumped in to defend him. That was when other Tibetan men joined the fight and chased the paddy wagon and police patrol. They fought with the policemen until PAP reinforcements arrived, complete with riot shields and helmets. Then men and monks began throwing rocks at them.

Tibetans' narratives usually skipped from here to the arrests and beatings of laymen and monks by security forces later that night. Narrators were particularly upset at what many felt was the excessive force used by security forces. Everyone was talking about the old nomad man whose eye was put out and the young monk whose back was broken, sent to Xining and then to Beijing for medical care. Everyone seemed to know someone who had been arrested and beaten, including many young Tibetan laymen from surrounding villages. But an ex-pat man I knew who had witnessed the fighting from the other end of the street said he saw the PAP initially just letting the rocks bounce off their shields. He said that when Tibetan laymen and monks started attacking police cars and overturning them and he heard retaliating gunshots, he decided it was time for him to get out. Later, Tibetan male friends who had stayed told him that, unbeknownst to the crowd of rock throwers, the local PAP had sent in cars behind them to corner them. Then, when the PAP launched tear gas, the men scattered into nearby urban courtyards. They said that the laymen and monks who were chased down were dragged back to the street, where they were made to kneel, then handcuffed and beaten before being taken to jail. I was told that all but a few of the monks were released by the next afternoon, just hours before the monastic dance was finally performed.

By now, I'm amazed at how even this sketchy summary of this one event far exceeds the length of the short vignettes given in foreign media accounts of the Tibetan unrest. Complexity is always hard to put on paper, especially when urgent times require capturing the attention of restless global readers. But brevity is not the only reason why foreign accounts of that first clash in Tongren vary greatly from what I saw and heard on those days. In fact, the date of this event, weeks before the explosion of unrest in Lhasa came to dominate the significance of everything that came before it, gives us a chance to consider not only the complexity of motives and causes in the unrest but also the ways in which people caught up in crises come to "frame" or reinterpret events after the fact in order to make sense of them. In this case, I found that similar framing processes were at work both locally in Tongren and in foreign media coverage.

Given the "early" date of the event (the local state media referred to it as "the 2-2-1 incident," but in my notes I was calling it the fifteenth of the first because the lunar year frame was more relevant to Tibetans), it doesn't figure strongly in foreign analyses of the Tibetan unrest writ large. But brief accounts of it do appear from the day after all the way to the most recent ones I've seen from August. Its reappearance in different venues over the past six months pointed up the ways that a media story, in citations and paraphrases in the aftermath of crisis, seems to take on a life of its own. When such things happen in Tibetan regions of China, most often the only way to get the word out is for locals to take great risks and talk to foreign media on the phone. This was especially true after Chinese authorities barred foreign journalists from Tibetan regions in March. I myself, so conspicuous as one of the only foreigners in town, was too afraid of endangering my friends or being kicked out to contact anyone.

Two accounts of the February 21 event in Tongren, seemingly based on different local sources, appeared within days, one a very brief blurb by a Reuters reporter, the other an equally brief transcript of a local's call to Radio Free Asia (RFA). Here's the Reuters account:

Tibetans, Chinese police clash over balloon prices
Posted Mon Feb 25, 2008 12:23am AEDT
Updated Mon Feb 25, 2008 12:22am AEDT

A dispute over the price of balloons in an ethnically Tibetan town in western China has sparked a clash between thousands of residents and police, a source with knowledge of the incident said. Several thousand Tibetans in Tongren, Qinghai province, threw stones and attacked police for over an hour during Lunar New Year celebrations on Thursday night, the source, who declined to be named said.

The clash happened after a group of Tibetan youths were involved in a scuffle with a Muslim trader of the Hui ethnic group, the source said. "Members of the crowd . . . tried to intervene, and then beat the policemen, who ran away. Rumours that the police had beat up some local youths spread through the crowd, and many other police were beaten or chased away, leading to large-scale unrest," the source said.

A contingent of People's Armed Police, or paramilitary force, later arrived to restore order, firing tear gas and detaining about 100 people. Up to 20 of the police, who were all Tibetans, were taken to hospital, and two police cars were overturned during the rioting, the source said. Authorities released 90 of the detained, and the remaining 10 were freed the following morning, after protesters gathered outside government offices and monks at local monasteries threatened to boycott new year rituals and dance ceremonies scheduled for later that day.

"This suggests the local Government also decided the incidents were a reaction to excessive force, not a protest about China's role in Tibet," the source said. A notice from Tongren county authorities called for calm and said police were holding "people whose mistakes are considered heavy for further investigation." "The county Government asks all nationalities . . . voluntarily to protect the security of the county," the statement said. Calls placed to Tongren Government offices seeking comment went unanswered.

Relations between mainly Buddhist Tibetans and the Hui, a Muslim minority numbering about 10 million in China, have long been tense. Ethnic tensions between Chinese minorities and the dominant Han, who account for about 90 per cent of China's 1.3 billion people, regularly spill over into violence, particularly in the country's unsettled western regions. In November, an altercation between a Han Chinese shopowner and Tibetan monks in rural Tibet's Naqu district led to hundreds of Tibetan herdsmen smashing shops owned by Han Chinese. (*Source*: http://www.abc.net.au/news/stories/2008/02/25/2171075 .htm?section = justin)

And here's the RFA call-in transcript, reprinted in an online chronology:

Chinese authorities sent in three truckloads of armed police after a clash erupted between Chinese authorities and hundreds of Tibetans at the annual Monlam prayer festival attended by thousands of spectators; the authorities "ordered the prayer festival stopped"; paramilitary police fired tear gas. Two hundred Tibetans, mostly monks, were detained, many of whom "were participating in a masked dance performance so they couldn't perform the dance."

Up to 200 armed and unarmed police "were sent into the crowd, possibly to prevent anti-Chinese protests." When police questioned one man, other

Tibetans gathered around him, and a group of Tibetans outside a restaurant began "shouting slogans and attacking police with sticks and stones." When the police detained "some monks," the people protested more intensely. Under the pressure of a massive Tibetan demonstration, the local government "had to" release all those who were arrested on the first day of protest. Many of them had been severely beaten and tortured; two of them were taken to Xining for treatment. This further enraged Tibetan demonstrators who "refused to stop." Other protests erupted "around the same time"; the crowds damaged seven Chinese government vehicles; authorities sent in more police, and around 200 people, mostly monks, were detained but most have since been released. During the clash and protests, many Tibetans raised independence slogans and prayed for the long life of the Dalai Lama. The demonstrations went on until about 10pm.

The head lama of Rebkong monastery intervened, and the demonstration came to an end; "even the traditional mask dance was also performed." The local government posted a statement in the town saying: "Local Tibetans gathered for the Monlam festival protested when police interrogated a Tibetan. Those Tibetan youths who were involved in the protests were interrogated and those who were slightly injured were handed over to their parents for advice and guidance. So the county is peaceful as before." (*Source*: Reported by RFA, February 22, 2008, https://www.tibetinfonet.net/newsticker/entries)

Of course there is much to notice in the differences between these accounts of the same incident, such as the different claims about numbers, the type of relevant festival event, and the nature of the security forces involved. But most striking to me in the Reuters account is the absence of any statement that police beat Tibetans, whereas in the RFA transcript it's the lack of a linear chronology, typical of oral narratives, and the absence of any mention of Hui–Tibetan fighting. I don't know the details of what really happened in Tongren that day, only the broad contours of events emerge from the fog. I'm convinced that security forces did indeed brutally beat arrested Tibetans; that the brawl was sparked, perhaps intentionally, by a squabble between a Tibetan and a Hui merchant over a balloon; and that monks, in the minority, joined the fighting and were among those who began to call for an uprising. And I'm convinced that monks initiated a peaceful demonstration the next day, even though Tibetan laymen attacked an unwise Hui motorcyclist there.

But the effect of the Reuters version of the event, set in the secular context of celebrating the lunar New Year, is to portray Tibetan participants as rioters, engaged in local ethnic conflict brought under control by police. The effect of the RFA version, set in the Buddhist context of the Prayer Festival, is to portray Tibetan participants as monk-led demonstrators, protesting the arbitrary interference of state security forces in Buddhist ritual and calling for independence from Chinese rule. It would seem that in the days immediately following the incident, the competing poles in claims about Tibetan participants' motives in unrest had already emerged in the media. But the explosion of unrest in Lhasa and across Tibetan regions a few weeks later raised the stakes and widened the scale for gathering and framing accounts of clashes. All subsequent references to February 21 in Tongren came after major clashes in Lhasa (March 10–16) and after monks at Rongbo monastery in Tongren staged their own Buddhist demonstrations and public long life prayers for the Dalai Lama (March 16–17), only to be stopped by beefed-up military forces that had been sent into Tongren in anticipation of March 10.

As far as I can tell, the February 21 incident in Tongren was mentioned some fifteen times in the foreign media in the following five months. All such mentions then framed the incident, its motives, and its causes as background to the March uprisings. But there is little consensus on details except for the broadest of outlines. This is remarkable given that Tongren was one of the very few places that foreign journalists could actually visit. From the media reports (I never met them while there), I counted a total of five foreign journalists who visited, two in March and three during the summer months. Of those who were reporting from abroad, only one reporter relied on the original Reuters piece; the rest cited the RFA transcript as their main source.

Of those, perhaps the most interesting account of the February 21 incident is that of the courageous Tibetan woman poet and blogger named Woeser (like many Tibetan writers, she uses a single name), who is based in Beijing. Beginning in March, at great risk to herself (she and her husband were under house arrest in Beijing by mid-March), Woeser followed the unrest closely and blogged updates in Chinese, which were then translated and circulated in the foreign media. Her account of February 21 in Tongren was posted on April 17, the very day that Tongren saw the bloodiest and most traumatic of clashes. I was not there. I was on the next street over being stopped by police. On that day, I was told, monks protesting the previous arrests of their peers and the increasing military presence in town were themselves arrested. When other monks and laity intervened, their encounter with national PAP troops on a main street turned into a melee of beatings and arrests. Tensions in town had been high since March, but now they heightened again; Tongren was under de facto martial law. Already by the third week of March, prefecture and county authorities, initially relatively lenient, had begun their own reinterpretation of the incident of February 21. An official notice was posted throughout the prefecture and aired on local television calling for the rearrest of all those who had participated and offering cash rewards for anyone who would turn in photos identifying them.

In this context came Woeser's account of what happened in February:

> As early as two months ago, i.e. on the evening of February 11, because the military police disrupted the religious ceremony held by the local monastery in Rebgong (Ch. Tongren) County in Tsolho (Ch. Huangnan) Prefecture, Qinghai Province, it caused great resentment among the local monks and lay people.

Thus, they shouted slogans demanding freedom of religious belief and wish a long life to the Dalai Lama. Consequently, they were dispersed by the local government with tear gases, and madly arrested over 200 monks and lay people. The next day, this prompted several thousand monks and lay people to stage a demonstration at the county seat, demanding the local government to release the monks and lay people who were arrested. Under the pressure, the local government had to release all those who were arrested, but three monks and one old man were severely injured resulting from beating, and had to be sent to the emergency room so as to save their lives. Soon afterward, the authorities transferred special police from Xining and Zhengzhou (in the local hotel there are banners on which such words as "welcome the special police from Zhengzhou to stay at our hotel") to Rebgong. Suppressed by the massive forces, the "Incident of February 11" happened in Rebgong was temporarily calmed down, but we can say this is the prelude to the series of incidents happened after March 10 in Lhasa and protests which spread to all Tibetan areas. (Posted April 17, 2008, in Chinese)

It is not clear who her source was, but it seems that Woeser picks up the original RFA call-in, and she reiterates major aspects of that version here, including the numbers and the setting of the event at the Prayer Festival and not at the secular new year celebration in town, but gone is any mention of Tibetans attacking anyone. Monks here participate as they did in later demonstrations: they lead nonviolent demonstrations against state interference. Given the traumatic events of March and April, when Woeser first learned of the February incident in Tongren, it is no wonder that she comes to frame it this way. But something else interests me more about this account. Inexplicably, she gets the date wrong, placing the event ten days earlier, at a time before the Great Prayer Festival had even begun in Tongren. And rather than catch the mistake (several accounts had already dated it accurately), some reporters abroad, including Reuters, picked it up and reported it as is, so that the original RFA framing of the event *came to be reported as a separate event* in Tongren. Thus, for example, in the Tibetinfonet online chronology of Tibetan unrest, accounts of the same event in Tongren are listed under two dates: February 11, where monks protested interference at a Buddhist ritual, and February 21, where the clash between the Hui and the Tibetan over the balloon is mentioned.

What has happened, it seems to me, is in the midst of the unprecedented scale of unrest and military crackdown in Tibetan regions, a "shadow event" was established for the problematically complex incident of February 21 in Tongren, a kind of mirror twin, rendered concrete on a separate day, that distills it down to motives and causes that seem to make sense in the face of such awesome state terror. That process illustrates to me that such motives and causes for Tibetan unrest are more persuasive outside of China than, say, those claimed in the original Reuters account. Hence the August 6 International Campaign for Tibet report on the spring 2008 unrest repeats in summary form the version of February 21 in Tongren in which police arbitrarily disrupt a monastic ritual at the Great Prayer Festival.

The truth? I find it escapes my grasp like the balloon escaped someone's grasp that night. This is not because people are necessarily deliberately manipulating facts. After living through that time in Tongren, I feel strongly that the incredible lightness of knowledge is the direct outcome and indeed the most important goal of state violence. Life in the valley in the spring and summer of 2008 was not a relentless series of public clashes. Instead, under de facto martial law and the quiet unspoken threat of military posts and patrols, the psychological engineering of state terror had me, like everyone else, grasping onto daily routine, curtailing my movements, and looking over my shoulder. Terrified to endanger anyone and determined to stay, I learned of events only through snippets of rumor and furtive conversations.

And yet, as I turn to face this past year and try to make sense of it, I am convinced that relative truths are still crucial. To really grasp the implications of "the Olympic Year" in Tibetan regions of China, we need to at least try to understand the complexities of historical events as well as the (often unconscious) interpretive processes we use to represent them. The events of February 21 in Tongren were indeed a precursor to the widespread Tibetan unrest that broke out in March, but it also emerged out of a boiling soup of simultaneous motives, both short and long term, both local and global. Indeed, February 21, "early" as it was, was not a starting point for the 2008 Tibetan unrest. Instead, I see it as part of a much longer-term process of Chinese state efforts to globalize the local politics of China's western frontier. This was intensified first by the Great Develop the West campaign in China, launched in 2000, and then sharpened to a point in 2008 by the intense national face politics of the Olympics. There is indeed a long history of ethnic conflict between Tibetans and Hui, but those hair-trigger resentments were set in motion by the deep disparities of recent development processes favoring the monied and the connected in China. In this sense, the February 21, 2008, unrest in Tongren should be placed in a lineage that includes the Hui–Tibetan brawl that broke out some six years earlier in the neighboring county of Jianzha (called "gcan tsa" in Tibetan). In that 2002 incident, Tibetans fought both Hui townsmen and Tibetan police, whom they thought had been bribed by wealthy Hui merchants.

Tibetan politics in China has arguably been a global politics for a long time but especially since the Dalai Lama escaped to India in 1959 and established a government in exile. The Dalai Lama is the face of the global for Tibetans across regions in China. Clashes between Tibetans and state security forces in Amdo Tibetan regions (including Tongren) and in Lhasa had already happened in October 2007, when the United States defiantly honored the Dalai Lama with a Congressional Medal and Tibetan monks' celebrations were stopped by police. For Chinese central authorities, October 2007 was already the homestretch of a long process of ramping up for the world coming-out party of the Beijing Olympics, a process that, among other things, involved increasing militarization out west, that is, the creation and training of special "antiterrorist" units and the construction of new highways and railways that, among other things, would move them around quickly. This led to a process in Tongren that seems to have been replayed throughout Tibetan regions in 2008: a tragic ballooning of violence, the escalation and spread of violence as all players anticipated the global media scrutiny accompanying the Olympics. Beefed-up provincial and national military forces were then immediately called in after more localized clashes, and some Tibetans, knowing the world was watching as never before, defiantly protested their presence and their use of force, airing a variety of demands and goals.

I will perhaps never know exactly what happened on February 21, 2008, in Tongren. But my whole experience there this past year has had a profound impact on me. I've come away with a visceral sense of what it means to live through a period of massive militarization, when an autocratic state mobilized to simultaneously crush dissent and consolidate control over its western regions. And this helps me to better appreciate the wide range of often conflicting and disorganized motives and aspirations of the Tibetans who must make their lives under such conditions. The global media has moved on, but the situation they struggle with remains. I, for one, will continue to grapple with it and with my own role in representing it.

Chapter 3

Meanwhile, across the Straits . . .

THE ELECTION IN TAIWAN

Yong Chen

As American attention is captivated by the war in Iraq and, more recently, our own upcoming national election, another important event is about to take place on the other side of the Pacific Ocean: the presidential election of Taiwan on March 21 (March 22 local time). This event is of great importance to the United States for a number of reasons. First, there is the economic significance of Taiwan, America's ninth-largest trade partner in 2007, which has emerged in recent decades as an important player in the global economy, especially in the information technology sector. Second, there is the geopolitical significance of Taiwan. American links to Taiwan are a vital factor in the often fragile but increasingly mutually dependent relationship between China and the United States.

The election will decide who will lead Taiwan for the next four years. The choice is between two candidates: Frank Hsieh and Ma Ying-jeou. The former represents the Democratic Progressive Party (DPP) and the latter the Kuomintang (KMT). A crucial difference between the two parties is their respective policy on Taiwan's relationship with mainland China. The DPP advocates independence, while the KMT wants to maintain the status quo.

If public polls in Taiwan are any indication, a majority of voters in Taiwan prefer the status quo, which has benefited Taiwan, at least economically. Trade with China's thriving economy has become a lifeline for Taiwan's ailing economy. In 2007 trade across the Taiwan Straits exceeded U.S.$100 billion, and such trade activities gave Taiwan an annual surplus of over U.S.$46 billion. Meanwhile, in its effort to develop its modern and global economy, China continues to need the investment dollars and the technological and managerial know-how that pours into the People's Republic of China from Taiwan.

The election in Taiwan has also been a heated issue among Chinese Americans, dividing them in recent years. At the end of the day, however, when the noise of election quiets down, ordinary people will realize that it is peace and prosperity, not political rhetoric, that best represents their interest.

Posted 3/21/2008 at 08:44:00 AM

With all eyes on Beijing in 2008, few Taiwan stories made major headlines in U.S. media. Even so, the threat of explosion lurked, as always, in any issue that sparked interest and opinion on both sides of the Straits, including the spring's presidential election. The banal assertions that the Olympics would bring the world together aside, the Olympic Games provided continual friction between China and Taiwan. Before the year even began, Olympic preparations created controversy in the Straits. In the spring of 2007, Beijing Olympic organizers proposed that the Taiwan leg of the international Olympic torch relay come just before the Hong Kong and Macau legs, grouping all three cities together as "overseas Chinese cities." Taiwan rejected the torch's island appearance, asserting that unlike Macau and Hong Kong, which are under Chinese rule, Taiwan remains independent and should be part of the international torch circuit, not tacked onto the domestic route.

Taiwan's presence in Beijing as "Chinese Taipei" went smoothly (despite a disappointing medal showing), but tensions simmered. Even while Beijing talked tough on Taiwan independence, bristling at the mention of it in international settings and holding to the line that Taiwan is part of China, China watchers at home and abroad noted that Beijing's stance seemed more about placating Chinese nationalists than about actually reclaiming control over the rogue island. The Taiwan–China relationship was, in fact, largely stable this year. As in years past, relations between the two, ahem, political entities were predictably rancorous, impassioned, and hostile. For instance, in response to the September announcement of a proposed U.S. arms sale to Taiwan, China canceled a series of talks with the United States. It is unlikely that the State Department was surprised by that response.

Though Taiwan–China relations are, at this point, something like a choreographed dance, Taiwan remains enormously important to China, economically, politically, and rhetorically. In 2008, Paul Katz chronicled Taiwan's stories for China Beat, filling readers in on the island's large and small issues. This chapter includes a selection of his writings.

Selection of Readings on Taiwan ☆ Paul R. Katz

WHAT SHALL WE DO WITH THE DEAD DICTATOR?

One of the thorniest problems facing fledgling democracies involves how to cope with memories of their former dictators. Attempts to assess this aspect of a country's history are especially problematic because the trauma many citizens have suffered is tempered by the lingering impact of indoctrination and hero worship. Add to this mixture of emotions the spices of identity formation and electoral politics, and its volatility can increase exponentially.

Since 2007, Taiwan has been grappling with the legacy of former Republic of China (ROC) President Chiang Kai-shek (1887–1975). One aspect has involved a "rectification of names" (*zhengming*) campaign (for example, renaming CKS International Airport as Taiwan Taoyuan International Airport), which also includes affixing the word "Taiwan" to as many state organizations as possible (a case in point being the *Taiwan Post*). At the same time, government officials and scholars have been striving to achieve some degree of transitional justice by holding Chiang and other former ROC leaders accountable for human rights abuses, especially the death and imprisonment of thousands of Taiwanese during the 228 Incident of 1947.

The debate over these issues reached a crescendo in December 2007, when the government renamed and redesigned the sacred space of the Chiang Kai-shek Memorial Hall (now National Taiwan Democracy Memorial Hall) while also withdrawing funding and the military honor guard from the Cihhu Presidential Burial Palace in Dasi, where both the elder Chiang and his son, former President Chiang Ching-kuo (1910–1988), had been temporarily laid to rest. Both of these sites are powerful symbols of the presence the Chiangs continue to exert over Taiwan. The mammoth Memorial Hall, modeled after the Sun Yat-sen Mausoleum in Nanjing, was constructed over a three-and-a-half-year period extending from 1976 to 1980, with the imposing bronze statue of Chiang weighing in as the fourth largest in the world. The Cihhu mausoleum was built on land originally belonging to the renowned Lin family of Panchiao, which was presented to the state in 1955 and used as a site for one of Chiang's residences from 1959 onward.

Plans to rename the Memorial Hall were announced in May 2007, but the formal opening of the new site and the replacement of the renowned characters adorning the site's main gate, "Great Centrality and Perfect Uprightness" (*dazhong zhizheng*), with "Liberty Square" (*Ziyou guangchang*), did not take place until the end of the year. There had also been fears that Chiang's statue would be demolished or enclosed in an iron cage, but when the hall reopened on New Year's Day, it was found to have been surrounded by kites and photographs commemorating Taiwan's arduous struggle toward democracy. Even these alterations caused considerable furor, especially after strongly worded statements in their favor by leading officials from the Ministry of Education and Government Information.

The government's decision to withdraw its support from the presidential mausoleum, which was made at the same time the Memorial Hall was being rectified, sparked a different set of rhetorical fireworks, especially when Chiang Ching-kuo's third daughter-in-law proposed having both Chiangs' remains reburied in their native home of Fenghua, in the mainland province of Zhejiang. President Chen Shuibian immediately voiced his outrage, pointing out that the government had already spent NT$30 million (approximately U.S.$925,000) in taxpayers' money to build permanent tombs for the former leaders in a suburb of Taipei. With elections fast approaching, the above issues became subjects of an increasingly acrimonious debate. One of the few voices of reason was none other than one of Chiang Kai-shek's descendants, Demos Chiang, who posted thoughtful entries on his own blog pointing out that while his great-grandfather had been responsible for great suffering, he neither merited deification nor deserved demonization.

As election fever subsided, so did the controversy over the Chiang legacy, although some have blamed the Democratic Progressive Party's (the DPP, often associated with the Taiwan independence movement) stunning defeat in part on the clumsy way the government handled this issue. The transformation of the National Taiwan Democracy Memorial Hall was largely complete, although several months later the website still featured the hall's former abbreviation. The mausoleum is now being managed by the Taoyuan County Government, while a new park in Dasi has been built to hold hundreds of discarded statues of Chiang Kai-shek. The wounds caused during his rule remain, but many still regard him as a great leader, and there is even some nostalgia for the rule of his son. However, the question of how to come to grips with this facet of Taiwan's modern history remains unanswered. While archives have been opened and studies published, the past has been politicized by both the DPP and the Kuomintang (KMT), and Taiwan's sole "Truth Commission" was created by the pro-KMT camp merely to investigate the shooting of President Chen Shuibian and Vice President Lu Hsiu-lien prior to the 2004 election. However, while both democracies and dictatorships attempt to manipulate the past to serve the present, Taiwan deserves credit for allowing such topics to be the subject of free and freewheeling discussion.

TRAUMA AND MEMORY—228 IN TAIWAN TODAY

In 2008, Taiwan commemorated the sixty-first anniversary of the February 28 Incident (hereafter referred to as 228),[1] an uprising against KMT authoritarian rule initially sparked by the beating of a female vendor in Taipei for selling untaxed cigarettes. During the ensuing military crackdown, tens of thousands of Taiwan's elite were arrested, tortured, and murdered, with the violence lasting into the spring of 1947 and helping usher in the era known as the White Terror.

The untold suffering of 228 has led to decades of division in Taiwan society because while the conflict's victims included both Taiwanese and Mainlanders, the KMT brought the full brunt of state violence to persecute innocent men and women. 228 remained taboo for decades under Chiang Kai-shek's dictatorial rule, with the first scholars to lecture on this subject writing their wills before heading off to class. It took until 1995 for then KMT President Lee Teng-hui to offer the first official apology, with the Legislative Yuan making 228 an official holiday in 1998.

Regrettably, the commemoration of 228 is increasingly turning into a formal-

---

1. My thoughts on 228 benefited from reading editorials in the *Taipei Times* and *Taiwan News Online*. Thanks also to Kevin Chang (Chang Ku-ming) for his advice and inspiration.

ity. This year's anniversary in particular was highly politicized, coming amid a tightly fought presidential race featuring Frank Hsieh of the ruling DPP and Ma Ying-jeou of the KMT. Thousands of DPP supporters marched through the streets of Taipei starting at 2:28 P.M. before proceeding to an evening rally, in part in hopes of rekindling the spirit of the Hand in-Hand Safeguard Taiwan Rally, which attracted over 2 million participants back in 2004. Ma, who was leading Hsieh by at least ten points in opinion polls, attended a 228 concert in tribute to the victims. In a concerted drive to appeal to the 70 percent non-Mainlander element of Taiwan's 23 million people, Ma often prefers to use Taiwanese instead of his native Mandarin when offering apologies for the past. His years of effort have moved some family members of the victims to take part in KMT-sponsored events.

However, for many people the KMT art of apology still seems to be little more than mere lip service. One reason why some people might feel skeptical is that the KMT has co-opted a significant number of Taiwanese local factions, including some with close ties to the victims. For example, pan-blue local officials in the Kinmen County Government and Taya Township Office in Taichung County chose to ignore government regulations that the flag be flown at half mast nationwide, with Taya's mayor publicly expressing his dissatisfaction with the DPP government's decision to deemphasize holidays such as Retrocession Day while choosing to focus on 228 instead.

Apologies aside, much remains to be done before the trauma of 228 can be fully healed. Taiwanese scholars like Hsu Hsueh-chi and Lai Tse-han have done pathbreaking research, while Stephen E. Phillips has published an important book-length study. In addition, institutions like the 228 Memorial Foundation and Taipei 228 Memorial Museum are working to shed new light on the past. Another interesting development is that some Chinese historians (including a sizable number of Mainlanders) who had never previously shown any interest in Taiwan history are now starting to publish their own interpretations of 228. However, many critical files housed in government and KMT party archives still lie beyond the reach of critical scholarly research.

During a visit to a 228 victim's family, Hsieh urged that both he and Ma promise to fully open all relevant files collected by the National Security Bureau, the Taiwan Garrison Command (now under the Ministry of Defense), and the Investigation Bureau (now under the Ministry of Justice). One hopeful sign was that Ma pledged to build a national 228 Memorial Hall and continue promoting research on the tragedy and that he placed the blame squarely on his own party. However, in response to complaints over the KMT's continued blocking of the budget for the Statute for the Handling of and Compensation for the 228 Incident in the Legislative Yuan, Ma chose to criticize the Cabinet for listing the budget under the Ministry of Education instead of the Ministry of the Interior. Inasmuch as the KMT now holds a commanding majority, it remains to be seen how much progress will actually take place.

In the midst of all this politicking, perhaps the greatest tragedy is that many victims' families (Taiwanese and Mainlander alike) still have no idea why their loved ones perished or where their remains lie. Many people believe in the need to establish an independent and impartial "truth and reconciliation commission" with the authority to investigate unjust martial law verdicts and unsolved state political crimes in order to achieve the long-term goal of transitional justice and genuine reconciliation. However, others fear that a truth commission seems hopeless now, as one side of Taiwan's polarized political spectrum might automatically reject any rulings considered favorable to the other. And, even if a truth commission proved viable, the fact remains that virtually no material in local school curriculums performs the vital function of educating Taiwan's youth about 228.

All of this casts a shadow over the way in which 228 will be remembered in the future. At a memorial service held at the Taipei 228 Memorial Peace Park, President Chen Shui-bian said, "If we cannot face the past, we cannot construct the future." Or, as Nobel laureate Elie Wiesel so eloquently stated during his 1986 Peace Prize acceptance speech, "if we forget, we are guilty, we are accomplices." It seems particularly noteworthy that the 228 Memorial Foundation set the theme of this year's official commemorations as "Taiwan Stands Up," urging people to overcome the tensions wrought by 228 and five decades of authoritarian rule by rallying to the defense of Taiwan's hard-won democracy. However, Taiwan's democratic triumphs will surely lose their luster if politicians continue to use the past in the service of the present and the next generation proves apathetic about this dark side of their nation's history.

THE RETURN OF THE TWO NATIONALISMS

One fascinating aspect of the KMT regaining political dominance in Taiwan is the reappearance of two forms of nationalism that have been central to that party's political ideology, namely, Greater China and anti-Japanese resistance. Both have enjoyed a certain degree of legitimacy in the context of modern Chinese history, yet each carries its own risks as well.

The theme of Greater China found clear expression in President Ma Ying-jeou's inaugural address, which emphasized the idea that the residents of both China and Taiwan were part of a greater "Chinese nation" (*zhonghua minzu*). It also seemed significant that Ma made no mention of Japan, as well as the issue of whether Taiwan (or the ROC for that matter) is a sovereign state. From a diplomatic perspective, the skirting of such issues in order to enhance cross-strait negotiations makes considerable sense, as can be seen in the successful conclusion of agreements on direct flights and tourism. However, the question of who will benefit from these policies is unclear, and there are also concerns about the costs. One example is Ma's agreeing to be addressed as "Mr. Ma" when he meets China's Association for Relations Across the Taiwan Strait Chairman Chen Yunlin later this year. While such compromises have a reasonable chance of furthering future ties between China and Taiwan, one cannot help but think of other leaders from the previous century who were willing to make all manner of sacrifices in the interest of "peace in our time."

Anti-Japanese sentiments made a dramatic comeback in Taiwan's political arena during a diplomatic row with Japan that ensued after the June 10 sinking of a Taiwanese fishing vessel by a Japanese patrol boat in disputed waters surrounding islets known in Taiwan as Tiaoyutai and in Japan as the Senkaku Islands. Both Taipei and Tokyo claim these islets and their surrounding waters, in part because of their abundant fishery resources and potential natural gas deposits. Japan subsequently apologized and offered to negotiate compensation for the fishing boat's captain, but the immediate aftermath of the incident was marked by highly provocative comments, including Premier Liu Chao-shiuan allowing himself to be goaded by hard-line KMT legislators into saying that he did not "exclude war" with Japan.

Perhaps more importantly, in addition to recalling Koh Se-kai, Taiwan's de facto ambassador to Japan, the Ma government scrapped the Committee on Japanese Affairs, a body that had played a key role in improving Taiwan's ties with Japan. Established in 2005, this committee comprised experts who reported directly to the foreign minister and provided recommendations on Taiwan–Japan relations. The presence of this committee contributed to steadily improving yet unofficial links with Tokyo, with Japan overtaking the United States as Taiwan's second-biggest trading partner after China in 2006 and the two nations becoming each other's top foreign tourist destinations.

Now that this committee has been axed, one wonders who will be responsible for managing ties with Japan and whether the links between these two countries will improve or continue to deteriorate. If the Ma administration continues to play on emotional anti-Japanese sentiments, the people of Japan might well conclude that years of friendship with Taiwan are now at risk. Such sentiments are already being expressed in editorials in the Japanese media, which point to the rise of Greater China and anti-Japanese sentiments as harbingers of what could be a "nightmarish" future.

There have also been signs that these tensions are infecting Taiwan's own domestic arena. On June 18, following a meeting with former president Chen Shui-bian, Koh Se-kai was struck by a protester who claimed to be a member of the prounification Patriot Association. This assault followed highly charged comments by KMT lawmakers, who labeled Koh as a "Taiwan traitor" (*taijian*) and "a Japanese, not a Taiwanese." There have also been reports of Japanese students being beaten up, and there is now enhanced security at the Taipei Japanese School.

It seems particularly fascinating that both of these forms of nationalism have also helped shape Chinese Communist Party (CCP) ideology, which suggests that they might serve as a common ground for future negotiations. Moreover, both the CCP and the KMT found it useful to exploit such sentiments in order to distract attention from other issues. In Taiwan the stock market plummeted 15 percent after Ma's inauguration, while prices continued to rise. In addition, the new government was plagued by controversies over its members having until recently enjoyed dual citizenship or permanent residency, including the current foreign minister, who somehow managed to apply for a green card while serving as ambassador to Guatemala. As a result, the administration's popularity steadily declined, and a June *United Daily News* poll showed Ma's own rating at 50 percent, down from 66 percent in May.

Finally, there were disturbing indications of politics once again extending its claws into academia. One example is the decision by National Chengchi University not to extend the contract of former Ministry of Education Secretary Chuang Kuo-jung on charges of "conduct unbecoming of a professor." While Chuang made some highly offensive remarks about Ma's father, he had subsequently apologized, and the department and college faculty review committees had only recommended a suspension, only to be overruled by the university review committee in favor of the harsher punishment. During the past ten years, there have been 106 instances of contract termination at Taiwan's universities, but those that involved charges of "conduct unbecoming of a professor" tended to be cases of sexual harassment, rape, and corruption and usually followed the accused faculty member's being convicted in a court of law. There have also been difficulties surrounding the proposed reappointment of former Representative to the United States Joseph Wu at the same university. These events, combined with reports that many officials appointed by the Chen administration are now in danger of losing their jobs, suggest a return of the "cicada in winter effect," by which opposition voices gradually fall silent.

One hopes that the above instances are merely aberrations and that the KMT's return to power, combined with the understandable quest for improved relations with China, does not come at the price of rampant nationalism and the abandonment of the democratic freedoms that so many men and women fought so hard to achieve.[2]

---

2. Some of the contents of this post were inspired by Max Hirsch's June 17 article titled "Goodwill between Japan, Taiwan Fading after Key Committee Scrapped."

Chapter 4

Nationalism and the Torch

FOLLOW THE BOUNCING TORCH

Jeffrey N. Wasserstrom

It can become numbing to try to keep up with all the stories about the torch and keep track of where exactly it has been and is going next. Still, it remains fascinating to see how the responses to it have varied from place to place. Fortunately, for those who want a quick visual reminder of what's happened so far, as well as a guide to where the flame is headed, there's a handy interactive map in the *Financial Times*.

FT's visual time line of China's involvement in the Games includes a re-minder of the now often forgotten moment in 1960 when an element of protest came into the Rome opening ceremonies because of a flap over how Taiwan's team had to describe itself. So much for the tired notion that the Games have never been politicized before or have only been politi-cized in a few hot-button years, such as 1936 and 1980.

Posted 4/27/2008 at 06:43:00 AM

The torch run's problems started with the Tibetan riots and protests. In a perfect example of how domestic problems can rapidly become international headaches, Beijing's perceived hard-line response in Tibet mobilized activists around the globe. Some groups, such as those like Save Darfur, who strongly criticized China's relationship with the Sudanese government, were already planning Olympic torch protests before the Tibet crisis occurred. These small-scale demonstrations were quickly eclipsed as the response at each torch stop was bigger than the last. The torch's progress was delayed, disrupted, or canceled in Paris, San Francisco, Nagano, London, Islamabad, New Delhi, and Seoul. In many other cities, such as Buenos Aires, Canberra, and Hong Kong, large groups of protesters gathered along the route, though the torch continued its circuit uninterrupted.

While the pro-Tibet crowd garnered most of the media coverage, protesters weren't the only ones along the parade routes. Instead, small numbers of protesters were often greeted by thousands of overseas Chinese (supplemented by students from the People's Republic of China studying abroad) who waved flags, cheered the torch, and, occasionally, got into scuffles with anti-China demonstrators.

At home in China, there was enormous anger over attempts to disrupt the torch's run. After one protester in Paris attempted to wrest the torch away from wheelchair-bound Jin Jing, a paralympic fencer, Jin became a national hero. Photos of her using her body to shield the flame from the grasping protester, a Tibetan flag tied around his head, became emblematic of China's feelings about the torch relay. This was supposed to be, they felt, a triumphal moment for the Chinese nation. The torch embodied China's sacrifices and perseverance to reach a point where the world recognized it with an Olympic berth. The disrespect shown the torch reflected an international disrespect for China and its herculean efforts to throw a stunning party. Grouping this disrespect into the several centuries of "national humiliation" that schoolchildren are taught China has been subjected to, many Chinese felt angry and disheartened by the anti-China protests. The Olympics, it began to seem, might not bring China international respect after all.

Torching the Relay: An Interview ☆ Geremie R. Barmé[1]

The following remarks were written in response to a series of questions from writers at Woroni, *the paper produced by students at the Australian National University. They were drafted on April 28 and revised on May 3, 2008.*

---

1. My thanks to Tom Swann of *Woroni* for inviting me to respond to his questions and to Jeffrey Wasserstrom for suggesting that *China Beat* post this material.

WORONI: In general, the article will be asking, Why was there such a power-ful expression of Chinese nationalism in the Australian national capital, Canberra? We are guided by our personal observations that much of the protest-ing was overtly political and often antagonistic, which we think was not fully brought out in the media coverage.

GEREMIE R. BARMÉ: Chinese demonstrators in Canberra would claim that they were giving voice to righteous patriotic (rather than the more negative "nationalistic") sentiment in the face of deliberate distortions of the real situa-tion in Tibetan China resulting from the "Western media" demonization of the People's Republic of China and the way the media had handled the March dis-turbances in Lhasa and elsewhere in what, for want of a better expression, I would call Tibetan China (that is the areas including the "Tibet Autonomous Region," Qinghai, parts of Gansu, Sichuan, and Yunnan with large ethnic Tibetan populations). In the days leading up to the Canberra leg of the Olympic torch relay, Chinese organizers (both official and nonofficial) made the case to their fellows that Canberra is a city with a small population and that if patriotic Chinese did not turn up in numbers then protesters—"Tibet splittists" (to use the Chinese jargon), adherents of Falun Gong and a rag-bag of "anti-Chinese elements"—would make a big showing of "anti-Chinese" fervor in front of the national and international media. Only a large vocally patriotic Chinese presence could counter this.

Furthermore, the demonstrators who made themselves so noisily felt and heard in Canberra had been inflamed by the disruptions of the relay in London, Paris, and San Francisco. They were also outraged by talk of a boycott of the Beijing Olympics opening on August 8 this year. These boisterous—and also very physical demonstrations—had been reported in the Chinese media and blo-gosphere with a level of emotional intensity bordering on the hysterical. Accounts in the official Chinese media were also highly colorful and employed the histrionic style of high-Maoist China, that is, the liberal use of morally laden terms of vituperation and condemnation—something I have written about in the chapter "Totalitarian Nostalgia" in my book *In the Red: On Contemporary Chinese Culture* (1999). During this process, the Olympic torch, something that should by all rights be regarded as a global symbol that belongs to the world community, increasingly became in the minds of many people a symbol of China and China alone. Indeed, the torch, or "sacred flame" (*shenghuo*) as it is referred to in Chinese (and for that matter Japanese, in which it is called *seika*), became a quasi-sacerdotal symbol of supernational Chinese identity. (I would refer read-ers to the recent biting comments made during a visit to Australia by the Beijing-based artist Ai Weiwei on what I would call the "hijacking of the sacred" by Beijing propagandists and those in their thrall in *The Australian* on April 30, 2008.)

As we have witnessed in recent weeks, the issue of the Olympic torch relay has now become one of Chinese global pride, integrity, and national unity. The official Chinese media has also encouraged a kind of by-proxy witch-hunt to determine which among the foreign countries of "the West" (an ill-defined category to say the least), their media, politicians, and public figures are, to use expressions first coined in the U.S. media in 2005, "panda huggers" (*xiongmao pai*, pro-China), "dragon slayers" (*tulong pai*, anti-China) or "panda hedgers" (*xiongmao qiqiang pai*, undecided). Such terminology militates against subtlety of argument, nuance, shades of difference, or complexity on "both sides." I would also note that the "unified caliber" (*tongyi koujing*) of Beijing-authored attacks on the "Western media" constitute a deliberate decision by the highest power in the land to use this opportunity to mount an all-out offensive on reporting on China by the independent media worldwide. I would speculate that this is a strategic decision made with the short-term tactical aim of neutralizing international media reports on China before and during the Olympic period—a time during which China has undertaken to allow unprecedented access of the international media to the country. The long-term ramifications of this decision will be profound.

WORONI: Are you able to provide any information about how it was reported and viewed in China? More generally, how is the torch relay being reported?

BARMÉ: Overall, the relay in Canberra was reported as being a celebration of China and a resounding success. Large crowds waving flags of the People's Republic of China and toting various slogans were shown on TV news. Naturally, within Australia there were many proud participants—and I think of Gill Hicks (who walks on prosthetic legs after having lost hers in the July 7 London bombings) and Ian Thorpe. However, as I remarked above, it is noteworthy that the torch relay has now been constructed as more a reflection of China's global presence than merely being an activity supported by and crucially involving the international community.

Chinese commentators have also noted that since the "Western" (Euramerican and Australian) media is basically run by prurient sensationalism and commercial concerns, it is hardly surprising that the story of protests surrounding the Olympic relay has concentrated on shrill protests and the activities of what are invariably referred to as a "small handful" of "Tibetan splittists" and other "anti-Chinese elements." More broadly, the Chinese state and semi-independent media have spoken darkly of the existence of an "international conspiracy" against China, one that covertly reflects irrational fears of China's rise as an economic and political superpower. According to this logic, the contretemps surrounding the Beijing Olympics is merely the latest platform for the conspirators. Many Chinese writing on the Net or who I have encountered since March (I was in Beijing during the original Lhasa disturbances and have traveled to a number of cities in China since then on a second trip—for reasons unrelated to these issues) also point out that they feel that China is not given due credit for the extraordinary changes that have swept the nation in recent decades that have seen the mass alleviation of poverty and the rapid modernization of the largest nation on earth. However, while conspiracy theories make for good copy, they don't help us understand the situation or the long-term causes of the present rhetorical extremes both in China and elsewhere. Indeed, I would hasten to point out that media paranoia and hysteria is hardly something limited to China, and it would appear that many commentators and opinion makers internationally have joined in the fray with enthusiasm.

The early reports of the London and Paris melees in the Chinese media moved from avoiding mention of the disruptions to propagating the righteous outrage of the international Chinese community (much of which consists of mainland Chinese students living and studying overseas) and the heroic spirit of martyrdom evinced by Jin Jing, the handicapped torchbearer who was lunged at during the Paris relay (she quickly fell from grace when she had the temerity to oppose a mainland Chinese boycott of the French-owned Carrefour chain—critics widely attacked her: "not only doesn't she have a leg, she doesn't even have a brain!" was a commonly heard tagline). The Chinese media treated these early protests as the disruptive activities of "a small minority" (*yi xiaocuo*) worthy of nothing more than contempt. It should be noted that after the spontaneous protests in China itself against Carrefour in mid-April, the authorities began to calm things down by calling on people to engage in "rational patriotism" that did not impinge on the economic weal of the nation. This is a common tactic that we have seen deployed any number of times.[2] For their part, the owners of Carrefour were quick to claim their pro-China, pro-Olympics stance and express outrage and disgust at the events in Paris.

WORONI: What does the Olympics mean to the Chinese people? (Many of the protesters and people in the media talked in terms of one-world spirit and so on.)

BARMÉ: Put simply, one could argue that the 2008 Beijing Olympics have been turned into a celebration of the People's Republic of China's emergence as a major global force. Years of propaganda, educational hype, and commercial spruiking[3] by the Chinese party-state, the commercial media, and international corporations who want to make a buck (or two or millions) have added to the crescendo of hope, pride, and national hubris bound up in a heady embrace during this the Olympic year. Extraordinary investment has gone into the physical sites of the games as well as into the redevelopment (and further despoliation) of Beijing. Voices of discord, disagreement, or doubt have never enjoyed any airtime. Those deprived of their homes or livelihoods as a result of the grand plan for the Olympics are generally mute, and "Olympic doubters" are in a minority. Those who might have concerns have no way of knowing how widely held their disquiet may be. China is not a pluralistic society, its media is guided,

---

2. See, for example, my 2005 article "Mirrors of History."
3. "Spruik" is of Australian origin and means "to promote in public."

and its public opinion is manufactured (again, this is a topic about which I have written at length elsewhere). So-called public sentiment (*gongzhong yulun*) is, I would argue, the result of long years of careful engineering. What is particularly unsettling for the uninformed observer is that those who mouth with unanimity views supported by the party-state are relatively complicit in their unreflective cooptation. I observed in my 1999 book *In the Red* mentioned earlier:

> As the children of the Cultural Revolution and the Reform era come into power and money they are finding a new sense of self-importance and worth. They are resentful of the real and imagined slights that they and their nation have suffered in the past, and their desire for strength and revenge is increasingly reflected in contemporary Chinese culture. Unofficial culture has reached or is reaching an uncomfortable accommodation with the economic if not always the political realities of contemporary China. As its practitioners negotiate a relationship with both the state in all of its complex manifestations and capital (often, but not always, the same thing) national pride and achievement act as a glue that further seals the pact. The patriotic consensus, aptly manipulated by diverse Party organs, acts as a crucial element in the coherence of the otherwise increasingly fragmented Chinese world.[4]

WORONI: How is the issue of Tibet viewed within China? Or other geopolitical issues with which China is involved? By Chinese outside of China? Many have said that they think that the Western media is deliberately manipulating coverage of how China proceeds in its political issues.

BARMÉ: The issues of Tibet or, more generally, of "Tibetan China" (that is, the territories in China with large ethnically Tibetan populations in Qinghai, Gansu, Sichuan, and Yunnan) are extremely complex. While the Chinese official story fixates on the bloodshed of March 14 and the activities of agitators for Tibetan independence, it judiciously avoids discussion of the protests in the other dozens of towns and cities with large Tibetan populations or the state violence and extrajudicial punishments meted out in the process. Nor is any real attempt made to help the public understand how or why such widespread and, in the main, peaceful protests could have taken place apart from ascribing them to the "premeditated plots" of the "Dalai clique." In the Chinese media there is now a propaganda push to extol tirelessly China's constant contributions to the Tibetans and their material prosperity; there is scant evidence of there being any willingness to concede that there could be any reason whatsoever for anyone to protest about anything. No one asks whether the aggressive modernization foisted on the Tibetans (and enjoyed by many but concomitantly a process that has created numerous iniquities and problems) should be questioned. With that as

---

4. From the chapter "To Screw Foreigners Is Patriotic," which, when first published as an article in July 1995, bore the subtitle "China's Avant-Garde Nationalists." *In the Red: On Contemporary Chinese Culture* (New York: Columbia University Press, 1999), 277. See also the same book for the appendix titled "Screw You, Too," 365–77.

the rhetorical backdrop to all reporting in China, then protest, even if peaceful and moderate, must invariably be depicted as the result of the callous manipulations of the dreaded "Dalai clique" and their shameful desire to see China rent apart or for a restoration of the old lama-dominated theocracy of pre-1950s Tibet.[5]

Most people know nothing more of the Tibetan realm than a few songs and dances, a few famous spots, and glib ideas about Tibetan Buddhism. They certainly know little about the economic displacement that seems to be a major issue for some protesters or of the effects of forced sedenterization of nomad communities or the new party control of the selection of reincarnated lamas, all issues of great importance for people in the Tibetan areas. Chinese comments I generally hear are of a kind that we in Australia are familiar with from the days of Pauline Hanson (a right-wing parliamentarian active from 1996 who helped during the long years of the Howard Coalition government to shift public debate to the right): remember when Aborigines were derided for being bludgers on the social security system of "mainstream Australia"? Remember too that for all of the social and economic problems of Aboriginal communities, they were blamed for their own dire straits and attacked for "having it so good" while "average Australians" were "doing it hard on strugglestreet"? Similarly, I have often heard people say in recent weeks that the Tibetans have it so good and are freer than mainstream Han Chinese; they should be grateful for all the largesse they enjoy. Issues of socioeconomic importance or questions of legitimate cultural and religious concerns seem to be virtually ignored in the mainstream Chinese media, nor are the actual on-the-ground policies debated in the public realm (they are daresay the subject of far more considered discussion behind closed doors). That the public is deprived of informed information and open discussion is an inevitable reality in a constrained media environment.

On this same anecdotal level, I have encountered common expressions of contempt for Tibetans as an ethnic group (that is, that they are "backward," have "low IQs," and are "dirty" and "resistant to modernity") since I was first a student in China in the mid-1970s. But I would also note that Tibet fascination—for its culture, landscape, religion, and social relations—has also been a common feature of Han culture (alternative and mainstream) since the mid-1980s.[6] It is also said that there are numerous Han converts to Tibetan Buddhism, people who are among the many who are searching for some greater human meaning beyond the arid landscape of material acquisition that is the predominant feature of mainstream consumerism.

One of the crucially complicating factors related to events since the initial

---

5. For an excellent article on the rhetorical (and policy) dead end that results from this kind of argumentation, see Isabel Hilton's April 12, 2008, article "Ditch the Tatty Flag of Nationalism."

6. See, for example, the material that John Minford and I included in the 1988 second edition of our *Seeds of Fire, Chinese Voices of Conscience.*

demonstrations in Lhasa on March 10 (these were peaceful protests that preceded the mob violence of March 14 and the widespread unrest and crackdown
ever since) was that the Chinese authorities enforced a blackout that kept the
Western media out of Lhasa and then restricted access to virtually most of
Tibetan China. A lack of media freedom and sensationalism as well as state-
guided propaganda and emotionalism have added to the escalation of rhetorical
violence and blind prejudice all around. For many Western media outlets, the
media blackout and sensational circumstances of the torch relay have fed the
frenzy. A cogent and measured reflection on the official responses to March 14
is the twelve-point petition issued on March 22 by leading Chinese intellectuals
and public figures (which called on the government to stop oppression in Tibet
and calls for an end to violence). It remains essential reading.

WORONI: Some protesters were angry that white/non-Chinese Australians
were protesting in the name of Tibet. Can you shed light on this?

BARMÉ: This is an added unpleasantness to an already unpalatable situation.
Regardless of where one stands on issues related to the Tibetan question, freedom of speech, peaceful protest, and demonstration are guaranteed under Australian law. It is unfortunate in the extreme that in my home city of Canberra,
Chinese protesters—the majority of whom it would seem are not Australian
citizens, although they naturally enjoy basic rights guaranteed under Australian
law—have attempted to curtail or deny others the right to protest peacefully on
non-Chinese sovereign soil. Sadly, perhaps even tragically given the scale of the
perceptions now generated, many observers feel they have seen a sort of "export
authoritarianism" masquerading as Chinese patriotism. A lot of work will have
to be done to ameliorate this distasteful impression. It is noteworthy that some
bloggers in China are also disgusted by the self-indulgent rhetorical hysteria of
their (generally) middle-class countrymen and women overseas. They say that
they'd like to see them go back to China and fight for political reform, media
freedom, and human rights on home turf rather than making an hubristic spectacle of themselves internationally. Indeed, if China enjoyed true intellectual,
media, and political pluralism, it would be possible to have a more rational and
reasonable discussion of whether non-Chinese or non-Tibetan Australians have
a right to express publicly their views on matters of international concern. Given
the present state of affairs, this is simply not the case.

WORONI: Some have claimed that Tibet has long been part of China. Why?
Or would you say there is any academically recognized truth in this?

BARMÉ: The era of the nation state began for the territory of the Qing
Empire (the last Chinese dynasty, 1644–1911) in the mid-nineteenth century.
Like other modern countries, "China" is a relatively recent construct as a modern nation-state. Prior to this time the sway of imperial rule, the relations
between different imperial courts and bordering states or tributary states, is what
determined issues of territory. To project anachronistic views regarding the territory of the present People's Republic of China into the distant past is a dubious

undertaking at best. Similarly, to claim a unique independence for the territories of "Tibet" or "Greater Tibet" in the context of the imperial era is spurious. Although there were moves for an independent nation-state status for Tibet during the first half of the twentieth century (especially under the influence of the British imperium), such a status was not achieved in practical terms. For a study of the relations of the Tibetan areas of contemporary China to dynastic empires from the Mongol Yuan era (thirteenth century) to the high Qing (mid-eighteenth century), I would refer your readers to the excellent work of the late historian F. W. Mote of Princeton University.[7]

Furthermore, I would note that there is a dearth of independent scholarship on this subject of note in the People's Republic, as all historians and their research must conform to the official party-state line when dealing with issues of Chinese territorial integrity. This makes it particularly difficult for readers of Chinese alone to acquaint themselves with the rigorous, objective, and painstaking research that has been done on such issues by international scholars (not just English-language scholarship), especially as the work of such scholars when produced in Chinese translation is usually censored or "cosmetically edited" when it touches on sensitive issues.

WORONI: Can you say anything about the concept of "motherland"?

BARMÉ: The "motherland," or, in Chinese, "*zuguo*," which could also be translated as "fatherland," a term with uncomfortable connotations in English, actually means "land of [one's] ancestors." It is a term and concept created in Japanese and Chinese during the era of Western imperial politics in the nineteenth century. It has gained increased force in China over the past twenty years as the Chinese party-state (that is, the nation that is run by a one-party system) has promoted patriotism as a positive unifying force, in particular through constant "patriotic education" (*aiguo jiaoyu*) classes from primary school onwards and popular movements that see party propaganda, patriotic sentiment, and slick commercialism combined.

WORONI: We find it ironic and concerning that many protesters were rejecting politicization but responding with further, at times quite explicit politicization; that they were responding to claims of violence on behalf of their government with antagonism and intimidation; that they were protesting for the cause of an autocratic government under the protection of a foreign democratic one. Do you think Chinese political culture is cognizant of such contradictions?

BARMÉ: One of the underlying elements of mob patriotism/nationalism in any highly charged environment is the lack of self-reflection. We see careful thought abandoned; there is an indulgence in emotionalism and the mindless drift towards extreme and simplistic responses to what are generally complex issues. The politics of the Games itself are fraught—and now more so than ever.

---

7. See his *Imperial China, 900–1800* (Cambridge, MA: Harvard University Press, 1999).

The Chinese media in the People's Republic of China has never been clear about the various undertakings that were made to the international community to ameliorate the human rights situation in China prior to the 2008 Games, and so most people have no idea that the constant news of human rights abuses coming from China have formed over some time a very negative backdrop to the recent Tibet issue.[8]

It has been a great source of regret to many of us that the strident and vociferous activities of large mobs of Chinese "patriots" since London and Paris have so profoundly tarnished the image of China's young people internationally. Furthermore, some have pointed out that the high-decibel denunciations of any who voice opinions not in keeping with what is dubbed "mainstream [Chinese] opinion" (*zhuliu minyi*) have created the impression that people in China and abroad are expected to support unquestioningly the People's Republic of China, and all of its policies, regardless. Doubts, questioning, and informed discussion are, at present, not tolerated. Independent commentators in China have noted that while rabid patriotic Chinese demonstrators have enjoyed the right to protest internationally under the protection of the police of their resident countries and with the full enjoyment of democratic freedoms that Western bourgeois democracies allow, in China they would enjoy no such freedoms.

WORONI: Questions of violence and intimidation aside, would you say that the show of support for China's Olympics, the sense of national pride, and the sense of the need to protect it internationally is shared by most Chinese?

BARMÉ: It is impossible to gauge what "most Chinese" think or feel, as there is no means of making such assessments. I would imagine that there is widespread pride in the Olympics and a fervent hope that the year passes without further incident. However, I would note that a people that has had a history of mass movements, agitations, rallies, and mob agitation for nigh on a century now will not resile from further displays of collective anger and raucous protest. The Olympics will now be fraught, and there will inevitably be extreme official paranoia generated by the fear that some athlete, visitor, or even playful prankster will unfurl a Tibetan flag or shout "Free Tibet" at some moment during the Olympics—be it in the main sports venues or anywhere in Beijing. Everyone will have to pay the price for this in advance through overzealous security measures and a virtual state of martial law. This will make for a baleful environment indeed. But elsewhere I have pointed out that "harmonious society" is a laden concept, one that consists of political tutelage, social quiescence, and commercial frenzy, among other things.

I would further point out that many Chinese interlocutors are often more than happy to tell you what "We Chinese" feel or believe on any given topic.

---

8. The appalling Hu Jia case being only the most recently well-advertised case: see the enlightening article "Hu Jia in China's Legal Labyrinth" by Jerome A. Cohen and Eva Pils in the early May 2008 issue of *Far Eastern Economic Review*.

Given the lack of media freedom or true transparency in the Chinese public realm (added to by the shifting rhetorical ground of Internet bloggers and commentators), claims that assert that individuals are able to represent anything but personal (even if it is "bestowed") opinion are, needless to say, risible.

Chinese Protesters Extinguish Olympic Torch in Protest? ☆Adam J. Schokora

Emphasis was placed on torch protests abroad, so foreign media were attuned to the possibility of protests at home too. Before the Sichuan earthquake (after which Chinese called on the government to temporarily halt the torch relay out of respect for the suffering of affected people), Asia Sentinel first reported, then retracted, that the torch was extinguished by protesters during its run through the southern city of Shenzhen. After the initial report, China-focused blog Danwei.org's commentators tried to piece together the events. According to their comments, Asia Sentinel's first report was indeed erroneous, but readers' comments also illustrate the contentious nature of conversations about the torch at the time, as well as differing notions of what constitutes "censorship." Here is a transcript of their exchange.

As reported by *Asia Sentinel*, the Olympic torch has apparently been extinguished by local Chinese protesters while making the rounds in Shenzhen earlier today. Despite efforts to find local sources collaborating details of the story, nothing has turned up on the Chinese Internet. Pictures, video, and text all seem to have been effectively harmonized. *Asia Sentinel* has told Danwei it has and is preparing video footage of the incident for release.

Posted by: Adam J. Schokora at Danwei.org | May 8, 2008 6:08 PM

UPDATE 1:
See the comment by Spelunker below for an eyewitness account.

UPDATE 2:
Asia Sentinel has updated its original story with a long-awaited video of the purported incident of local Chinese crowds extinguishing the Olympic torch in protest. However, the video doesn't appear to support the story's original claim.

UPDATE 3:
The latest from *Asia Sentinel* on its original story, quoted from its website: "*Asia Sentinel* is removing our story on the seizure of the Olympic torch in Shenzhen from the website. Although it was supplied by a heretofore reliable Chinese

reporter who obtained the details and video from a Chinese eyewitness, we have determined that it is not sufficiently verifiable. We apologize."

COMMENTS:
protesters? I didn't see any.
Posted by: Anonymous | May 8, 2008 11:19 PM

Today, the fact is ;8000 000 [*sic*] shenzhen local people celebrate and welcome the torch. The truth is ; there is [*sic*]
Posted by: selina | May 9, 2008 12:05 AM

Adam, I know only "protesters" can fit into your predetermined narrative about the Beijing Olympics. Unfortunately, that was not the case in Shenzhen. The torch was disturbed not by protesters but by too many supporters who could not keep a good order.

By the way, I would like to provide you with an excellent example of censorship. The Pope's good wish to the Beijing Olympics was censored by the Reuters, the Associated Press, and the *New York Times* in their reports of the performance of a Chinese orchestra in Vatican yesterday. On the contrast, BBC did not censor the pope's good wish, while the AFP made it a title of its report on the same event.
Posted by: wenwu | May 9, 2008 7:23 AM

Considering that your website is quite influential among many people, I thought it would be prudent for you to report on things only after they have been confirmed. Otherwise you may be instrumental in spreading rumors. You are, after all, not a journalist under time pressure to publish certain articles by a certain deadline.
Posted by: no sensationalism | May 9, 2008 8:25 AM

It seems to be overexciting people, not protester against torch relay.
Anyway, the 'harmonization' of pictures is stupid.
Posted by: Lark In Cloud | May 9, 2008 9:26 AM

This is Spelunker reporting live from Guangzhou. I witnessed the torch relay twice in Guangzhou (Zhongshan Memorial Hall and Beijing Pedestrian Street) and saw local TV coverage of the Shenzhen relay.

Allow me to present the facts:

1. No foreign media are allowed to accompany the torch route in China, as only local Chinese press are allowed in the media vehicles that travel along the torch relay route.

2. The Olympic flame was extinguished 4 times in Guangzhou, and the torch route was changed twice due to overcrowding conditions. The live TV

broadcast did briefly show torch bearer #197 as his torch went out, but there was no live broadcast of the torch when similar problems developed elsewhere along the route because TV broadcasts cut away to commentary by studio folks.

3. Local daily newspapers provided adequate explanations on May 8 for the 4 torch extinguishments and 2 minor route detours in Guangzhou.

4. There were no protests of any kind in Guangzhou.

I really doubt the Shenzhen torch extinguishments were due to any type of local protest, instead it is more likely due to overcrowding as was the actual case in Guangzhou.

The police perimeter was changed in front of Zhongshan Memorial Hall. This occurred just an hour before the torch relay was due and upset local residents who waited for 4 or 5 hours at this prime viewing location. There was a brief scuffle between police and some feisty elderly Chinese who refused to move, but I did not stay to see the end result of that battle.

At Beijing Pedestrian Street I was able to enjoy a pleasant tug-of-war between police and an enthusiastic crowd that tightly sandwiched the narrow Olympic thoroughfare. This was definitely one of the best venues for getting a close-up view of the torch relay if you don't mind being a sardine for several minutes. I held up a big sign with 4 Chinese characters "You Er Ge Ge" as the torch relay runner and torch attendant brothers jogged by. Many photographers took pictures of me and my sign (I wore my "Lei Feng" T-shirt as well) but I haven't seen myself on TV, in newspapers or on the Internet yet.
Cheers from Guangzhou!
Spelunker
Posted by: Spelunker | May 9, 2008 10:46 AM

What's "You Er Ge Ge"?
Posted by: lost in your sign | May 9, 2008 12:11 PM

It's the allegedly drop-dead gorgeous Torch guard, the second (Er) brother (Ge Ge) on the right (You).
Posted by: Leah | May 9, 2008 5:07 PM

Guangzhou police officers were also confused by my sign, as they had to listen to a funny foreigner explain *youergege* to them as well.

It seems to be strictly an Internet phenomena, as the term did not appear to be well known among those I encountered on the streets of Guangzhou and Hong Kong. (I also attended the torch relay in Wanchai on May 2 and held up the same sign.)

Posted by: Anonymous | May 10, 2008 10:59 PM

Why Were Chinese People So Angry about the Attempts to Seize the Torch in the International Torch Relay? ☆ Susan Brownell

In late July 2008, I returned from five days in the earthquake disaster zone in Sichuan province, where I was a member of the "People's Olympic Education Promotion Team" that visited Deyang city to conduct "Youth Olympic Games Re-Enactments" at six local primary and secondary schools. There I realized that for the people we encountered, The Torch is a sacred object. I call it The Torch because that is what they called it—*huoju*—as if there were only one, and no further adjectives were necessary.

The project expressed the mission of Donnie Pei, a professor at the Capital Institute of Physical Education, and Zhou Chenguang, a primary school physical education (PE) teacher, to take the Olympics to the grassroots. Pei could not come with us, so our team leader was Zhou. The member who attracted the most attention everywhere was Sun Yiyong, a songwriter and a torchbearer during the Inner Mongolia torch relay, who was called simply The Torchbearer (*huojushou*). The other members, who paled next to his luminance, consisted of Wu Ji'an, China's "King of Games," who creates and collects games and teaches them to schoolchildren and teachers nationwide; Zhou's son Bowen; myself; and three support staff. We came from Beijing, Shanghai, Chengdu, and Deyang and were self-funded but for the "soft implements" (discus, javelin, hammer, hurdles, and epees made out of flexible packing foam) funded by the Haidian District government in Beijing. Thus, we were a determined "people's" (*minjian*) group and not an "official" (*guanfang*) group. As Zhou put it to the local city officials, we were the three "have-nots": have no organization, no discipline, and no funding. Such a group had probably never been seen in the area before in this form, although the earthquake relief effort had accustomed the locals both to nongovernmental organizations and to roaming foreigners.

We were received—initially, as we realized, with considerable skepticism—by the Education Bureau of the Deyang city government as part of its current work in "psychological intervention." As the reality of postdisaster life is setting in, children are realizing that they have no parents for whom to study hard, parents whose lives revolved around their one child feel that they have no reason to live, people who lost limbs are realizing that they are a burden on their families, and volunteers are suffering posttraumatic stress syndrome from what they saw. And so there are starting to be suicides. As a result, a major initiative in psychological intervention is being carried out in the schools and communities, utilizing Young Pioneers counselors, visiting expert psychologists (including foreign experts), and others.

Our assigned task was to bring the Olympic spirit into the schools in order to aid the recovery. When we arrived, we were received by the chief of the Students Section, Mr. Zeng. He told us with intensity, "I hope that we can do our best to solve the conflicts as fast as possible. Of course we cannot solve all the conflicts. But let us do our best to solve the ones that we can solve." As we concluded our dinner, he told us, "You cannot fail."

The next day we drove to the disaster zone and saw the site of the collapsed school where fifty of two hundred students had survived, pile after pile of brick rubble, acres of newly created prefabricated communities, and the clocktower in Hanwang whose clock had stopped at 2:28. We spontaneously stopped at one of the schools that had been relocated into a prefab complex because their school building had collapsed, and there I first observed the power of The Torch.

Each torchbearer gets to keep the torch that he or she carried, minus its internal mechanism. Because it was a National Treasure, Sun Yiyong carried it with him everywhere he went, inside its special box cradled in a yellow silk case sewn by his mother, which he slung over his shoulder. As he told us, "When I got my own torch it was not at all like the others. It's like your own child—you feel differently toward it compared to the others, it's special." When we introduced ourselves to some of the students standing in the concrete walkway between the prefab classrooms, they wanted to see The Torch. Sun Yiyong took it carefully out of its box, and the students began to crowd around to touch it. They started streaming out of their prefab classrooms. To allow each student a chance, Zhou asked them to line up and pass it from hand to hand until each student had touched it. Because we were taking them away from their classes, we apologized to the teachers who came to see what was up and left as they asked us to come back.

The next day at the sports field of the Oriental Power Primary School, we conducted our first Youth Olympic Games reenactment for one thousand of the three thousand students at the school, building on the model developed by Pei and Zhou at Yangfangdian Primary School in Beijing. We played our "meet song," "Pass on the Flame's Spark," which Sun had written as a eulogy to the Olympic torchbearers, and conducted a little opening ceremony, following the protocol common in China. My role was to be the International Person. I delivered a short address in Chinese, in which I said that the Olympic spirit is a spirit of mutual respect, mutual understanding, fair play, and the pursuit of international friendship and world peace. As a member of the big family of the global village, I sincerely wished them success in rebuilding their happy homes and hoped that the Olympic spirit of "swifter, higher, stronger" would help them in their effort.

After the flagbearer entered the stadium bearing the Olympic education banner designed by Zhou and Pei, the Olympic Angel, Zhou's son Bowen, entered in a white robe adorned with real feather wings and a green wreath on his head. The Olympic Angel was an inspiration of Donnie Pei, who wondered how to reduce the philosophy of Olympism to a level understandable by primary school students. He believed that Olympism should make you into a good person and that an angel embodies goodness. Also, the white robe and wings recall the figures of Nike, winged goddess of victory, in the athletic scenes on ancient Greek amphorae. For him, the angel symbolized ancient Greece and was not a Christian symbol. And so as our Olympic angel entered the stadium carrying a cardboard reproduction of the Olympic torch, it was announced that it was bringing the flame, symbolizing hope, from Mount Olympus in ancient Greece to China.

Finally, The Torchbearer entered the stadium, wearing his red-and-white official torchbearer's shirt and shorts and carrying the real Lucky Clouds torch, images that were easily identified by the children because the real torch relay was being broadcast daily on Chinese TV as it passed through China. Deyang had originally been scheduled for a stop, but it had been eliminated after the earthquake, a source of great regret to local residents. Sichuan had been moved so that it was the last province on the relay before the torch returned to Beijing. As a result, ours was the first Torch to reach Sichuan. But the local education officials were looking forward to the fact that after the relay left Sichuan, Deyang would have its own Torches, since several locals had been designated to carry it.

What happened next took us all by surprise. A high-pitched cry of excitement rose into the air as the children recognized The Torch, and one thousand children began spontaneously streaming toward it. They surrounded Sun Yiyong as he rounded the field and for a while they were allowed to follow, but they began pressing so hard to get near and touch The Torch that it became difficult for him to move and he was afraid he was going to step on a child. The situation was rapidly becoming dangerous. The school's PE teacher (PE teachers are the ones who keep order in Chinese schools since they lead the recess exercises) grabbed the microphone and began shouting, "Children! Maintain order!"

Eventually order was restored, and Sun Yiyong walked the periphery of the crowd while the students looked without touching. But we had learned a lesson. At subsequent events, a group of four boys clothed in red and yellow T-shirts jogged with him and acted as bodyguards for The Torch, as had the Blue Men who were so maligned in the Western media during the international torch relay. For these boys it was an honor to protect The Torch. But in the following five events, each time The Torchbearer appeared at the entrance to the sports field, the high-pitched cry would go into the air, and the children would start moving toward it like metal shavings being pulled toward a magnet. The idea of allowing large numbers of children to touch the torch was abandoned, and at subsequent events about ten to twenty "outstanding students" were invited to stand at the front of the crowd. First they passed the reproduction torch down the line, and then they passed The Torch along. Finally the reproduction torch was used to "light" The Torch (neither was actually aflame, though the reproduction torch had red construction-paper flames coming from its top), and they exited the scene.

After a reading of Pierre de Coubertin's "Ode to Sport," Zhou conducted the activity called "We are all Torchbearers." He asked, "Who is a Torchbearer?" answering, "I am a Torchbearer! You are a Torchbearer! We are all Torchbearers!" Each child had been asked to bring a paperback textbook and had been given a square of flame-red crepe paper. By rolling up the textbook and sticking the crepe paper into the top of the cone, each child had a little torch which she or he waved in the air. Zhou explained, "Take your knowledge and your strength and twist your book to make it into a torch, then put your torch into your heart."

On our second night several members went to a school that had been cobbled together from students from several different schools and relocated into prefab buildings. Unfortunately I missed it—it turned out to be one of the most moving events of the trip. As they told me later, the curfew arrived, and the electricity was cut off as they were in the midst of passing around The Torch. Zhou said to the students, "Are you afraid?" and they said, "Yes." He said, "Don't be afraid. Remember The Torch. The cinders are in your heart and will always be there, even when it is dark." They concluded by signing autographs to the light of a flashlight, and then Zhou led them in shouting, "Go China! Go Sichuan! Go Deyang! Go School!" One of the children added, "I tell myself to go!" (*wo wei wo jiayou*), which Zhou considered to be one of the most inspiring events of the trip because it showed the child had taken the Olympic spirit inside himself and made it his own.

At each stop, people wanted to touch The Torch, and the teachers and officials were more aggressive about it than the children. They wanted to take photos of themselves holding The Torch or of groups of people each with one hand on The Torch. They seemed to feel, at least at some level, that touching the Lucky Clouds Torch would bring them good fortune. The undisputed star of our group was The Torch. After that, The Torchbearer. And after that, the International Person (me). (I also got mobbed for autographs and had to be rescued by a bodyguard.)

During this time, I learned that in Chinese, a flame is a living thing with an anatomy like a plant. At its base are the "seeds of fire" (*huozhong*), or cinders, which represent hope and are the thing that one holds in one's inner heart. Out of the seeds come the "sprouts of fire" (*huomiao*), or tendrils of flame. It grows into a full flame (*huoyan*). It sends off "star fire" (*xinghuo*), or sparks, which symbolize the passing of inspiration from one person to another. All of this was metaphorical—our torches did not have fires because that would be too dangerous for children.

We organized Olympic reenactments at two schools per day for three consecutive days, a total of six schools and over three thousand children. Our status in Deyang increased each day. Local education officials held a meeting midway through our second day to assess our achievements. The head of the Deyang Education Bureau, Mr. Mao, observed, "The Olympic spirit is the spirit of conquering the disaster. Could we recover so quickly without the spirit of 'swifter, higher, stronger'? This is also our spirit. . . . Our students' psychological wounds are serious. We will organize our students to get into motion. We humans cannot stop, our spirit cannot stop."

After three days and six schools, we were completely exhausted. At our farewell lunch, Section Chief Zeng observed that we had accomplished psychological intervention on a large scale. The standard psychological intervention reaches people one by one, so the experts who had been brought in could only reach about one thousand people per week. We had reached over three thousand students in three days. Zhou later explained, "Psychological intervention opens up a hole in your body and then sews it up again. It takes a long time to recover. We don't open up a hole to do surgery. We let the sun shine on them and they absorb it into their bodies and keep it there. Chinese medicine is not in favor of doing operations, so this method is appealing."

When I first began studying anthropology, I took part in the famous seminar of Victor Turner, one of the most influential anthropologists of his time. He was then experimenting with ritual reenactments, which we conducted in the seminar. He believed that ritual action and the handling of symbolic objects function to channel human emotions like a laser beam. He believed that rituals could have this effect on humans even when the rituals were not their own and our reenactments tested his theory. He was also interested in the use of rituals in healing processes.[9] Like many of his former students, I have carried on this tradition in my own teaching. Every year my theory class repeats the experiment by reenacting a ritual of their choice. Without further belaboring the complicated theory behind this, I will just note that I regularly see and feel the transformative power of ritual reenactments, which seem to be able to exert at least some effect on some people no matter how impromptu they may be. It was in this spirit that I entered into our Youth Olympic Games Re-enactment. Did we "solve the conflicts that could be solved"? Hard to say, but I do think that we made a small difference.

In my classroom reenactments, I am often surprised at the effect on myself, and in Deyang I experienced the sudden insights into my own culture that Turner says are a potential of ritual (a product of "liminality"). Against the background of the furor over the international torch relay, observing the reverence and emotion for The Torch and The Torchbearer made me suddenly see how cynical we are, more often than not, in the West as a product of our secularized, rationalized society in which there are only small spaces in which it is acceptable to express reverence for symbols. A picture appeared in my mind that is an exaggeration but perhaps with a kernel of truth: in China, the majority of

---

9. For the theoretical background, see Turner's *The Ritual Process, The Anthropology of Performance,* and *From Ritual to Theatre.*

public expressions take place in a vast field of rituals and symbols, while the protest zones that were announced for the Olympic Games were small, circumscribed spaces where critical analytical thought is expressed. In the United States, the majority of public expressions take place in a vast field of critical analytical thought, while ritual expression takes place in small, circumscribed places like churches and, arguably, sports events. I realized that at least part of the anger that many Chinese people felt at the disruptions of the international torch relay was the result of the (to them) appalling and uncivilized lack of respect for a nearly sacred object.

In the West, the Olympic Games have struggled with a loss of idealism due to challenges like commercialism and doping. The Chinese Olympic organizers and many Chinese people held an idealistic faith in the transformative power of the Olympic Games, believing that they could facilitate China's integration with the world and benefit its future development. The West duly regarded this with skepticism. According to Turner, a balanced social process requires rituals. The global village needs its ritual, and the Olympic Games are currently serving that function. But also, according to Turner, ritual has the potential to either increase solidarity or initiate irreparable schisms.

In Deyang it was possible to foresee the closing of this cultural gap between China and the West. Everyone agreed that our final performance at the elite Foreign Languages Middle School in Deyang was the "most orderly"—and all but myself and the artist Sun Yiyong considered this a good thing. The children did not mob The Torch or me. They spoke very good English, and they paid 40,000 yuan per year in tuition. Apparently for such privileged children, The Torch and The International Person had already lost some of their luster.

Pass On the Flame's Spark (The Torchbearer's Song)

Pass the flame's spark, from you on to me
Grand relay of peace and fraternity
Pass the flame's spark, let passion flow on
Its unending journey of harmony

Sacred fire's seeds, lit from the sun's rays
In matchless glory, your flames leap up high
All will remember this twinkling day
Five lands below, five rings in the sky

Hot blazing torch will light up the stars
Linking countless hearts' desires
The whole world is passing on one dream
All can see the great acts it inspires

Lyrics and melody: Sun Yiyong
English translation: Susan Brownell
Singer: solo Shang Zixing
Song for 2008 Youth Olympic Games Re-enactment, People's Olympic
  Education Promotion Team Beijing Olympic Torchbearers

Chapter 5

Earthquake and Recovery

GIVING LONG-TERM RELIEF

Yong Chen

May 12, 2008, will enter the history of China and the world as a day of sadness. At 2:30 P.M. local time, a devastating earthquake, registering 7.9 on the Richter scale, hit Wenchuan near Chengdu, the provincial capital of Sichuan, and the confirmed death toll has soared to more than 41,000.

This is also a moment of perseverance. There are countless stories of surviving victims of the catastrophe—grieving parents, husbands and wives, children, coworkers, neighbors, classmates—doing all they could to rescue and help others. This is a moment of compassion and humanity. China acted swiftly, sending relief workers, volunteers, and soldiers along with relief materials to the hard-damaged and difficult-to-reach areas in the midst of continuous aftershocks. The enormous disaster in the distant mountainous areas in inland China has also touched the entire world, as people in many countries are providing assistance in various ways, donating money and sending relief teams.

People in all Chinese communities throughout the world, including Southern California (where I am based), responded immediately. According to incomplete numbers gathered by the Chinese-language newspaper *Qiaobao,* Chinese Southern Californians raised more than U.S.$3 million by May 20, while their counterparts in New York raised U.S.$2.3 million. These numbers do not include the money sent to China directly or through various overseas and mainstream U.S. charity organizations.

A friend of mine, a victim in Mianyang, another area hit hard by the earthquake, whose family has survived the disaster but whose house has become inhabitable, said recently, "We will rebuild." She was talking about rebuilding not her home but her community and city. With such resolution and with all the help from China and the rest of the world, the damaged areas will stand up again from the rubble.

Posted 5/23/2008 at 08:00:00 AM

On May 12, 2008, a 7.9-magnitude earthquake centered in northern Sichuan province shook buildings as far away as Shanghai and Hong Kong, more than a thousand miles to the east and south. Closer to the epicenter, the effects of the earthquake, the strongest to strike China since the 1976 earthquake at Tangshan, were devastating. Thousands of buildings collapsed within the first few minutes, including many schools. Roads were destroyed and repeated aftershocks weakened dams throughout the region, fueling fears of flooding. Some villages near the quake's center were almost entirely leveled. The earthquake left almost 70,000 dead and an estimated 5 million to 10 million homeless.

In the hours and days to follow, the world watched as rescuers attempted to dig out the tens of thousands who were buried in collapsed buildings. The Chinese media, typically kept on a short leash by the government, reported freely, largely without any limitations in the first few days of the disaster. Prime Minister Wen Jiabao arrived in the region and was shortly thereafter dubbed "Grandpa Wen" for his efforts to comfort parents who stood vigil outside their children's shoddily built and now collapsed schools, hoping their loved ones might yet be alive. Nationwide and around the world, people held vigils and collected donations to aid in the rescue and rebuilding efforts. Following a tough spring—with the riots in Tibet and then the controversial and disrupted international torch run—the earthquake softened international opinion toward China. The Chinese government's quick and authoritative response to the disaster earned accolades abroad, while the disaster itself strengthened national spirit and resolve.

At China Beat, *many of our May postings were attempts to keep our readers abreast of breaking news and commentary, but we also published a number of pieces from scholars who took a longer view of the relationships between the Chinese state, society, and natural disaster. Commentators in other venues were apt to see the Chinese government's response to the earthquake as unprecedented, particularly in comparison to the dismal response and cover-up of the 1976 Tangshan earthquake. Our writers, with a longer historical lens, argued for the relevance of earlier stories to understanding the context for and response to the Sichuan earthquake.*

Rumor and the Sichuan Earthquake ☆ S. A. Smith

One of the intriguing aspects of the appalling crisis created by the earthquake in Sichuan on May 12—whose death toll rose to more than 60,000—was the role played by rumor. Just four days before the quake, the Sichuan provincial government issued a notice designed to quell "earthquake rumors." On May 15, three days after the quake, Xinhua news agency announced that seventeen people had been arrested for circulating malicious rumors, while the Ministry of Public Security revealed that its bureaus in eleven provinces and municipalities had discovered more than forty messages on the Internet that "spread false information, made sensational statements and sapped public confidence."

In the weeks leading up to May 12, warnings of an imminent earthquake emanated from various quarters. Most significantly, Li Shihui, a scientist at the laboratory of geomechanical engineering of the Chinese Academy of Sciences, claimed on his blog that in April the seismologist Geng Qingguo, vice chair of the Committee for Natural Disaster Prediction at the China Geophysical Institute, had predicted a quake of 7 or more on the Richter scale in the Aba Tibetan and Qiang autonomous prefecture of Sichuan. On April 30, he claimed, the Committee for Natural Disaster Prediction had passed on a confidential report about his prediction to the China Seismology Bureau. Others less qualified than Li posted warnings of an earthquake on their blogs, although most were vague on detail. On May 7, a geological worker from Wuhan posted a notice on the Internet predicting that an earthquake would strike on May 12: "the epicenter should be quite near Wuhan. I hope Wuhan residents who see my blog will inform all relatives and friends and take precautions." Another blogger claimed to have an uncle working in the Sichuan Seismological Bureau: "Even when there were already signs indicating an earthquake, the Sichuan Seismological Bureau still suppressed and failed to report the information, completely disregarding people's lives." On the basis of Internet chat and reports in the press, a slew of rumors began to circulate that caused many citizens to contact their local earthquake prevention and disaster relief boards. Anxiety seems to have run particularly high in Aba County, specifically mentioned as the epicenter in Geng Qingguo's unpublished report and, significantly, a major center of pro-Tibetan riots a couple of weeks earlier. The authorities were quick to deny the rumors. On May 9, the Sichuan provincial government issued a statement:

> May 3, 8 p.m. The Abazhou Earthquake Prevention and Disaster Relief Board got calls from members of the public, asking whether news that an earthquake would strike Suomo town in Maerkang county was true. The authorities quickly demanded that the Maerkang Earthquake Disaster Prevention Bureau take measures to find out where the rumor came from and to refute it, so as to stop the rumors from spreading further. . . . The Abazhou Earthquake Prevention and Disaster Relief Board and the other cadres managed to clear up the misunderstanding in time, and life of the locals is back to normal.[1]

On May 12, the day of the earthquake, the statement was pulled from the provincial government website.

Much public concern was stirred up by rumors—some of them fed by reports in the press—about animals behaving strangely. In Mianzhu, sixty miles from the epicenter in Wenchuan County, bloggers reported that over a million butterflies had migrated weeks before the quake. According to a report in *Huaxi*

---

1. "Earthquake Predicted but Quashed as Rumour," *Epoch Times*, May 13, 2008.

Dushi Bao (Western China City News) on May 10, thousands of migrating toads descended on to the streets of Mianyang, the second-largest city in the province, many being crushed to death by vehicles and pedestrians. On May 13, 2008, *Dajiyuan* (the Chinese-language version of *Epoch Times*, the Falungong-sponsored newspaper) published a photograph of thousands of toads crawling out of the Tongyang canal in Taizhou, far away in Jiangsu province, crossing the Dongfeng bridge "in orderly fashion." According to the *Chutian Dushi Bao*, other omens, not involving animals, were that on April 26 the Guanyin pool in Enshi in Hubei was suddenly drained of 80,000 tonnes of water. Whirlpools began to form at about 7:00 A.M., a roaring noise was heard, and within five hours the pool had dried up.

Many of the rumors and Internet postings claimed authority on the basis of science. Scientists have long hypothesized that animals can predict earthquakes, suggesting variously that they can sense the ultrasonic waves generated by a quake, that they can pick up low-frequency electromagnetic signals emitted by subterranean movements, or that they can detect changes in the air or gases released by movements of the earth. The U.S. Geological Survey, which has conducted many studies of the phenomenon, remains skeptical. Chinese earthquake scientists, by contrast, who are among the best in the world, generally give greater credence to these hypotheses. Indeed, during the Cultural Revolution, such hypotheses acquired almost the status of scientific certainty. Zhang Xiaodong, a researcher at the China Seismological Bureau, has confirmed that his agency has used natural activity—mainly animal activity—to predict earthquakes twenty times in the past twenty years. This, however, represents a fraction of the earthquakes that have beset the country in that period. The most famous case in which scientists predicted an earthquake on the basis of unusual animal behavior and changes in groundwater levels occurred in Haicheng, a city of a million people in Liaoning, on February 4, 1974. From the preceding December, people reported dazed rats and snakes that appeared "frozen" to the roads, cows and horses that were unusually restless, chickens that refused to enter their coops, and domestic geese that had taken flight. As a result, the authorities evacuated the city just days before the 7.3-magnitude earthquake struck. However, the following year, serious doubt about the capacity of animals to give warnings of earthquakes arose when the second most lethal earthquake in history, measuring 7.6 on the Richter scale, hit Tangshan in July 1976.

The discourse about animals and earthquake prediction appears to be highly modern: it circulates via the press and the Internet, it invokes scientific argument, and it raises uncomfortable political questions about the culpability of the authorities in not responding to warning signs and the advice of scientific experts. Yet it is rooted in a much more ancient discourse about omens. For thousands of years, Chinese people have attributed supernatural significance to unusual or destructive natural phenomena, such as earthquakes, comets, or eclipses. These phenomena are systematically recorded in the *Hanshu*, an impor-

tant ancient Chinese text, alongside facts of political importance, and are interpreted variously by chroniclers as warnings of coming danger, as warnings to the
Son of Heaven not to undertake a certain course of action, and, not least, as
divine punishment for actions the emperor has undertaken. As is well known,
the Mandate of Heaven rested on the emperor's ability to maintain humankind
in harmony with heaven and earth; the occurrence of freakish natural phenomena was thus easily interpreted as a sign that the emperor had invoked divine
displeasure. I do not wish to suggest that the majority of Chinese today interpret
natural phenomena in this way, but I would suggest that there are millions—
especially in the countryside and among the elderly although by no means confined to these groups—who take it for granted that unusual or destructive
natural phenomena are omens of some sort, that is, that they have some supernatural meaning in excess of their naturalistic explanation. At the time of the
Tangshan earthquake, for example, talk of supernatural omens was rife, with
many connecting the earthquake to the deaths of Zhou Enlai and two other
famous Communist Party leaders (Kang Sheng and Zhu De), which occurred in
the preceding eight months, and to the death of Mao, the Great Helmsman
himself, which occurred six weeks after it.

The salient characteristic of omens is that they have no fixed and obvious
meaning, and it is through rumor that people debate that meaning. If most of
the rumors surrounding the current earthquake appear to draw on an essentially
"secular" discourse, it is evident even from press reports that older discourses of
omens are also being mobilized in the bid to explain the warnings that "heaven"
gave in the weeks running up to May 12. The account in *Dajiyuan* (the Falun-
gong-affiliated newspaper alluded to above) about the toad migration in Mianyang, for example, tells us that the immediate reaction of many village people
was "What kind of omen of disaster is this?" It tells us that many rural people
were anxious and that the forestry department sought to assuage their fear by
explaining that the toad migration was entirely natural, caused by the fact that
rising temperatures and substantial rainfall had led to unusually high levels of
breeding on the part of the toads. In Taizhou, scientists offered a slightly different
explanation, saying that the toad migration was due to a rise in temperature and
a lack of oxygen in the ditch water where the toads normally spawn. But the
response of bloggers to these reassurances was dismissive. "It's obviously an
omen." "Officials say that there are environmental factors behind it, but that
just shows how ignorant they are."

Why do many consider toads so especially ominous? After all, compared
with the fox or the snake, the toad occupies a rather marginal place in China's
rich tradition of folklore, drama, opera, and song. Moreover, as a creature of
warty mien, associated with dark, damp places, it does not obviously inspire
affection. In "Talking Toads and Chinless Ghosts: The Politics of Rumor in the
People's Republic of China, 1961–65," an article that appeared in *American Historical Review* in 2006, I discuss the symbolic associations that toads conjure up.

The subject of that article was a rumor that circulated between 1962 and 1963 across a huge swath of China, starting in the northeast and reaching Shanghai a year later. It told of a conversation overheard between two toads that prophesied that old people would perish within the year unless young people baked toad-shaped buns for them. The most obvious message of the rumor, which came in several variants, was that the young should take better care of the elderly in circumstances where, in the wake of the Great Leap Forward famine, many old people felt their entitlement to food was no longer secure.

More relevant to the rumors surrounding the current Sichuan earthquake, however, is my argument that it is the symbolic meaning of the toad rumor that is all-important, rumor being an inherently emotional form of communication in which the affective charge is all-important. In Chinese folklore, the toad is linked to Chang E, goddess of the moon, and this sets up a chain of signifiers that links water, darkness, and the moon. Each of these signifiers is powerfully coded as *yin* within popular culture, and I suggested in the article that the sub-liminal message of the toad rumor of the early 1960s was that there was an alarming surge in the power of *yin* forces. Since 1949 and especially since the Great Leap Forward, it had become increasingly difficult for people to observe the traditional rituals that serve to make *ling*—the power of supernatural enti-ties—efficacious in the world and, by extension, that serve to ensure cosmic balance. The toad rumor reminded people that unless these rituals were observed, further chaos, such as that that had resulted from the famine, could be expected. I have come across no evidence in current reports about the Sichuan earthquake that indicates that the toad migrations are being interpreted in exactly this way. However, as powerful signifiers of *yin* forces, it seems reasonable to infer that the toad migrations play on fears that the natural and social worlds are out of kilter: a fact dramatically highlighted when chaos erupted from the bowels of the earth.

It is not possible, of course, to conclude that this is the "real" meaning of the stories about migrating toads, but it is a reading that is easily overlooked when the discourse about the portents of the earthquake appears on the surface to be largely secular. Moreover, the response of bloggers suggests that at least some prefer a supernatural explanation of this omen to a naturalistic one. That said, we must acknowledge that since 1949, scientific or quasi-scientific explana-tions of natural phenomena have gained huge ground within popular culture. During the Cultural Revolution, for example, the idea that animals can foretell earthquakes became widely understood as proven fact, for ordinary folk were encouraged to watch for strange behavior on the part of animals and report it to the authorities. At that time, this fit with the political campaign for ordinary people to take scientific endeavor out of the hands of "bourgeois" experts. It thus seems likely that the assumption that animal behavior can predict earthquakes is widespread among the public. Yet such a scientific assumption can exist—with

a greater or lesser degree of felt contradiction—with more supernatural understandings of earthquakes.

In "Fear and Rumor in the People's Republic of China in the 1950s," published in *Cultural and Social History* in 2008, I examine two types of rumor that
flourished in the 1950s, both of which served to disseminate fear and anxiety
among the populace. The first were secular rumors of an imminent third world
war or an atomic attack; the second were supernatural rumors about demonic
invasions. In this article I reject the temptation to see the first as a "rational" type
of rumor and the second as an "irrational" type, arguing instead that millions of
people in the 1950s, especially in the countryside, made little distinction between
the two, seeing both as reflecting the fact that the cosmic order that regulates
interaction between the human and spirit worlds was out of kilter. In the inter-
vening half century, it is quite likely that supernatural explanations of natural
phenomena have lost much of their attractiveness, for increased technological
control over nature, combined with more widespread scientific education, has
helped to entrench the conceptual distinctions characteristic of the post-Galilean
world between man and nature, the natural and supernatural worlds, and cause
and effect within popular culture. Nevertheless, the rumors around the Sichuan
earthquake testify to the fact that many can accept such distinctions and continue to believe that supernatural beings or forces regularly intervene in the
realm of nature.

The harsh response of the authorities to the current bout of rumor-monger-
ing reminds us that even the weirdest rumors can be seen as an implicit—if
not always intended—challenge to authority. Rumor flourishes in situations of
uncertainty, where people feel that it is dangerous not to know what is going on.
A critical element in the current crisis around the Sichuan earthquake—at least
in its buildup—was the absence of information that ordinary people considered
reliable or credible. Sharing stories about the strange behavior of animals created
spaces in which they could share knowledge and gain a measure of psychological
control over an ambiguous and threatening situation. Given that the government
puts a premium on the control of public discourse, even the strangest supernatural rumor may be seen as political insofar as it represents a form of unauthorized
speech—"an attempt at collective conversation by people who wish to enter their
sentiments into a public discourse" (Anand Yang). Regardless of the intentions
of the rumor-mongers, rumors ipso facto represent an objective challenge to the
regime's monopoly of news and information. Unlike official news, moreover,
rumors travel horizontally rather than top down, setting up a "chain pattern
of communication" that bypasses the vertical lines of communication of the
centralized party-state.

It is clear that some who are circulating "news" via the Internet or the press
are engaged in a much more conscious effort to discredit the government, particularly by suggesting that it deliberately suppressed information about the
impending earthquake in a bid to avoid panic in the run-up to the Olympic

Games. In the past, earthquakes have regularly stoked up distrust of the government in this way. It is widely believed, for example, that leading scientists and geological monitoring centers issued warnings in advance of the Tangshan earthquake in 1976 but that neither the China Earthquake Association nor the government took them seriously. Popular confidence in government was further undermined in the wake of the Tangshan earthquake when party leaders refused to acknowledge the scale of the calamity or accept international relief.

In the wake of the current earthquake, at least one blogger was quick to look back to that time: "I am one of the survivors of the Tangshan quake," he wrote. "Tangshan people are extremely hostile towards the National Seismology Bureau because of their failure to predict such a devastating earthquake. . . . Now 32 years later, they have again failed to predict the Sichuan quake. The head of the bureau should resign." Meanwhile, Chang Ping, recently sacked deputy editor of the Guangzhou-based *Nanfang Dushi Bao*, has used the current epidemic of rumors surrounding the earthquake to argue in the pages of that newspaper that it reflects the need for much greater freedom of information in China. In a context where the Chinese government has been applauded around the world for its openness in handling the crisis, however, such criticism will probably come to nothing. Nevertheless, history suggests that earthquakes in China often have unanticipated political fallout.

Earthquake and the Imperatives of Chinese Mourning ☆ Donald S. Sutton

Disasters like the great Sichuan earthquake of May 12, 2008, expose not only mass suffering but also the imperative of proper treatment of the dead. Long before the founding of the People's Republic in 1949, governments in China had concerned themselves with such matters. Today, ranking only behind the weighty practical matters of rescue, flood prevention, and caring for the injured and homeless, sensitivity to mourning is a key measure of the government's performance, one complicated by ethnic diversity, rural/urban differences, and the government's own commitment to reform those practices it regards as superstitious.

For all the simplification of death rituals, a strong Chinese belief persists that survivors have to repay obligations incurred in life.[2] The party-state has not

2. For Chinese death ritual traditions, see James L. Watson, "Of Flesh and Bones: The Management of Death Pollution in Cantonese society," in Maurice Bloch and Jonathan Parry, eds., *Death and the Regeneration of Life* (Cambridge: Cambridge University Press, 1982), 55–86; Watson Rawski and Evelyn S. Rawski, eds., *Death Ritual in Late Imperial and Modern China* (Berkeley: University of California Press, 1988); and Donald S. Sutton, "Death Rites and Chinese Culture: Standardization and Variation in Ming and Qing

always done right by the dead. For the sake of party authority and social harmony, the regime did little to commemorate the ordinary victims of the famine years of 1960–1961 or the Cultural Revolution (1966–1969). And it did nothing at all to honor victims of the military suppression in the Tiananmen Square democracy movement of 1989—aside from some soldiers, that is, who lost their lives. But in the earthquake crisis, China's leaders showed greater sensitivity.

The most elementary obligation, not of course uniquely Chinese, is to identify the dead and dispose of them properly: rural Chinese still widely practice burial, despite the government propaganda for cremation. After the quake, the government resorted to advance DNA testing to identify bodies initially given collective burial in order to prevent epidemic disease. In remote towns and villages cut off by rockfalls, recovering the dead under the ruins must have taken many weeks.

Another obligation is to settle the souls. The dead are still thought, at least by many rural people, to pass through the underworld courts with the help of forty-nine days of periodic ritual observances. (The dangers presented by wronged, wracked, and ignored souls are the subject matter of innumerable folk operas and movies.) At the site of building collapses, firecrackers were exploded as each new body was dug up, and the family members burned spirit money for the use of their dead in the hereafter. Proper mourning had to wait.

Yet another long-standing obligation is to express one's bereavement with sincerity, in the case of women, vocally. Bereaved women were photographed wailing at quake sites displaying photographs of their loved ones. Some (for example, at Dujiangyan in Wenchuan County) called angrily for investigation into shoddy building practices at some of the schools where a total of nine thousand children and teachers died. Such demonstrations are usually proscribed, but given the moral resonance of mourning along with the presence of foreign reporters, the police let them continue for several days. Calls for legal remedy, however, have been ignored, and it is yet to be seen whether investigation will uncover laxity or corruption among local party officials, who are part of the leadership's base. The obligation to condole sincerely is equally Chinese. While official ceremonies favor speeches and dirges, Premier Wen and other officials, realizing this obligation, found ways to display arduous commitment and genuine emotion. A Chinese journalist's account of "Grandpa Wen" refusing to treat his abrasions when he slipped in the rubble is strongly reminiscent of imperial officials who fasted and braved the elements during drought and other emergencies in order to share their people's suffering. In another echo of the past, a local official, feeling the need to take personal responsibility, dramatically kowtowed in apology in front of marching parents.

Times," *Modern China* 33, no. 1 (2007): 123–53; for a view of recent death rituals, see Ellen Oxfeld, "'When You Drink Water, Think of Its Source': Morality, Status, and Reinvention in Rural Chinese Funerals," *Journal of Asian Studies* 63, no. 4 (November 2004): 961–90.

Emergency conditions, then, interfered with normal mourning, and local and official extemporizations also reflected different conceptions. What is proper mourning is also complicated by China's ethnic diversity. It is at first sight curious that so little was said about the Qiang minority, which dominates Wenchuan County near the epicenter and must have sent many of its best and brightest to the collapsed middle school. Tourists who have visited nearby Taoping hamlet must be wondering how the great unmortared stone towers in which many locals live could have withstood the earthquake, and indeed Taoping is on the list of affected places. Such communities used to mourn their dead with a shaman's martial performance and, in the case of deaths by accident, cremated the bodies. But the Qiang are relatively assimilated; while their colorful traditionalism and picturesqueness are normally played up for tourists and in TV performances for national holidays, government reports in the crisis preferred to underline the nation's solidarity behind all of its citizens.

Coming in the same year as the great southern snowfall and just two months after the Tibetan disturbances, the Sichuan earthquake must have reminded some Chinese of 1976, the year of the Tangshan earthquake. Historically, national disasters were signs of imbalance in the world, cracks in the political firmament, even harbingers of a new regime, as the heavenly mandate shifted to a new dynastic pretender. Even in 1976 these ideas were archaic, for the last emperor of the Qing (1644–1911) had abdicated some sixty-four years earlier, but people could not help noticing that two leading revolutionary leaders, Zhou Enlai and Zhu De, died in the months shortly before that earthquake. When Mao Zedong died that September, followed by the removal of the radical group now cursed as the Gang of Four, the pattern seemed to be confirmed. Within two years Deng Xiaoping's reforms were inaugurated. An earthquake had signaled vast political change.

Today's leaders, in more secure and prosperous times, must have remembered the inadequate response of the radical leadership in 1976. The Gang of Four had seen the relief as a distraction from the current political campaign against Deng Xiaoping, then temporarily out of power, and it had been Mao's recently designated heir Hua Guofeng who went a week after the Tangshan quake to take command of the relief work, an act that won him great political credit and may have helped the overthrow of the Gang of Four after Mao's death. Premier Wen Jiabao came within an hour and a half to supervise relief, and unlike Hua Guofeng, who in those post–Cultural Revolution days preached self-reliance, Wen after a few days opened China's disaster to foreign help and media transparency in a spirit of globalism suiting the year of the Chinese Olympics. Proof that 1976 was on the leaders' minds came when they set mourning for the 70,000 earthquake dead at three days, beginning with three minutes of silence nationwide, concurrent with the sounding of factory and ship sirens and horn blasts—exactly the same as for Mao Zedong. (Deng Xiaoping in 1997 got only the sirens and horn blasts, with six days of pro forma mourning.)

Some of the national mourning was clearly under official direction: a Japanese news team reported a CCTV producer carefully instructing relief workers to dig, pause, and doff their caps just before the three minutes of national silence. Such coaching in the ways of modernity recalls the sedulous efforts, in anticipation of the Olympics, to reform the city manners of Beijing inhabitants. Yet China's 200 million netizens faithfully observed the silence of their own accord, reducing Google.cn traffic almost to zero.[3] Old customs were spontaneously modified: in some places the candles customarily floated on streams on June 7, the eve of the Duanwu festival, were specially dedicated to the victims of the May 12 quake. Other national means of mourning sprang up—parades of young people shouting patriotic slogans, urging the survivors to take courage, and sitting after dark around candles in the shape of "5/12."

There was a huge expansion of condolence pages on the Internet: on one combined site 70,000 people selected virtual flowers and left a brief message. The principal theme of these Web messages was to wish for the fortitude of the bereaved and urge the Chinese people to be strong and united. Many Internet users offered consolation that the dead children are already in heaven; maybe, say some, they are already reborn—a surprisingly Buddhist sentiment for the city folk who make up most Internet users. Besides overseas contributions, huge sums of relief money were collected in China, and orphaned children found sponsors or adoptive parents. The outpourings of sympathy were infused with an evidently spontaneous patriotic fervor that reminded foreign reporters of Han Chinese reactions to criticisms of China's Tibet policy a few weeks earlier. Anticipatory pride in China's upcoming Olympics fortified these very varied expressions—patriotic expressions of *jiayou* (Go!) and *wansui* (Ten Thousand Years!) by sympathetic netizens foreshadowed the enthusiastic chants for Chinese athletes at Olympic venues in August.

National solidarity, not individual stories of misfortune, was also the theme of the official media. One of the strangest events was the solemn burial (with speeches and food offerings) of the only panda that died at the Wolong reserve in the quake zone, but it made sense, given the panda's ubiquity as a collective symbol of Sichuan and the Chinese nation. Wenchuan parents' anger at building code violations in schools—as distinct from other multistoried public buildings, which often survived intact—was picked up in a Sina.com blog headed "Who killed our children?" but the issue was kept out of the official press. The ongoing investigation into the school collapses does not seem to be looking for culprits; the Ministry of Education has focused on the safety of the remaining schools and the proper rebuilding of those destroyed. In a much-publicized blog, the writer Yu Qiuyu, who enjoys the semiofficial status of a public intellectual specializing in cultural policy, called upon bereaved parents to stop protesting so as

---

3. According to "Bob" in a comment on *China Beat*, giving the reference http://www.googlechinablog.com/2008/05/blog-post_22.html.

not to give an opening to "anti-Chinese" elements.[4] The year 2008 was supposed to be one of national pride. The focus of official mourning shifted to soldiers martyred while doing patriotic rescue work in the earthquake rubble, and the Olympic torch relay, suspended for the mourning period, resumed its proud passage around China. The imperative was not private mourning but national solidarity and certainly not finger-pointing.

Recalling the earthquake, the party leaders may have mixed feelings: they seem to have coped well with the crisis, notably the earthquake lakes. They proclaimed victory in the battle with nature in a high-tech makeover of Maoist efforts, having mobilized the People's Liberation Army, in particular, with notably more success than in 1976. With the help of unaccustomed flexibility from the Propaganda Department as it reached out to an international audience, they rode on a wave of popularity that the Olympic Games certainly enhanced. But as they remember the public's spontaneous reactions to the earthquake, including the practical intervention of Chinese nongovernmental organizations and private car owners who organized to bring relief from Chengdu to the quake zone, they might harbor some worries: Will future mass tragedies be so easily translated into national solidarity? Will independently channeled emotion in the public sphere inevitably back the party-state in future crises? Will other leaders have to take up the unconventionally populist style that Grandpa Wen has adopted so successfully in this time of mourning and recuperation?

Chinese Responses to Disaster: A View from the Qing ☆ Kathryn Edgerton-Tarpley

Media reports published in the immediate wake of the devastating May 12 earthquake in Sichuan highlighted trends seen as impressive and new in terms of responses by the People's Republic of China (PRC) to disaster. Certainly the quick response of state leaders—symbolized by Premier Wen Jiabao's much-heralded arrival in the disaster area only hours after the earthquake hit—stands in stark contrast to the PRC's handling of major catastrophes during the Mao era. During the Great Leap Famine of 1959–1961, Chairman Mao and other top leaders failed to act on reports that people were starving to death by the thousands. An estimated 30 million people died as a result of that famine, making it the most lethal famine in world history.

The willingness of the Chinese government to accept international aid and even rescue teams from Japan, Taiwan, South Korea, and Singapore provided an equally sharp contrast to the Mao-era government's determination to keep news

---

4. For a translation of his "tearful" appeal and sharp rebuttals by other writers in Chinese, see http://en.chinaelections.org/NewsInfo.asp?NewsID = 17932.

of the Great Leap Famine a secret, even if that required increasing grain exports to neighboring countries during the disaster rather than requesting foreign aid. The rapidity of the response and the massive scale of the government-led relief effort—one hundred rescue helicopters dropping soldiers into remote areas and 130,000 soldiers and medics mobilized for relief work within three days of the earthquake—impressed Americans as well, particularly those who recalled how victims of Hurricane Katrina waited for a full week before 50,000 members of the U.S. National Guard were finally dispatched to the disaster area.

While helicopter drops and the acceptance of Japanese rescue teams are new for China, however, other facets of the immediate postquake relief effort display interesting similarities to relief campaigns carried out in late imperial China. As a historian of famines in nineteenth-century China, I was intrigued to read that just as the rulers of China's last dynasty, the Qing (1644–1911), sought to shore up social stability during disasters by seeking to regulate grain prices in famine areas, on May 15 China's current government imposed temporary controls on food prices and transportation fares in the quake-hit areas of Sichuan, Gansu, and Shaanxi in an attempt to stop hoarding and speculation. Officials even punished seventeen people for profiteering.

Some American media reports (for example, a front-page *Los Angeles Times* article from May 17) took the PRC's proactive response as evidence that the government is at last beginning to govern "in a manner befitting a modern 21st century state." A broader historical perspective, however, suggests that in fact the current PRC government is acting in the tradition of imperial China's Confucian rulers, who often responded with alacrity during natural disasters out of a sense of both responsibility to nourish the people and a mindfulness that failing to do so might cost them Heaven's mandate and popular sanction for their rule.[5]

Shortly after the quake China's state-run media also reported that victims can depend on the government to pay their medical expenses. In late imperial China, officials and local literati argued that disasters were a result of the interaction of natural and human forces. While Heaven might send the original drought that led to a crop failure, for instance, it was believed to be a combination of people's failure to prepare for disaster beforehand and the selfish and greedy behavior of low-level officials and underlings that allowed a drought to escalate into a major famine. The earthquake in Sichuan is obviously a natural rather than man-made catastrophe. Nevertheless, PRC officials seem as anxious as their late Qing counterparts to ensure that what starts as a natural disaster is not

---

5. Important scholarly accounts of famine relief in pre-twentieth century China include Lillian M. Li, *Fighting Famine in North China: State, Market, and Environmental Decline, 1690s–1990s* (Stanford, CA: Stanford University Press, 2007); Pierre-Etienne Will, *Bureaucracy and Famine in Eighteenth-Century China*, trans. Elborg Forster (Stanford, CA: Stanford University Press, 1990); and Pierre Etienne Will and R. Bin Wong, with James Lee, Jean Oi, and Peter Perdue, *Nourish the People: The State Civilian Granary System in China, 1650–1850* (Ann Arbor, MI: Center for Chinese Studies, 1991).

transformed into something even worse on their watch. As Deputy Health Minister Gao Qiang explained when taking responsibility for preventing the outbreak of large-scale epidemics in quake areas, "We should not add to the losses caused by natural disasters and let people suffer more just because we have not done our job well" (*China Daily*, May 16, 2008).

The involvement of large numbers of private citizens provides another parallel between late Qing famine relief efforts and the current relief campaign. During the North China famine that killed roughly 13 million people during the late 1870s, wealthy philanthropists from cities throughout the Jiangnan region (in the lower Yangtze River valley) worked together to raise relief money for their starving compatriots in North China. As I demonstrate in *Tears from Iron: Cultural Responses to Famine in Nineteenth-Century China*, some enterprising southern literati even traveled to the northern provinces themselves to distribute grain, bury bodies, build schools for famine orphanages, and redeem women who had been sold by their starving families. While some of these men later received state recognition for their relief work, their relief activities were separate from the Qing state's official relief campaign.

Media coverage of the current disaster has highlighted the Chinese government's response and the PLA's crucial role in relief work. A few reports, however, show that private citizens are responding to the disaster in impressive numbers as well. The *People's Daily* reported that by May 14, just two days after the earthquake, Beijingers had filled the city's blood bank, so hundreds of additional would-be donors were asked to leave their cell phone numbers and wait until more blood was needed. The *Guardian* observed that wads of cash and piles of donated food and water were driven into Sichuan not only by army vehicles but also by private or company-owned cars "adorned with red banners proclaiming the names of the donor company or work unit." The *Los Angeles Times* reported that although the government "has at times warned do-gooders to stay clear and let the army and police do their jobs," Chinese individuals and businesses have continued to play an active role in relief efforts. "The outpouring of help from the people and the speed with which many groups became involved underscored a fundamental shift in recent years as more individuals and companies take the initiative, eroding the traditional government-led approach," commented the *Times* (May 15). In a particularly vivid example of citizen activism, on May 14 a group of eighteen mountaineers from Beijing, among them doctors and business owners, flew to a quake-stricken county to rescue victims by putting their survival skills into practice, thus following in the footsteps of the late Qing literati who traveled to northern provinces to distribute relief (*China Daily*, May 15).

Chinese philanthropists leapt into action in the 1870s because by that point the beleaguered late Qing government no longer had the resources to carry out the type of massive relief campaign that Confucian rhetoric and eighteenth-century precedent demanded. The current PRC state, in contrast, is a strong state that thus far has proved to be quite capable of conducting a highly effective relief effort. The degree of initiative displayed by nonstate actors during this crisis, however, demonstrates that the state no longer fully controls—and perhaps no longer feels a need to fully control—individual and company-sponsored relief efforts. The late Qing government reluctantly allowed foreign relief workers— many of them Anglo-American missionaries—and Jiangnan philanthropists to distribute relief in famine areas because by the 1870s it was simply too weak to deal with a major crisis by itself. The present Chinese government, on the contrary, accepted foreign rescue teams and private initiative from a position of relative strength. The assistance of Japanese relief workers or Chinese citizens is no longer viewed primarily as a threat to an insecure state but as a way to improve ties with neighbors and further unify the nation.

China and the Red Cross ☆ Caroline Reeves

Caroline Reeves has conducted extensive research on the history of the Chinese Red Cross and late Qing and twentieth-century Chinese relief work, so China Beat *asked her to comment on the 2008 efforts in light of that historical research. Here is a selection from her postings; for more, please visit our website.*

Among the scenes of devastation—small bodies in shrouds, crumpled buildings and bridges, dazed survivors—another image flashes across the screen: something familiar, something reassuring to international viewers. Out of the chaos appears the symbol of the Red Cross, on the arm of a medic, on the side of an ambulance: a sign that there might be some hope—or at least some comfort—for these victims of China's horrific earthquake.

As we watch the unreal footage of a natural disaster that has, so far, claimed almost 30,000 lives, we are brought back to our own comfort zone by the presence of that familiar symbol, the Red Cross. This is something we "know," something that needs no translation from cryptic Chinese into English, or German, or whatever our language. But what we are looking at is not "our" Red Cross but the Red Cross Society of China, *Zhongguo Hongshizihui* (RCSC). This is an organization with its own history and its own imperatives, a society whose background gives us important insights into the China we cannot pull our eyes away from today. . . .

Its existence reveals two important aspects about Chinese society often overlooked in the world's media coverage of that country: first, the Chinese people's desire to help their compatriots personally and directly, despite authoritarian governments or social systems, and, second, China's overwhelming desire to be included in the great international movements of the last 150 years, including the international humanitarian movement embodied by the international movement of Red Cross and Red Crescent Societies. . . . The media often portrays China as a monolith, "where the state decides everything and group-think predominates," but today, when China is quite literally falling apart, it is precisely these two aspects that prevail.[6]

Resistance Is Useful ☆ Rana Mitter

In the days after the tragic Sichuan earthquake of May 15, 2008, the *People's Daily*, the official news and propaganda organ of the Chinese Communist Party (CCP), ran nonstop coverage of the rescue efforts. Pictures of heroic soldiers sat alongside images of grim-faced survivors who had been pulled to safety. And in the headlines, over and over again, China's citizens were reminded that they should not be merely passive spectators to the tragedy. The party was (of course!) in the lead when it came to earthquake relief, but all Chinese were supposed to make a contribution. The phrase that appeared repeatedly in those days to summarize this ethos was *kangzhen* ("resistance to the earthquake").

The phrasing struck me as rather unusual. Earthquakes are not the sort of thing that one "resists" in the usual sense. They are natural phenomena, to be endured or overcome, but "resistance," with its implications of human agency used to fight back against some other human force, seemed slightly out of place.

And yet in another sense, there was a strange sense of familiarity. The images of soldiers, of traumatized evacuees, the language of a national struggle against an implacable enemy—all of these brought to mind the imagery of China's titanic struggle against Japan during World War II. This conflict was known in China at the time, and is still known today, as "China's War of Resistance to Japan"—in Chinese, *Kangri zhanzheng*, or *kangzhan* for short. *Kangzhan*, of course, sounds very much like *kangzhen*.

Is it fanciful to suggest that there was a deliberate attempt by the propaganda arm of the CCP to encourage a link in readers' minds between the struggle against Japan between 1937 and 1945 and the aftermath of a dreadful natural disaster in 2008? It would be hard to prove, without pinning down one of the ever-elusive linguistic engineers in Beijing's media world, but the resemblances are real and uncanny. China has, after all, had a very complex and often strange

6. Jeffrey N. Wasserstom, "One, Two or Many Chinas?" *openDemocracy.net*, February 19, 2008.

relationship with its wartime past. For most of the Mao period, the war against the Japanese was mentioned only in very restrictive terms: it was fine, indeed essential, to suggest that the CCP had come to power because its patriotic anti-Japanese stance had won it converts throughout Chinese society.

In this narrative of the war, the officially recognized government of China, the Nationalists (Kuomintang or Guomindang) under Chiang Kai-shek, were corrupt and had done little to resist the invaders. Furthermore, the most toxic part of the historical legacy—the collaboration with the Japanese by some Chinese leaders under occupation—was mentioned hardly at all, and then only in terms of treachery that needed no further analysis. After 1949, Mao's government was not concerned that Japan would invade again because the United States had occupied and demilitarized it. In contrast, they were deeply concerned that Chiang Kai-shek, who was still on Taiwan, might decide to invade the mainland. So it became more important to vilify Chiang's contributions to the wartime effort than it did to make a major issue of Japan's wartime crimes in China.

From the 1980s on, however, the story within China changed. Chiang and Mao died within a year of one another (in 1975 and 1976). From 1978, China entered Deng Xiaoping's period of reform, where the command economy and deep penetration of the state and party into Chinese society were loosened and confrontational ideology was changed into a pragmatic view of "socialism with Chinese characteristics" (meaning, it seemed, anything that would make markets work without having to cede political control). In this atmosphere, China got richer, but many leaders worried about how the population might become purely materialistic, with no wider sense of community or citizenship.

Into this spiritual gap came the idea that China should turn back to its wartime experience. For eight long years, China had fought—and successfully resisted—the Japanese invaders. All Chinese had fought together, whether Nationalists or Communists (again, the collaborators with Japan were still kept out in the historiographical cold). Now, it was time once again to recall those glorious days of resistance and use them to inspire and warn a generation of Chinese born not only long after the war but also after the death of Mao. As an added bonus, the new stress on the similarities rather than the differences between Chiang and Mao meant that reunification with Taiwan might become more likely, as the Cold War rift that had divided the Taiwan Straits became less severe. (Unfortunately, Chiang Kai-shek's stock in China started going up just when it was dropping sharply in democratizing Taiwan, where his brutal repression of dissent was at last being discussed openly on the island.) As a result, from the mid-1980s, new monuments to this history of China's War of Resistance appeared across the nation. In Beijing, a massive museum to the war was built, containing a statue of a fallen soldier who represented both Communist and Nationalist troops. In Nanjing, half a century after the notorious "Rape of Nanking," a museum commemorating the massacre was finally erected. (Both museums were given a major revamp in 2007 on the seventieth anniversary of the war's outbreak.)

But the new version of history had a particular piquancy in one part of China: Sichuan province. After the Japanese invasion, Chiang Kai-shek's Nationalist government had retreated to Chongqing (now an autonomous city but then part of Sichuan), and it had been China's wartime capital from 1938 to 1945. Chongqing was constantly bombed by Japanese air raids during that period, tens of millions of refugees fled to the region, and the population faced starvation and massive social upheaval. Yet after Mao's victory in 1949, the province had to keep quiet about its history of genuinely heroic resistance because it had been carried out not under the victorious Communists but under the now-despised Nationalists, about whom nothing good could be said. The turn in historical interpretation in the 1980s and 1990s allowed the region to make up for lost time. Books on Sichuan's wartime record, local art and historical exhibitions about the sufferings of Chongqing and Chengdu, and oral histories of the events were all given huge publicity, particularly around the sixtieth anniversary of the end of the war in 2005. *Kangzhan* was finally back at the center of Sichuan's identity in the early twenty-first century, just as it had been in the 1930s.

Into this atmosphere burst the horrific earthquake of May 15, 2008. In some ways, its arrival was politically fortuitous for the Chinese government. The upcoming Olympic Games were coming under international pressure from groups concerned about the violent events in Tibet in March of that year and continuing international concern about China's role in the Darfur conflict. The earthquake changed the global narrative to one of sympathy for China's suffering and also admiration for its swift and efficient responses to the disaster. Internationally, the aftermath of the earthquake probably did help to neutralize anger at China in the international community, and in fact the Olympics went off very successfully overall.

But the *kangzhen* phrasing was not meant for the international community, and the imagery of soldiers and evacuees was not primarily aimed at CNN or the BBC. Rather, it seemed to speak directly to the new connection between the wartime past and the patriotic present that distinguishes a Chinese party which is no longer ideologically communist but is still keen to project an image of communal endeavor and national strength to its own people in the face of external threats. The Nationalists and Communists had both done something very similar during the 1930s when Japan invaded. For that reason, the links between *kangzhen* and *kangzhan* are much closer than just a linguistic similarity.

And it works. One of the most notable fights in the Chinese cybersphere in the months after the earthquake concerned a young woman who complained online about what she called the constant whining and complaints of the earthquake victims. Hadn't China heard enough from them? she asked. It seemed that she might symbolize precisely what the propagandists had worried about: a young, selfish urbanite who cared nothing for wider society but only about material goods and her own well-being. If so, she would have been surprised at the firestorm of criticism that was aimed back at her. Whether they saw the links between wartime and earthquake or not, China's netizens (to use a word beloved of the English edition of the *People's Daily*) did indeed see "resistance to the earthquake" as a communal endeavor for all Chinese.

After the Earthquake: Former Students
Report on the Disaster ☆ Peter Hessler

Mr. Hessler, the Internet connection has been broken for 30 hours, I just opened my email, thanks very much for writing to me. I am sorry to say my parents' house collapsed, but they are fine, when the earthquake happened, they were working in the field, but my niece was badly wounded when she was at school. My parents are with me in the city center. We are busying go to and coming back to hospitals to see our relatives. my house is full of people, my uncles, my aunts, and many other. I am too busy to write, I will let you know more when I am free. Thanks.

David

At my home in Colorado, I received David's e-mail early Tuesday morning as the news about the earthquake in southwestern China worsened. As of now, the official death count is more than 13,000, and that number will undoubtedly rise in coming days. I hope that I continue to hear from friends who are safe. David was a student of mine in the mid-1990s, when I was a Peace Corps volunteer in Sichuan province; that was the English name he had chosen for himself. Like most of my students, he had grown up in the countryside. Many of the e-mails I'm now receiving indicate that people in rural settlements have generally fared better than city residents. A young man named Willy described his wife's village in northern Sichuan:

In Nancy's home town . . . their parents were dealing with the newly picked tea and they found the house shake, and they ran out of the room, and the tiles fell off, the windows shook hard, and the water in the jars in their yard jumped out of the jar. People found it very hard to stand and many of them just took hold of the trees to keep balance.

But the truth is that nowadays rural Chinese villages are home mostly to the very old and the very young. Virtually everybody of working age has migrated, and the population of urban centers has exploded—the National Bureau of Statistics estimates that 130 million rural Chinese are now living in cities. Construction is fast and often slapdash; during a recent visit to Lishui, a city in Zhejiang province, I was told by workers that it generally takes fifty days to build a two-story factory. This is the kind of structure that has collapsed in cities such as Mianyang, which is close to the epicenter of the quake. A former student named Lucy wrote,

> We are really sad to see China is experiencing so many bad things. . . . I called one of my friends in Mianyang, and she told me the things there are very bad. Many people are under the broken buildings. Many students are crying for help. Many children are also crying because they have not eaten anything for 28 hours. Today, when I called her again, I could not reach her. I really hope all the things will be better soon.

In the minds of many Chinese, major earthquakes are often connected with political events. This week's disaster is the largest since 1976, when a quake in eastern China killed more than 240,000 people. That was the year that Zhou Enlai and Mao Zedong both died and the Cultural Revolution ended. At that time, Willy was a newborn in rural Sichuan, far from the epicenter, but even there his parents felt the tremors. His mother was bathing her two sons and her first instinct was to put some clothes on them—later, she said that she couldn't stand the thought of them dying naked. In a neighboring village, the peasants slaughtered all the pigs, even the smallest ones; they believed that it was best to enjoy what they had before the world ended.

This week, Willy told me that many people are responding in similar ways to China's recent string of disasters. First, brutally cold weather in January and February caused major transportation-related delays and deaths and disrupted the Spring Festival holiday, then the protests occurred in Tibet and during the Olympic torch relay overseas, and now the earthquake has devastated parts of Sichuan province. He wrote,

> People here are likely to connect it with the Olympics. Almost everyone thinks that this year gives China disasters and it is a bad year. Interesting enough, when the snowstorm occurred, when I was watching TV, I just said for fun to Nancy that the year of 2008 was so bad that possibly an earthquake might happen in China. It seems that my sixth sense is right. And the authorities in Sichuan just predicted that there would be severe drought during the summer.

In China, when bad things happen, they happen in places like Sichuan. The province is landlocked, remote, and rugged; it's always been heavily populated, and it's always been poor. When I was in the Peace Corps, Sichuan was home to 110 million people, a staggering figure: roughly one of every fifty human beings on earth was Sichuanese. Since then, the central government has divided the region into two parts, Sichuan province and Chongqing municipality, but that has done nothing to change the sheer sense of massed humanity. And the recent earthquake is by no means unusual. If you've lived in Sichuan and continue to follow it in the news, you become accustomed to terrible stories—floods and landslides and collapsed bridges. Periodically, I'll receive an e-mail that stops me cold, such as the one that Kevin sent last May:

> I am sorry to tell a bad news. My town is called Yihe in Kaixian County in Chongqing. Two days ago, a big thunder hit my wife's village school. It killed 7 students and wounded 44 students. It was not my wife's class. But when the tragedy happened, my wife was teaching her students. . . . I am sorry to tell you about the bad news. These days my wife and I are both sad and scared at home.

The Chinese often believe that human beings are shaped by the land around them. After my time in Sichuan, I came to agree; I had never lived among people who were so tough. The Sichuanese are natural workers, and they dominate construction crews in many parts of China. They are patient and tireless and determined, and they're famous for pragmatism—Deng Xiaoping came from Sichuan. The people are also surprisingly good-natured and optimistic. Maybe that's what happens when you're a survivor, and maybe that also accounts for their sense of humor. On Tuesday, I received another e-mail from Willy:

> . . . a minor quake measure 6.1 occurred again in Chengdu at around 3:00 and I called my friend there, they said when it happened yesterday, the whole house was like a swing. But this afternoon, when I called him, he said many of his colleagues (some teachers) were playing mahjong happily in the wake of the terrible quake. . . .
>
> Do you still remember my uncle, who went to Gansu as the early migrant worker? His son survived the quake. . . . He was a college student in Aba Teachers' College, which happens to be located in the epicenter. He is going to graduate in July, but he found a job for Yanjing Beer Company, the company asked them to go to Guangxi to get training instead of going back to school to study, so when the quake happened he was on the train to Guangxi not knowing that Yanjing Beer Company had saved his life.

This week, it's unlikely that there will be much good news coming from China. But the rescue crews will, one hopes, make progress, and there may be reason for some Sichuan-style optimism. First, it seems that the Chinese government has been relatively open about news coverage, and it doesn't seem to be restricting e-mails and phone calls. Second, the scale of destruction could easily have been worse. The epicenter was near the city of Dujiangyan, which in May 2001 started construction on a massive hydroelectric dam on the Min River. Big dams are common in China, and Dujiangyan was one of the nation's "Ten Key Projects" aimed at producing electricity and better water supplies.

By 2003, there were signs that the government was quietly expanding the project, and silt had begun to accumulate at a second location on the river. Dujiangyan is home to a local irrigation system that has functioned for more than two thousand years and has been declared a World Heritage site; it would have been effectively destroyed by the new dam. The city's World Heritage Office opposed the project, contacting journalists from Chinese publications. The press was allowed to report with relative openness, in part because it portrayed the dam as destructive of cultural heritage. But one of the local entities that openly opposed the dam was the Dujiangyan Seismological Bureau.

In August 2003, dam construction was forced to stop. In the history of the People's Republic, this represented the first time that an engineering project on such a scale had been cancelled because of public pressure. (For a full account, see "Unbuilt Dams," by Andrew C. Mertha and William R. Lowry, published in the October 2006 issue of *Comparative Politics*.) Today, with Dujiangyan in ruins and the government struggling to respond, there's some small consolation in the fact that at least there wasn't another major dam on the site. And maybe later, after the emergency has passed, officials will remember the importance of the press and the seismological experts in stopping the dam. Sichuan's greatest resource has always been its people, and sometimes the government just needs to listen to them.

Letters from Sichuan II ☆ Peter Hessler

On May 13, I filed a web report on the *New Yorker* site, based on what I heard from former students in the early days of the disaster. Since then, I've continued to receive notes, and I've copied a few below.

When I lived in Sichuan, I was most impressed by the sense of place. The landscape was rugged and beautiful, and the people had a distinct character. They seemed more emotional than in other parts of China; they laughed more freely, and their street arguments were more vicious. It wasn't any surprise that in 1999, after NATO bombed the Chinese embassy in Belgrade, the most violent protests occurred in Chengdu. People sometimes blame it on the spicy food, which seems a shallow explanation. I sensed it had something to with the land itself—so many mountains and rivers, so many people. Emotions have always moved fast in Sichuan, and over the past week they've moved even faster.

May 14, 2008

Mr Hessler, When I am writing the e-mail to you. I am really sad and my heart is still blooding. My school was destroyed, and many of my students were killed in the earthquake. In my hometown, Guangyuan, the earthquake is really bad, I was teaching in class when I heard the terrible sound, all of us ran out of the classroom. Then the school is in trouble. I heard students crying sadly. I saw the teaching building fall down, we had two floors, I was on the ground floor, most of us escaped the building before it fell down. In our school, there are 400 students and so far 27 students died and about 40 were badly wounded, some of them are in Guangyuan, and some of them are in Mianyyang. I am now with my husband in my sister's home in Neijiang City. I really miss my students at school, I think I will go back tomorrow morning. How I wish I could be with my students, my headmaster told me in my class 6 students died. They are all my favorite students. They died so young and small, around 14 years old. If I can make calls in Guangyuan, I will call Mr Dai and tell him the news, I want him to email you, I have no internet connection in my school area.

I wish that everything will be fine
Yours
Olivia

May 15, 2008
Pete—

My father called me, he told me that it had been raining the whole day. People in Sichuan's Bazhong City said that the fowls and the animals are running like mad, people say that there will be aftershocks. So my family are still very terrified. My nephew has stored the computer I sent him and the TV set in the cupboard. My whole family has to sleep in the chicken house which can be used as the shelter because it is low, and even it collapses, it does no great harm, my parents are afraid that the quake is like the one in 1976 in Tangshan.

Take care,
Willy

May 16, 2008
Thanks for your letter.
This is my experience in the earthquake below. Close to the earthquake.

5.12 noon. Our group leader said: "The ground is shaking, earthquake!" My office is on the first floor. We ran out of the office and shouted to students on the 2nd, 3rd, 4th floor "ran, ran, ran to the playground." In fact, at that moment we should stay under the desk. My student hold my clothes and cried "Will it shake again, Mr Yu?" I said "Never. Don't worry. Just stay in the playground. Don't move." That moment my thinking was very simple: If the children in our school are OK, my daughter Zoe will be OK. Fortunately, all people around me are OK.

No doubt we are luck enough. Not far away, Qingchuan, a county of Guangyuan, the mountains were down, the river was up, the road was broken. The teaching buildings were down. Many students and teachers were covered under the teaching buildings. It was not hopeful for most of them to be saved.

In Guangyuan downtown 80 or so persons were killed in the earthquake. The first night we slept on the playground, we dared not go back home, some building were down, some building will be down. The whole city were camping. No tents, the second day we slept under the color-strip cloth, which was set for rain.

My cousin's daughter who is almost 2 years old, was frightened. She cried all night "Dad, let's go home. Dad, let's go home." Du Yiquan, our school's computer teacher, he took his son Zouzou to the playground, Zouzou did good, he just said softly to his Mum "Mum, My nose is uncomfortable" and repeated the sentence again and again. My daughter Zoe is just 50 days, she didn't know what happened, slept in my wife's breast. Many of my colleague said "poor child! How poor the baby is." My nephew, 7 years old, is studying in our school. I told him "Your house fell down in your hometown." He didn't know it means too much, at least no place to live. And he continued to play in the playground happily.

Our school cooked porridge for the victims of the earthquake. I realized if there was not enough food for my wife to eat, my little Zoe would not take the breast. So the second day I sent them back to my wife's Laojia (hometown), where her parents once lived. There the earthquake did not affect the peasants too much. They slept outside at night because of the earthquake and got up early the second morning to harvest their wheat. In hometown I watched TV and knew many people died and tears came to my eyes.

Many volunteers went to the earthquake area. The 4th day after the earthquake, I went back home. I checked my email. When I was writing to you, my Mum in next room shouted to me "it is shaking again." The chair I sat was shaking and I felt it. But I don't care. I am accustomed to it.

Today I subscribed, anyway I am still alive and I can write e-mail. I went to school and prepared for beginning class again later.

Thanks again, I will be OK. Zoe will be OK. Everybody will be OK.

Roger

May 18, 2008

These days I am really sad for the situation in Sichuan and Chongqing. Tonight's show really moves me, I am really proud that China is getting stronger and stronger, and I really think Chinese government is so open and tries its best to help the people in the earthquake. I think the people in the disaster areas will get all the problems over. By the way, I am fine, all my students are fine, the earthquake did not affect us so much, but we are still afraid of it, some people say there may be one quake in Chongqing soon.

Jackson

May 19, 2008

Mr Hessler, these days too many tears ran down from my eyes. These days I have been so proud of being a Chinese, I am proud of the government's quick actions, and I am proud of the unity in China. Last night I watched the CCTV Charity Show, I was deeply moved, and today China held the national mourning day for the victims. I was touched again. I am sorry for Sichuan People, I know we will have a hard life for a long time, but I am willing to overcome the difficulties with my students. Thanks so much for caring us, we are very fine.

Chuck Du

May 20, 2008

Hi, Pete. Here the people in Yueqing are having all kinds of activities to send condolence to the death in Sichuan. I am really sad to see the rising death toll and I am really moved by the policy about the National Mourning Days for the victims. And these days I am likely to shed tears for my hometown fellows. Yesterday when it was the time for us to show condolence in silence, I taped the scene on the express way, what I saw made both sad and happy, most of the cars and bus did not stop and they ran very fast as usual, only a few did. But I think all of the cars and buses tooted their horns at least, which is the drivers' favourite (It is like what you wrote in River Town, maybe several hundred times a minute.) My school had a grand donation rally, and the school raised around 500,000 yuan, it is a big deal as for a school. Many people had their eyes full of tears when the host mentioned the sad stories during the quakes.

And these days, it seems that the aftershocks come one after another. People in Sichuan are still living in terror. All the people fled their home in Nanchong, they either go to the countryside or sleep near the Jialingjiang River. Nanchong has become a ghost city, my mom told me that the gate of my apartment in Nanchong is completely open the whole day, and the security guards have also fled leaving the whole area empty. The tents are sold 500 yuan compared to the price 50 yuan not long ago.

Friends in Nanchong told me yesterday evening the International food chain shop—McDonald's in Nanchong was smashed by some young people, some people said some university students were behind the incident. The restaurant was named the TieGongji (iron cock) or miser. It is said that some people are taking actions against the Nokia Agency in Nanchong because it also falls behind others when it comes to the recent donation for the victims in Sichuan.

Willy

Chapter 6

Shanghai Images in Beijing's Year

A BETTER LIFE IN NEW SHANGHAI?

Maura Elizabeth Cunningham

Now that the Olympics have passed, China has begun gearing up for the country's next big international event: the 2010 World Expo to be held in Shanghai beginning May 1, 2010. In addition to massive Expo-related construction projects and infrastructure development, Shanghai officials are also testing the city's Expo readiness by hosting smaller meetings and performances designed to attract international crowds. Broadway shows are now coming to Shanghai, and the city has been a tour stop for foreign musical acts as diverse as the Rolling Stones, Linkin Park, and the New York Philharmonic. Currently, visitors to the seventh annual Shanghai Biennale can ponder artworks centered on the theme of "mobility related to the urban, economic, and social developments"; next March, dozens of international authors will participate in the sixth year of the Shanghai International Literary Festival.

Despite this vibrant cultural scene, however, while attending last year's literary festival at the swanky M on the Bund restaurant, I felt a bizarre sense of dislocation as I looked around the room. Chinese waiters unobtrusively cleared away empty coffee cups and wine glasses while festival ticket holders—almost all foreigners—milled about and discussed the latest goings-on in the Shanghai expat world. Rather than signifying Shanghai's move toward a "Better City, Better Life" (the Expo's tagline), the event instead felt like an exclusive gathering open only to those fluent in English. Holding the festival on the Bund, the most visible reminder of foreign entry into China, only intensified my discomfort.

This, then, is the contradiction in Shanghai's efforts to promote itself as a cosmopolitan metropolis: the city is becoming the venue for more and more international events, but participation in such gatherings is generally limited to a thin slice of the populace. While all city residents must deal with the upheaval generated by Expo preparations, they do not always have the opportunity to reap the benefits of Shanghai's new interest in placing itself on the world stage. With eighteen months now left until the 2010 Expo begins, Shanghai city officials still have far to go to create a "Better City, Better Life."

Posted 11/3/2008 at 08:00:00 AM

Within China, Shanghai has a special status. It is where Chinese people go to get a taste of Europe by taking a turn on the Bund, with its stone facades as backdrop, or walking down the planer tree–lined streets of the French Concession. It is also where they go, if they can afford it, to shop, on once and now again fashionable streets such as Nanjing Road. It is a city that is widely admired for its stylishness and excitement, but also disparaged, with many Chinese from other parts of the country viewing the Shanghainese as haughty, materialistic, and superficial.

For foreign visitors, though, one source of fascination is the city's cosmopolitan past represented by sites such as the massive clock of the 1927 riverfront Custom House (once known as "Big Ching," a nickname suggesting that it was a Chinese counterpart to London's Big Ben); another is its increasingly futuristic cityscape, especially in the Pudong (East Shanghai) district that stands across the water from the Bund. The maglev train, skyscrapers, and unlimited neon of this metropolis, which now contains several times as many very tall buildings as Manhattan, suggests a possible shape of things to come. Shanghai is a city constantly under construction—at one point it was estimated that a quarter or more of the world's cranes were being used in Shanghai. In recent years, that construction has meant the rapid demolition of many of Shanghai's distinctive multifamily houses and close-knit lanes. A similar process happened in Beijing in preparation for the Olympic Games, and it has sped up in Shanghai as well as that city approaches its 2010 World Expo, which will be China's first world's fair.

In this chapter, journalist and photographer Howard French shares a selection of the photographs he took in Shanghai while he served as New York Times *bureau chief from 2003 to 2008. Captivated by the lane life of Shanghai, constantly under threat from encroaching developments, French began to photograph them. His photos capture the bustle and casual familiarity of these close-knit neighborhoods but are tinged also by the melancholy of their impending extinction.*

Disappearing Shanghai ☆ Howard W. French

The rise and fall of cities, like the nations that produce them, is a banal fact of history.

Rare though is the great city that vanishes before our eyes, its old structures torn down and replaced almost instantly by new ones as if in completion of a single gesture.

This is a new kind of spectacle; a variant on that highly familiar theme: made in China.

As a reporter for the *New York Times*, I had the dumb luck to arrive in Shanghai at the very apogee of this transformation. In fact, my earliest hint of the scale of the undertaking came to me during my first ride into the city along a dark and dusty highway from Pudong Airport in 2003.

The road itself was still so new that no lights had been turned on, and the signs for exits had not yet been marked. As we got close to the city, all manner of vehicles joined in the commotion, from heavy trucks spewing black exhaust into night air that hung thick with pollution, to rickety three-wheel vehicles that were more motorcycle than automobile, to men bent forward in the backbreaking labor of hauling overloaded trailers by their own raw manpower. The remaking of Shanghai was a twenty-four-hour-a-day project.

Yet even with strong first impressions like these, it would be some time before I really grasped the scale of what was going on here.

My first six months in Shanghai were spent studying Chinese full time, not reporting. Weekends were a time of sheer recovery for me, and as I spent my free hours wandering the city I gradually came to understand how to walk the streets was to take an excursion in history—a very particular history.

Older Chinese cities came into existence over millennia as settlements that grew into villages, villages that grew into towns, and finally towns that grew into major urban centers as the numbers of their inhabitants and the density of inhabitation grew.

Beijing, the old imperial capital and Shanghai's latter-day rival for the title of China's greatest city, is the most remarkable example of this kind. Its genetic fingerprint unmistakably remains that of an imperial village, one that radiated and steadily grew from the hems of the imperial compound.

On the visual evidence alone, Shanghai is a very different creature. It seems thoroughly modern in its commercial and industrial roots, as though it were stamped almost from its birth by the forces of globalization. It is a myth that Shanghai was a mere "fishing village" prior to the establishment of Western settlements after the Opium War (1839–1842); by that point it was already a walled city with temples, a bustling market district, and perhaps a quarter of a million inhabitants. Still, the speed with which it developed from that point on remains dramatic.

Oddly for a country so steeped in history, "old" in Shanghai often means not the remnants of the sections that existed before the Westerners arrived but rather reminders of the early twentieth century, the period in which it became China's first modern city and, one might argue, Asia's first great world city as well. With only about as many people as Old Beijing in 1900, by 1937 Shanghai had bulged to include some 3.7 million people, more than twice the population of its northern rival, and had become the sixth-busiest port in the world.

When I arrived, the rusty old sinews and lineaments of this old Shanghai, by turns stately, creaky, and crumbling, were still everywhere on display. These were the vestiges of the extraordinary boom of a century earlier that prefigured the explosive growth of China and its cities today.

The most famous relics of this age are, of course, the imposing and palatial buildings of the Bund, the Huangpu waterfront that the British built up, in a flourish of imperial and entrepreneurial shock and awe.

"What pangs of regret and remorse ought to be awakened among these proud, unenlightened men, when, in their moment, if any, of honest reflection, they cast their eyes upon this 'Model Settlement,' and perceive that a handful of outer barbarians have done more than they themselves, with their highest efforts, have achieved anywhere in their own wide Empire during all the untold centuries of its fame," once mused the British photographer John Thompson, displaying a sense of satisfaction shared by his fellow foreigners.

Those less enamored of the West's lust for conquest—and not all of the critics were Chinese—saw the Bund as emblematic of the artificiality of the foreign settlements in China. Its pompous mishmash of architectural styles, for one, struck the author Harold Acton as a "ponderous parody" of authentic Western thoroughfares; the ornate structures, he said, "do not look man-made: they have little connection with the people of China; they are poisonous toadstools raised by anonymous banks, trust and commercial firms. Imposing from the river but essentially soulless: no court or government had designed them and given them life."

My own discovery of the organic vestiges of the legendary boomtown of the late nineteenth and early twentieth centuries that I had read so much about came not on the Bund rather but in the rapidly disappearing neighborhoods of the old city, where internal migrants have flocked in waves by the millions, from Anhui and Zhejiang and further afield in search of a foothold in Shanghai's new and booming cash economy.

This discovery came about on a crisp Saturday afternoon in the early winter of 2003—a day that I'll never forget because it changed my life in some important ways, not least prompting me to recommit myself to a lifelong but sporadic practice of photography.

The first of the neighborhoods to draw me in began on Luxiangyuan Lu, just south of Renmin Lu. At first, it was the narrowness of the street that beckoned me. As I wandered in a bit further, I was drawn by the buzz of activity, uncommon even for bustling Shanghai.

On what passed for sidewalks and spilling into the street were people who made their living as scavengers, banging away at metal refuse with hammers, salvaging whatever they could for resale. Then, a few yards further down the lane, I found an entire street converted into an open-air produce market.

What I began to discover that afternoon was an almost secret world, accessible through discreet little alleys and backstreets that look deceptively drab at first glance. You set out down these paths, though, and on lucky days what opens up for you is a realm of magical illusions, places that appear and reappear, on subsequent visits, as if they had been served up from another age, suspended in amber, frozen and preserved for all time.

But, of course, it is not frozen, much less preserved. It is a world that is fast disappearing, a place of unavoidably brief and tragic loves. No sooner than you think you've learned and memorized every single face and worked out every nook and cranny, these places are steamrolled, demolished—gone and lost forever. And in Shanghai, the process of which I speak is happening like a train of cascading dominoes—hence the title of my attempt at tribute: Disappearing Shanghai.

The rhythms of life in the private little worlds I've documented here, the songbirds and the crickets lovingly raised in their cages, the street markets and the foods, with their smells and colors that change so suddenly and so crisply according to the season, the eternal tending of laundry from long bamboo poles, the wildly screeching bicycle brakes, the lusty throat clearing, the world-weary lounging about on beach chairs and in pajamas, the very appearance of the people's faces, weathered by a century of immense and often brutal change, like the old man in the faded Mao suit I saw on a street corner this afternoon looking for the life of him like an apparition lost amid the onrush of the new—it is all on its way out. It is all being swept away in the pursuit of a new template of modernity, a Hong Kong without hills but with steroids and, to judge by the gaudiest patches of Pudong, on psychedelics, too.

Why mourn this fact, for, after all, what is history? What is urban civilization—that most fantastic achievement of mankind—if not an engine of ceaseless change?

Another Shanghai is rising up fast, and one day it will disappear too, won't it? Not, of course, before throwing up its own portraitists, its own poets, its own bards.

This may be all true in a literal, bookish sense. But as I explored this world with camera in hand, my senses protested. They told me there was no way the world in creation would have anything like the texture of the one it is replacing, and for that reason, as the old city turns to rubble and dust, its disappearance should interrogate us.

That old Shanghai, the disappearing one that seems so scarcely cherished by its own hurried and nostalgia-free denizens, is the product of a wave of globalization that preceded the word. It is a world of taxi dancers and singsong girls, of pedicabs and "coolies," of financiers and speculators of every stripe, from every shore. Of big capital and cheap labor. Of gangs and gunrunners and drugs, a place of intrigue of every kind.

It is a world full of stories and legend and lore and of history all being erased right now to drag the city into the planners' vision of a twenty-first-century metropolis. The narrative is tightly controlled from above, and no room will be left for loose ends, for layering and for texture, and, above all, for a place whose resonances as a playground for exploitative foreign capitalists and later for invading Japanese goes against the grain of a national narrative that is all about triumph and resurrection, overcoming and redemption.

I've spoken of hurried and nostalgia-free denizens, but that is not altogether correct. Unless they grew up in the old city, most Shanghainese have little sense of it. For many, even before it was steamrolled, it was all but invisible. People have long been encouraged to celebrate the new and to put what is faded and all too flawed out of mind, and in this, by and large, the people have obeyed their cues.

Countless times I've been asked, "Why are you taking these bad images? Are you trying to embarrass us?" Sometimes the question comes in a nominally helpful voice: "Why don't you take pictures in a nice part of town?"

Equating the old city with an insalubrious eyesore serves several purposes. It has helped engineer consensus for the bulldozing of huge swaths of central Shanghai without taking into account the wishes of the residents of the areas targeted for redevelopment.

How, after all, could anyone wish to live in a designated eyesore?

It is also critical for the narrative of redemption, cleverly eliding the issue of historical responsibility. The message rings forth: the state is upgrading the lives of its citizens as progress marches steadily forward, without permitting a pause to ask how the central city had ever been allowed to become an insalubrious eyesore. Rummaging around in questions like that could get quite messy.

The truth about the feelings of the residents of the old city is complicated. It is my hope that some of this complexity is evident in the images themselves.

Yes, Shanghai people, like people everywhere, value running water inside their homes, just like they value private bathrooms and kitchens. It is true that, for many, these old dwellings are too crowded and too run down to imagine saving.

But there are social and social justice questions that, for many, are equally if not even more pressing. Part of the untold story of Shanghai is the summary evictions and nonnegotiable compensation packages that have been "offered" to these inner-city residents who have then been bundled up and shipped off to new lives in distant and unfinished satellite towns.

There are the corrupt land deals between the city and developers that proceed in total opacity, without open or public bidding. There are the residents, the very people who figure in my images, who live in uncertainty from month to month, knowing that their neighborhoods exist on borrowed time but given little or no forewarning by the city of when the wrecking ball will strike, to keep them off balance and prevent them from protesting the terms of their relocation.

And there is the loss of community that person after person has wept about as we have spoken while I photographed them. Often, the tears have come in the next breath after fond dreams of modern plumbing.

Nostalgia

Disappearing Shanghai

The Reader

Girl with Bottles

The Rumor

Short Porch

Oriental Pearl

Just Us

Lookout

Off Shanxi Road

Chapter 7

Tiananmen Reconsidered

REVOLUTIONARY ANNIVERSARIES

Kate Merkel-Hess

Few Westerners will take note that this week it is time to celebrate Chinese revolutions. October 1 will be the fifty-ninth anniversary of the founding of the People's Republic of China (celebrated as National Day). Ten days later, on October 10, Taiwan celebrates its National Day (also known as Double Ten Day and on its ninety-seventh go-round). October is clearly a time for revolutions.

Even so, these aren't the Chinese revolutions that matter in the West. Chinese are understandably exasperated with the continued Western fixation on the traumatic Cultural Revolution, as well as, when it comes to anniversaries, the June 4 one linked to 1989. The student-led protests of that year were in part a broad-minded demonstration of democratic ideals (though other aspirations and grievances were in play as well), and this is certainly how they are remembered in the West, with the crackdown seen as symbolizing authoritarian insensitivity at its worst.

In China, however, the protests of 1989 are more important as a marker of shifting expectations of the Chinese government. The context that precipitated the demonstrations was pocketbook practicality: in the first decade following Deng Xiaoping's sweeping economic reforms (begun in late 1978), the government began to dismantle its social safety net, and one of the first bits to go was guaranteed jobs for university graduates. Coupled with inflation and unpleasant living conditions on university campuses, the calls for increased political participation that had been in the air for almost a decade took on new life.

Following the movement's violent end, there were more practical decisions to be made. The Chinese people chose the go-slow approach of increasing wealth (though not for everyone at the same time) and slowly expanding civil rights (though not without periodic retrenchments from time to time). Increasingly it seems, even to some of us who express outrage at specific abusive practices and endemic corruption, that the choice of stability was a prescient one and one that could lead to a steady expansion of civil rights without the devastating violence of a revolution.

Posted 10/1/2008 at 08:00:00 AM

In July 2008, Beijing News published a piece to honor the recent publication of a book by photographer Liu Heung Shing, accompanied by photos in both its online and print editions. Finding that the three photographs editors had selected to accompany the piece were not enough, a young copy editor at the paper went online to locate a fourth. The copy editor found a photo called "The Wounded" that Liu had taken when working for the Associated Press in 1989—it shows two young men, inert and with blood on their shirts, being rushed along a street on a bicycle cart— and inserted it into the story. The government reaction was swift—as any mention of the 1989 protests is forbidden, the website of the newspaper was censored, and the paper quickly attempted to recall all the distributed copies. Media watchers speculated that the young copy editor, who was reportedly in his late twenties, simply didn't realize what the image depicted.

While the reaction shows the continued sensitivity of 1989's events, the photo's publication illustrates that the government's blockade has been effective in inoculating some young Chinese to knowledge about the protests. This is not to say, however, that those who are interested in talking about 6/4, as the events of June 4, 1989, and the weeks of protest that led up to it are referred to in China, have no forums in which to do so. In recent years, Internet chat rooms, bulletin boards, and blogs have all outpaced government attempts to censor discussions of 1989, and each spring they fill up with debates and remembrances about the event. It is the rare educated Chinese citizen, of any age, who does not have an opinion about how the event should be remembered.

Those who write about 1989 have often argued that, in a society now characterized by unprecedented economic growth, the ideals of the protesters are dead. In this chapter, however, Jeffrey Wasserstrom points out that, in fact, the student protesters and the many more numerous workers who joined them were motivated not just by democratic ideals (though that was important) but also by a desire to fully participate in global culture. Almost twenty years later, many young Chinese increasingly see that opportunity within reach.

Tiananmen's Shifting Legacy ☆ Jeffrey N. Wasserstrom

It is three weeks since the nineteenth anniversary of the massacre of June 4, 1989, in Beijing, forty-nine until the symbolically potent twentieth. The routine in advance of the event, by now well established, was again witnessed in full this year: security around Tiananmen Square is tightened; a candlelight vigil for martyrs is held in Hong Kong (still the only part of the People's Republic of China [PRC] where open discussion of June 4 is allowed); Ding Zilin of the "Tiananmen Mothers" organization submits an open letter to the Chinese authorities, calling on them to abandon their "big lie" about 1989 and admit that those, like her son, who were slain by soldiers were not "counterrevolutionaries" or rioters but ordinary urbanites; and human rights activists, former student leaders, and China specialists issue statements or write commentaries assessing the legacy of 1989 or proposing a new way to honor the dead.

The lead-up to the latest anniversary followed this familiar pattern, but there were some novel twists—"novel" rather than "surprising," given how unusual a year 2008 had already proved to be and promises to remain.

This time, for example, some activists included a call for an "Olympic pardon" in their June 4 commentaries, suggesting that a moment just weeks before the start of the games would be a particularly appropriate one for the authorities to release political prisoners. The Hong Kong vigil was given a distinctive 2008 cast via efforts to combine honoring the martyrs of 1989 and mourning the victims of the Sichuan earthquake. In a similar vein, when local police asked Ding Zilin a week or so before the anniversary if her annual letter was ready, she said (according to reporter Mary-Anne Toy) that she had submitted it early but had a postscript to add, presumably inspired by how earthquake victims were mourned: "When will the national flag be lowered for our children?"

These are only some of the ways that ties between 1989 and 2008 have been and can be established for political reasons. They also suggest that it might be worth pondering how the events of the two years can be connected in historical terms too. Does a look back to Tiananmen help us make sense of what young Chinese have been doing in 2008? Can the recent behavior of China's leaders be understood as reflecting lessons they learned from the events of 1989? What, for example, should we make of the role of Wen Jiabao in each of these critical periods: as the inspirational prime minister who comforted victims and impressed millions of citizens in the earthquake's aftermath and as the man who went into Tiananmen Square to meet with protesters in 1989 in the company of his then-boss Zhao Ziyang (who would be purged and placed under long-term house arrest for taking a softer line on the student-led movement than paramount leader Deng Xiaoping)?

At first glance, these questions may seem odd ones. It might appear, for example, that there are only contrasts and no parallels between the nationalistic young Chinese of today and their 1989 counterparts or that the Chinese government's refusal to allow open discussion of the June 4 events must mean that it has no interest in learning any lessons from the upheaval. In fact, however, it is possible to see ties between the two generations of youths and to appreciate just how much, even in defeat, 1989's protesters altered Chinese political patterns.

History's Bridge

In order to do this, it is necessary to clear away some common Western misunderstandings of Tiananmen. Here are five of the most important points:

- All protesters and all martyrs were not students; a great many of both were workers.
- Chinese protesters' ideological outlook was not identical to their counterparts in east-central Europe in 1989. In Beijing—in contrast to, say, Budapest or Bucharest—many people called not for an end to Communist rule but rather for party leaders to do a better job living up to their own professed ideals. This helps explain why there was division at the top over how to respond to the protests. The demonstrations began in mid-April, but it was not until mid-May that it became clear that Zhao Ziyang and others favoring a soft line had lost the fight within the upper echelons of power.
- It is misleading to think that China's 1989 had everything to do with democracy and nothing to do with patriotism or nationalism. The Western media of the time were fascinated with symbols such as the Statue of Liberty–like "Goddess of Democracy," but in fact anger at nepotism and corruption was a more central theme in Chinese wall posters and manifestos of the time than demands for elections, and criticism of these failings was framed in terms of official selfishness endangering the nation.

  The most powerful tactic adopted by the students, which brought them an enormous outpouring of support from members of other social groups, was launching a hunger strike—an act with special meaning at a time when lavish banquets were a potent symbol of corrupt behavior. Students insisted that for China to become great again, it required leaders willing to engage more fully with the outside world and pay more attention to the needs of the people. It is revealing in this respect that a main anthem of the movement, Hou Dejian's "Children of the Dragon," had strong nationalistic overtones.
- The economic background to the protests is often forgotten. Chinese protesters in 1989 did share with their east-central European counterparts a keen awareness that people living in capitalist lands were enjoying a much higher standard of living. To look from East Berlin to West Berlin or from Canton to Hong Kong was to become aware of the contrast between drab, backward cities and glittering, modern ones.
- There was a significant generational aspect in the demonstrations. China's young people (and again this is a point of similarity with those in other Communist societies) had a sense of being unable to take part fully in attractive and increasingly global forms of popular culture. Many also felt that the state's interference in their private lives hindered their ability to express their individualism and do the things that would help define themselves as members of a distinctive generation.

These last two sides of the 1989 movement are summed up in comments that Chinese student leader Wu'er Kaixi made in *The Gate of Heavenly Peace,* the award-winning documentary film by Carma Hinton and Richard Gordon. He first lists ways that his generation's beliefs and desires differ from those of their parents and even their older siblings and then poses a rhetorical question: "So what do we want?" His answer: "Nike shoes. Lots of free time to take our girlfriends to a bar. The freedom to discuss an issue with someone."

When Tiananmen is reconsidered with these factors taken into account, it becomes easier to trace links between the young people who took to the streets in 1989 and those who flock to Internet chat rooms, earthquake-relief campaigns, and shopping malls in 2008. Behind the surface differences there are connecting threads: an intense love of country and a desire to make their mark as a generation, for example. True, the outbursts of anger in 2008 directed against foreigners who are chastised for being disrespectful toward China in one way or another marks a great contrast (even if it has precedents in China's history), but there have been signs that this sense of moral outrage could easily turn, as it did in 1989, toward corruption and selfishness closer to home.

History's Threads

The contrasts between then and now can also be seen as due, in part, to the Chinese Communist Party taking stock of lessons it learned from 1989—both as that year unfolded in China and as it unfolded in other regions. Three are notable. First, the party has understood the importance of material goods. In a China that has enjoyed high growth rates and embraced consumer culture, the contrast between Shanghai and Hong Kong lifestyles is now much less stark than that between East Berlin and West Berlin before the wall came tumbling down.

When it comes to educated youths in particular, the government has done more than just give them the chance to buy the "Nike shoes" that Wu'er Kaixi mentioned. It has also made it possible for them to partake in global youth culture. And it has backed off from micromanaging campus daily life and that of the educated classes generally, thus allowing more latitude for discussion of ideas and travel abroad. In short, if Tiananmen was fueled by a frustration over the limited choices that Chinese urbanites had, the post-1989 period has been characterized by a dramatic expansion of the choices open to educated city dwellers—apart from certain closed-off realms, such as picking who governs their metropolis and their nation.

A second lesson that the Chinese regime has learned is that the biggest threat to its longevity comes from movements capable of drawing together members of disparate social classes, as Solidarity did in Poland and Tiananmen did in China. This helps to explain, at least partially, the severity of the crackdown against Falun Gong, in a country where the authorities are increasingly willing to make concessions to protesters whose struggles are very localized and affect only a single class.

A third, more indirect lesson from Tiananmen is visible in the series of efforts by the regime to position itself as capable of steering rather than becoming the target of patriotic and nationalistic emotions. It has done this by ramping up patriotic education drives and by leaping ahead of and trying to channel youthful outbursts (such as the one in May 1999 when NATO bombs hit the Chinese embassy in Belgrade, killing three citizens of the PRC).

The love of country continues to be a difficult thing to control completely. There is always a chance that this double-edged sword will turn against officials. In a milieu where corruption is still (as in 1989) seen as a great national blight, the authorities must show repeatedly that they are concerned with more than simply maintaining their positions of power at all costs and furthering selfish agendas. They also have to show that they care about the whole nation, not just one part of it.

This "purity test" presents an ever-present danger, reflected in a couple of tense moments the Chinese authorities faced after the Sichuan earthquake, even amid the general goodwill their impressive response secured. The first tremor came right after the disaster, when angry bloggers chastised China's leaders for continuing to show celebratory images of the Olympic torch relay on state television at the very time when people in Sichuan were suffering so deeply. The second came soon after when talk began to circulate about the disproportionately large number of school buildings that had collapsed, in many cases because of shoddy construction linked to official corruption.

Beijing defused the first moment when it introduced a minute's silence for earthquake victims to the relay and then called a short moratorium in the ritual. The government also showed its sensitivity to earthquake victims and their families by lowering flags to half-mast, an unprecedented move in China for a case like this. The second danger was deflected in a different way, as Beijing's effective response to the disaster meant that most of the anger at corruption was directed at local officials.

With the People

If the Chinese regime's road from 1989 to 2008 is interesting to ponder, so too is that of man of the hour, China's prime minister, Wen Jiabao. It remains a mystery to many how the reputation of Wen continued to rise despite his association with the disgraced (in official terms) Zhao Ziyang after the latter's role in the Tiananmen events of 1989. In this context, however, the question of what lesson he has drawn from his trip to the square is moot.

Here's one thought: when Zhao met with students on the square in 1989, one thing he reportedly said to them was, "I came too late." The confession of bad timing carries a possible implication that he and perhaps the movement would have been better served if he had taken the initiative earlier on, made a bold gesture in support of the protests, or simply met with demonstrators sooner. Perhaps it is appropriate then that one thing that Wen has consistently done in other circumstances is to show an acute sense of timing, exemplified in the fact that his words and deeds after the earthquake were not just evidently heartfelt but were made quickly and spoke immediately to popular concerns. Here, perhaps, is a third connective thread with 1989, one that links leadership and people in a way that is full of political symbolism.

The Gate of Heavenly Peacemaking ☆ Pär K. Cassel[1]

Two months before the opening of the Olympics, the nineteenth anniversary of the suppression of the student movement of 1989 passed. Although the anniversary passed more quietly than usual, Tiananmen keeps its special place in our minds, and few places in China can compete with the stature of the gate and the square that bears its name.

For five hundred years, the gate was an important site for official functions during the Ming and Qing dynasties,[2] and following the fall of the last empire, the gate has grown in prominence. When the republic was inaugurated in 1912, the first president, Yuan Shikai, used the gate as a venue for the kind of public pageantry that was expected of a modern nation-state. On May 4, 1919, the students of Peking University chose the gate as the stage of a forceful protest against the Treaty of Versailles, and they were followed by a number of demonstrations well into the 1940s. It was here that Mao Zedong proclaimed the founding of the People's Republic of China in October 1949. Ten years later, the expansion of Tiananmen Square took place, creating the massive monument-filled plaza we know today.[3] The gate also adorns the Chinese national coat of arms, and every Chinese schoolchild can recite the patriotic verse, *Wo ai Beijing, Tiananmen* ("I love Beijing, Tiananmen").

Now close your eyes and tell me what English expression comes to your mind when you hear the name *Tiananmen*. Although the gate has many connotations, it is very likely that you would think the "Gate of Heavenly Peace," which is the standard translation of the name in English. In most Western languages,

---

1. I am grateful to my first teacher of Manchu, Professor Mark C. Elliott, for directing my attention to the Manchu name of Tiananmen in the first place. I am also grateful to an anonymous Manjurologist who responded to this piece when it was first posted to *China Beat* and shared some observations regarding the grammar of the Manchu term. The responsibility of the contents in this essay belongs to me only, of course.

2. Jonathan Spence, "The Gate and the Square," in *Children of the Dragon* (New York: Macmillan, 1990).

3. Wu Hung, *Remaking Beijing: Tiananmen Square and the Creation of a Political Space* (Chicago: University of Chicago Press, 2005).

Tiananmen is rendered in different versions of "Gate of Heavenly Peace," all of which propagate different shades of the idea of peace and serenity. In French it is called *La porte de la Paix celeste* and in German *Tor des himmlischen Frieden*, and in my native Swedish tongue, which has two closely related words for "peace," we usually call it *Himmelska fridens port* or *Himmelsfridens port*, which are close to "Gate of Heavenly Tranquility." When I hear the Swedish expression, I often think of Göran Malmqvist's translation of Wen Yiduo's poem, "Tiananmen," which narrates an atrocity perpetrated by the Guomindang near the gate.[4]

It is not clear to me exactly when Westerners decided that Tiananmen was a gate of peace and tranquility. In his work *The Middle Kingdom*, Samuel Wells Williams translated the name as "Gate of Heavenly Rest,"[5] and you sometimes find old English-language books using the term "Gate of Heavenly Tranquility." A quick search on Google Books shows that the name "Gate of heavenly peace" was used as early as 1874, which indicates that the name may have been coined in the decades after foreign legations were established in the capital in an area not far from the gate itself.

Given the fact that many violent events have taken place in front of the gate, quite a few writers have succumbed to the temptation of pointing out the supposed dissonance between the pacific name of the gate and the not-so-peaceful events that have transpired there. Already in 1935, L. C. Arlington and William Lewisohn said the following in their classic study of Beijing:

> Since the establishment of the Republic the square in front of the gate has repeatedly been used for political meetings that have often led to minor riots rather belying the name of "Heavenly Peace." The radical and democratic speeches made on such occasions would have sounded very strange to the ears of the great Ming and Manchu Emperors of the past![6]

Thankfully for us China historians, who cherish complexity and make a living writing about it, things are of course not quite that simple. First of all, the name Tiananmen is of relatively "recent" origin; when the gate was originally built in the 1420s, the imperial government gave it the name "Chengtianmen," which roughly translates as "Gate of Receiving the Mandate of Heaven." It did not get its present name until after it was rebuilt in 1651, a couple of years after the Manchu conquest of Beijing.

More importantly, we also need to consider the fact that the Qing Empire

---

4. Wen Yiduo and Ai Qing, *Dödvatten och gryning: Två röster från Kina: dikter*, Swedish translation by Göran Malmqvist (Höganäs: Wiken, 1983).

5. Samuel Wells Williams, *The Middle Kingdom: A Survey of the Geography, Government, Education, Social Life, Arts, Religion, &c., of the Chinese Empire and Its Inhabitants* (New York and London: Wiley and Putnam, 1848), vol. 1, 60.

6. L. C. Arlington and William Lewisohn, *In Search of Old Peking* (reprint; Hong Kong: Oxford University Press, 1987), 31.

was a multilingual empire and that virtually every official name had a Manchu equivalent, be it the name of a building or the reign name of an emperor. As the Manchu language is a fully inflecting language, the Manchu officials who coined these names had to be explicit about the relationship between the words forming an expression, and, as the German sinologist Erich Hauer pointed out in a seminal article from 1930, the "Manchu versions of names often reveal the true meaning of the names given."[7]

In our postmodern era, we are perhaps a bit wary of talking about the "true meaning" of anything, but the fact remains that many of the first Manchus who ruled in Beijing were not very proficient in Chinese, and we should take Manchu names as serious expressions of what they were thinking, not just as translations of the "real" Chinese name. When I started to study Manchu eight years ago, my teacher used the Manchu name of Tiananmen as a way of showing the importance of the Manchu language to understanding Chinese history.

So, what was the Manchu name of Tiananmen? Unlike its brief Chinese counterpart, it was rather wordy, just as one might have expected: *abkai elhe obure duka.*

Now, let's analyze the name word by word. The first word is the Manchu term for "heaven" in its causative/genitive form and can be translated as "by heaven" or "of heaven," depending on context. The second and third words form a verbal expression meaning "to make peace" or "to pacify." And the final word is just the Manchu word for "gate," nothing more and nothing less. Taken together, the name of the gate should more properly be translated "The Gate of Heaven's Pacification" or, perhaps more accurately, "Gate of Heavenly Peacemaking," as Hauer put it in his article.

In other words, Tiananmen is by no means a peaceful name but a name rather fitting to a fledging empire that anxiously protected its claims to legitimacy and busied itself with suppressing rebellion and dissent wherever they showed up. This should not come as a surprise to anyone familiar with the history of the Qing dynasty—or any subsequent regime for that matter. Now if we take a second look at the Chinese name, the Sinologist in us quickly realizes that the second character in Tiananmen, *an,* can both be a noun meaning "peace" and a transitive verb meaning "make peace" or even "suppress." Indeed, many Chinese-language guides to the gate explain that Tiananmen is an ellipsis of the much longer phrase *shou ming yu tian, an bang zhi guo,* which roughly translates as "receiving the mandate of heaven, pacifying the realm and ruling the people."[8]

Is "Gate of Heavenly Peace" an erroneous name that should be replaced by a better translation, such as "Gate of Heavenly Peacemaking"? Or shall we follow

---

7. Erich Hauer, "Why the Sinologue Should Study Manchu," *Journal of the North-China Branch of the Royal Asiatic Society* 61 (1930): 162.

8. Lu Bingjie, *Tian'anmen* (Jinan: Shandong huabao chubanshe, 2004), 40.

the trend of using native names and just call the gate Tiananmen, hoping that Sinologists and better-informed tour guides will impart the "truth" about the name to the public? I do not have a ready answer to that question, and I am reluctant to change well-established and catchy names, even if they are basically incorrect. But I think we need to think more about the role of language in Chinese history and the tremendous power that the written word in general and Chinese characters in particular have over our minds.

Chapter 8

The Road to the Olympics

VIETNAM'S YOUTH GIVEN A RARE CHANCE TO PROTEST— AGAINST CHINA

Caroline Finlay

Ask a random Vietnamese person, "Which country do you hate the most?" and the answer will most likely be, "China!" The neighbors have put aside their differences in favor of trade, and in 2005, seventeen years after China last invaded northern Vietnam, China became Vietnam's biggest trading partner.

The Vietnamese have had another opportunity to vent their anti-Chinese feelings with the visit of the Olympic flame to Ho Chi Minh City, but unlike anti-Chinese protests in the West, their complaints have nothing to do with Tibet. Popular democracy and freedom protests tend to not be covered in Vietnam's state-controlled media, and mention of Tibet and of the monks' protests in Burma was minimal. Instead, the Vietnamese are fixated by the Spratly and Paracel islands, of almost negligible land area but with potential oil deposits, located in the South China Sea between Vietnam, China, Taiwan, and the Philippines. All four powers claim and occupy a few of these bits of land sprinkled across one of the most traveled seas in the world.

Blogger haivuong63 posted this article outlining an effective protest at the torch relay: "According to me, the protest must have a clear goal and an appropriate manner, which is to raise our voices about China's invasion of Vietnam's sea and land areas . . . specifically in our beloved Spratly and Paracel islands. Because of this we shouldn't act wrongly by hampering the torch procession. . . . We must intend this to be a gentle protest for Spratly and Paracel. We shouldn't oppose the Olympic torch even though it has been taken advantage of by Beijing."

The Vietnamese people feel empowered at the opportunity to protest a historically bellicose neighbor, but that highlights the fact that protests at home are few and far between. Now that Vietnam has entered the World Trade Organization, it doesn't face the international human rights pressure it used to, and at the same time Vietnam is under pressure from trade partner China. This is a combination that may even eliminate the one doorway for Vietnamese youth to practice activism—anti-Chinese activism.

Posted 5/6/2008 at 08:40:00 AM

When it was announced in July 2001 that Beijing had been awarded the 2008 Olympic Games, Chinese all over the world watched the announcement live on TV and cheered along with the 200,000 people who had gathered in Tiananmen Square. Some foreigners applauded the move, expressing the hope that just as the 1988 Seoul Games had accompanied a democratizing wave in South Korea, the Olympics would contribute to a Chinese political thaw. As organizers in Beijing swung into action, however, international newspapers increasingly registered a cautious, sometimes even negative response to the International Olympic Committee's decision. Activists in Tibet and Taiwan feared that the pick would be seen as affirmation of China's policies. European critics, using an example that would become familiar to China watchers in the coming years (and get a high-profile American backer in actress Mia Farrow), predicted that the Chinese Olympics would be a propaganda exercise like the 1936 Berlin Olympics.

Beyond political concerns, there were many practical details to work out in planning Beijing's biggest-ever party. Air quality needed to be improved, massive stadiums built, and the airport refurbished. Erroneous English signs around the city had to be corrected. Run-down buildings along major thoroughfares had to be torn down or large walls built to hide them. Beijing's population was mobilized to make the city's transformation possible, though, as Susan Brownell argues in this chapter, these expressions of "Olympic spirit" were often genuine, not Communist Party propaganda. From moving out of the slated-for-destruction houses to being friendly to foreigners (as Mary Erbaugh discusses in "How to Talk to Strangers"), Olympic organizers urged patriotic cooperation.

While many residents were excited and involved in Olympic preparations, some were bitter about the sacrifices asked of them. New limits on car driving in the city crimped transportation as well as some cabbies' incomes. Proposals for air pollution limitations scared local factory owners. And owners of some condemned houses refused to leave and tried to stop the city from bulldozing their historic homes.

At China Beat, *writers raised questions about the (often negative) international response to China as Olympic host as well as how China reacted to international opinions, as in Jeffrey Wasserstrom's "The Boycotts of '08 Revisited" and Lijia Zhang's "Hand Grenades and Olympics." In the end, the two weeks of the Games passed largely without a hitch, and not a few commentators marveled at the remarkable mobilization that had made the Games possible.*

China's Olympic Road ☆ Susan Brownell

Susan Brownell was China Beat's *in-house Olympic expert. A professor in the Department of Anthropology at the University of Missouri–St. Louis, Brownell spent the 2007–2008 school year in Beijing on a Fulbright grant, conducting research on the Olympic Games. Brownell's interest in Chinese sports extends beyond academic research—as a student in Beijing in 1986, she represented the city in the Chinese National College Games and set a national record in the heptathlon. Here, we have chosen selections from Brownell's many posts at* China Beat *in the months leading up to the Olympics. You can find the complete essays at the website.*

HISTORICAL PRECEDENTS: PUTTING THE BEIJING GAMES IN CONTEXT

For multiple reasons, I do not subscribe to the current fad for drawing parallels between the 1936 "Hitler" Games and the 2008 Beijing Games. If one is looking for actual historical connections, then I would argue that the 104-year connection between the United States and China through Olympic sports, which dates back to the 1904 St. Louis Olympic Games, is today exerting a much greater influence on the shape of the Beijing Olympics than is the legacy of a now-defunct German regime.

The third modern Olympic Games were held in St. Louis in 1904 alongside the Louisiana Purchase Exposition (world's fair), and while China did not take part in the sports (it would send its first Olympic athlete to the 1932 Los Angeles Games), the Qing dynasty sent the first official delegation that it had ever sent to an international exposition. It was motivated to do so by concerns about the negative national image of China promoted by the unofficial exhibits at previous fairs, such as the opium den exhibit at the 1893 World's Columbian Exposition in Chicago. The 1904 Olympics were apparently the first Olympics to be reported in the press back in China.

The world's fair was America's coming-out party as a world power. It had just acquired the former Spanish colonies of the Philippines, Puerto Rico, and Guam as a result of the Spanish-American War in 1898. At the fair, it presented itself as an expanding power, with an extremely large display devoted to the Philippines. Another large section of the exposition grounds was devoted to displays intended to demonstrate that the government was succeeding in civilizing American Indians.

That the Old World was not completely happy about the emerging New World is evident in the European criticism of the Olympic Games. International Olympic Committee (IOC) president Pierre de Coubertin said that awarding the Games to St. Louis had been a "misfortune" and recalled, "So the St. Louis Games were completely lacking in attraction. Personally, I had no wish to attend them. . . . I had a sort of presentiment that the Olympiad would match the mediocrity of the town." He complained about "utilitarian America." He also labeled as "embarrassing" the "Anthropology Days," in which natives who had been brought to the fair for the ethnic displays competed in some track-and-field events and pole climbing, and their performances were unfavorably compared with those of the "civilized" men who took part in the Olympic Games.

While the Americans were generally satisfied with the Olympic Games, even to this day European historians consider the St. Louis Games and the associated "Anthropology Days" to be one of the low points of Olympic history. It is often said that the 1906 Intermediate Olympic Games in Athens "saved" the Olympics. Historian Mark Dyreson has observed that after St. Louis it became clear that American notions of what purposes Olympic sport should serve differed quite dramatically from the notions of the European nations that made up the core of the IOC's leadership. The conflict would remain for the rest of the twentieth century.

The first published calls for China to host the Olympic Games appeared in two YMCA publications: a 1908 essay in *Tientsin Young Men* and an item in the report to the YMCA's International Committee by C. H. Robertson, the director of the Tianjin (Tientsin) YMCA. Robertson stated that since 1907 a campaign had been carried on to inspire patriotism in China by asking three questions:

1. When will China be able to send a winning athlete to the Olympic contests?
2. When will China be able to send a winning team to the Olympic contests?
3. When will China be able to invite all the world to come to Peking (Beijing) for an international Olympic contest, alternating with those at Athens?

These three questions are now famous in China because it has taken almost exactly one hundred years for China to realize this Olympic dream. Robertson went on to note enthusiastically, "This campaign grips in a remarkable way the heart and imagination of the Chinese officials, educators, and students, and I believe it is a thing in which American boys will want to have a definite and practical part."

Olympic sports were introduced into China in the late nineteenth century by the YMCA and missionary-run schools and colleges. The YMCA continued to play a major role in China's sport system, and its influence was still being felt until recently since many sports leaders were YMCA trained. The last of these leaders have passed away in recent years. The IOC co-opted the first Chinese member in 1922; he was C. T. Wang, who was active in the YMCA and a Yale University graduate.[1] The third IOC member in China, Dong Shouyi (Tung Shou-yi) (co-opted in 1947), attended Springfield College, the YMCA's college in Massachusetts.

China imitated the St. Louis model. In 1910 the Nanyang Industrial Exposition in Nanjing was China's first attempt at an international exposition on Chinese soil. Held in conjunction was a sporting event organized by the YMCA that later came to be known as the first national athletic games of the Republic of

---

1. "Co-optation" is the IOC's word for its process of selecting its members.

China (ROC; founded in 1912). The American YMCA used the Philippines as a launching point to spread sports throughout East Asia, and in 1913 the first Far Eastern Olympiad was held in Manila. They were so successful that the IOC was worried that they might be a rival to the Olympic Games—so it requested that the term "Olympiad" be removed, and they were thereafter called the Far Eastern Championships. They were the first regional games in the world and at various times included athletes from the Philippines, Japan, Malaysia, Indonesia, China, and Hong Kong.

One hundred and four years after the United States hosted a world's fair and an Olympic Games as its coming-out party, China will host the Beijing Olympic Games as its coming-out party. What we will see in Beijing in 2008 is what the model for promoting a national image to the world has evolved into after a century in China. The Olympic slogan "One World, One Dream" expresses this ideal: we are all part of one world, and we share the dream of prosperity and strength. As the United States did over a century ago, China will try to display the success of its civilizing mission among its frontier minorities. It will try to display its wealth through monumental architecture and exhibitions of economic wares. In 1904, train stations were one of the major ways of displaying wealth—the St. Louis Union Station completed in 1902 was one of the largest and most opulent train stations in the world. In 2008, sports stadiums have replaced train stations, and China will have its Bird's Nest stadium. The St. Louis world's fair was the biggest of all time, just as the Beijing Games may well be the biggest Olympics of all time. When a superpower holds a coming-out party, it is a hard act to follow.

The most relevant historical lesson from 1904 is that existing powers do not necessarily welcome newcomers with open arms. As happened to the United States, there are suggestions that Chinese views about the purposes of Olympic sport conflict with the "correct" (i.e., dominant) views. It may happen that future Olympic histories written by Westerners will record that the Beijing Games were a low point in Olympic history and that London 2012 "saved" the Games.

These days, if it sometimes seems that Chinese ideas about national image contain some throwbacks to the turn of the twentieth century, there is probably good reason. In the meantime, the West has changed the rules of the game by adding new factors such as human rights, while China is still trying to win by playing more or less according to the rules it learned in the early twentieth century. Of course, as long as the West controls the rules of the game, it can keep changing them to ensure that newcomers never win.

COULD CHINA STOP TAIWAN FROM COMING TO THE OLYMPIC GAMES?

Actually, this was a trick question. Chinese leaders strongly desire for Taiwan to attend the Olympic Games and other major sports events because they are the most important venue in which Taiwan is displayed to the world as a dependent part of Chinese national territory.

Global politics usually don't change as quickly as we would like, but they do change. One year ago I was one of many people who thought that the biggest political threat to the Beijing Olympic Games was the movement toward independence in Taiwan. Now it appears that the Taiwan situation is comparatively stable. But the symbols associated with Taiwan—including words—remain one of the most politically sensitive areas of the Olympic Games.

The readmission of the People's Republic of China (PRC) into the IOC was achieved in 1979 when the general membership approved the Nagoya Resolution, known as the "Olympic formula." The admission to the IOC hinged upon approval of only five items—name, flag, anthem, emblem, and constitution. Officially, the identity of a national Olympic committee (NOC) is reduced to these and only these five elements. As a result of the Olympic formula, neither the phrase "Republic of China" nor its associated flag, anthem, and emblem may be used in venues conducting IOC-approved activities. Mainland Chinese have been known to object to the presence of Taiwanese symbols or proindependence ideas at venues like the International Olympic Academy in Greece or the 2004 Pre-Olympic Congress in Greece, knowing that the Nagoya Resolution supports them. From the PRC's perspective, the intent of the resolution is to symbolize Taiwan as a dependent territory of the PRC and the Olympic committee on Taiwan as a territorial branch of the Chinese Olympic Committee. Thus, Chinese sportspeople do not like the English phrase "national Olympic committee" because they believe that Taiwan is not a nation. In the PRC, the phrase used is "national and territorial Olympic committees (*guojia he diqu aoweihui*). The current Olympic Charter, on the other hand, specifically states that "NOCs have the right to designate, identify or refer to themselves as 'National Olympic Committees' (NOCs)."

Obviously, Taiwan's status within the IOC is complicated. From the point of view of the IOC, it is an NOC equivalent to the other NOCs, and Taiwan has often pressed for its due rights on that count. However, from the PRC's perspective, the Chinese Taipei Olympic Committee has an equivalent status to the Chinese Hong Kong Olympic Committee, and neither is allowed to act contrary to the interests of the mainland. So, for example, China has argued that the Chinese Taipei Olympic Committee does not have the right to bid for the Asian Games and Olympic Games—a right possessed by all the other NOCs. Taiwan's response was to bid for the World Games, the world's biggest contest of non-Olympic sports, which will be held in Kaohsiung in 2009.

During the Beijing 2008 Olympic Games, in accordance with the Nagoya Resolution, China's national laws, and China's diplomatic agreements with 168 countries, China will symbolize Taiwan as a province of China, and if history repeats itself, sometimes Taiwanese people will attempt to subvert this. When the route of the torch relay was introduced in April 2007, Taiwan insisted that it could receive the torch only if it entered and exited via a third, independent country and did not come or go directly from the mainland or from Hong Kong or Macau, as this would have symbolized that Taiwan is a part of China.

The Beijing Organizing Committee for the Olympic Games (BOCOG) anticipated attempts to display ROC symbols in Olympic venues. In Atlanta in 1996, at the finals in women's table tennis between China's Deng Yaping and Chinese Taipei's Chen Jing (who had won the gold medal in 1988 representing China), a Taiwanese student spectator unfurled the flag of the ROC and was ejected by Atlanta police, while another Taiwanese student (who was also an Olympic volunteer) was arrested for assaulting the officer when he tried to protect the first student and spent several hours in jail. This was possible under American law because the back of the admission ticket contained fine print prohibiting, among other things, "flags other than those of participating countries" and giving the Atlanta Committee for the Olympic Games the authority to "eject any Spectator who fails to comply with these rules." The backs of the Beijing tickets contain fine print stating that "Chinese laws and regulations prohibit you from carrying certain articles to the Venue. You should not carry . . . flags of countries or regions not participating in the Games."

This background returns me to the question of whether China could stop Taiwan from coming to the Olympic Games.

Actually, the legal right to determine the invited countries does not rest with the host city. According to the current Olympic Charter, the IOC approves the list of NOCs that will be invited to the Olympic Games. The host city contract requires compliance with the charter. Thus, the host city cannot alter the IOC's invitation list. (By the way, the charter now gives the IOC the right to punish NOCs that accept the invitation and then withdraw, i.e., boycott.)

In today's litigious environment, a breach of the host city contract might result in a lawsuit. But these days the IOC has the Nagoya Resolution in place. In sum, the lay of the land is quite different now, and it's doubtful that China could get away with excluding Taiwan, even if it wanted to.

But it doesn't want to. Since at least the 1970s, it has been the PRC's policy to invite Taiwan to major sports events, including the quadrennial Chinese National Games. "Taiwan" has often been represented by a team, but where the athletes actually come from is often unclear. This facet of China–Taiwan relations is not given much attention in either the mainland or Taiwan, and so most people don't know much about it. Apparently the first such invitation was issued to Taiwan for the 1972 Asian Table Tennis Championships in Beijing, which were part of "ping-pong diplomacy," with no response. A team composed of Taiwanese living in Japan and the United States competed in the 1973 Asia-Africa-Latin America Table Tennis Championship. The website of one of the eight legally recognized non-Communist parties, the Taiwan Democratic Self-Governance League (Taimeng), states that in 1975 Taimeng co-organized the first team to represent Taiwan in the Chinese National Games, a delegation of 297 people, including 190 athletes. They were described as "Taiwan nationals" (apparently born in Taiwan or with relatives there) living in the mainland, Hong Kong, Macau, and abroad. The team leader was said to be from New York. Other reports state that a "Taiwan" delegation also took part in the 1979 National Games. But Taiwan is not listed in the medal count for either the 1975 or the 1979 Games.

By the 1983 and 1987 National Games, the policy of organizing pseudo-Taiwanese teams seems to have changed because media reported that an official invitation had been issued to Taiwan by the State Sports Commission, but apparently no "Taiwan" team took part in either Games. Sports led the way in the establishment of cross-straits exchanges, and He Zhenliang represented the Chinese side in the top-secret negotiations initiated in 1988 that allowed Taiwan to send a large official delegation to the 1990 Asian Games in Beijing. In 1991, for the first time a song and dance troupe and a dragon boat team from Taiwan attended the Minority Nationality Sports Games, and delegations have participated in all subsequent Minority Games; a delegation of sixty attended the 2007 Games in Guangzhou. From 2000 onward Taiwanese teams have taken part in the National Farmer's Games and from 2003 in the National City Games. With the exception of the 1990 Asian Games delegation, these groups are sponsored by civil cultural exchange organizations and not by the government. But most Chinese people are not aware of the difference.

In sum, after thirty-five years of a Taiwan presence in Chinese opening ceremonies, for most mainland Chinese people it would be unthinkable that Taiwan, in their minds an inalienable part of China, would not march into the stadium during the parade of athletes in the opening ceremonies of the Beijing Olympics.

WHY CAN'T THE CHINESE AUTHORITIES ALLOW A LITTLE SPACE FOR PROTESTS DURING THE OLYMPICS?

Of course, the easy answer to this question is, Because there is almost no freedom of assembly in China and there are big restrictions on freedom of expression. But I realized that this answer is too simple. The people I talked to, even well-educated and international people, have a gut reaction to the idea of public protests that is unfavorable.

Before the Games, I discussed the issue of protests with Chinese colleagues, friends, and acquaintances from academic, government, and corporate backgrounds. The people whose views I summarize here are college educated (in China), middle class, internationally informed (but not educated abroad), and between the ages of thirty and fifty-five. I would guess that their political stance is close to the mainstream (though since Chinese people don't vote for top leaders, there's no clear barometer of their political stances like "Republican" or "Democrat").

Some of them expressed that the protests surrounding the torch relay presented a new view of the West because they did not fully understand that such protests are common there. My guess is that while they knew about them, perhaps they had never seen so many visual images on TV and in the media. However, it seems to me that the way in which this coverage was handled in China left many people with the false impression that protests like these occur in London and Paris nearly every day, a portrait they regard with distaste. Let me try to outline the system of beliefs that produces this reaction.

First, there is the cultural background of host–guest relations. There is a highly refined protocol between a host and a guest in China; this also extends to Chinese conventions for the expression of mutual respect between states, which historically were more highly developed than those of the West. Chinese people see large sporting events as part of the cycle of host–guest reciprocity: when I host a major sport event, I invite you to my home as my guest, and there I put you in the seat of honor, feed you the special foods, and give you the special gifts unique to my hometown. The cultural performances in the Olympic opening ceremonies are said to be like the unique foods that you receive as my guest, which are not available in your hometown. In the summer of 2006, He Zhenliang, China's senior member in the IOC, spoke passionately to me about hosts and guests when I interviewed him for an essay that the IOC had invited me to write for their official magazine, *The Olympic Review*.

For Mr. He, the Beijing Games were China's opportunity to return the hospitality of the other host nations who had previously invited China into their homes and to welcome the world as a guest to China's home. He anticipated that there would be negative Western media coverage, and he explained to me that Chinese people see this as disrespectful because it is as if the host invited a guest to his home and the guest responded by criticizing the host. He cited Pierre de Coubertin's notion of *"le respect mutuel"* and stated that journalism that serves the West's appetite for "curiosities"—highlighting China's differences with the West rather than its commonalities, its deficiencies rather than its accomplishments—is disrespectful to China and to the Olympic ideals.

In conversations with more average Chinese people, I encountered the same reaction. In the Chinese tradition, host–guest meetings are highly ritualized and ceremonial and are not supposed to be occasions for straightforward debate. Or, put another way, the Olympic Games are an occasion when the guest should respect the "face" of the host. The image of protests taking place outside the Bird's Nest stadium, where a splendid ceremony of international friendship is supposed to be taking place, would be "ugly" or "not good to look at" (*bu haokan*). Everyone recognizes that this means they are engaging in "appearance-ism" (*xingshi zhuyi*), which is said to be a key feature of Chinese society (sometimes jokingly, sometimes with some bitterness). The proverb that "family shame should not be made public" (*jia chou bu ke wai yang*) is often quoted to express it.

As one of my colleagues put it, it's like when there is a wedding in the family.

Actually, the members of the family do not get along with each other. But they put on a show for outsiders during the wedding. I noted that Americans have similar feelings, but she countered by stating that Chinese people have particularly strong feelings about this. As a result, if someone chooses to disrupt the proceedings, it is an indicator that the internal conflicts are so great that the collective is threatened. And in China this is a thought that seems to evoke fear.

Needless to say, this is the context within which protests by Chinese Tibetans during the Olympic Games would be judged. Perhaps this is one reason that the Dalai Lama, who should understand Chinese culture well enough to know this, has recently come out with strong statements against the disruption of the Olympic Games through protests.

An acquaintance who has a degree in international relations further observed that in China the custom is to *first* invite the guest to your home to allow him or her to "understand" you and build trust and only later to try to talk through differences. "Mutual understanding" (*huxiang lijie*) facilitates the later negotiations. To try to work out all differences ahead of time would be ridiculous. I probably don't need to add that this particular custom is one that many Westerners are forced to learn in dealing with Chinese partners—but having been forced to learn it, they find that it is actually a better way of forming human relations. It is also probably a more accurate description of what is happening through the Beijing Olympic Games—they are more accurately perceived as the starting point for a closer relationship between China and the outside world than a nuptial ceremony marking a permanent intimate bond.

A related factor is the negative Chinese attitude toward criticism. On this point, cultural differences with the West are difficult to pinpoint because there are many frames in which Chinese people seem freer with criticism than Westerners. For example, a friend who runs into you on the sidewalk will say, "Your expression is bad" or "Have you put on weight?" The Xinhua sport reporter Qu Beilin has written a series of essays in the past year trying to help Chinese people understand Westerners because, having covered the 1993 and 2001 IOC Sessions that voted on Beijing's Olympic bids, he had an urgent intuition that China did not understand the West and that it had better try to do so before the Beijing Games. In his essays, a recurring theme is that the reason Chinese people don't understand what Westerners really think about them is that Westerners are too polite to criticize you to your face. Nevertheless, Chinese people generally seem to feel that "critics" are negatively regarded in China.

People in official leadership positions very often do not grasp the concept that criticism can have a constructive function, either, and that is why they do not appreciate the watchdog function that a free media could play if it were free to criticize them. Even less so do they appreciate that Western media criticism of China could have a constructive function. I feel that in evaluating their viewpoints, it is important to keep in mind that the current cohort of leadership in China, which is fifty to sixty years old, came of age during the Cultural Revolution, when they were exposed to practices of extreme criticism that were very destructive. A constructive response to criticism is based on mutual trust. As a teacher, I have noticed that most of my students must learn to engage with and respond to criticism rather than to get angry and retreat, which seems to be the human knee-jerk reaction. There is a generation of people in power in China right now in whom a healthy approach to criticism may never have been cultivated.

There is also a pragmatic reason that my Chinese acquaintances do not think that "protest zones" are feasible. They all subscribe to what I might call the "powder-keg" theory of Chinese society. They feel that because of growing inequities Chinese society is unstable and that one public protest could ignite another and another, and soon the whole country would be protesting and everything would collapse. That in the West it might be common for one group to hold public protests while everyone else just walks by on their way to work is hard to comprehend. They state that the problem of "surrounding onlookers" (*weiguan*) is common in China. If there were a protest zone outside the Bird's Nest stadium, soon a crowd would gather. Before you know it, you'd have a riot.

I have to admit that I have some sympathy to this view. In the 1980s I was trapped three different times in Chinese crowds that were on the verge of losing control, and it was a scary experience. But crowds seem much better behaved these days, and anyway no security forces were present on those occasions. Westerners see protest zones as a way of ensuring that demonstrations are controlled and *do not* lead to widespread rioting, but my Chinese respondents did not hold this view and across the board felt that they would spark rioting rather than control it. They also do not subscribe to the Western theory that allowing a space for protest can defuse a conflict by "letting off steam." One colleague argued that the custom of protesting is different in China and that Chinese protest only when they have been pushed to the point of no return. Therefore, it is not possible for protests to perform the function of "venting" (*faxie*) on a limited scale. My acquaintances stated that the social problems facing China today are too complex to be solved immediately and that is why it would be better to keep the lid on protests for the near future. They felt that continued rapid economic development is the only hope for the resolution of these problems.

I would like to make clear that what I have tried to do here is to outline common Chinese attitudes about public protests during the Beijing Olympics. These ideas are not my own, and I am not saying that they are accurate from a social-scientific perspective—but that is another question. And I have not analyzed the real power differences and political structure that are another important part of the picture—people in leadership positions don't have to accept media criticism because their job security depends almost entirely on the leaders above them who appointed them and not on public transparency. However, it seems to me that this political structure is at least partly supported by a cultural context that is not supportive of public protests such as are common in the West.

THE GAMES AND PROPAGANDA: PROPPING UP THE PARTY?

Olympic education" is the IOC's label for the educational efforts that are supposed to be an integral part of the Olympic movement as required by Fundamental Principle #1 of the Olympic Charter, which states that Olympism is a philosophy of life that blends sport with culture and education. Between 2005 and 2008, China carried out the largest-scale "Olympic education" campaign in history. There were academic and professional conferences, textbooks and courses for public schools and universities, educational television and radio shows, magazine and newspaper essays, websites, and more.

In the fall of 2007, I was added to the "experts team" of Beijing City's Olympic Education Standing Office, and so I saw its workings from the inside. I attended meetings of the Standing Office, took part in ceremonies at schools, interviewed teachers and principals, and count the people mentioned below as my friends.

From this perspective I offer the following observations to contradict the notion that the Beijing Games were simply propaganda fodder for the Communist Party.

The Initial Impetus for Beijing's Olympic Education Programs in the Schools Came from "the People" (*minjian*), Not the Government

At the 2000 Postgraduate Session at the International Olympic Academy (IOA), Donnie Pei was inspired by the Dean, Kostas Georgiadis, who led the Olympic education projects for the 2004 Athens Games. After the success of Beijing's bid in 2001, Pei, who had worked as a physical education teacher for ten years before going to Canada, began visiting schools in Beijing to try to persuade them to start Olympic activities. He found that most principals and teachers were uninterested because they believed the Olympics were nothing more than sports, but finally on his tenth attempt he ran into physical education teacher Zhou Chenguang at Yangfangdian Primary School. Zhou was immediately attracted by Pei's discussion of the Olympics as a way of teaching values because of his own crisis of conscience:

> In the 1980s we still understood physical education as the Soviet Union. We required students to line up in straight lines. [For the recess exercises] I was very proud when one thousand children lined up straight. I would put a lot of effort into it. I'd stand on the platform to direct them, jump off and run up to them to straighten them up [motions hands as if adjusting a child's torso], run back to the platform, and so on. I had put out so much effort. I started to wonder what had I trained them for? They would go out into society and what would they do with what they had learned? Did it have any use? I had produced little soldiers. What had I accomplished? They knew how to be obedient. It was a big machine for producing cabbages. I started to feel as if I had harmed them.

In 2002, Pei and Zhou initiated China's first Olympic education school activities, a reenactment of the ancient Greek pentathlon. Pei had gotten this idea from the IOA, where it is an annual tradition created by Ingomar Weiler, a professor in classics at the University of Graz. For Pei, the ancient Greek ideal of all-around education was the remedy for the overemphasis on testing that was plaguing China's educational system. He says, "Olympic education is a movement, but it's a moving movement. Humans need to be moved—materialism is not enough. Olympic education emphasizes balance, which is found in the Chinese Way of the Mean as well as in the Greek ideal of harmonious education. China needs this now, as did late 19th/early 20th century Europe in Coubertin's times after industrialization. The idea has value because of a social need."

By 2005, Yangfangdian Primary School had already held four installments of its annual "mini–Olympic Games," and each time Zhou Chenguang had faxed multiple invitations to BOCOG with little response from it or other official VIPs. But in that year, BOCOG stepped up its operations and started to pay attention to fulfilling the Host City Contract's stipulations on educational programs, which China took more seriously than host nations usually do. The Beijing Municipal Education Commission, working together with BOCOG, formed the Olympic Education Standing Office. They designated 200 primary and secondary schools in Beijing City and another 356 schools nationwide as "Olympic Education Demonstration Schools" and Yangfangdian as their "Pioneer." Principals and teachers from around Beijing were invited to three forums to learn from the experiences at Yangfangdian. By the end of 2007, hundreds more schools had engaged in "hand-in-hand sharing" with the Demonstration Schools, taking the total number of schools that had carried out Olympic activities to 1,100. It is estimated that these programs touched 400 million students nationwide.

The Heart-to-Heart sister school program was organized among 210 schools in Beijing. This program was based on the "One School, One Country" program first initiated at the Nagano Olympics in 1998. Each school established a sister school relationship with one of the 205 National Olympic Committees as well as with five National Paralympic Committees.

In addition, a teacher training program reached about 10,000 primary and secondary school teachers in Beijing.

Thus, what began as a "people's" initiative was picked up by the government. But the intellectuals generally regarded this as a positive development because without the support of the government, there would have been no way to implement their ideas on such a broad scale. As Pei put it,

> There is no conflict between them and us. They give us a lot of recognition. We do not take the credit. As scholars we must rely on the government. We cannot be too naïve. We are members of social life, we cannot isolate ourselves. We must have an open mind. The government needs our knowledge. We should not be the "lonely flower admiring itself" (*gufang zishang*). If the government

understands, then we shut up. "The flames reach higher when people from all around add kindling to them" (*zhou ren tian chai huo yan gao*). It's teamwork.

What is most important to Pei is that "in the end my ideas go to the children. This is what I want." In 2008, Pei was recognized as a "Model Worker" for Beijing City, the highest form of recognition by the Beijing government.

The Specific Content of Olympic Education Is Almost Completely Nonpolitical

Schools were given complete freedom to design their own Olympic education activities, and the resulting variety is amazing. Students formed their own organizing committees (following the organizational chart on BOCOG's website) or conducted bid competitions like the Olympic bid. They organized mini–Olympic Games with a parade of athletes in the opening ceremony featuring students dressed as the different nations of the world. They produced a huge amount of artwork in every conceivable medium, even beans or bottle tops glued to posterboard. They developed innumerable performance types, including the "Olympic angel chorus" at Yangfangdian, which performs a moving rendition of Beethoven's "Ode to Joy" or the "Olympic Volunteer's Song" while wearing angel wings. Students at the Information Management vocational school, most of whose parents are migrant laborers, spent two years of their after-school time producing a computer-generated animated film in which the Fuwa mascots introduce Olympic history.

Teachers I talked to felt that Olympic education was *nonpolitical* and thus contrasted with the previous character education campaigns in the national curriculum. As one teacher told me, "After the national leaders have stated the policy, if the only way you can think to implement it is to shout slogans, it becomes irritating after a while." With Olympic education, they could use concrete activities to teach children fair play, teamwork, mutual respect, selfless service, international friendship, the pursuit of world peace, and many other concepts. And unlike the previous character education, their students enjoyed the projects.

The words "communist" and "socialist" are almost completely absent in Olympic education materials and lectures. In mid-May, I sat through one and a half hours of presentations by teachers at local schools considered to have the best examples of Olympic education, and I did not hear the words "communist" or "socialist" once. Last week I attended a meeting of the Olympic Education Standing Office to plan a book that will summarize and analyze the thousands of activities carried out under its umbrella. The success of the Olympic education effort is being judged not by whether it promoted loyalty to the party or nation but by whether it motivated the students and produced creative results. I also attended several of the lectures delivered in the teacher training program and to the volunteers. Like the content of the school programs, these lectures largely impart knowledge about *the world outside China*.

The most political content I have seen was at a meeting run by the Communist Youth League (CYL) of the Beijing Forestry University, which was a training lecture for college student participants in the Green Long March project to promote environmental awareness across China. A few speakers almost casually mentioned the support of the party and government for the various volunteer projects organized by the CYL, but that was it.

I do not feel that the party and government are explicitly claiming responsibility for organizing these games—on the contrary, public statements claim that the games belong to all people, that "everyone can participate" (China has placed particular importance on the Olympic creed that "the most important thing is to participate"). The strongest argument that one could accurately make is that the Games *implicitly* support the Communist Party. But if one wants to venture into the realm of implicit messages, there are many others that contradict this one. I believe the major message in Olympic education is that there is an exciting and colorful world out there, and China is about to join it. And this is in accord with the major goal of Olympic education, which is to produce a next generation of Chinese people who are better prepared to be active citizens in that world than the current adults, who are all too conscious of their limitations.

Beijing's Olympic Education Depoliticizes the Olympics

Actually, I think it is more accurate to conclude that the Olympic Games have been *depoliticized* in China's Olympic education efforts. And this, in my opinion, is part of a backlash against the politicized national curriculum. Ren Hai reached this conclusion in a recent essay:

> Today's world lacks an education that focuses on a global horizon and is firmly based on the interests of humankind as a whole. It was precisely this lack that sparked the emergence of Olympic education. Olympic education aims to cultivate qualified citizens of the "global village," to help them break through the various limitations of their respective societies, to impress the seal of a world citizen on top of the existing identity of a national citizen.[2]

Enduring social change only occurs when the ideas in people's heads change. In my opinion, Olympic education is one of the most important dimensions of the Beijing Olympics, one whose effects will be felt for decades to come. But we will never be able to prove them or measure them, and so what is going on in this realm will be unlikely to make headlines, and its place in history may never be recorded.

I once witnessed Donnie Pei become irritated at a reporter asking him ques-

---

2. In the forthcoming *Olympic Studies Reader*.

tions about political issues surrounding the games. He stood up and passionately told him in English,

> The Olympic Games are a congregation, a celebration, a holiday—it's a festival. If some Westerners take this time to raise political issues, tell them they're stupid. Even if it's George Bush—tell him to go to the IOA and receive an Olympic education. Olympism is respect for any culture, any people, any nation. That's why the Olympic Games survived one hundred years until now. We are promoting love between people. I don't want to promote hatred, such as the Tibet and Taiwan protesters. We are China. We should understand each other better through the Olympic Games.

The Boycotts of '08 Revisited ☆ Jeffrey N. Wasserstrom

It was springtime in the eighth year of a young century, and the Olympics would begin soon in an old capital. No medals would be awarded until the summer, but the '08 Games were already shrouded in controversy because of talk of a boycott linked to the host country's policies in a territory it controlled. Meanwhile, a different sort of boycott call had gone out several weeks earlier when Chinese people grew angry at a foreign power.

This sounds like a recap of the China events that were making headlines before the tragic earthquake hit Sichuan. But the paragraph applies equally well to the situation exactly a century ago, when the start of the first London Olympics neared, some Irish athletes threatened not to compete, and Chinese were boycotting Japanese goods.

And there would soon be another 1908 occurrence, a gesture of defiance during the opening ceremonies, which could have a 2008 counterpart. When the American team paraded, they refused to bow before the king.

Reading newspaper accounts from 1908 can cause déjà vu, though it also reveals many contrasts between those days and ours.

It shows, for example, that the Olympics were not then what they are now in terms of the attention generated and the sports involved. Only a fraction of the teams and journalists converging on Beijing went to London in 1908, and the athletic competition that generated the most controversy that summer was a "tug-of-war" contest.

There's also much that differentiates Ireland's history from Tibet's. To cite just one example, many Irish nationalists demanded complete independence in 1908, while in 2008 the Dalai Lama is simply asking for more cultural autonomy for Tibetans.

The recent call by some Chinese for a boycott of French Carrefour stores—partly to demonstrate displeasure with France because a Chinese torch carrier was roughed up by protesters in Paris—is also different from the 1908 struggle against Japan. That earlier boycott, for example, was much bigger and had nothing to do with the Olympics.

It began when the Chinese authorities seized a Japanese ship headed toward the Portuguese colony of Macau. Convinced the vessel was carrying arms to revolutionaries seeking to overthrow the Qing dynasty (1644–1911), officials replaced the ship's Japanese flag with a Chinese one and sailed it to Canton. The boycott call came after Japan pressured the Qing into paying an indemnity for taking the vessel and making a humiliating apology for showing disrespect toward Japan's flag.

Given the existence of these and other contrasts between 1908 and 2008, does looking back a century have more than mere curiosity value? And with so many analogies and comparisons already in play in the debates about Tibet and about the Olympics, where supposed similarities between Beijing 2008 and Berlin 1936 or Moscow 1980 are often mentioned, do we need more to ponder?

These are fair questions. But looking back to 1908 is not of just antiquarian interest. One reason, ironically, is precisely because of how many Olympic analogies and Tibet comparisons are circulating. Some of these have been used well, but even the best have sometimes encouraged us to misunderstand how long or how complex the lineage of a current tactic or dilemma actually is.

How exactly can looking back a century help clarify understanding of 2008? Here are five specific illustrations:

1. It reminds us that the modern Olympics have been politicized for much more than just a few decades and that even using the opening ceremonies to make a political statement, often talked about as though it were a novel tactic, has long-term precedents.

2. Irish–Tibetan comparisons, though imperfect, help us guard against overstating the uniqueness of Beijing's dilemma when it comes to trying to control borderlands containing people who speak their own language and have divergent religious beliefs. Moreover, in Ireland then, as in Tibet now, resentment of relative newcomers doing well economically helps generate discontent.

3. Some foreign commentators have framed the Carrefour action as imitative, a knee-jerk response to Western talk of an Olympic boycott. The case of 1908 reminds us that boycotts have been used by many generations of Chinese protesters.

4. A look back to 1908 also reveals that the international reach of Chinese nationalism is no novelty. Long before Chinese based abroad were swept up in the current patriotic fever, merchants living in North America, Hong Kong, and Southeast Asia lent support to antiforeign boycotts, including that of a century ago.

5. And if we want to appreciate why Chinese officials opposed the targeting

of Carrefour stores, even though the regime has been displeased by the West's behavior during the lead-up to the Games, casting our eyes back a century can help.

The 1908 protests began as loyalist actions. But as would happen again and again in the twentieth century, some of those involved would eventually start expressing their love of country by saying that the nation needed officials who were more capable, less corrupt, or simply more determined to place the welfare of the people above all other concerns.

This reminds us that nationalist fervor and patriotism could be then, as they can be now, double-edged swords. This was revealed earlier this month when, in the immediate aftermath of the horrific Sichuan earthquake, Chinese bloggers objected to the continuation of celebratory official press reports of the torch relay, at a time when so many people of the nation were suffering. Netizens who not long before had been calling on a boycott of France switched to calling for a shift in treatment of the relay to demonstrate official concern for their suffering compatriots—something that led, almost immediately, to such things as the introduction of a moment of silence into subsequent rituals involving the traveling flame.

Looking back to 1908 won't provide simple answers to complex questions like whether calls for an Olympic boycott are justified or foolish. It can, though, help us think more clearly about the contemporary situation. And this is really all that historical analogies and comparisons generally can do.

And there's an added payoff: it brings a fresh sports metaphor into the mix. The Chinese government's efforts to ride out Olympic controversies have been likened to a gymnast struggling to stay atop a balance beam. But wouldn't it be at least as fitting to think of it as trying to compete successfully in a symbolic tug-of-war?

How to Talk to Strangers: Beijing's Advice ☆ Mary S. Erbaugh

American parents warn their children, "Don't talk to strangers!" But Chinese adults traditionally avoid even superficial greetings to strangers. This preserves a distinction between insiders and outsiders (*nei wai you bie*) that honors insiders but deflects con artists and unwelcome requests. People remain wary until they know someone's title, surname, and background through networks of connections (*guanxi*) with kin, classmates, and colleagues. People do not say "hello" even to neighbors on the street. In stores, restaurants, train stations, taxis, post offices, or clinics, customers request service without pleasantries: "Pork chop noodles!" "To the east bus station!" Good service focuses on a quick but silent response. Strangers remain lonely and vulnerable to rudeness, as any Chinese bus rider knows.

Mandarin classes and phrase books for foreigners stress phrases that are supposed to be equivalents to English "hello," "please," "sorry," "thanks," and "good-bye." But surprisingly, such phrases are not universal. The Mandarin versions turn out to be very recent, unfamiliar translations from European languages. Using them can sound as awkward, conversation stopping, and potentially sarcastic as saying *bon jour* in a Mississippi gas station.

Yet the Beijing government has launched the biggest propaganda campaign since the Cultural Revolution to press people to use exactly these "five courteous phrases" (*wuge limao de ci*): "hello" (*nin hao*), "please" (*qing*), "sorry" (*duibuqi*), "thanks" (*xiexie*), and "good-bye" (*zai jian*). This deliberately innocuous effort repudiates the painful political labels of the Cultural Revolution in hopes of a public sphere that is depoliticized; harmonious; hygienically free of trash, spitting, and public urination; and internationally recognized as a world-class "civilization" (*wenming limao*).[3]

The shift toward using the five courteous phrases fills a historically recent gap in greeting foreign visitors. But the phrases are beginning to catch on locally to bridge a gap in Chinese social relations. Hundreds of millions of Chinese have suddenly found themselves as strangers in new factories and high-rise neighborhoods where 40 percent of people surveyed don't know the names of their neighbors. Self-help best-sellers, arguing that talking to strangers can be good business, coach readers on how to use the phrases.

Adding the phrases onto traditional insider courtesy is a slow process, especially outside the metropolis. Each phrase carries problematic historic overtones. English "hello" or "hi," translated as *nin hao*, sounds closer to "greetings to the honored people," adapted from ceremonial group greetings, such as leaders reviewing the troops from Tiananmen Square or students greeting their teachers. "Please" (*qing*) is a verb, traditionally restricted to a superior making an offer to an inferior, "might I invite you to do X." Customers who say *qing* sound contradictory. Service workers are reluctant to say it, for it risks both cheekiness and assuming responsibility for situations that are often out of their control, such as running out of stock.

"Sorry," translated as *duibuqi*, is literally "I cannot rise to face you," closer to "I beg you to forgive me. How can I make it up to you?" It takes responsibility for serious wrongdoing, which demands reparations. For minor lapses, people often say, "[I'm] embarrassed" (*bu hao yisi*), or borrow the widely understood Cantonese phrase for "[I] shouldn't/sorry/excuse me/please/thanks" (*m goi*). In the United States, people say "sorry" or "excuse me" to request attention. In Mandarin, "may I ask . . ." (*qing wen*) is often less confusing. "Thank you," translated as *xiexie*, comes from "[I] refuse [it]" and the necessity to refuse any

---

3. For details, see Mary S. Erbaugh, "China Expands Its Courtesy: Saying 'Hello' to Strangers," *Journal of Asian Studies* 67, no. 2 (2008).

offer three times. Waiters and clerks find it confusing. "Good-bye," translated as *zai jian*, sounds more like "farewell" or even *bon voyage* to people you never expect to see again. Family, friends, and colleagues do not tempt fate by saying it; they simply say, "[I'm] leaving" (*zou le*).

What are you supposed to say instead of the five phrases? The title ("teacher," "manager," even a fictive kinship title like "grandpa"), plus surname, plus a situational comment: "Have you eaten?" "You must be busy," "Where are you going?" American visitors often feel that their privacy has been invaded but respond literally: "Well, I had breakfast rather late" or "I'm going to my friend Lee's house." But situational comments are usually merely pro forma efforts to establish a connection. Only a vague response is needed: "I've eaten," "Very busy," "Going out." The less people have seen foreigners, the more curious they are. Decades ago as a student in Taipei, passersby exhausted me by yelling, "Foreigner!" "How old are you?" "Are you married?" "How many children do you have?" "Where do you live?" "What did you pay for those socks?" A recent propaganda poster in the Beijing neighborhood near Tiananmen Square lists "Eight 'Don't Ask' Topics for Foreigners": age, marital status, occupation, income, health status, politics, religion, or personal experiences.

Chinese do ask each other specific questions both from curiosity and to establish common ground when they are first introduced, especially hometown, school, and employer. Even the politest Chinese try to establish a connection with questions that American visitors may react to as annoying or clichéd: "What country are you from?" "How long have you been in China?" "Can you use chopsticks?" "What do you think of China?" China values the right phrase for each situation. Americans can grow impatient when a Chinese says, "I'm happy to be in . . . the Big Apple/the Windy City/Nanjing, one of China's 'three furnaces' of hot weather/Hangzhou by the beautiful West Lake/at the Hai'er Company, China's biggest maker of home appliances." But to Chinese ears, conventional comments show sensitivity to where you are and what to say. Americans relish political debate. But Chinese are unlikely to exhort Americans to close Guantanamo, free Puerto Rico, or pay reparations for African American slavery. Ironically, Olympic sports talk offers situational comments with a very simple vocabulary: team names, nationalities, scores, and good wishes.

Learning English, Learning Chinese ☆ David L. Porter

Judging from recent interviews on Beijing streets that were broadcast during the Olympics by American TV and radio journalists, the city-wide cram courses in Olympics English were proving popular.

The current craze for English in China, where seven-year-olds study the language daily and charismatic English teachers achieve the status of rock stars, reflects both these impulses. To speak a foreigner's language, even if it is only a few phrases, is to show due respect to a friend come from afar. But it's also a sign of increasing confidence and worldliness of outlook, a reflection not so much of China's opening to the world as of the world, at long last, opening to China.

A Chinese journalist covering the Summer Olympics in Atlanta in 1996 would have had a considerably harder time turning up a local resident who could offer so much as a cliché of cosmopolitan hospitality in the journalist's native Chinese. There have, however, been some signs of change. In the United States, Chinese is now the second most widely used foreign language after Spanish; 200,000 students are learning Chinese at 1,000 colleges, 300 elementary and secondary schools, and 600 Chinese-language schools across the United States. These numbers have been rising rapidly: from 1998 to 2002 (the most recent year for which the statistic is available), the number of college students electing Chinese as a foreign language rose by 20 percent; more recently, the number of K–12 students studying the language increased eightfold between 2000 and 2007 to approximately 40,000.

This growth has been supported by the U.S. federal government, which has designated Chinese as a "critical language" and has awarded 90 percent of foreign language development grants under the National Security Language Initiative to Chinese-language programs. States have begun to jump on the bandwagon as well: a recent law passed in Utah stipulates that all public middle schools in the state require Chinese-language instruction beginning in 2007.

Current enrollment numbers, while increasing, are still minuscule compared to the number of people learning Chinese across the world, which China's Ministry of Education currently places at 30 million, with a projected increase to 100 million by 2010.

These students have clearly taken to heart the kinds of greetings we heard this summer on the streets of Beijing, and they are, much to their credit, determined to respond in kind.

Hand Grenades and the Olympics ☆ Lijia Zhang

When I was at school, sports lessons included an exercise where we threw hand grenades (made from wood topped with metal to resemble the real thing) against a wall over which a red slogan had been stretched offering the reason for such a militaristic pastime: "Exercise our bodies and protect our motherland." We feared that China might be invaded one day by the American "imperialists" or Soviet "revisionists." Indeed, the whole West held evil intent toward us. Living in a closed country, we had little idea about the outside world.

I went to school in Nanjing in the early 1970s, when the revolutionary fever of the Cultural Revolution was calming down. A few years earlier, my father had been banished to the countryside for criticizing the government. My grandfather, a small-time grain dealer, had committed suicide, as he worried his not-so-politically-correct background would land him in trouble. These were the darkest of times for my family as well as for our nation. China has come a long way since then, yet the image of those dark days remains deeply imprinted on Western minds. I wonder whether the West is a little too keen to report the negative stories. Or perhaps the West feels more comfortable hearing such stories?

That's my impression, as a Chinese who has lived abroad but has returned to Beijing. Even during those days throwing grenades, I dreamt of becoming a journalist and writer. That dream was shattered when I was sixteen and my mother dragged me to work at a state-owned missile factory.

My journalistic career started with the Olympics. In 1993, on the night when the result of the first bid was announced, I was at Tiananmen Square. I recall the fountain going off as we thought China had won the bid. It was heartbreaking to interview the bitterly disappointed crowds. But, in truth, China wasn't really ready. The memory of the bloody crackdown in 1989 was still fresh.

I was also in Beijing eight years later when China did win the bid. In our neighborhood, grannies spent the whole afternoon practicing their dance steps and their husbands beat drums and gongs. This time, we were not disappointed. The wild celebration, the deafening noise of firecrackers, laughter, and ecstatic cries went on the whole night. I was interviewed by the BBC. I said, "In the ecstatic cries, I heard Chinese people's longing for the recognition and respect from the world."

I was just as happy as everyone else. Ever since the economic reforms, China has lifted millions of people out of poverty. An incredible feat. As a child, I used to roast cicadas to satisfy my craving for meat; now my nineteen-year-old nephew, a student in Nanjing, drives his own car. People are enjoying a great deal more personal freedom. As a girl in the rocket factory, I had to endure so many rules. I worked there for ten years. I was never promoted, partly because of my naturally curly hair—my boss thought I wore a perm. Back then, only those with a bourgeois outlook would curl their hair. These days, young women curl their hair, shave off their hair, or change the colors of their hair whenever they want. It's not a small thing.

Over the past few years, I have seen how the capital has been transformed. State-of-the-art buildings—not just Olympic buildings such as the Bird's Nest and the Water Cube—have popped up like mushrooms after a spring rain. With only a few days to go before the opening ceremony, Beijing, having undergone a facelift, has never been so beautiful, clean, and quiet.

Huge efforts and sacrifices have been made. To ensure the best possible air quality, polluting factories around Beijing have been shut down, construction work has been halted, and cars have been taken off the roads (the results, admittedly, have been mixed). Other measures are excessive: beggars, the homeless, and migrants without documents have been driven out. Petitioners who bring their grievances to the Supreme People's Court have been stopped from entering the capital. Potential troublemakers are being monitored or are under house arrest. Such has been the stance the authorities adopt while dealing with uncertainty.

Yet Beijing's Olympics will be a success because the majority of the population want them to be, not just because the government wants to use Olympic success to gain legitimacy. Xia Fengzhi, a sixty-seven-year-old retired worker and a volunteer, told me how happy and excited he is about the Games: "I want foreigners to see what China has achieved. We were called the 'sick man of Asia.' Now we are strong and rich enough to hold such a major international event."

No doubt there will be many more negative stories abroad, criticizing China's human rights abuses, the lack of media freedom, and the overtight security. Of course, some Chinese have no access to the reports, but those who do tend to dismiss them as grumbles from anti-China forces. In a survey conducted by the Pew Research Center, China's people ranked first among twenty-four nations in their optimism about their country's future, buoyed by the fast economic growth and the promise of the Olympics.

There is, I believe, another factor—the timing. The survey was conducted this spring, just after the unrest in Tibet and during the troubled Olympic torch relay, when China experienced a surge of nationalism in response to what many Chinese regarded as an "anti-China feeling" in the West and "biased" Tibet reports.

I have no problem with the negative stories, but I think it's wrong for the West to stand in moral judgment, especially when some of the accusations are not true. For example, what happened in Lhasa, in my view, was far more complicated than "the Chinese government's ruthless crackdown on Tibetan protest." There was a peaceful protest, but there was also a violent racial riot, one that I doubt would be tolerated in any country.

As a journalist, most of my stories criticize the government, which seems to have little idea as to how to present itself. Blessed with such domestic support and armed with skills in mass organization, the authorities could have taken a more relaxed approach to this festival of sport. Why didn't it make the Olympic Games a fun event—China's big coming-out party? It didn't need to cause so much interruption to people's lives. It would have been far better to let the world see China as it actually is.

I can't help feeling there's been a missed opportunity on more important matters, too. Our leaders could have made use of this to address the real issues: cracking down on corruption, improving the rule of law, relaxing media control, and opening the country further.

But don't doubt our support of the Beijing Games. The Olympics are meant to be an occasion to bring different people with different views together. It'll provide a chance for China and the rest of the world to understand each other. Although I can understand how China's undemocratic political system and lack of transparency make the West uneasy, especially when matched with the country's rise, much of the fear is generated by ignorance.

Today's schoolchildren enjoy far more sophisticated sports than throwing hand grenades. They know a lot more about the outside world. I wonder if Western children know as much about China. And if they did, would there still be the same fear? Maybe the Olympics will bring us closer.

Chapter 9

The Olympics as Spectacle

PAINTING OVER MAO
Notes on the Inauguration of the Beijing Olympic Games
Geremie R. Barmé

Most observers noted that Mao, the party chairman who founded the People's Republic in 1949 and led the country until his death in 1976, was absent from Zhang Yimou's Olympic opening ceremony paean to China's past civilization. Of course, they might have missed the pregnant absence of the dead leader in the heavily rewritten "Song to the Motherland" (*Gechang zuguo*). The original of the song featured the dead leader, but he was gone from the version mimed by nine-year-old Lin Miaoke (the real singer was Yang Peiyi, who was excluded on the grounds that she was not suitably photogenic). However, in reality, the Great Helmsman did get a look-in, if only obliquely.

On the unfurled paper scroll that features center stage early in the performance, dancers trace out a painting in the "*xieyi*," or impressionistic, style of traditional Chinese art. Their lithe movements create a vision of mountains and a river to which is added a sun. To my mind, it is an image that evokes the painting-mural that forms a backdrop to the statue of the Chairman in the Mao Memorial Hall in the center of Beijing. That picture is, in turn, inspired by a line from Mao's most famous poem "Snow" (February 1936) that reads, "How splendid the rivers and mountains of China" (*jiangshan ru ci duo jiao*). The poem lists the prominent rulers of dynastic China and ends by commenting on how all these great men fade in comparison to the true heroes of the modern world: the people. The poem is generally interpreted as being about Mao himself, the hero of the age.

In their opening ceremony design, what Zhang Yimou and his colleagues achieved, be it intentional or not, is a rethinking of this reference. . . . A Chinese landscape, with its coded political references, is transformed into something that is suffused with a new and embracing meaning by the global community. It offers a positive message for the future of China's engagement with the world not only to international audiences but perhaps also to China's own leaders.

Posted 8/12/2008 at 03:00:00 PM

Filmmaker Zhang Yimou, assisted by an international team of advisers that initially included Steven Spielberg (until the Hollywood impresario pulled out), planned a stunning opening ceremony for the Olympic Games. Despite the fireworks, fancy stunts, and cast of thousands, the show on the floor of the "Bird's Nest" was arguably not the most dramatic of the night. It had to share that title with the conference between Russian Prime Minister (and former president) Vladimir Putin and U.S. President George W. Bush—"animated," at times, according to Australian Prime Minister Kevin Rudd, who was sitting two rows behind them. This was because the announcement that Russia had invaded Georgia came during the Opening Ceremonies.

The timing—it was postulated that Russia had specifically scheduled the invasion for the day when all media eyes would be on Beijing—was only one more piece of evidence that 2008 was a year when news watchers were overwhelmed by the confluence of major international events. Though reports rolled in from Georgia over the next weeks, however, the Olympic Games were the story to follow. Astounding American swimmer Michael Phelps netted eight gold medals; Chinese hurdler Liu Xiang, on whom Chinese hopes were riding, pulled a tendon and withdrew from the competition; the Chinese female gymnastics team won gold; and the Beijing skies were clear, most days.

While what did happen in Beijing was important, what didn't was equally so—there weren't, for instance, any large-scale protests or disruptions. Our contributors, however, noticed a lot of other things that were missing—any imagery of Mao Zedong, for one, aside from occasional television shots of his giant portrait looking down on Tiananmen Square. In its carefully crafted messages about China's past, the Olympic "spectacle" also told us a great deal about China's present and its future.

It's Right to Party, En Masse ☆ Haiyan Lee

The most clichéd way of referring to the 2008 Beijing Olympic Games in English-language media has been "China's coming-out party." The slightly condescending undertone is nonetheless mingled with well-wishing that the debutante will give the world a heck of a party, the glitches and heartaches in the run-up notwithstanding. For this precious moment, China chose Zhang Yimou, arguably its most talented film director, to chaperone itself onto the world stage.

By all indications, it was a good choice. The fifty-minute multi-milliondollar extravaganza was so spectacular that the only appropriate response, it would seem, was a WOW! Or to wonder in amazement, like one American volleyball player did, "How did they do that?" Any more parsing would seem pedantic. But, alas, this is the age of "have computer, will blog." So let's begin with the *New York Times* piece (August 9, 2008, by Jim Yardley) that hails the event as a wild success with "signature Chinese touches." There is no denying that the lavish ceremony was first and foremost about China. And the China it celebrated was ancient (the five-thousand-year history), civilized (the arts and crafts), inventive (the four great inventions), entrepreneurial (the silk roads), hospitable (the Confucian chant about cherishing guests from afar), technologically accomplished (the astronaut), diverse but united (the fifty-six nationalities), and innocent and hopeful (the schoolchildren). It wore love, peace, and harmony proudly on its sleeve. What more could the world ask for?

Dutiful commentators will likely remind us what this dazzling propaganda blockbuster glosses over: the human rights abuses, the suppression of ethnic/regional autonomy, the rise of xenophobic nationalism, the environmental degradation, the widening gap between rich and poor, the unholy alliances with authoritarian regimes elsewhere, and so on. However, not every skeleton has been stuffed into the national closet. In fact, the ceremony openly paraded the specter of another China that should in theory jar the domestic revelers and besotted observers alike: Mao's China.

Everything about the Beijing Olympics was meant to sweep you off your feet. But above all, it was the number of performers—close to 15,000—in the opening ceremony that probably caused many an eye to pop and jaw to drop. Given how much of the "Chineseness" in the program belonged to the category of "invented" or at least airbrushed tradition, the surreally synchronized movements of thousands of people was perhaps the most "signature" of the Chinese touches. The antecedents are much closer in history and more vivid in memory: we need only recall the images of mass formations dressed in regulation garb, singing in unison, marching in lockstep, waving the *Little Red Book*, or doing what George Orwell calls "physical jerks" to the accompaniment of bombastic loudspeaker music. To date, only the North Koreans can rival the Chinese in staging such spectacles of sheer numbers. It is the totalitarian aesthetic at its most beguiling and frightening. It is the power of mass ritual.

A new book called *Ritual and Its Consequences: An Essay on the Limits of Sincerity* (2008) argues that ritual is a quintessential human activity because it creates an "as-if" world in which identities are (re)made, boundaries tested, and human potentialities stretched. It can be used by rulers to shore up the existing order or by the malcontent to imagine alternative worlds. The Chinese Communist Party, since its days of fighting guerrilla warfare in the countryside, has tapped the power of ritual with consummate skill: it famously invented the ritual of *fanshen* (turning over) to denounce the ancien régime and the social order it presided over; and it mandated (and to some extent still does) mass participation in a numbing array of state-orchestrated rituals to cultivate loyalty and conformity.

The party understands well the transformative power of ritual: it can goad a timid peasant to point an accusing finger at a local despot, inspire saintly acts of self-sacrifice in an ordinary person, or make schoolgirls savagely beat their teacher to death. Zhang Yimou, too, has understood this well since his days as a cinematographer. The 1980s classic *Yellow Earth* (directed by Chen Kaige, with

Zhang as cinematographer) already gives us a good taste of Zhang's passion for mass rituals enhanced by bold colors and searing music. In a brief but powerful scene set in Yan'an, the party's headquarters during the war of resistance against Japan, a large assembly of men in peasant jackets and white turbans dance to the stirring beat of waist drums, kicking up clouds of dust and a delirious atmosphere of festivity. They are sending off new Red Army recruits who file past with red ribbons tied across their torsos—after the bridegroom's fashion at rural weddings. The scene is a potent reminder that it was the party's ability to absorb folk arts and rituals into its political theater as much as its Marxist-Leninist ideology and military know-how that enabled it to sweep into power in 1949.

To be sure, the film ends on a subversive note of skepticism, showing a huge gathering of peasants prostrating on the parched yellow earth in a rain-seeking ritual and then surging forth in a direction *away* from the far horizon where the protagonist and Communist soldier Gu Qing has reappeared after a period of absence. The ending suggests that the party saves neither the girl (Cuiqiao) from the fate of arranged marriage nor the peasants in general from the blight of poverty and ignorance. Such discordant moments, however, are rare in Zhang's later, martial arts epics. Beginning with *Hero*, Zhang seems enthralled by what Susan Sontag calls "fascinatin' fascism," or power dressed up as splendid spectacles. Repeatedly, he knocks our socks off with glorious shots of ancient humanity, surprisingly agile in their quaintly cumbersome accoutrements not unlike those worn by portions of the opening ceremony performers, carrying out the will of a tyrant with unstoppable menace. These are the films that have at last turned a profit for Zhang and endeared him to the authorities. They are seductive in the same way that films about the Nazi aesthetics of pomp and violence have perversely held audiences' attention worldwide for decades.

It is no accident that a *New York Times* profile of Zhang Yimou calls him China's Leni Riefenstahl (August 8, 2008, by David Barboza). Whether or not the analogy is fair, Zhang's success owes as much to an iron-fisted regime that loves grandeur as to our irrepressible fascination with aestheticized and ritualized politics, particularly its ability to galvanize people to achieve the seemingly impossible. In comparison, democratic politics is hopelessly drab and tedious (except when it resorts to imperialist, shock-and-awe–style violence against a "rogue" state). How on earth does one turn C-Span into a visually stunning and emotionally rousing spectacle? The same book on ritual mentioned earlier asserts that modern Western societies cling to the virtue of sincerity and authenticity out of a profound distrust of ritual. Ritual appears to many as empty formality devoid of genuine feeling. But this doesn't mean that we are immune to its lure of creativity, theatricality, and communality or its promise to lift us out of our private, atomized, and irrelevant existence.

No sooner had the ceremony ended on the magical night of 8/8/08 than both domestic and foreign media showered kudos on Zhang Yimou and the performers (many of whom were soldiers of the People's Liberation Army

[PLA]). The Chinese press, in particular, was full of moving stories about the hardship endured by each performer for the sake of perfection. Foreign enthusiasm, however, was occasionally punctured by misgivings about turning humans into mechanical patterns.[1] In a candid interview with *Southern Weekend* (August 14, 2008, by Zhang Ying and Xia Chen), Zhang defended his deployment of the "number's strategy" (*renhai zhanshu*) on artistic grounds, arguing that it was indispensable to plaza art (*guangchang yishu*). He also noted wistfully the tremendous concessions he did have to make to appease his habitual critics, such as avoiding the use of drums and lanterns, even though these "Chinese cultural elements" (*Zhongguo yuansu*) could have taken the show to new acoustic and visual heights.[2] Instead, the obscure *"fou"* was chosen as the percussion instrument, and red lanterns were conspicuously absent. All this was done to deprive his detractors of the opportunity to throw lines like "Here come Zhang Yimou and his lanterns again" at what was after all a collective project. Looking ahead to the closing ceremony while the games were still ongoing, he revealed that it would be more relaxed and fun, more of a carnival than a work of stagecraft.[3]

Although self-conscious about the disquiet his art can elicit and willing to make accommodations, Zhang Yimou clearly believes that there is a time and place for the solemn majesty of size and pattern and that there is a time and place for the casual charm of street art. The closing ceremony garnered nearly universal approval for being appropriately carnivalesque, with its rough-hewn "tower of memory" and firefighters whooshing up and down the scaffold "like insects on a giant ear of corn," according to one imaginative viewer. Visual pleasure was still plentifully supplied by beautifully executed human body formations in the style of Busby Berkeley, but mass art was eclipsed by towering celebrity figures such as Plácido Domingo, Song Zuying, Jackie Chan, Wang Lee Hom, and others, who, together with the nonchalant London segment, eased the audiences back to the familiar territory of bourgeois art as a weapon of mass distraction (as opposed to mobilization). The world breathed a collective sigh of relief. Better to party en masse than to flex massive military muscles; better to deck out the PLA soldiers in fluorescent catsuits and make them undulate in the Bird's

---

1. See, for example, *New Yorker* film critic Anthony Lane's "Letter from Beijing" dated August 25, 2008: "In the course of a long evening, billions of viewers were induced not so much to revise their opinion of China as to realize that its formidable manpower could be harnessed to the cause of astonishment. . . . If, deep below the spectacle, there was an unspoken suggestion that it would be an extremely bad idea to go to war against this nation, it never rose to the surface." And, "we . . . ask ourselves, what kind of society is it that can afford to make patterns out of its people?"

2. Zhang Yimou was widely skewered for his fondness for these self-exoticizing "cultural elements," particularly for tacking an invented lantern ritual onto his 1991 film *Raise the Red Lantern*.

3. The series of lengthy interviews labeled "Cracking the Mysteries" ("Jie mi") can be found at http://www.infzm.com/content/15982 and http://www.infzm.com/content/15903.

Nest than to have them drive tanks into Tiananmen Square and mow down demonstrators. It is not often that China is faulted for trying too hard to please. No one, really, minds being mesmerized by (soft) power.

Where Were China's Women on 8/8/08? ☆ Nicole E. Barnes

The opening ceremony of the Beijing Olympics, televised to the world on August 8, 2008, was magnificent and awe inspiring. Vancouver and London certainly have their work cut out for them when they host the Games in 2010 and 2012, respectively. Yet as I watched a string of stunning performances of Chinese men—banging on brass drums both in unison and in visually fascinating patterns, doing quasi-qigong dance moves, and executing a painting with their bodies while dancing on the world's largest LCD screen, all capped by the appearance of seven-foot-six-inch-tall basketball superstar and flag bearer Yao Ming—I wondered, where did China's 640 million women go? Sure, nine-year-old Lin Miaoke sang a patriotic song, and another nine-year-old girl floated over the mixed-gender group of children who were presumed to represent the fifty-six recognized nationalities (though many and perhaps all were actually members of the majority Han ethnicity). The group of schoolchildren in the end was also mixed gender, but adult women were minorities in the evening's performance. I kept squinting at various performers in an attempt to ascertain their gender, but the fact that I had to look so hard indicated that something was wrong.

During one portion of the ceremony hundreds of gorgeous women lilted around the stage in modified Tang costume, moving very delicately, as if they actually were dolls made of porcelain (or perhaps as if their huge dresses were unbearably hot and heavy in Beijing's August air). The plump women of the Tang elite who played central roles in court politics and polo on horseback were not represented. A single woman floated out on a magic carpet-type platform supported by dozens of people beneath her, and her entire performance of swirling colored scarves around herself while she "floated" lasted about two minutes. Another handful of women actually did float like angels over the 90,000 spectators in the Bird's Nest (suspended from the ceiling by cables, of course), with lights illuminating their ever-smiling faces of serene beauty. But that was about it. In his world-class exposé, Zhang Yimou cast women as docile, delicate, and demure.

In this regard, the opening ceremony stands in stark contrast to the performance of the Chinese athletes. Forty-eight-kilogram Chen Xiexia was anything but demure when she lifted 117 kilograms—more than twice her own body weight—over her head without breaking a sweat. She won China's first gold medal with this stunning feat. And when the final tally was counted, women had secured fifty-seven of China's one hundred medals (twenty-seven gold, eleven silver, and nineteen bronze). Yet in all the nonsporting Olympic "events," women and girls were judged by their looks. The women who gave medals to the world's athletes, for example, had to conform to exact height and weight specifications (tall and thin). And we learned soon after 8/8/08 that the nine-year-old "singer" Lin Miaoke was only lip-synching; the actual vocalist, Yang Peiyi, was kept backstage because of her allegedly less-than-perfect looks (her adult teeth were just beginning to develop).

China has never had full gender equality (no country has), but it is worth remembering that it has in the not so distant past made very real advances in that direction. Shouldn't that have been recognized and celebrated somehow on its global opening night? Apparently the creators of the opening extravaganza didn't think so. They lost a wonderful opportunity to challenge the stereotype of submission that plagues Asian women everywhere.

Another interesting omission, noted in other chapters of this volume, was temporal. The ceremony showcased key moments in Chinese history but jumped over almost the entire twentieth century, most notably the years when Chairman Mao ruled the nascent People's Republic (1949–1976). From an ideological standpoint, the absence seemed to reflect official repudiation of Maoist politics and its socialist, planned economy in favor of the market reforms of Deng Xiao-ping and his successors, who have built the so-called socialism with Chinese characteristics that has catapulted millions of Chinese into the comfortable middle class. But from a gender standpoint, omitting the Mao years was in keeping with the sidelining of women in the opening ceremony. For all of his faults, Mao did preside over many advances in gender equality that can be summed up in his famous adage, "women hold up half the sky" (admittedly always a goal rather than a reality but an important goal). During the early Communist era, women kept their right to choose their marriage partners and also could choose to divorce them, entered characteristically male professions by the millions, earned equal pay for equal work, and had secure jobs to return to after giving birth (with all medical costs covered, of course). Now, say many Chinese feminists, a lot of these gains are becoming losses, and career women hit their heads on glass ceilings and gender-biased pay scales.

But even the most vocal feminists, in China and other places alike, now have to fight to get airtime on these kinds of issues. Chinese women became electri-cians and joined the All-China Women's Federation in the 1950s and 1960s, and American women demanded equality and read *The Feminine Mystique* and *Ms.* magazine in the 1960s and 1970s. Feminism is over now, a standard line goes, and women are all free to do as they please. When I was growing up in the United States in the 1970s and 1980s, this message was so loud as to cause a deafening silence on the remaining barriers to full gender equality—and the new barriers to it that sometimes arose. There is now a countermovement under way, with women located in varied parts of the world crafting a new feminism and insisting that—especially in underdeveloped countries—women should not have to live off the dregs of the world economy while producing the majority of the goods from which it profits. If many—but certainly not all—women in developed nations prosper (myself included), it is because economic and sexual exploitation rests on the backs of poor women halfway around the globe and in our own backyards.

Millions believed in the power of Mao (in the Chinese setting) and free love and good intentions (in the American one) to heal all wounds. Recognizing that gender inequality has not been solved, even after capitalism has spread wealth farther and deeper than any other economic system, can be gut-wrenching. So when I first posted a much shorter blog post version of this piece at *China Beat* (August 9, 2008), I received fifteen comments, many of which were critical and negative. I was blamed for creating "a problem where there isn't one" and "whining about nonissues." People pegged me as a Eurocentrist who always harps on China's imperfections while dismissing its every victory.

Just like Olympic planners in London and Toronto, feminists of the new generation face a Sisyphean task. We must convince the skeptics that sexism is alive and well and do so in a way that allows them to trust our judgment instead of dismissing it as petty and misplaced. We must keep these issues in the public eye, constantly challenging our own and others' complacency. Most importantly, we must remember that there is always hope, and this struggle does matter. If her emotional strength matched that of her body, that would be something Chen Xiexia could do in an instant.

What Would Mao Think of the Games? ☆ Jeffrey N. Wasserstrom

China specialists make a parlor game of imagining what Mao Zedong would make of the People's Republic of China (PRC) today, with its capitalist-friendly Communists and young people more familiar with the theme song from *Titanic* than the song "The East Is Red."

In my book *China's Brave New World*, for example, I ruminate on a revivified Mao's likely response to my favorite Nanjing bookstore, where the philosophy section has nary a copy of his *Little Red Book* but does contain Bertrand Russell's *History of Western Philosophy* and studies of abstruse French theory, like the optimistically titled *Understanding Foucault*. Some of my colleagues have taken this motif a step further, bringing into the mix the chairman's archrival, Generalissimo Chiang Kai-shek, who died in exile on a Nationalist Party–run Taiwan that was both capitalist and authoritarian.[4] In *Modern China: A Very Short Introduction*, for instance, Oxford historian Rana Mitter writes, "One can imagine Chiang Kaishek's

---

4. See, for instance, Jeremiah Jenne's June 14, 2008, post, "Mao and Chiang Kai-shek are walking down a street, and Mao says . . ." at his blog *Jottings from the Granite Studio*.

ghost wandering around China today nodding in approval, while Mao's ghost follows behind him, moaning at the destruction of his vision."

If the Olympics mark a turning point in the history of the PRC, isn't it time to play this game with the Games? What would Chairman Mao and Generalissimo Chiang make of the Beijing that has played host to athletes, journalists, fans, and political leaders? How would the opening ceremonies have struck them? What about the media coverage and sporting events that followed?

Let's start with the ghosts of two competitors arriving in a pre-Games Beijing. Much about the look of the city would shock them since neither had governed a metropolis with skyscrapers and megamalls. News that the metropolis was gearing up to host the Olympics would surely be a welcome surprise. Both Mao and Chiang had long lamented the fact that China of the early 1900s was derided as the "sick man of Asia," a play on earlier Western references to the Ottoman Empire in Europe—each a once-proud place that now could be bullied. Both leaders stressed the importance of exercise, insisting that China's lack of a strong tradition of vigorous sports had contributed to it being laid low by Western and then Japanese imperialism. The dream of China hosting the Games dates back to the early 1900s, so each leader would be pleased this long-time wish had been granted.

Once the ghosts got their bearings, their reactions to Beijing would begin to diverge. Mao would be delighted to see his face on most currency but maybe a bit put off by the fact that some new banknotes feature the Bird's Nest stadium instead. And he'd be pleased to see that a giant portrait of his face still looks down on Tiananmen Square. These same things would infuriate the generalissimo.

As a Christian who had made the birthday of Confucius an official holiday during the Nationalist period (1927–1949), the religious situation would be somewhat gratifying to the generalissimo and annoying to the chairman. It is true that the only Christian churches offering services now are carefully selected officially sanctioned ones, like that recently visited by "Xiao Bushi" (Little Bush, as George W. is sometimes called to distinguish him from his father). The unofficial but increasingly popular "house churches" remain illegal. Still, the situation is quite different than it was on the mainland late in Mao's life, when all manifestations of Christian belief were driven underground.

As for Confucius, reviled by Mao as a feudal thinker, temples devoted to the Sage that were destroyed by Red Guards have been refurbished and new statues honoring him installed. Seeing such objects erected in the kinds of places where statues of Mao himself once stood (though there are still plenty of those around, too) would be hard for the chairman's ghost to take.

The prominence of Confucius in the Olympics opening ceremonies is also relevant. He was invoked early on in the show, via a famous quotation of the Sage's about the pleasure of having "friends come from afar" and a contingent of performers dressed as his disciples. This would have been a source of comfort to the generalissimo's ghost, an outrage to Mao's. If any ancient figure deserved to be celebrated, according to the chairman, it was the first emperor of the Qin, known for, among other things, his disdain for Confucian scholars and their books.

Neither ghost would have minded seeing those segments of the ceremonies that Western commentators have criticized as evocative of Nazi or North Korean rituals. The generalissimo fought the Axis powers during World War II, but he was drawn at times to fascism; the chairman and North Korea's leaders often had similar approaches to spectacle. Moreover, both Mao and Chiang presided over National Day parades on their respective sides of the Taiwan Strait that involved large numbers of people moving together in lockstep.

What would have disturbed both was the quick march through China's history, in which director Zhang Yimou skipped straight from the Ming dynasty, represented by the giant ships of explorer Zheng He, to the late 1970s. This made it seem as if the antidynastic 1911 Revolution of Sun Yat-sen, the Japanese invasions of the 1930s (that both Mao and Chiang resisted), the Long March (that saved the Communist Party from extinction at the hands of the Nationalists), and the period from 1949 to the mid-1970s when Mao ruled the mainland (and Chiang ruled Taiwan) had never happened. The events of the twentieth century were of epic importance for China; to see most of it airbrushed out of the Olympic gala would disturb not only the ghosts but all who understand the dangers of a selective telling of history.

Moving forward to the sporting events, there are four things worth noting, especially relating to Mao's ghost:

He would've liked seeing China besting America in the collection of a valuable kind of mineral (though the United States with 110 ultimately had ten more total medals than China; China had fifty-six gold medals to thirty-six for the United States). The disastrous Great Leap Forward he launched, which contributed to a famine with a staggeringly high death toll, was aimed, after all, at catching up with and ultimately surpassing Western countries in steel production.

We should remember that Mao touted the importance of female equality via slogans such as "women hold up half the sky" and the introduction of a new, much fairer Marriage Law in 1950. As such, surely his ghost would have taken pleasure in the success of China's female athletes.

As someone famed for his swims in the Yangtze River, Mao might have been delighted by the aquatic stadium and swimming and diving events. But he did value a governing party's ability to control the news and give it a nationalistic spin—something that Chiang, also no slouch as a proponent of censorship, prized as well. And so, Mao's ghost would have understood why the exploits of domestic athletes got more attention than did those of Michael Phelps on Chinese television.

Most significantly, Mao's ghost would surely have been pleased to learn that, while athletes based on Taiwan can still compete as their own team, they cannot use their national flag or have their national anthem played during the Games. This is just one of many aspects of Beijing in 2008 that shows the degree to which it is the Communist Party's spin on the "one-China" theme, not the Nationalist Party's one, that remains dominant.

In the end, then, Mao would be the one most satisfied by the games. Geremie Barmé, an Australian Sinologist who is a leading authority on both Mao and Chinese film, argues that there were subtle ways that the opening ceremonies invoked the Chairman. He notes that director Zhang Yimou took one of the Chairman's watchwords ("using the past to serve the present and the foreign to serve China") as his guide throughout.

This is doubtless true, but there is nothing subtle about some aspects of the Games that would have pleased the Chairman, including the makeup of the crowd. After being humiliated on 1950s trips to Moscow, forced to play supplicating "little brother" to patronizing Soviet leaders, Mao was eager to see a day when foreign heads of great powers would come to Beijing on Beijing's own terms. So Mao's ghost would surely have liked the sight of Putin and Bush sitting in a Chinese stadium awash with red PRC flags, watching a spectacle that most foreigners found impressive, even if at times also a bit disturbing. And as Barmé reminds us, though there were allusions to Confucius in the show, many of the choreographers and performers responsible for it were from an organization that was always very dear to Mao: the People's Liberation Army, which he had once led into battle and ultimately led to victory over the forces of Chiang's Nationalist Party.

☆ The Olympics around the World ☆

Many China-centered English-language websites (China Beat included) tend to focus their coverage on China and the United States (or, rather, coverage of Chinese media and then coverage of China as it is discussed and written about in the United States and perhaps the United Kingdom as well). In recognition that the Olympic Games are a global event, we decided in August 2008 to feature a series of short pieces from China Beat contributors around the world on how the Olympics were being covered in their neck of the woods. Here is a selection of those pieces.

Wishful Reporting in England ☆ Pierre Fuller

My tea nearly dropped to the table here in Leicester, England, when I saw *The Independent* headline. "Beijing 2008 Olympics: Tiananmen orchestra fails to drown out clamour of protests," it read, conjuring up images of Richard Gere and a chorus of Tibetan monks chanting a hundred violinists off a Tiananmen stage. So, it'd finally come, the wellspring of protest of the regime had burst, I thought. I started to read. An orchestra of 2,008 musicians was flown in from all over the world, I learned, while "foreign and local groups . . . have been told to give plenty of notice" for permission to protest. Little news there. I read on. More on the orchestra and then a paragraph on the fact that "China's critics are keen to use the Olympics" to put issues in the spotlight. Fair enough, but there were stories on that years back when Beijing won the contest to host. . . .

The only mention of protest left in the story was the fact that "despite ongoing pressure over human rights and pollution"—without a single example of who, in what form, and where in the entire article—"the normal business of the Games is continuing to gather steam."

So if the official orchestra steamed ahead after all, where's the "failure" in the headline? The "clamor?" Even the "protests?" Certainly the ambush of police killing sixteen in Kashgar on Monday was one. Maybe *The Independent* could have waited for an event like that to "drown out" the two-thousand-piece orchestra. Or maybe it's just a case of wishing protests into existence. Since when is that reporting?

Vancouver: Host to Winter 2010 Olympics ☆ David Luesink

It is interesting to note the similarities between criticisms of Olympic preparation in Vancouver and Beijing. Although the famously beautiful city of Vancouver is still two years away from hosting the winter Olympics in conjunction with the mountain village of Whistler, we are already running into the standard problems and criticisms familiar to Olympic planners of the past few decades. . . .

Although the Olympics claim to bring people together to celebrate the best in sport apart from politics, the clear links between corporate sponsorships and nationalism as a distraction from the increasing gap between rich and poor in countries like China and Canada are only too obvious in the difference between those who can afford tickets and those who must be content to watch events on television. As in Beijing, many Vancouver residents feel that the Olympics will only exacerbate the problem of housing prices for lower- and middle-income earners. The city government reneged on early promises for increasing social housing, so some critics claim there will be more homeless people than athletes for 2010.

Perhaps the most interesting Olympic-related story of the past few days in Vancouver is the announcement by the head of Vancouver's Olympic Committee that Vancouver's Olympics will not organize an international torch relay so they can avoid the kind of protests that marred China's relay in London and Paris. Perhaps that is as it should be, given the rather monumental job of overcoming the apathetic attitude of many Canadians toward Olympic events unrelated to gold medals in hockey.

Nobody (?) Likes a Spoiler ☆ Miri Kim

On July 31, SBS, a major South Korean broadcast network, aired a short clip showing details of the carefully guarded rehearsals for the opening ceremony of the 2008 Beijing Olympics. As the news (and the clip) spread on the Web, Chinese and Korean news, portal sites, and users on blogs and message boards expressed, to put it mildly, consternation. On popular Chinese portals like sina.com and 163.com, polls show that a large percentage of the respondents supported revoking the offending station's broadcasting privileges or investigating who bore responsibility for the leak and levying a heavy fine on the station.

Korean reactions on blogs and comments I saw ranged from dismay, embarrassment, and strong condemnation of SBS, to defensiveness and indifference, and even to excitement at the promise of the beauty of the opening ceremony captured by the footage. In what is one of the most tech-savvy societies in the world, South Korea's wired citizens, or "netizens," can be found at the cutting edge of any controversy, and the SBS incident is no exception. Furthermore, Korean users are just as if not more mindful of developments on Chinese-language sites than Internet users in predominantly English-speaking countries like the United States and, true to form, followed this issue very closely on both international and home fronts. . . .

The Korean media's coverage of the leak tended to reflect one subset of sentiments expressed by individual netizens in various discussions—regret and concern over the possible loss of respect from other nations at this perceived breach of media etiquette—in relation not only to China but to everyone who would participate and tune in to the Beijing Olympics.

China's economic growth in recent years has brought both opportunities and worries domestically and internationally. Many countries around the globe share a similar sort of anticipation where China is concerned, but particularly in South Korea, there is a widespread feeling that the Beijing Olympics may decisively raise China's international profile, perhaps to the effect of marginalizing its East Asian neighbors. There are precedents for the first notion—the Tokyo and Sapporo Olympics in 1964 and 1972 and the Seoul Olympics in 1988 also served to showcase the economic and political development of Japan and Korea on an international stage. . . .

A View from Aotearoa–New Zealand ☆ Paola Voci

There I was watching it all on TV like billions of others, an Italian "Sinologist" turned Chinese film and media researcher in the United States, who ultimately landed in New Zealand five years ago to teach about China in Dunedin, at the very bottom of Aotearoa's South Island. . . .

China is still strangely a remote country here. I say "strangely" not only because Prime Minister Helen Clark was the first "Western" leader to sign a free-trade agreement with China but also because Chinese are the first minority in Aotearoa and are likely to surpass Maori in numbers in the next few years. Yet multiculturalism and intercultural communications are still slow to grow in a country where *bi*culturalism, although officially embraced, is still very much contested. For instance, despite their growing presence—especially in Auckland—and their impact on national culture and economy, the Chinese in New Zealand have not yet found a strong diasporic voice in Kiwi culture (with very few exceptions in the world of the arts: the poet/writer Alison Wong or the filmmaker Roseanne Liang). In New Zealand media, Chinese and Asians more broadly are seldom visible. In other words, yesterday was quite an exceptional day, as China literally occupied national media as a mighty protagonist for several hours and the Olympics literally acted as a rush introductory course on Chinese culture. . . .

From the United States to China, by Way of Israel ☆ Shakhar Rahav

I have recently returned to my native Israel after a long sojourn in the United States. One of the things I have been looking for here is the way in which China is covered and portrayed in the Israeli media and what images of China arise in local discourse. . . .

There are no Israeli China correspondents who report from China on a regular basis. Yet the Olympics have of course prompted some independent coverage. Most talk centers on the sports and the competitors and also on "our athletes." But during the ceremony coverage some remarks betray a fascination with the host country and anxiety about it. . . . The machine-like precision of the opening ceremonies made some reporters anxious, and they spoke of the kind of state and regime that is necessary to produce such a highly disciplined performance (echoes of Nazi Germany and the Soviet Union to these reporters' minds). . . . And the funniest remark, covering one of the duller moments in the ceremony, was the TV anchor who remarked on the huge amount of restaurants in the city and then added, "they have a huge appetite." So it is, evidently—large countries produce large appetites.

And it is appetite that brings me to the most striking presentation of China that I have encountered here. A McDonald's ad campaign presents a George W. Bush look-alike, who in a commercial clip is surrounded by American-speaking security personnel dressed in suits and dark glasses who hurry the president to a McDonald's at an undisclosed location in Israel. After the president satisfies his urges by ordering a Big Mac, he offers a couple of Israeli children tickets to the Olympic Games in "Beijing." The American president consequently adorns posters in McDonald's and holds out two tempting tickets at the customer. And so, "America," the agent of globalization, the major force and cultural ideal, presents us with food and with entertainment. It is via the United States that we the customers are invited to China. The United States and China are thus mixed, both representing perhaps the larger international community and the "cool" of our globalized age. The images are enhanced by McDonald's clever agreements with the film *Kung Fu Panda* and with the Olympic Games it sponsors. McDonald's now opens the door to an internationalized China offering kung fu, noodles, and burgers.

America opens the door to China. It was perhaps an understanding of this wisdom that gave basketball player Yao Ming the symbolic role of flag bearer for the Chinese Olympic delegation. The athlete, whose stardom is derived from his success in the world of the American National Basketball Association, leads the symbol of national pride, and so America paves the road to China, even, perhaps, for Chinese.

From Lovers to Volunteers: China's National Anthem ☆ Liang Luo

Prior to the Olympic Games, the Chinese government and many ordinary Chinese citizens hoped that one particular song would make an impression on television viewers around the globe: "March of the Volunteers," the country's national anthem. It was played not only during the opening and closing ceremonies but also every time a Chinese athlete won a gold medal, and expectations ran high that this would happen a lot (as it did).

Even if international audiences grew accustomed to the sound of the tune, they were unlikely to know that the national anthem is actually a film's theme song that antedates the founding of the People's Republic of China (PRC) by a decade and a half, a film that was just as much about Chinese nationalism as it was about sentimental young lovers and their struggles in troubled times.

"March of the Volunteers" was designated the temporary national anthem for the PRC in 1949. This "temporary" national anthem was in use for more than a decade and a half, until the Cultural Revolution, when "East Is Red" and "Sailing the Seas Depends on the Helmsman" in reality replaced "March of the Volunteers" as national anthems. During the Cultural Revolution in the 1960s and 1970s, though the tune could still be played, the lyrics of "March of the Volunteers" were banned. After the Cultural Revolution, new lyrics were written in 1978, ending with the following lines: "We will for generations / Raise high Mao Zedong's banner / March on!"

I have no recollection whatsoever of the new lyrics. When I started elementary school around 1980 in a Sichuan mountain village, it may have been too backward to quickly adopt the recent changes in the lyrics of the national anthem. More likely, I was simply too young to take notice of such changes. After I transferred to a bigger city in 1984, the lyrics of the national anthem that I heard and sang at the weekly flag-raising ceremony were the original, which, I now know, was reestablished as the national anthem in 1982.

My personal encounter with the national anthem coincides with the first meaningful participation of the PRC in the Olympic Games, in 1984. When Xu Haifeng won the first gold medal in Los Angeles and "March of the Volunteers" was heard for the first time in the history of the Olympic Games, the PRC announced its Olympic dreams to the world.

Beijing's Olympic Weather: "Haze," Blue Skies, and Hot Air ☆ Alex Pasternack

Pictures cannot reflect reality.

—Du Shaozhong

It's really good for everybody . . . to keep such clean air, that's fantastic.

—Haile Gebrselassie

Ethiopian running legend Haile Gebrselassie may have been the only person to curse the skies in Beijing on August 24, 2008. Five months earlier, the reigning world record holder in the marathon decided to pull out of the event over concerns that the city's choking smog would trigger his asthma. As the International Olympic Committee (IOC) had done in private, the runner called on China publicly to address the smog for the sake of athletes and its own citizens. "I was here in February, I didn't see no blue sky," the Ethiopian runner told a Reuters reporter at the Games.

But on the morning of August 24, Gebrselassie gazed up at a rich blue sky, capping Beijing's least polluted month in a decade. Later that day, another runner would complete the marathon in record Olympic time—but not faster than Gebreselassie's record. "Since I came here everything is perfect." He added with a chuckle, "They should tell us."

For years, Beijing officials did tell the world that its skies would be blue for the Games. Reports said the air was cleaner than ever, and, in the spirit of banning things (protests, spitting, and unofficial cultural events were nixed), the city announced it would implement a sweeping antismog policy. A two-month stoppage at construction sites and polluting factories, along with vehicle restrictions that would cut traffic in half, coupled with attempts to trigger rainfall, promised to banish smog for the Games.

But Gebrselassie might be excused for being skeptical. Aside from the choking, gray skies that the Ethiopian runner saw over the capital when he first visited Beijing and again on the day of the opening ceremony, keen observers had other reasons to be suspicious. For the years and months leading up to the Games, official pollution data, propagandistic pronouncements, and temporary fixes left a portrait of pollution as murky as the skies themselves.

August 2008 will likely be remembered as one of Beijing's least polluted months. But for smog watchers, it was also one of the city's most unpredictable and confusing, too. In July, a series of sudden thunderstorms, reportedly triggered by the government's arsenal of rainmaking rockets and abetted by cold fronts, led to a rash of clear skies. When the smog returned in full force four days before the opening, the government made an announcement that betrayed its desperation: a possible "emergency contingency plan" would extend restrictions on cars and factories.

But at a press conference one week before the Games, Du Shaozhong, deputy director of the Beijing municipal bureau of environmental protection, used another tactic to disperse the smog: rhetorical alchemy. "Clouds and haze are not pollution," he told foreign journalists following the smog story. "This kind of weather is a natural phenomenon. It has nothing to do with pollution. If we were sitting in a bathhouse, there'd be a lot of steam. But no pollution." He insisted that photographs that purported to show smog were misleading and, echoing the party's insistence on scientific development, urged the media to "analyz[e] the data scientifically."

The IOC backed him up. Arne Ljungqvist, chairman of the IOC's medical commission, said, "The mist in the air that we see . . . is not a feature of pollution primarily but a feature of evaporation and humidity. We do have a communication problem here."

To be sure, a foreign press corps looking for "gotcha" moments has been eager to underscore Beijing's pollution problem with ugly images. Beijing's air is not always terrible. On some days, the ancient city's streets pulsate with life under heartwarming blue skies. The relative rarity of these gorgeous days—and the prospect of perhaps more to come—gives them an added beauty that a similar day in New York cannot claim.

But the "steam" that director Du referred to was, in fact, caused by pollution. A few days later, the BBC's own analysis found that Beijing was breathing in air with a PM10 concentration of 269 micrograms (mcg) per cubic meter (m³)—168 percent above the standard of the World Health Organization (WHO) for short-term exposure, a smog level the Beijing government once called "unhealthy." The government's typical insistence that "there's nothing to see here" came true on opening day, when smog shrouded the Olympic green beneath a veil of white. At moments, the city and even the massive Bird's Nest stadium practically vanished before my eyes.

Since 1998, when Beijing was ranked as having the third-worst air quality in a global ranking of 157 cities, the city has made great strides in reducing pollution sources, if not pollution levels. The government has sought to phase out high-emission vehicles, transitioned much of the inner city from coal-fired to electric heat, and deployed a fleet of clean natural gas buses. It has also succeeded in getting cars off the roads in the world's grandest antipollution experiment, thereby reducing emissions in the city by 20 percent, the government says. To clean up the city for the Olympics, it says it has spent $17.6 billion on environmental projects—projects it says will leave a permanent mark on the city.

But longer-term and systematic issues have not been addressed. There remains considerable debate, for instance, over the sources of the city's pollution. Is it the automobiles that in recent years have hit the city's roads at a rate of one thousand per day? The volatile organic compounds that small factories exhale into the atmosphere? Many point to the high emissions of old trucks—sometimes equivalent to that of twenty new cars—that have lately been banned from the city center. Others single out the pollution and dust that blows in from neighboring provinces. Even straw-burning farmers in the suburbs have been a popular culprit.

In 2007, exasperated environmental officials announced they were launching a long-awaited survey of pollution sources to get to the bottom of the problem. But like many other orders from the top, finding and rooting out sources of smog faces an uphill struggle against China's biggest enemies, including corruption, an official emphasis on economic growth, and the usual accomplice to many of the country's ills: censorship.

In the tense lead-up to the Games, the air was thick with chicanery. Du Shaozhong's doublespeak—this insistence that pollution was haze—is not a rarity but rather the norm. In 1997, for instance, a new term was coined in official documents to describe the city's pollution. The old term, *wuran*, was too descriptive; *wumai*, or "fog haze," sounds better.

But no euphemism in Beijing's green vocabulary may be as fraught as "blue sky" day. Launched as part of a pollution rating system in 1998, the "blue sky" designation has nothing to do with the color of the sky. Rather, it is given to any day, blue skies or not, with an API, or Air Pollution Index, reading of 100 or lower. To be more specific, that's when the air contains 150 mcg/m³ of fine dust or less.

But this threshold for a "blue sky" day is still three times more polluted than WHO's short-term exposure standard for fine dust (also known as PM10): a concentration of 20 mcg/m³. That means that a "blue sky" day isn't just lacking in blue skies: it's not necessarily a good day for breathing either. Even days with actual blue skies can be dangerous because of ozone (O_3), a colorless gas with a harmful effect on the lungs. Still, Beijing doesn't release figures for ozone.

Even more worrisome is that when Beijing was bidding for the Olympics in 2000, the national government lowered—lowered—its standards for ozone and for nitrogen dioxide (NO_2). When I asked Mr. Du about this, he responded that NO_2 and O_3 standards were raised "in accordance with Chinese law." He did not explain why Beijing does not release figures about ozone.

To clear that up, a "blue sky" day isn't necessarily blue and, by WHO standards, can still be heavily polluted. Meanwhile, a day with actual blue skies and even low particulate levels can also be polluted because of ozone. But to most Beijing citizens and visitors enjoying a "blue sky" day, these fine details, like fine particles, go largely unnoticed.

If the name is misleading, its usage can be much worse. In 2007, the government met its "blue sky" day target of 246 because of an abundance of days when the API reading was exactly 100. Setting aside the question of whether these days could even be considered healthy, more than a few people simply wondered if some pollution readings weren't shaved off the top to meet the official goal.

This number massaging piqued the interest of Steve Andrews, an environmental researcher in Beijing on a Princeton-in-Asia fellowship. After some digging into official pollution data, Andrews found that the environmental bureau wasn't just widening the goalposts. It was moving them. Literally. Officials had relocated smog monitoring stations to areas away from roads and to places outside the city, creating the impression that pollution was decreasing.

In a paper published in *Environmental Research Letters*, Andrews found that if the same monitoring station locations used from 1998 to 2005 continued to be used in 2006, thirty-eight "blue sky" days would have exceeded the "blue sky" standard. He went on to pick apart Beijing's claim that pollution levels had dropped between 1998 and 2007, concluding that the improvements, as measured in "blue sky" days, were due to "irregularities in the monitoring and reporting of air quality and not to less polluted air." As he told me then, "The impact of the new monitoring stations in Huairou and Changping on 'improving' Beijing's air quality for this year cannot be overstated." (Andrews's study focused only on Beijing, but it raises questions about the monitoring of pollution in other Chinese cities where the "blue sky" rating is used, including Chengdu, Shanghai, Nanjing, and Guangzhou.)

When I and other reporters asked Mr. Du repeatedly why Beijing had moved its monitoring stations, he would switch between condemning Andrews's findings or mumbling something about "improvements" to the monitoring network. Numbers were not being fudged, he said, though he did concede that "we need to enhance observation and enforcement and supervision" of the air-quality data.

But the readings released during the Olympics left much to be desired. The first few smoggy days of the Games, for instance, government-issued numbers on pollution would not only hover suspiciously below the "blue sky" cutoff but also vary wildly from analyses made at populous areas.

On the day of opening ceremonies of August 8, the official API was a "blue sky" 94, or a PM10 concentration of 138 mcg/m^3. That afternoon the BBC measured PM10 concentration of 156 mcg/m^3—just above the "blue sky" cutoff of 150. Later that day, the Associated Press measured a PM10 concentration of 345 mcg/m^3 at mid-afternoon at the Olympic green. Two days later, when the Beijing Environmental Protection Bureau (BJEPB) reported a PM10 concentration of 114 mcg/m^3, the Associated Press and BBC reported PM10 concentrations of 278 and 604 mcg/m^3, respectively. Even in the months after the Games, the BJEPB declined to release details about what was in the air in August, hampering efforts by researchers to verify the number of "blue sky" days or to help target pollution sources down the road.

One morning in the middle of August, as the Games began to hit their stride, Beijing awoke to a dreamy blue sky that would, with the exception of a few thunderstorms, persist for weeks. Pollution indices dropped to almost unheard-of levels. The government's antismog measures, one of the grandest environmental experiments in history, seemed to have worked. Intense debate about the future of the car policy ensued on the Internet—commuters liked it, car owners didn't—and the government eventually announced it would continue an amended version of the policy for a six-month trial period. Each day, a fifth of the city's cars would be taken off the roads. "Beijing will be built into a livable city," Minister Du said at the close of the Games.

But as crucial as restricting cars may be in helping Beijing breathe easier, the use of such a blunt instrument represents a failure in Beijing's multipronged fight against pollution. Like a recovering drug addict, the city will need to first come clean about its problem before it can get clean.

The city's pollution problem is so substantial, researchers say, that even "quitting" cars cold turkey has a limited impact on the pollution. More important is something the government cannot control (at least not completely): weather patterns. Kenneth Rahn, an atmospheric scientist who has studied Beijing's pollution problem, has concluded that because of polluting factories, coal use, and weak emission standards in areas south and west of Beijing, strong winds and rain are the only way to flush out the city's smog. "They better start praying to the Mongolian weather gods," he told me a few months before the Games. In August, Beijing did indeed enjoy a cold front that washed into the city just after the opening ceremony.

Some officials did in fact pray to the gods—but in the hopes that rain would not hit Beijing. (When an official from the Beijing Meteorological Bureau was asked in 2007 what the chances were of rain during the opening ceremony, he ended his answer uncharacteristically for a Communist Party official: "God bless Beijing.") In an ironic but symbolic twist, the city's need for smog-clearing rain ran up against a pledge to keep the Games dry.

Indeed, on the damp, smog-smacked night of the opening ceremony, as thousands of fireworks ringed the stadium, an onslaught of over one thousand rainmaking rockets were containing thunderstorms in the far outskirts of the city. Untouched by rainfall, the show shimmered in front of a TV audience of millions. To those of us inside the stadium, in spite of the spectacle, the night was weighed down with humidity and smog.

As the rockets were slamming clouds far out of sight, the opening ceremony reached its middle section. In a segment titled "Nature," children painted a landscape at center stage and recited a poem as *taiqi* masters twirled around them.

> The air is warming. The ice cap is melting . . . We plant trees.
> We sow seeds. The earth turns green. The sky is blue indeed . . .

For all of Beijing's "scientific" emphasis on eliminating sources of pollution, it was a drastic last-ditch policy, weather patterns, and perhaps a bit of luck that ultimately cleared the air for the Games. Meanwhile, a Potemkin village campaign to varnish the city's green image for the Olympic period foiled more substantial improvements. If the city hopes to extend the legacy of the "green" Olympics, it needn't depend on luck and blunt instruments. It needs to be honest in its reporting of pollution rather than leaving everyone guessing. To borrow the words of would-be Olympic champion Mr. Gebrselassie, "They should tell us."

Beijing Soundscape: Volunteerism, Internationalism, Heroism, and Patriotism at the 2008 Games ☆ Daniel Beekman

Beijing's Olympic campaign impressed and enraged, altered and preserved, inspired and imprisoned. Then, at eight in the evening on August 8, the 2008 Games finally began.

Sitting in the stands, I listened to dunks, spikes, and splashes. A genuine appreciation for sport gripped China.

Only in flashes—Lebron James's chatty Chinese grandma, calls for Messi at Worker's Stadium, a dismayed Bird's Nest, a marathon through silent streets—did the din from Beijing's Olympic campaign penetrate.

Powerful and press-credentialed Chinese flocked August 8 to the Bird's Nest—a spectacular new national stadium. Millions settled around television sets blaring success for China.

I squeezed onto a subway car, squeezed up a shopping mall escalator, and squeezed into a sweaty, flag-waving throng to watch the opening ceremonies.

When 2,008 drummers first appeared on the Wangfujing pedestrian street jumbotron, thousands of college students cheered.

Sitting cross-legged in the street, climbing slender eucalyptus, swaying into "Go China!" chants, they drenched Wangfujing—east of the Forbidden City—with patriotism.

Chinese music, then dance, calligraphy, and kung fu—director Zhang Yimou's spectacle won the throng's approval. We heard "Ode to the Motherland" and "March of the Volunteers." A hundred foreign heads of state smiled—or attempted to smile.

Beijing's Olympic campaign I'd grown to know. Beijing's Olympic campaign I'd devoured in a thousand snarky newspaper columns. Beijing's Olympic campaign I'd discussed and debated for nearly a year.

Beijing's Olympic campaign—reflecting and regenerating all the hopes, confusions, and fears ever born between East and West.

"People in the West don't understand China," a Beijing college student and Olympic volunteer told me in July. "I visited Switzerland and someone asked me if all Chinese still rode horses and wore robes. So you see, I can't wait for the Games to begin."

Beijing's Olympic campaign shot forward in 2001 when, encouraged by an economic explosion, the International Olympic Committee awarded China its first Games.

Oligarchs, shopkeepers, and laborers from Guangzhou to Harbin celebrated the Games as China's chance to bury that insulting colonialist moniker—"The Sick Man of East Asia."

Beijing's Olympic campaign would reveal a prosperous, approachable China—a gentle superpower. To that end, trees were planted. Skyscrapers constructed. Pop singers enlisted. Propaganda plastered.

Students at Yangfangdian primary school invented a chant: "East, west, south, north, middle / Olympic Games in our hearts / Jump for development / Discover so much happiness."

A week before the Games, I visited an archaeology exhibit dedicated to *Homo erectus pekinesis*, a prehistoric creature nicknamed "Peking Man." The exhibit appeared on Olympic tourist maps.

"Of course Peking Man would be happy for China," a staffer said. "Why? Now China is hosting the Olympics. Now China is strong."

When human rights activists from the United States and Europe challenged Beijing on behalf of exiled Tibetans and jailed journalists, many Chinese panicked.

"I hope the Olympics aren't boycotted," an elderly man said. "We've waited a hundred years for these Olympics and we need them."

Of course, the Games are an international affair; Beijing couldn't dodge foreign criticism regarding regulatory graft, property rights, or air pollution.

"Hosting the Olympics is like opening your window," remarked a tattooed Chinese rapper ahead of the Games. "When the wind picks up, you're covered in dust."

Beijing's Olympic campaign, in contrast to the 2008 Games, wasn't about sports—it was about ideas. It was about environmental protection, national sovereignty, and social harmony.

In June, after Beijing banned thin plastic shopping bags—an effort to reduce "white pollution"—I spoke with a middle-aged woman outside my neighborhood grocery.

"We brought our own bags today!" she crowed. "We want to protect the environment. We want to host a successful Games."

In March and April, many Chinese responded angrily to ethnic violence in Tibet.

"If you are Chinese, if you are a warm-blooded youth, let's support Beijing's Olympics and oppose the Tibetan splittists!" read a post to *Xiaonei*, an online, intercampus social networking platform similar to Facebook.

One frigid January morning, I approached two elderly women resting in a Beijing park.

"We're so happy for China. Before 1949 we were poor. We didn't have food, clothing or shelter. Now we'll host the Games and it's all thanks to Chairman Mao."

If he were alive in 2008, I wondered aloud, what would Mao Zedong—the Communist revolutionary—think of Beijing's Olympics?

"He'd love them, of course. In 2001, when it was announced that China had won the right to host the Games, we all cried. President Hu [Jintao] and Prime Minister Wen [Jiabao] gave wonderful speeches. Our leaders care about us—the common people."

I spent nine months digging at Beijing's Olympic campaign as a researcher and reporter. But until August 8, the athletes seemed an abstraction.

Now here they were, up on Wangfujing's jumbotron beaming, stepping into the Bird's Nest fleet of foot and strong of limb. Here were the 2008 Games.

Marvelous sports achievements marked the next sixteen days and elegant athletic action. I tuned into trampoline and handball on Chinese Central Television (CCTV).

Jamaican sprinter Usain Bolt and American swimmer Michael Phelps led an extraordinary crop of Olympians to forty-three new world records.

Bolt crashed the track in Beijing, overwhelming past medalists in the one hundred and two hundred meters. I caught his breakaway dash and flashy celebration from the smoky, dark depths of my favorite Internet bar.

Phelps won—and won won won won won won—coolly earning eight gold medals and adoration throughout China.

"I'm in love with Michael Phelps," a young Chinese programmer admitted. "He's a champion."

China handled all comers in badminton, a prime-time East Asian sport that Americans reserve for family reunions. Chinese paddlers won eight of eight possible gold medals in table tennis.

The People's Republic nearly swept diving as well. A twenty-year-old Aussie, Matthew Mitcham, ambushed ten-meter-platform favorite Zhou Luxin on a sparkling final dive. Still, China won seven out of eight medals in diving.

Male gymnast Zou Kai struck gold in the floor exercise and horizontal bars, bounding precisely, chalky, taut forearms smeared with blood from repeated WHAP WHAP blows to the bars.

It was pocket weightlifter Chen Xiexia, however, who stole sobs from Chinese patriots. Chen "clean-jerked" her way to stardom on August 9, nabbing the Games' first gold medal. Her cherub face and stirring squats headed CCTV montages from then on.

Chinese archer Zhang Juanjuan snapped South Korea's twenty-four-year monopoly on women's individual golds. Even opening ceremonies flag bearer Yao Ming won applause; his basketball squad beat Germany, 59 to 55.

China's gold medal landslide—fifty-one total—stunned Olympic fans around the world—fans unprepared for the stunning success of Project 119, a government-financed push into medal-heavy sports like rowing, swimming, track, and sailing.

"China won't win the overall medal count in 2008," one of my Chinese friends predicted in April. "We don't have many great runners or swimmers. Our bodies are suited for tumbling."

On August 14, unheralded Liu Zige surged through the pool at Beijing's bubbly National Aquatics Center—the "Water Cube"—to claim China's first-ever swimming gold.

I regret missing Liu's performance; I wasn't on hand for a single gold medal event in Beijing. I hadn't the luck or the money.

Beijing's Olympic organizers did raffle away cheap seats. I scored a pair of women's water polo tickets for sixty yuan—nine U.S. bucks. But truckloads of tickets disappeared through corporate back doors. Magnates clamored to see Roger Federer and Ronaldinho. Resale values soared.

"No tickets, no problem," my neighbors assured me. "We'll watch the Games on TV—cheap, convenient and comfortable."

Millions of working-class Beijingers opted out of the ticket crush altogether; assuming high prices, assuming dirty deals, they never applied.

Fittingly, my first live encounter with 2008 Games arrived via *guanxi*—social connections.

A Chinese friend and Olympic volunteer summoned me through slanting rain to men's volleyball at the Capital Gymnasium. Bulgaria versus China was already under way when I claimed her extra ticket.

I quickly warmed to the Bulgarians' implausible hops. The stands resounded with "*Zhongguo jiayou!*"—"Go China!" or literally "Add gas!" Everyone enjoyed the "wave."

It was a doubleheader—Germany versus Poland in the nightcap. But China lost, and thousands clambered to exit.

A few rows of Chinese remained—grandmas and grandpas in yellow T-shirts, slapping plastic "boom sticks" to the rhythm of Beijing's Olympic campaign. "Civilized Workers Cheering Squad," their shirts proclaimed in Chinese and English.

A squad member turned to me.

"Are you American?" Ms. Zhu asked. "Are you a basketball fan? China is playing your Dream Team tonight."

Ms. Zhu then rattled off the starting lineup of the United States: *Zhan Musi* (Lebron James), *Ke Bi* (Kobe Bryant), *Ji De* (Jason Kidd), *Huo Huade* (Dwight Howard), and *Kameiluo Andongni* (Carmelo Anthony).

Ms. Zhu had spent the China-versus-Bulgaria match in a state of perpetual agitation. Now Poland's giants went to work on Germany, and, Chinese flag folded neatly in her lap, Ms. Zhu relaxed.

She sat with her work unit, smiling for newspaper photographers. In exchange for free tickets, Ms. Zhu and her coworkers had promised to generate Olympic atmosphere all night—proud proletarians, mobilized in support of Beijing's image.

Chinese volunteered by the thousands after a devastating earthquake rocked Sichuan province in May. Some Westerners praised China's relief effort, forecasting the growth of a healthy civil society.

Others scoffed, arguing that relief workers were conscripted from the Communist Party and Communist Youth League, as in Mao's day.

As for Beijing's Olympic campaign? Nearly 1 million college students served as 2008 Games volunteers. Some dumped summer internships to join the corps under pressure from professors and party officials.

Was Ms. Zhu a volunteer or a conscript? How populist was Beijing's Olympic campaign?

"This has been fun," remarked Ms. Zhu. "But I wish we were watching *Wei De* (Dwayne Wade) and Yao Ming play instead. They're great."

Expectations of change characterized Beijing's Olympic campaign. Diplomats of the International Olympic Committee (IOC) argued that a strong dose of Olympism would transform China into a liberal, humane state.

Hu, Wen, and Olympic chief Liu Qi promised that the 2008 Games would catapult China's service industry into the twenty-first century, bolster high-tech investment, and resuscitate Beijing's sick ecosystem.

Most Beijingers guessed the Games would change Western perceptions of China as starving, Maoist, and culturally isolated.

Many non-Chinese tendered a similar argument, predicting that foreign athletes, organizers, and journalists would force China to internationalize. Olympic watchers on both sides imagined the Games would expand on Deng Xiaoping's "Open Door" doctrine.

In fact, internationalization was a visible feature of Beijing's Olympic campaign.

In January, I visited Huajiadian Experimental Primary School. Students there formed a mock IOC. I watched them present on German beer, Korean architecture, and the staple crops of North America.

Even at an unheated school for the children of migrant workers—farmers turned urban laborers who number 5 million in Beijing alone—students drilled for the global economy. "England, Brazil, America!" they shouted in unison, bundled up like marshmallows.

"The [Chinese] government has really pushed Olympic education," Dr. Susan Brownell, an American anthropologist, told me last Christmas Day. "In the context of Beijing, Olympic education has meant training China's next generation to be international.

"What does 'international' mean?" Brownell continued. "Good question."

Fast-forward to August 13, in Beijing. Climbing carefully past Colombians and Italians, Worker's Stadium beer slopping onto my hand. Serbia-versus-Argentina men's soccer and kickoff approaching. Jazzy West African trumpets setting the mood.

One in three Chinese fans sporting an Argentina jersey; *qiumi* ("ball fans") go wild for soccer's perennial powers. The crowd chanting "MESSI MESSI MESSI," desperate to see Argentina's wonder-boy striker play.

For the South Americans, a meaningless match. Winners against Côte d'Ivoire and Australia, already through to the Olympic tournament's second round.

Messi resting on the sidelines. With twenty minutes to go, the crowd turning on Argentina. Argentine defenders flicking balls backward to a smatter, then a chorus of boos.

I heard Beijing's Olympic campaign fulfilled August 13 when Argentina held possession and Worker's Stadium jeered. I heard internationalization, when Serbia thrust forward to cheers.

Here were Chinese grade-schoolers and grandpas alongside Nigerian trumpeters, screaming for a Serb goal. The 2008 Games may or may not have changed China. Regardless, China on August 13 sounded decidedly international.

Arguably, Liu Xiang led Beijing's Olympic campaign. Liu Qi organized the 2008 Games. Aging diplomat He Zhenliang helped China win the right to host them. But handsome hurdler Liu was the campaign's face from 2004 on.

For Liu, the 2008 Games were a different story. I witnessed his fall from grace and heard Beijing's Olympic campaign deflate temporarily below a stunned Bird's Nest audience.

Liu won a gold medal for China at the 2004 Summer Olympics in Athens—racing 110 meters in 12.91 seconds. Among runners, he remains the country's only Olympic gold medalist.

Overnight, Liu became an advertising and media darling, charming reporters and consumers alike. In early 2008, beaming Liu Xiang billboards endorsed Nike, Cadillac, and Coca-Cola. Yili, a Chinese dairy corporation, signed Liu at 10 million yuan (U.S.$1.5 million) per year.

This spring, the *Wall Street Journal*'s Geoffrey Fowler asked, "Where have you gone, Lei Feng?" declaring Liu "a new breed of Chinese hero: the global champion."

"Traditionally, hero making has been the job of the [Chinese] state," Fowler wrote, "and most state heroes are idealized former leaders and soldiers who exemplified the Communist ideals. But in an era of commercialized media, China's emerging icons are looking less like heroes of the state than heroes of the people."

Lei Feng was a solider of the revolution and China's favorite son during the 1960s. Born an orphan in 1940, Lei died tragically in 1962. A reliable soldier—noble, hardworking, and helpful—he became a role model.

Liu Xiang, born in 1983 to a truck driver and a waitress, competed at high jump until his state-sponsored sports school "gave up on him." That's when Liu switched to hurdles, breezing past local competition.

According to his coach, Liu was initially an awful hurdler but determined. He won the 110-meter hurdles at Beijing's 2001 World University Games. In 2007 he briefly held track and field's triple crown—world record holder, world champion, and Olympic gold medalist in the same event.

Liu, whose given name means "take flight," dedicated the 2004 gold to his grandmother. In April, Chinese youngsters voted Liu "most popular athlete." He beat out Yao and soccer's David Beckham.

Few athletes have shouldered so much pressure, however. The country expected Liu to repeat in 2008. These Games were China's Games—winning in Beijing mattered. If he won, relief. If he didn't . . .

"Silver? It means nothing here; you might as well finish last," Chinese rowing coach Igor Grinko, a Russian, told the *New York Times* this summer.

"To see Liu win is the dream of my entire family," one fan told the *Beijing News* last year. "We are confident that he'll lead the pack and make our long wait worthwhile."

When the moment finally arrived—a first-round heat on August 18—Liu didn't win, didn't lose. He pulled up lame on a competitor's false start and walked away. Hours later, television cameras captured teenage girls sobbing.

But inside the Bird's Nest, I saw no one react that way. I saw people stand to stare at the track. They stared hard—hard so that Liu would know to return, so hard he'd have to run.

"Liu is China's pride," a retired schoolteacher lectured me. "We Chinese all love him. We tell our kids—look at Liu Xiang. Work to improve your body. Do your best. Practice. Don't worry what other people say."

An injured Achilles' tendon robbed China of the summer's most anticipated event. The 110-meter final was supposed to represent peaceful competition *and* a resurgent China, the 2008 Games *and* Beijing's Olympic campaign.

I didn't hear sobs. I heard purses zip and fathers cough. I heard short, paralyzed breaths. I heard the Bird's Nest empty.

"Oh no!" whispered a young fan, shaking his head, "Oh no!"

Purportedly, NBC captured Phelps's power, Zou's poise, and China's ancient beauty. So what was different, experiencing the 2008 Games live? What did television viewers in the United States miss?

Beijing's silent marathon, perhaps.

It was August 24—the last day of the Games. Energized for the men's basketball title—America versus Spain—I jumped out of bed.

An eight-lane street lay between me and my destination, the Water Stone café. Getting across Zhongguancun was always difficult. Now barricades blocked the street's pedestrian *tianqiao* ("sky bridges"). I waded through a curbside crowd.

"What's going on?" I asked a policeman.

"*Malasong,*" he replied. Marathon.

I decided to wait for the front-runners. Ten minutes later they began to glide past. I clapped, excited. "*Jiayou!*"—"Add gas!" I shouted in Chinese. "You can do it!"

But something was wrong. My neighbors weren't clapping. They weren't shouting. The pajama-clad restaurateur. The cyclist in frightening stilettos. The silver-haired phlegm machine. The chunky twins from next door.

My Chinese neighbors ignored a pair of lithe Kenyans, a Russian, an Egyptian. I felt angry. These were the globe's fittest, toughest athletes—they deserved our applause and attention.

"Why aren't you cheering?" I spun a middle-aged man around.

"We're cheering . . . or we will. Our Chinese runners still haven't come."

Seething, I stalked away from Zhongguancun and the 2008 Olympic marathon. Then it hit me—why my neighbors weren't clapping or shouting.

Instead, they were listening. My Chinese neighbors were straining to hear the patter of Chinese feet flying down Zhongguancun.

In their silence I recognized Beijing's Olympic campaign, a seven-year lesson in volunteerism, internationalism, and heroism but most of all patriotism.

Chapter 10

China after the Games

AFTER THE OLYMPICS, WHAT?

Nicolai Volland

In the run-up to the Summer Games, China has been placed in an undeclared state of emergency. Special regulations affect almost every aspect of daily life. Taxi drivers had to brush up their English and study brochures that explained how to be courteous to foreigners. Vehicle traffic in the capital will be reduced for the time of the Games, and industrial production is being brought to a standstill across vast regions of northern China in order to ensure blue skies over Beijing and reduce the city's notorious smog.

Travelers from abroad as well as foreign residents in Beijing had to deal with drastic new visa rules: embassies issue no more multiple entry visas, foreign students can no longer extend their visas and must leave the country, and tourists must now produce return air tickets and hotel reservations to obtain their visas.

Restrictions on civil rights for Chinese are more worrying. Repression of human rights activists and lawyers has increased while Beijing has issued orders to the provinces to keep any forms of social unrest under control and stem the flow of petitioners seeking redress in Beijing. Internet and press controls are likely to be stepped up in early August.

Chinese and foreigners alike have accepted the heightened degree of control with some grumbling. The common perception of the new measures as temporary in nature, lasting just a few weeks, makes them acceptable. However, will things go back to what they were after the end of the Games?

The stricter handling of local forms of resistance has enhanced the power of the central state, and the Chinese Communist Party will be unlikely to give away its increased leverage. There is also little to be gained for the party-state from easing controls in the area of civil liberties, and the forms of repression we witness currently might, at best, be allowed to fizzle out. It is likely, thus, that the central government will find it desirable to perpetuate at least some of the "emergency" powers gained in the name of a one-time event.

Posted 7/10/2008 at 04:02:00 PM

Pundits were eager to predict the many ways the Beijing Olympics would change China. Some thought that after Beijing's fourteen days there would be greater openness, better international communication, and more respect for China. Pessimists saw increased security restrictions, crackdowns on dissidents, and rising nationalism. In fact, the most immediate outcome was China weariness. China commentators and scholars ran themselves ragged in the lead-up to the Games and, after the closing ceremonies, retreated for a much-needed rest. In the United States, as election news and stories about the financial crisis dominated the news cycle, yet another big 2008 China story—about tainted milk and tens of thousands of sickened babies—hardly cracked the front pages.

But, as contributors noted at China Beat *and elsewhere, the Olympic Games had important implications for China and the world. For one, several contributors (see, for instance, the piece by James Farrer in this chapter) noted that Chinese people and those elsewhere in the world viewed very different Games. Farrer, writing from Japan, analyzes the conflict between the unifying vision of the Games and the often nationalistic tenor of Olympic coverage.*

Below this tension, there were further questions about Beijing's sincere belief in the ideals—harmony, equality, fraternalism—mouthed during the Olympics. As Pallavi Aiyar notes in this chapter, the rights of many Chinese had been sublimated to the goal of getting the Olympics on track. It is still unclear if the government will find other national reasons to justify intrusive regulations on things like urban development and security checks or if the government will slowly peel back the Olympic infringements.

One Bed, Different Dreams: The Beijing Olympics as Seen in Tokyo ☆ James Farrer

Mo Bangfu, a Chinese columnist writing for the liberal *Asahi Shimbun*, used his weekly column the day before the closing ceremonies to award the Beijing Olympics a symbolic "silver medal" for its overall organization (August 23, 2008). Despite accusations of fakery, the opening ceremonies and the Olympic volunteers both deserve "gold medals," as do the ordinary Beijing residents and migrant workers who had to put up with massive everyday inconveniences.

The government, however, deserves a "disqualification" for not allowing any demonstrations in the designated demonstration areas, for restricting the access of normal citizens to the Olympic venues, and also "poor marks" for the large numbers of empty seats at events. As a whole, Mo suggests, the Beijing Olympics deserve a "silver medal," perhaps summing up the generally positive appraisal of some of the more liberal media voices in Japan. Conservative papers, however, gave the Beijing Olympics much lower marks.

Seeing the Olympics as a watershed event, Japanese commentators have speculated about a "post-Olympic" China, and their prognoses are generally darker than the more optimistic views in the U.S. media. Influenced by Japan's own postwar experience, columnists ask whether the Beijing Olympics will serve the purpose of integrating China into global society, in the same way achieved by the former Axis powers in the postwar Rome, Tokyo, and Munich Olympics and later by Seoul in 1988. Most answer negatively. Despite a consensus "silver medal" for a brilliant (if somewhat flawed) show, the Olympics were regarded as a political failure by most Japanese commentators, at least when judged by democratic norms. More darkly, some conservative papers suggest, the Olympics should be seen as a great "success" for the legitimacy of authoritarian rule in China.

In a front-page summary of the impact of the Olympics on China, the conservative *Sankei Shimbun* suggested that the Olympics were a celebration of dictatorship and the effectiveness of totalitarian government, "a celebration turning its back on democratization" (August 25, 2008). The article suggests that the Beijing Olympics should be compared to neither the 1964 Tokyo Olympics nor the 1988 Seoul Olympics, both of which led to greater democratization and the integration of Japan and Korea into the club of democratic states. Rather, the editors conclude, China's Olympics may in retrospect look more like the 1980 Moscow Olympics, which signaled political isolation and the internal disintegration of the Soviet Union. Like many conservative voices in Japan, the *Sankei* emphasizes the fragile state of the Chinese economy, predicting much bigger troubles, even a "hard landing" for China's "bubble economy" (August 25, 2008).

Even the more liberal *Asahi Shimbun* described the opening ceremony as a "political show for the party leadership" (August 9, 2008), pointing to the important role played by Communist Party leaders in every public event leading up to the Olympics. The article claims that in every city passed through on the torch relay, the first torch bearer was always the local party secretary. As the Games opened, *Asahi* guest columnist and liberal academic Fujiwara Koichi judged Zhang Yimou's elaborate opening ceremony as a "vacuous" political exercise. He writes, "It's a sad sight to see this brilliant director expending his talents on this exaggerated display of tradition and political propaganda."

Despite the emptiness of its political slogans, Fujiwara continues, it was important that the world participated in the Games in order to build bridges with the Chinese people, who can bring about real change in their government (*Asahi Shimbun*, August 24, 2008). The closing Olympic editorial in the *Asahi Shimbun*, although more moderate in tone, also called for political reform in China and asked the Chinese state to give some substance to the "One World, One Dream" motto by joining the global society in the fight against global warming (August 25, 2008).

Much of this criticism mirrors the English-language media, but there are some differences. Japanese media reports seem at the same time more critical and less condescending than their U.S. counterparts. Japanese seem to expect more of their giant neighbor but are also far more fearful and skeptical of it.

This dynamic is especially evident in the profound mistrust in Japan's mainstream media toward Chinese political leadership and the insistence by some conservative Japanese commentators that China is headed for a severe economic downturn. These pessimistic economic predictions are significant if only because Japan is the largest foreign investor in China, which is now Japan's largest export market. Of course, Japan's reports also say a great deal about Japan's own obsessions, including concerns about Japan's declining vitality and status in comparison with its increasingly powerful and affluent "neighboring country" (a term frequently used in Japanese media).

"One World, One Dream" or "One Games, Different Dreams"?

The motto of the Chinese Olympics was "One World, One Dream" (*tongyige shijie, tongyige mengxiang*). But it might be more appropriate to have named the Olympics after another expression, "one bed, different dreams" (*tongchuang yimeng*), a Chinese idiom used to refer to two people sharing a bed but dreaming different dreams. Looking at the hypernationalist coverage of the Olympics in the United States and China, Olympic historian David Wallechinsky (according to a *Los Angeles Times* blog) describes "parallel games," in which Americans and Chinese were essentially watching their own teams perform in highly selective national media coverage. But this "one games, different dreams" phenomenon is not limited to the hypernationalistic U.S. and Chinese media. Japan's media also focused almost exclusively on the events that featured participation by Japanese athletes.

The Olympics seen on Japanese television were fundamentally Japan's Olympics, just as the Olympics seen by Americans and Chinese were fundamentally nationalist versions of the same global event. It seems that even small countries are not immune to Olympic nationalism. A report in a *New York Times* blog (August 23, 2008) documents the "gold medal fever" in several countries around the world, including Mongolia, India, Indonesia, and Jamaica. Of course, some of the superstar accomplishments—such as Michael Phelps and Usain Bolt breaking records—were truly global media events, but for most viewers in the world, including those in Japan, this Olympics was a case of "same games, different dreams," in a televised experience characterized by highly selective media nationalism.

China's Olympic Run ☆ Pallavi Aiyar

For seven years the Beijing Olympics have provided the overarching umbrella under which Chinese authorities have sheltered while pushing through some of the most sweeping transformations of a society the world has seen.

With traditional beliefs like Confucianism having been battered by decades of Communist struggle and in turn socialism's egalitarian ideals punctured by an increasingly single-minded pursuit of mammon, Olympianism—the elevation of the Games to semisacred status to serve a variety of political ends—has emerged as China's new credo, its holy cow. The Games have functioned as a rudder for state policy, helped justify unpopular decisions, shored up the ruling Communist Party's legitimacy and rallied the nation behind the quest for international prestige and acknowledgment.

The Chinese Communist Party has officially acknowledged that even Chairman Mao was 30 percent wrong in his actions, but the Olympics have been deemed 100 percent right; to question them is the equivalent of blasphemy.

Since the time of the Roman Empire, large sporting events have served an important ritualistic and political function, helping to create a sense of common belonging and pride amongst citizens. So in China, the authorities have used the Olympics to create a nationalist glue that cuts across social divides and provides a sense of commonality at a time when traditional social moorings became unhinged by vertiginous development.

All of this begs the question, What will fill the Olympic-sized void once the Games end? Neither the World Expo in Shanghai nor the Guangzhou Asian Games, both scheduled for 2010, have the same rallying power to mobilize a nation. For the Chinese leadership, this is an issue that presents the need for some tightrope walking that even the skilled policy acrobatics of Beijing's top apparatchiks will find testing.

When I first moved to China in late 2002, I was somewhat befuddled by the overwhelming dominance of the Olympic Games in virtually every narrative strand I came across. Whether it was stock market analysts, antitobacco lobbyists, intellectual property rights lawyers, tourist officials, or foreign journalists, it was almost impossible to avoid the "O" word.

Animal rights activists talked of how the Games would transform Chinese attitudes to dogs away from viewing them as food and toward coddling them as man's best friend. Stock market analysts pointed to the economic buoyancy generated by the Olympics as the basis for bullish predictions, while taxi drivers grappled with English textbooks, determined to master their ABC's in time to welcome "foreign friends" in August 2008.

Over the six years that I went on to spend in the Chinese capital, Beijing was mauled by cranes and bulldozers, with large swaths of the ancient city smashed and rebuilt anew. The sparkling facades that emerged from the ashes of the old city not only sent a clear message about China's particular vision of modernity but also, in severing all physical linkages with the past, erased the city's collective memory. This was a phenomenon that helped sublimate the as-yet-unresolved wounds of recent history—including the emotional and physical devastation unleashed by Mao's Cultural Revolution—while focusing attention on a future ostensibly as bright as the dazzling Bird's Nest stadium.

Hundreds of thousands of people were dislocated in the process. Some protested, but many others I spoke to accepted their lot as necessary for the "New Beijing" that the Olympics would unveil.

The Games were projected as a stage upon which Beijing was to be recast architecturally and even temperamentally. The city's notoriously fetid public toilets became relatively fragrant, armies of senior citizens were invited to take free English classes, and fines for spitting were occasionally implemented. New museums and subway lines, a makeover for the zoo, and a ravishing airport terminal were all pressed into the service of the creation of the "New Beijing, New Olympics."

With their promise of bringing massive "face" to the country, the Games fed the flames of nationalism with considerable success, building confidence in the Communist Party's ability to deliver international recognition in the eyes of its domestic constituency. They also served as a powerful pretext for stilling dissent. If all the necessary accommodation, on occasion painful, to ensure a successful Olympics was deemed and accepted as patriotic, then those who questioned their value were of definition traitorous.

The utility of the Olympics to the Chinese authorities was illustrated by the manner in which the Games were used to distract from and silence criticism of the shoddy construction and deep-rooted corruption revealed in the aftermath of May's devastating earthquake in Sichuan province.

In several of the cities hardest hit by the earthquake, reenactments of the Olympic torch relay were organized. The idea, according to local media reports, was to use "the Olympic spirit in schools to aid recovery." Explicit statements equating the "Olympic spirit" with that of "the spirit of conquering disaster" or endurance and forbearance were made.

In many ways this strategy worked. Following decades of famine, war, foreign occupation, and revolutionary excess, hosting the Olympic Games was seen by significant numbers of Chinese as the moment when their country could finally hold its head up high to receive gold medal after gold medal.

Various short-term inconveniences were put up with without much protest, including electricity shortages in neighboring provinces, temporary economic losses suffered by businesses ordered shut during the Games, the clearing away of brothels and other "unsuitable" venues, and so on.

The idea that certain sacrifices were both necessary and worthwhile achieved a degree of popular currency. These "adjustments" included fundamental changes, such as the creation of a capital city in which many long-term residents found themselves symbolically and physically cast out to the fringes. New Beijing did not have space or patience for poverty.

As the Olympics euphoria comes to an end, bringing with it closure to the seven-year-long hype around the event, both short- and long-term contradictions swept under the carpet of the Games will find themselves rudely uncovered.

Along with the inevitable anticlimactic feeling that accompanies the end of any big party, the close of the Olympics will open a void.

From environmental degradation to the country's badly tattered social security fabric, the challenges confronting China today are hard ones for authorities to fit into the nationalistic discourse the Games had laced so well with. An aging demographic, health care reform, inflation, and corruption are issues that will become easier to hear without the overwhelming noise generated by the clarion call of the Olympics.

As a long-term resident of Beijing, the end of the Games has left even me with a sense of hollowness. After weeks of yelling, *"Zhongguo jiayou,"* or "Come on! China," as Chinese athletes won medal upon medal, there's a desire to continue cheering but no victories to cheer for.

I'm left wondering what will unite the country in the absence of the Games. What will distract from internal divisions and emergent tensions? Historically, sporting spectacles have been matched only by small wars as diversionary tactics. The likelihood of China taking that course in the near future is minute.

Nonetheless, the next few years will be crucial in determining how fragile or resilient the current regime in China really is. Faced with rising labor costs, an economy that is increasingly intertwined with the outside world, and growing pressure on resources from water to oil, China will need to devise new strategies to transform its economic model if it is to continue to grow at the double-digit rate of the past decade.

With the end of the Games, Olympianism's greatest failure—its overwhelming emphasis on unity to the exclusion of legitimate differences—will also no longer be as easy to obfuscate. Discontentment against Beijing's rule in Tibet and Xinjiang, which took center stage for a while in the run-up to the Olympics, will reemerge as formidable challenges for the authorities.

Without the Games and their prestige to drive home the necessity of "harmony" at any cost, China's ruling party will have to confront its greatest Achilles' heel—its inability to admit to the existence of real diversity and dissent—head-on.

For years now the Olympics have acted as a safety net for the juggling act China's ruling party is constantly engaged in. The post-Olympic aporia that the country is likely to experience spells higher risks with less-than-predictable outcomes. Expect some furrowed brows in Zhongnanhai.

Chapter 11

Follow the Leader

EARLY CRITICS OF DENG XIAOPING— A 1978 FLASHBACK

Jeffrey N. Wasserstrom

Americans associate bottom-up challenges to Deng Xiaoping with images of the massive 1989 protests. But those demonstrations were not the first acts of dissent Deng had to deal with by any means. More than a decade earlier, right after his reform era began, came the "Democracy Wall movement"—named for a Beijing area where critics started putting up posters (some of which warned of Deng becoming a dictator) in 1978. The term "democracy wall" had been used for comparable spaces back in the 1940s (when Chiang Kai-shek's authoritarianism was being attacked) and again during 1957's "Hundred Flowers" campaign. The 1957 precedent is particularly relevant because Deng responded to criticism in the late 1970s much as Mao Zedong had some twenty years earlier, first welcoming it as a healthy form of expression, then cracking down.

The Democracy Wall movement of 1978–1979 was not a single, coherent, organized struggle with a clear agenda but rather a constellation of activities by groups inspired by varied ideas. When remembered in the West, it tends to be simplified: treated as a liberal democratic project, even though the language of many posters was infused with Marxist concepts and ideals. There is more to keep in mind about Democracy Wall than the name of the unusually liberal Wei Jingsheng, who gained fame through crafting a powerful manifesto, "The Fifth Modernization," which said Deng's call for "Four Modernizations" (of agriculture, industry, science and technology, and education) left something out: democracy.

Today, however, focusing on Wei makes sense since his famous poster went up exactly thirty years ago. Interestingly, Wei presented democracy (the "fifth modernization") not as an abstract good but as a pragmatic necessity. Without it, he wrote, great obstacles would block China's material development. The fact that this year's first protests were the anti-maglev "strolls" underlines the gulf separating 1978 from 2008. There's a connecting thread: a desire for more transparent and responsive government officials. To worry about the damaging impact of a form of state-of-the-art technology is very different from talking about the obstacles that limit China's material progress.

Posted 12/4/2008 at 09:36:00 AM

China's national leaders were unusually prominent in 2008. While the Chinese people expressed widespread dissatisfaction with government corruption—named as the number one concern in recent years in several national polls—popular ire was largely focused on lower-level leaders. National leaders continued to enjoy widespread support, and in polls comparing levels of satisfaction with the government overall, a greater percentage of China's population than that of many other countries said they thought their nation was basically well run.

In 2008, Prime Minister Wen Jiabao put a sympathetic face on that national Chinese leadership. Calling himself "Grandpa Wen" after the Sichuan earthquake, he sat with grieving parents, exhorted children still stuck in the rubble to hang on, and cried when confronted by the personal tragedies of China's largest recent natural disaster. Wen's personal touch and his calls for government to communicate with regular people recalled earlier charismatic Chinese leaders. Richard Kraus discusses the ways Wen's Sichuan tour corresponded to historical expectations of Chinese leaders in his piece "Preserving the Premier's Calligraphy at Beichuan Middle School."

Wen's concern for the common people plays well, particularly in an age of increasingly personal media interactions. One such example is that, following his empathetic tour of Sichuan, Wen Jiabao's Facebook page shot up in popularity, gaining thousands of "friends" within days. Wen was not the only Chinese politician who used the Internet to makes friends and influence people—Hu Jintao participated in a low-content but highly acclaimed online chat with Chinese Internet users (the peg for Nicolai Volland's piece "Boss Hu and the Press" in this chapter).

While the Chinese people took advantage of increased communication with leaders like Wen and Hu, the death of an earlier Chinese premier passed with little media notice. Hua Guofeng died during the Olympic Games, but Chinese leaders didn't announce his death immediately. As Jeremiah Jenne describes in his reflection on Hua's historical importance, Hua Guofeng's seemingly inconsequential rule set the stage for China's late-twentieth-century reform and opening.

It wasn't just Chinese leaders who drew attention in China in 2008. As Geremie Barmé describes in "Facing Up to Friendship," Australia's new prime minister, Kevin Rudd, made an important speech at Beijing University in early April. Chinese were angry about the way Western media had covered the events in Tibet in March and were hurt by the international protests along the Olympic torch relay route. Speaking in Chinese, Rudd, who studied Chinese at university and was a diplomat in China, urged the students in the audience to confront a variety of issues, as their May Fourth predecessors had done. Rudd's assertion that he came to China telling the truth as only a "true friend" (zhengyou) could, was met favorably by the audience and in the Chinese media.

This year's actions by Rudd, Wen, and Hu point not only to a changing relationship between Chinese Party leadership and the Chinese people but also to changing expectations for international leaders in regard to their level of engagement with and understanding of China. As China's international strength and prominence grows, the Chinese people will almost certainly expect that international leaders will attempt to understand their desires and needs and not simply scold China for failing to meet international standards.

Facing Up to Friendship ☆ Geremie R. Barmé

On April 9, 2008, Australian Prime Minister Kevin Rudd made a speech to an audience at Peking University, China's preeminent university. Given the tensions over Tibet and the Olympic torch relay, as a practiced diplomat Rudd could have taken the easy path by speaking in platitudes about the strength of the bilateral relationship and any number of mutually acceptable and anodyne topics.

Instead, with finesse and skill, he chose to address the students on broad basis for a truly sustainable relationship with the economically booming yet politically autocratic state that is China. In doing so, he rewrote the rules of engagement in a way that can only benefit Australia and its relationship with this important country.

First Rudd acknowledged where he was: at a university that, more than any other educational institution in China, has helped shape that country's modern history, one known for its contributions to Chinese intellectual debate, political activism, and cultural experimentation. He mentioned some of China's twentieth-century intellectual heroes whose careers were entwined with Peking University. Some were involved in reshaping Chinese into a modern language capable of carrying urgently needed political, cultural, and historical debate. One was a leading democratic thinker.

He also made three references to Lu Xun (1881–1936), China's literary hero, unyielding critic of authoritarianism, and principled dissenter, noting that Lu Xun personally designed Peking University's crest. It would not have been lost on his audience that the prime minister's choice of intellectual exemplars acknowledged China's dominant Communist ideology while pointing to the traditions of free speech and debate that have made Peking University so important. Next year is one of many anniversaries, one of the most significant being of the ninetieth commemoration of the May Fourth movement. May 4, 1919, is remembered as an occasion when patriotic student and mass ire led to a boycott of Japanese goods. It was also the iconic moment in an era of cultural renewal and intellectual foment. It also marks a watershed in the rise of left-wing radicalism, something that would later bring devastation on the nation. But May Fourth also ushered in an era of mass political participation and youthful awakening in China. For the students of Peking University, the significance of Kevin Rudd's opening remarks would not have been lost; in a sense the Australian prime minister gave one of the first commemorative speeches at the university marking the ninetieth anniversary of May Fourth.

Rudd's strategy was thus first to honor the place where he was speaking and its connection to significant, complex historical and cultural figures. He went on to speak more personally of his own educational and political trajectory and about Australia's national interest. Appealing to his youthful audience to consider what positive role they could play in China's rise as a world power, he evoked the concept of harmony (*hexie*), embraced by the present Chinese leadership, before making a canny digression. This was to note that 2008 is the 110th anniversary of the Hundred Days Reform movement, during which an enlightened emperor struggled to enact a process of political reform and modernization similar to the Meiji Restoration in Japan that had taken place not long before. Rudd didn't need to say that this movement failed and its leaders were beheaded; his audience would know that. Instead he noted that one of the leading lights of the reforms, the thinker Kang Youwei, who survived by fleeing into exile, went on to write about "the Great Harmony" (*datong*), "a utopian world free of political boundaries." Thus, in a manner both subtle and eminently clear to a Chinese intellectual audience, he linked the officially approved concept of harmony to the broader course of political reform, change, and openness.

Rudd then spoke about China joining the rest of humanity as "a responsible global stakeholder"—a lead-in to addressing the pressing issue of Tibet. By framing his comments in such a manner, he established his right—and by extension the right of others—to disagree with both Chinese official and mainstream opinion on matters of international concern. There is a venerable Chinese expression for this position: "A true friend," Rudd went on, "is one who can be a *zhengyou*, that is a partner who sees beyond immediate benefit to the broader and firm basis for continuing, profound and sincere friendship."

The subsequent Chinese media discussion of Rudd's use of the powerful and meaning-laden term *zhengyou*—the true friend who dares to disagree—has been considerable. That is because the more common word "friendship" (*youyi*) has been a cornerstone of China's post-1949 diplomacy. Mao Zedong once observed, "The first and foremost question of the revolution is: who is our friend and who is our foe."

To be a friend of China, the Chinese people, the party-state, or, in the reform period, even a mainland business partner, the foreigner is often expected to stomach unpalatable situations and keep silent in the face of egregious behavior. A friend of China might enjoy the privilege of offering the occasional word of caution in private; in the public arena he or she is expected to have the good sense and courtesy to be "objective," that is, to toe the line, whatever that happens to be. The concept of "friendship" thus degenerates into little more than an effective tool for emotional blackmail and enforced complicity.

Rudd's tactic was to deftly sidestep the viselike embrace of that model of friendship by substituting another. "A strong relationship, and a true friendship," he told the students, "are built on the ability to engage in a direct, frank and ongoing dialogue about our fundamental interests and future vision."

The distinction was not lost on the Chinese. The official news agency Xinhua reported, "Eyes lit up when [Rudd] used this expression . . . it means friendship based on speaking the truth, speaking responsibly. It is evident that to be a *zhengyou*, the first thing one needs is the magnanimity of pluralism."[1] Of course, in the land of linguistic slippage it is easy to see that while for some *zhengyou* means speaking out of turn, for others it may simply become another way for allowing pesky foreigners to let off steam. After all, erudite historical references can easily be dismissed as "Sino-wank." They send a message of sincere engagement and competence to Chinese audiences and may too readily be taken to mean "We all talk the same language, I can disagree with you, but now let's get back to business." However, I believe that Kevin Rudd signaled something more, something that in another context I have called "a robust engagement with contemporary China and the broader Chinese world in all of its complexity, whether it be local, regional or global."[2]

Of course, there are dangers, not mentioned in the Chinese media. Perhaps the most famous *zhengyou* relationship of modern times was that between Mao Zedong and Liang Shuming, a Confucian thinker and agrarian reformer. Mao declared that although their politics were different, Liang was a true *zhengyou*. Liang advised Mao on rural policy from the 1940s into the early 1950s. But, in 1953, Liang dared to venture that class struggle was having a calamitous effect on rural life. He asked Mao whether he had the "magnanimity" to accept his views. The chairman shot back, "No, I don't have that magnanimity!" Shortly thereafter, Liang was denounced and silenced.

On the other hand, there are examples from Chinese history where a *zhengyou* has played a key role in bringing about good governance and prosperity.

The most famous *zhengyou* was Wei Zheng, a friend and critic of the emperor Taizong of the seventh-century Tang dynasty. Wei told the ruler that "if you listen to wise counsel all is brightness; if, however, you give in to bias darkness falls." When Wei died, some years later, the emperor bitterly mourned his death. He offered this tribute: "One looks at a reflection in a mirror to see if one's dress is in order. One studies history to understand the changing fortunes of time. And one seeks wise counsel to avoid mistakes. Wei Zheng has died, and I have lost my mirror. To have a *zhengyou* is to be fortunate indeed." The metaphor is used by China's leaders and the media even today. One can only hope that when they look in the mirror, they do not do so with eyes wide shut.

By introducing the term *zhengyou* with all of its liberating connotations into our dealings with China, Kevin Rudd has achieved something of considerable significance.

---

1. It is also noteworthy that in official accounts of the speech no mention was made of Hu Shi, the literary reformer, historian, and advocate of liberal democracy whom Rudd had listed among the leading lights of Peking University.

2. See my March 2005 essay "On New Sinology" online at http://rspas.anu.edu.au/pah/chinaheritageproject/newsinology.

Preserving the Premier's Calligraphy at
Beichuan Middle School ☆ Richard C. Kraus

The Beichuan Middle School lost a thousand students in May's devastating Sichuan earthquake. When Premier Wen Jiabao visited the school's temporary quarters, he wrote four characters on a blackboard to inspire the students: "distress rejuvenates a nation" (*duo nan xing bang*). After his departure, teachers and students could not bear to erase his chalk inscription, which was covered in plastic until the Sichuan Cultural Relics Bureau could devise a method for permanently preserving Wen's handwriting.

Although Premier Wen's chalk on a blackboard may seem difficult to preserve, China has a deeply established tradition of copying calligraphy. Many of the great works of past masters are known only by copies, often stone carvings, which astonishingly capture the most delicate brushstrokes in a medium that lasts for centuries. And newer technologies can be used to preserve Wen's temporary inscription for future generations.

The more interesting problem is political. The propagation of calligraphy by powerful men (never women) bolsters personality cults, as I show in my book *Brushes with Power*. Calligraphy is said to reveal the inner character of a person—one can detect the virtue of a writer by the beauty of his brushstrokes. Underlings have flattered their bosses for centuries by praising their calligraphy, leading to a secondary tradition of ghost calligraphers to create suitable inscriptions for those men of power who lacked a good classical education. For the powerful, spreading calligraphy around is a way to leave visible markers of their sphere of influence. Book titles, building signs, and newspaper mastheads have all featured inscriptions where politicians use the brush to display their patronage and extend their protection.

This ancient power–calligraphy bond was initially shaken in the twentieth century as modernists questioned the traditions of literati culture. But the practice instead grew to new extremes because Mao Zedong was both a serious calligrapher and the center of an unprecedented personality cult. Mao, whose distinctive writing style lives on today not only in artifacts from his day but also in a computer font inspired by it, wrote characters for causes and institutions he supported. Even those he did not often forged his calligraphy to strengthen their claims to legitimacy. Mao's characters graced the Bank of China, the *People's Daily*, and Red Guard armbands. Ardently revolutionary orchardists grew apples bearing the Chairman's calligraphy by ripening the fruit with stencils and sunlight.

The equation of good calligraphy and high moral leadership can be broken. Lin Biao, Mao's one-time ally, produced inscriptions for the *Little Red Book* of quotations from Chairman Mao and for a multitude of Mao statues around the nation. After Lin's shocking death in 1971, his characters were physically stripped from the plinths of the Mao statues. Indeed, the calligraphy of fallen politicians is sometimes seen as malign, casting a harmful shadow on society.

And after Hua Guofeng (1921–2008) succeeded Mao in 1976, he sought to replicate the chairman's cult, including a burst of calligraphic inscriptions. When Hua was felled from power by Deng Xiaoping (1904–1997), his humiliation included an aesthetic criticism of his clumsy handwriting. At the same time, Hua was derided for vanity when the Beijing Red Star Chicken Hatchery created a shrine around a calligraphic inscription he left during a visit.

The Leninist excesses of the Mao cult dampened the most flamboyantly self-promoting use of calligraphy, yet politicians continue to employ this deeply rooted cultural tool in relatively quiet ways. The effort to enshrine Premier Wen's chalked calligraphy may raise questions about his political ambitions or those of his supporters.

When Mao Zedong presented Pakistani mangoes as a sign of his favor to the worker-peasant propaganda teams in 1968, his fervent supporters desperately sought new technology to preserve the fruit. The mangoes ended up briefly worshipped but uneaten. Saving Premier Wen's chalk is a challenge more easily met, although it may raise eyebrows among cognoscenti of China's political culture.

Boss Hu and the Press ☆ Nicolai Volland

On June 20, Hu Jintao paid a high-profile visit to the *People's Daily*. His foray to the editorial offices of the Chinese Communist Party (CCP) mouthpiece was first announced in the form of what turned out to be all but a hoax: "General Secretary Hu chats with Chinese netizens!" The news spread like a wildfire, but surfers who rushed to the *People's Daily*'s "Strong Nation Forum" found themselves barred from entering. Disappointed, they vented their anger in the freely accessible Tianya forum. As is turned out, they may have missed little. Sitting in the offices of the *People's Daily*, "Boss Hu" (*Hu zong*—the slightly irreverent way Chinese netizens refer to Hu)[3] looked at a screen and was read three questions asked by what presumably were loyal and prescreened users of

---

3. Readers on *China Beat* have pointed out that *Hu zong* is an abbreviation of "Hu zongshuji" and should accordingly be translated as "General Secretary Hu." The netizen's use of the abbreviation, however, seems to imply a less the reverent attitude toward the office and its holder; since "zong" is also used as an abbreviation for "zongcai," or CEO, I have chosen the similarly informal "boss" as a translation. Ironically, Chinese surfers are forced by their government to use abbreviations when referring to Hu Jintao: the term "Hu zongshuji" is rejected by most software packages used by BBS providers, presumably to stop abuse and criticism of the nation's top leader on the Internet.

the forum. All questions were harmless ("Mr. General Secretary, what do you read on the Web?" "Mr. General Secretary, do you review many suggestions and proposals from netizens on the Web?"). Hu answered to one of the forum's editors, who keyed in the general secretary's answers. Thus, the "chat" was over, and Hu rushed on to other business—his real business.

It turned out that Hu Jintao's June 20 visit to the *People's Daily* was not accidental, and the "chat" was but a deft move to raise the publicity of his visit. So much became clear in the following days, when the Chinese media began to roll out a massive campaign relaying the importance of Hu's visit, with the *People's Daily* itself spearheading the movement. Hu Jintao used his visit to the offices of the paper to deliver a short but carefully planned speech to the newspaper's assembled staff; in fact, his target audience were not the several hundred employees of the Central Committee organ but rather the 3 million employees across China's vast media sector in general. Hailed as a "programmatic document" by the Central Propaganda Department, Hu's speech in fact set out the rules for the Chinese media not only for the Olympics, then just six weeks away, but in fact for years to come.

Hu's visit and the high profile attached to it is not without precedent. For more than half a century, the CCP's top leaders have made it a tradition to visit the party press and, in the course of "chats" with editors and journalists, to outline the party's policy toward the media. In April 1948, Chairman Mao visited *Jin-Sui Daily*, one of the CCP's wartime papers. His "Talk with Editors at Jin-Sui Daily" has been included in volume four of Mao's *Selected Works* and has since been a cornerstone of CCP press theory. In 1956, Liu Shaoqi held two meetings with journalists at the Xinhua news agency in which he signaled a significant relaxation on the ideological front that became known as the "Hundred Flowers" policy. Xinhua staff should not dogmatically copy the Soviet TASS agency but also see what might be learned from the news agencies in capitalist countries (Liu's remarks were quoted by radicals from Beijing media units during the Cultural Revolution and were taken as evidence of Liu's "crimes"). In 1985, then General Secretary Hu Yaobang paid a similar visit to *People's Daily*, as did Jiang Zemin in 1996.[4] Jiang's speech was given wide publicity, especially his attempts to balance the media's function as loyal mouthpieces of the party with their emerging role in "public opinion supervision" (*yulun jiandu*) through means such as investigative journalism. It is thus obvious that Hu Jintao tried to place himself within a long tradition of making major announcements of media policy through visits to the party's top media. So what are we to expect from the Chinese media in the coming years? A closer reading of Hu's June 20 speech tells us much about the core points of the CCP's media policy in the twenty-first century.

---

4. I am grateful to Alice Lyman Miller for the references to the visits of Hu Yaobang and Jiang.

First of all, what makes Hu's speech interesting is his acknowledgment of new developments in the Chinese media industry. In particular, Hu mentions the popular urban dailies (*dushibao*, such as the *Southern Metropolitan Daily*, the cutting-edge investigative paper from Guangzhou) and the Internet as crucially important new components of the Chinese media landscape. The rise of a popular press appealing to readers' tastes in a competitive market is probably the biggest change in the decade since Jiang Zemin reiterated the importance of the party papers. Hu elevates the product of the party's media reforms and the commercialization of the press sector and gives them legitimacy within the party-dominated public sphere. In a similar vein, the electronic and Web-based media are now officially incorporated into the CCP's media theory—as demonstrated by Hu's "chat" with surfers at the Strong Nation Forum.

However, Hu Jintao was quick to balance the newly emerging media and their counterpart, the party press, and laid down an authoritative definition of the respective roles of the two media types: "With the Party papers and broadcasting stations as the mainstay," the commercial papers are supplementing the role of the party press but are by no means supposed to replace the latter. In fact, the urban dailies and the Web-based media are what the party press is to the CCP: "propaganda resources" (*xuanchuan ziyuan*). Hu Jintao acknowledges the existence of a "multilayered public opinion" and the need to take all these layers into account in the party's propaganda work. That seems to be evidence for a more sophisticated and flexible approach to thought work and propaganda.

Propaganda, however, was the core theme of Hu's speech, and it remains the defining framework for the Chinese press of the twenty-first century. The overall parameters have changed remarkably little, and in these respects Hu's speech closely followed Jiang's 1996 address. Indeed, in the very first paragraph, Hu speaks of the "news front" (*xinwen zhanxian*), a term that is decades old; the militaristic vocabulary harks back to the CCP's perception of the media as a weapon in its struggle for power. Of all the media principles that Hu consequently invokes, the first and most prominent is *partiinost* (*dangxing*), a Soviet concept that has been the core of the CCP's approach to the media since the 1930s. Its reiteration in the current context is a clear signal that the basic line remains what it has been: the press—no matter whether party press or other media—must unwaveringly follow the line of the party center.

The third and fourth paragraphs of Hu's speech in particular are outright Cold War rhetoric. Hu declared that "news and public opinion are at the forefront of the ideological field," and in the next paragraph he explains that China finds itself amidst an intensifying ideological conflict with the West ("the struggle in the field of news and public opinion is getting more intense and more complicated"). The means of this struggle may be changing but not its nature. China's ideological conflict with the West remains as acute as ever in the eyes of the CCP's top leader. These are the external factors that determine the party's use of the media. In his explanations on *partiinost*, Hu says that "correct guidance of public opinion benefits the Party, the nation, and the people"; incorrect guidance, in turn, is prone to bring disaster: the CCP has learned its lesson from the democracy movement in 1989 and from the breakup of the Soviet Union. The CCP is not going to let it happen in China.

A crucial measure to ensure that the party stays in control of the media is journalism education. Again, Hu took his clue from Jiang Zemin, who had stressed the same point in 1996. As the gatekeepers in the media field (there is no prepublication censorship in the People's Republic of China, so journalists and editors are responsible to judge on what goes and what does not), journalists will be carefully watched; their ranks may be weeded from time to time to ensure that they stick to the role the party has assigned to them. Over the last few years, the CCP has driven an aggressive push to standardize registration and examination of prospective and practicing journalists, and in light of Hu's speech, more of the same may be in the offing.

In the run-up to the Olympic Games, the Chinese media had been in the headlines repeatedly. On the one hand, the party cracked down across the board, discouraging expressions of dissent before and during the Olympics. In particular, publications that have existed for many years in the cracks of the party-state, such as the popular English-language magazine *That's Beijing*, have been ordered to shut down or have seen takeovers by their Chinese joint venture partners. Experiments with new media forms are clearly not encouraged. On the other hand, much has been written about the surprisingly swift and broad coverage of the Wenchuan earthquake, when the Chinese media ignored an early ban on reporting and went into a nearly round-the-clock coverage of events, while Xinhua and the other paragons of the state media stood by. An emancipation of the Chinese press? Less so in Hu Jintao's eyes. The upsurge in earthquake reporting was quickly brought under control and was superseded by massive mainstream propaganda that focused on the heroic rescue efforts of the People's Liberation Army and the national party leadership. Controversial topics, such as construction problems at a school building that collapsed and corruption, were quickly suppressed. Well done: Hu Jintao congratulated the *People's Daily* staff on their extraordinary achievements during four major news events earlier this year: the winter storms that brought traffic to a collapse in much of southern China; the struggle to "protect social stability in Tibet," a euphemism for the government's crackdown in the nation's Tibetan areas; the preparation of the Olympics; and, finally, the Wenchuan earthquake. No fear of media openness, then; the CCP has demonstrated its ability to open up temporarily but quickly rein in the media once a return to its close control was deemed desirable.

So did the media heed "Boss Hu's" advice? It seems they did. The Beijing Olympics were executed in the spirit of "shock and awe," and the media played their part in the almost-perfect spectacle. With the Games safely stored away in memory, the Chinese media can go back to their bread-and-butter issues. The next big test, the Sanlu scandal that eventually morphed into a crisis involving the entire Chinese dairy industry and the nation's food safety system, showed the media in all the roles the party leadership had desired them to play. When the crisis broke in early August, the media effectively contributed to the cover-up, withholding news of the affair for the sake of the national priority—the Olympic Games. In so doing, they strictly followed the line issued by the Propaganda Department before the Olympics: no reporting on food safety scandals during the Games. Once the problem had been internationalized and the New Zealand–owned Fonterra company had blown the whistle, the party media went into a carefully considered overdrive, presenting Chinese audiences with pictures of the authorities in control, culprits being punished, and Wen Jiabao reassuring consumers that nothing like it would happen again. The media response looked carefully orchestrated and subsided just as fast as it rose, shifting attention to a more jubilant theme, the first spacewalk by Chinese astronauts.

Looking back to Hu's June 20 visit to *People's Daily* and his speech, it seems that both party media and their more popular counterparts have taken their clue and played their role within the party's concert on the "news and propaganda battle front" remarkably well. In his speech, Hu Jintao, or "Boss Hu," as the surfers at Tianya called him, summed up from the theoretical vantage point the experiences of the past decade and has staked out the direction for the next years: be open to the new but only once it is effectively co-opted and integrated into the party's existing framework of governance. We might have to get accustomed to the general secretary "chatting" with Internet users, but don't expect the Chinese media to open anytime soon.

Hua Guofeng: Remembering a Forgotten Leader ☆ Jeremiah Jenne

The week of the Olympic opening ceremonies, a rumor circulated among media types in Beijing that Hua Guofeng had passed away in a Beijing hospital. The news was met with all the stages of grief: confusion ("Who?"), denial ("He was still alive? Really?"), anger ("No . . . I'm being serious. He wasn't already dead?!?"), and bargaining ("Well, he might be dead, but let's hold off telling people because we wouldn't want to let anything spoil the Olympic Party."). We didn't reach the stage of acceptance until two weeks and a few dozen gold medals later when the Chinese Communist Party (CCP) finally got around to officially announcing that Chairman Hua, Mao's successor as the leader of the People's Republic of China from 1976 to 1978 (when Deng rose to preeminence), had died at the age of eighty-seven.

In the end it was all somehow sadly fitting. The Chinese press gave Hua a box with an undated photo and a couple of sentences below the fold, while the same week papers across China rolled out multisection full-color spreads devoted to the injured right ankle of Chinese hurdler Liu Xiang.

The foreign media were even less impressed. The *Washington Post* called him "an obscure functionary who briefly served as the handpicked successor to CCP chairman Mao Zedong." Mure Dickey, writing in the *Financial Times*, dismissed Hua as "an example of the slavish sycophancy Mao sought in his subordinates." Professor Kenneth Lieberthal told the *New York Times* that Hua was "more a figure who was there when Chinese politics pivoted than himself being a pivotal figure."

Let's face it, Hua Guofeng just never could get any respect: he's the Gerald Ford of Chinese politics, known more for following a larger-than-life figure (but only briefly) than for anything else. This is true even though Hua was something of a big deal. Mao had gone through a series of heirs apparent (Liu Shaoqi dead in prison, Lin Biao dead after a botched coup, Zhou Enlai simply dead, and Deng Xiaoping back in exile before his post-Mao return). Hua was last man standing, stamped with the Great Helmsman's endorsement: "With you in charge, I can rest easy" (Mao allegedly said to, uh, Hua, just before dying). After Mao went to meet Marx on September 9, 1976, it was Hua Guofeng who emerged as the leader of the Chinese people and was portrayed in posters occupying spots once given to the Great Helmsman.

Unfortunately, Hua went from busting up the Gang of Four and receiving the adulation of the masses to being shown a nice gold watch in just two short years. With Hua in charge, Mao might have rested easy, but when Deng Xiaoping returned to grace, Hua was quickly made redundant. The party let him linger on for a while, stripping away his leadership positions one by one until the early 1980s, when Hua was finally busted down to mere rank-and-file member of the Central Committee. By the end of the decade, he had faded into political oblivion.

Around the time of Hua's death, an old joke began making the rounds again: Mao, Deng, and Hua are walking across a bridge. The bridge suddenly breaks, and they are left clinging with their bare hands to the last rope. The three of them hang, suspended over a chasm, as the rope starts to unravel. The weight is too much; somebody has to let go. Deng speaks up and proclaims, "Chairman Mao should not let go because he is chairman, and Comrade Hua Guofeng should not let go because he is Mao's successor. I will sacrifice myself!" Hua is so moved by this that he turns and applauds Comrade Deng's revolutionary spirit.

I didn't say it was a good joke, but such is Hua's legacy. And it's not entirely fair.

The simple truth is, jokes aside, Hua Guofeng matters, and without him the trajectory of China's post-Mao history could have been very different. It's easy to forget now how close the Chinese government (and the country) came in the fall of 1976 to being ripped apart by the centrifugal forces of factionalism and ambition. Chairman Mao was gone, and ten years of Cultural Revolution had fractured the party and weakened the nation. Several groups vied for control.

There were reformers affiliated with the late Zhou Enlai and Deng Xiaoping. This group, many of whom were victims of the Cultural Revolution, feared and loathed the ideologues in the Cultural Revolutionary Leading Group that included Mao's widow Jiang Qing and the rest of the Gang of Four. The Gang of Four for their part was actively conspiring to take over the reins of government, even organizing and arming allied militias in Shanghai and other cities. There were other political blocs as well, all with their own interests and allegiances: the military, the state security apparatus, the Beijing faction, and the Shanghai faction, among the myriad cliques, cohorts, and cabals. In such a situation, for a polarizing figure like Deng Xiaoping to have immediately tried to assume power could have touched off a powder keg of intramural violence.

And then there was Hua.

In the critical weeks following Mao's death, Hua was . . . there. He was a man without strong factional ties, a blank slate hard to take seriously but difficult to oppose. In short: the perfect compromise candidate. Because Hua wasn't associated with the Cultural Revolution Leading Group, he was at least tolerable to the reformers and their allies in the military establishment, and while members of the Gang, especially Jiang Qing and Zhang Chunqiao, loathed Hua, his Cultural Revolution credentials and trump card of "with you in charge, I can rest easy" made it difficult to impugn him as "anti-Mao." In fact, Hua's elevation momentarily stymied the Gang's plans to seize power, buying time for the disparate forces arrayed against the Gang to coalesce.

Though Hua's role in the arrest of the Gang of Four remains a bit murky, he emerged in the aftermath with an impressive set of titles: chairman of the CCP, state premier, and, perhaps most important, head of the Central Military Commission, which controlled the People's Liberation Army. On October 24, 1976, over a million citizens and soldiers filled Tiananmen Square to greet their new chairman.

Once in power, Hua oversaw the gradual reversal of many Cultural Revolution–era policies. There was greater academic and artistic freedom. The party started to relax its grip on society. Schools reopened, and life began the long arduous trek back to some semblance of normal. Hua's government attempted to spur economic growth with an (overly) ambitious ten-year plan that combined pre–Great Leap Policies of the 1950s with a blueprint first put forth by Zhou Enlai and Deng Xiaoping in 1975 for modernizing agriculture, industry, technology, and the military. Hua also opened the economy to outside investment, a move that brought in billions in foreign capital, much of it from Japan.

For all the mockery heaped upon Hua's "Two Whatevers" Policy ("*We will resolutely uphold whatever policy decisions Chairman Mao made and unswervingly follow whatever instructions Chairman Mao gave*"), Hua might well have been dumb like a fox. Figuring that the economic reforms and modernization schemes of Deng and Zhou would be too much, too soon for some in the party to accept, he cloaked the beginnings of the Reform and Opening Era in Maoist rhetoric, setting the stage for the dismantlement of the Mao legacy while paying tribute to the chairman himself, including personally laying the cornerstone for a mausoleum in the heart of Tiananmen Square.

Hua's two years in power put China on the road to renewal, but Hua would not be around to see it through. His legitimacy rested on being Mao's chosen successor, but as the crushing yoke of the Cultural Revolution lifted, those who had suffered, like the urban intelligentsia, former Red Guards sent down to the countryside, as well as party rank and file who had been purged and persecuted, began to be rehabilitated. As this group returned to their homes and old positions, their sympathies naturally turned to Deng Xiaoping, whom they saw as a fellow victim, rather than Hua.

Hua soon discovered that being Mao's handpicked heir was more a political liability than an asset.

Moreover, while Hua had the titles, Deng had the connections and the ideas. If anything, Deng's ascendance and Hua's swift slide into political irrelevance demonstrated how titles mattered little; it was factional ties and political networks that dominated the often Byzantine world of post–Cultural Revolution politics, and Hua, the compromise candidate, had little support and few allies. There were no great purges; that Hua could be removed so thoroughly and without the need for violence or imprisonment suggests just how politically impotent he had truly become. Deng went on to open China to the world and set the country on a course for unprecedented growth and prosperity while Hua retired to a *hutong* in the Xicheng district of Beijing, rarely appearing in public.

Hua's death was greeted by a lot of "who cares?" and "so whats?" buried amidst the hype of China's Olympic summer. It's true: Hua was neither brilliant nor inspirational. But if we are to accept that the economic miracle that made the 2008 Beijing Olympics possible begins with Deng Xiaoping, we should also remember that Deng's rise to power was not inevitable. At a critical moment, Hua provided a steady hand on the wheel and (whether it was his intention or not) provided breathing space for the forces of reform to emerge and lead China into a new era.

Chapter 12

Things Seen and Unseen

WHY WAS YAO MING FINED?

Susan Brownell

A colleague here at the Beijing Sport University whom I have known for over ten years, Yi Jiandong, is one of the two most vocal media commentators on Chinese sports in the academic world (along with Lu Yuanzhen). He has reached an exalted status that an American professor like myself can only marvel at from afar. He is one of the "Big-Name Bloggers" on the Qzone blogsite, where he shares space with the likes of Feng Shuyong, head coach of the national track-and-field team (whose main purpose seems to be to report on Liu Xiang, 2004 gold medalist, 2007 world champion, and world record holder in the 110-meter hurdles), and Lin Dan (two-time world champion in badminton who writes his own blog).

Professor Yi also gets paid good money to blog, something that cannot be said of myself. Among his more than eighty posts since August 2007, the one that has gotten the most hits was on the topic "an explanation for why 'Japanese Don't Show Respect for Liu Xiang,'" which elicited 1,594 comments and 224,447 hits. Not only can a lowly American professor not aspire to his kinds of numbers and financial remuneration, I can't even expect that sports fans care about what I have to say. I take this as an illustration of the greater respect for university professors in Chinese popular culture generally and—in contrast to the United States—in the sports world in particular. . . .

Posted 2/6/2008 at 09:08:00 AM

The emergence of the pernicious phenomenon known as the "human flesh search" (ren rou sou sou) has been dated as far back as 2001, but this year this cyberbullying came under increasing scrutiny as the first human flesh search case wound its way through Chinese courts. The practitioners of the human flesh search mete out Internet justice to and facilitate the harassment of those who fail their moral and political tests. For instance, the first court case was brought by an unfaithful husband, Wang Fei, whose wife threw herself off their twenty-fourth-floor Beijing balcony after posting to her blog about her husband's cheating ways. In search of vengeance, netizens tracked down Wang's information, harrying him with threatening e-mails, phone calls, and even a Net-organized posse who showed up on his doorstep.

In the Western media, human flesh searching gained increased attention when Grace Wang, a Chinese student at Duke University, received death threats (and her family in China was forced into hiding) after she was captured on film attempting to mediate between pro-Tibet and pro-China protesters on the North Carolina campus in the spring of 2008. In both cases, searchers first discovered their target's identity and then published their personal information on the Web. Virtual and physical harassment followed.

It is ironic that the human flesh search developed in China since the country is best known abroad for its sophisticated Internet filtering systems and the thousands of Web monitors who keep tabs on China's more than 220 million Internet users. While the government may be monitoring its Internet users, the users themselves are equally adept at tracking down each other. As Yang Guobin explores in this chapter, it is thus difficult to establish trust in China's online world.

And while the Internet is the front battleground for control of information in China today, traditional media are still subject to controls as well. In this chapter, for example, Timothy Weston describes finding a sloppily censored magazine during a visit to China this year. At other times censorship is gracefully masked as paternalistic concern—a trope that David Bandurski takes to farcical heights in his satiric piece in this chapter.

But 2008 also saw a remarkable moment of reporting freedom. In May after the Sichuan earthquake, Chinese reporters rushed in and broadcast what they were seeing on the ground—at a time when American National Public Radio reporters were also allowed a surprising degree of access to the affected areas. The freedom of Chinese journalists to tell people what was actually happening lasted only a few days but was still a significant development. Again in September, news about the melamine-in-milk scandal broke online—and many millions flocked to Internet websites to learn what was not being reported in traditional media. The human flesh searchers may be good at ferreting out personal details, but many millions more Chinese Internet users are eager to get online in order to learn and read about the issues that matter in their lives, from government corruption to tainted milk. Increasingly, the Chinese government has wisely begun to engage in new media—as President Hu Jintao did this year when he participated in an online chat. Rather than simply *trying to shut it down, it appears that the Chinese government will attempt to manage the media to promote their own agenda.*

Digital China: Ten Things Worth Knowing about the Chinese Internet
☆ Kate Merkel-Hess and Jeffrey N. Wasserstrom

B y now, in the wake of all sorts of 2008 digital events, including China replacing the United States as the country with the most people surfing the Web, news-savvy Americans all know the Internet has become an important force in Chinese life—but they don't necessarily know what kind of force. Here are ten things to keep in mind whenever the Chinese Internet makes headlines.

1. *Optimists have long forecast—inaccurately—that the Internet will swiftly transform China into a completely open society.* Among others, George Will, Thomas Friedman, and Bill Clinton all predicted around the millennium's turn that the arrival of the Internet would inevitably and swiftly set China free. This hasn't happened. China's still run by a Communist Party that takes harsh measures against organizations that threaten its hold on power.

2. *Pessimists continue to suggest—also inaccurately—that Chinese political life hasn't really changed and cannot be said to have changed until the Communist Party falls. This ignores shifts in which the Internet has figured centrally.* China's leaders may not have to stand for reelection and certainly limit some forms of dissent, but the Chinese public sphere has become a more freewheeling, interesting, and chaotic arena for expressions of opinion than it was. This isn't all due to the Internet (crusading print journalists and activists have also done their part), but bloggers calling attention to official corruption or mocking government policies have definitely helped alter the political landscape. It's misleading to suggest—as the *New Republic* did in a 2008 special issue, "Meet the New China (Same as the Old One)"—that the realm of Chinese politics has remained static.

3. *It's misleading to imagine that the only Chinese Internet activity that matters politically involves "dissidents" and collective acts of protest.* Often, the politically significant things happening online involve forms of communication, such as calling attention to corrupt acts by local officials, that dovetail with policies that are promoted or at least given lip service by the central authorities. In many cases, these take the form of satirical discussions, which only gradually move toward anything like a "dissident" position. An illustration from the lead-up to the Beijing Games involved reports that pigs raised to be eaten by Olympic competitors were being fed a special organic diet to ensure that pork-consuming athletes wouldn't get so full of chemicals that they'd fail drug tests. This led to a flurry of Internet postings about the health risks ordinary Chinese faced when

eating "normal" pigs. First one and then scores of bloggers connected the dots between the regime's attentiveness to the well-being of athletes and seeming lack of concern for other groups, like miners. (There are scores of coal mining accidents each year, only some of which are officially acknowledged.) Many corners of the Chinese blogosphere were suddenly plastered with variations on the line "I'd rather be an Olympic pig than a man in a coal mine!"

4. *The political uses of the Chinese Internet that draw attention here and in China often differ.* Take, for example, Zeng Jingyan, wife of AIDS activist Hu Jia. After blogging about her experiences trying to free Hu from detention, she and her husband made *Time*'s list of the one hundred most influential people. But her actions haven't gained the kind of traction in her own country as, say, the Olympic pig stories did.

5. *A lot of what happens on the Chinese Internet isn't political.* Increasingly, Chinese Internet usage reflects the broad range of online activities happening in the United States, Europe, Japan, and other wired countries. Most Chinese Internet cafés are packed with students playing online video games, not checking out political websites. Online chat rooms are packed. Online commerce is growing rapidly. Online stock trading has taken off. And after the Sichuan earthquake, Chinese donated millions of dollars online.

6. *Though the Internet is thought of as an "international space," postings on it can be intensely patriotic, even jingoistic (in China and elsewhere).* Early Internet pioneers opined that the Internet would increasingly make national boundaries and identities irrelevant, especially among the wired young. But Chinese netizens can be nationalistic as well as cosmopolitan. In the spring, after the Tibet and Paris incidents, for example, *fenqing* ("angry youths") took to the Net, creating YouTube videos and blog posts that denigrated Tibetan rioters and railed against the French.

7. *Self-styled patriotic postings can make the government uneasy.* Unrestrained nationalism has often been a problem for the Chinese government. So officials are understandably wary when young people start to toss about nationalist slogans on the Internet and sometimes act quickly to rein things in. For instance, in April 2005, when anti-Japanese protests broke out across China in response to debates over the content of Japanese history textbooks (and their portrayal of World War II events), Internet censors quickly added the word "demonstration" to their list of banned words at QQ, China's most popular Internet messaging service. In the spring of 2008, the government initially allowed anti-French sentiment to build but soon was moving to tamp it down as online activists began calling for boycotts of international companies whose investment money Beijng has courted.

8. *Censorship is more complex than just "Big Brother" blocking sites or the "Great Firewall of China" keeping things out.* While Chinese Internet censorship is widespread, it's not a single unified system. There is some metalevel screening

of taboo words and images (like the Dalai Lama's name and face), but the "fire-wall" is actually a series of blocks—some at the national level, some at the local level. Universities, schools, and companies monitor and screen Internet traffic, as do Internet service providers and even individual websites. At the Chinese news blog Danwei, they've coined the catchy phrase "Net Nanny" to better reflect the Chinese government's efforts to prevent its citizens from being exposed to the wrong kinds of things. Some observers have noted the playful language games netizens use to circumvent the filters, but other discussions simply never take place, not only because of ham-handed interference but also because of self-censorship.

9. *China isn't always just following trends when it comes to Internet usage—it sometimes sets them.* This is true of software and technology developments for Internet censorship. It's also true of some creative areas. For instance, before the final installment of Harry Potter's adventures hit bookshelves last year, Chinese fans were able to read multiple versions online—written by Chinese authors riffing on J. K. Rowling's popular series—as well as several unauthorized translations of the real deal. Another example is that books made up of postings from popular blogs began making regular appearances on Chinese best-seller lists back in 2006, when these were still very rarely published in the West.

10. *You don't have to read Chinese to know what Chinese bloggers are saying.* You can go to Blog for China, a site started by a group of American-based Chinese students during the recent firestorm over alleged Western bias in media coverage of China, or visit sites like China Digital Times, Danwei, chinaSMACK, EastSouthWestNorth, Shanghaiist, and RConversation, all of which regularly translate posts from and track development relating to the Chinese Internet.

The Chinese Press in the Spotlight ☆ Timothy B. Weston

In the spring of 2008, the Chinese press struggled to cover a series of major and difficult stories while it was itself being watched and critiqued by the Western world with intensity and curiosity. What we saw in the Chinese press was a world in transition and flux.

First came the discussion in the Chinese press of the Tibetan demonstrations, its virtual refusal to acknowledge the validity of any foreign criticism, and its exposure of a reflexive, threatening, and brittle nationalism, especially among some Chinese youth. However, that was followed by its honest and educational reporting during the hand, foot, and mouth disease crisis in Anhui in April and May, and then came the biblical earthquake of May 12. The earthquake seemed to have shot fissures into the long-stalemated relationship between the Chinese media and the Chinese party-state. In the West, the earthquake—in large part because of the way the Chinese media reported it—opened up another Chinese face, one that, following on several months of largely negative coverage, could be loved. It appeared that the Olympics would not be the "It's Legit to Hate China Games" after all.

The Chinese government encouraged full coverage of the natural disaster domestically and around the world (very different from the kind of "anticoverage" it promotes in response to most *human-caused disasters*, such as mine collapses, about which I have written elsewhere). The coverage in Shanghai on CCTV starting the day of the earthquake itself was much like it might have been in the United States: the reporters wore resolved looks, humanized by a sense that they, too, were stricken by the sadness of the story. From what I saw, it seemed the network was truly trying to calm people, to be informative, and to be caring. The loops on the videotapes from the earthquake zone that first night were tight. Not many images had come out yet, so the coverage was especially numbing. It reminded me of American disaster news coverage—such as of Hurricane Katrina—which panders to our prurient interests by showing us searing and horrific images of what most of us fortunately will never experience personally. Somehow, though, in China this amount of information—tragic though it was—felt like a healthy thing. Most important, it felt open and thorough.

After watching the first few days of the earthquake coverage on Chinese TV, I returned to the United States on May 14. During the flight home I had a strange experience that made me think more about Chinese press liberalism and public relations. This involved the May 2008 special issue of *National Geographic*. I had taken that issue with me to China and started reading it but gave my copy of the magazine to an interested Chinese friend. So later, as I prepared to board my flight home at the sleek and modern Pudong International Airport in Shanghai just two days after the earthquake and the astounding openness of the early coverage, I bought a replacement copy of the special issue to read on the plane.

I was probably four hours from Shanghai and six from California when I came to a couple places in the magazine that had very thick pages, which I realized were actually several pages stuck together. They didn't just pull apart with a hissing static sound. They were really stuck together, with glue. They had been censored. I wondered, Why was someone or some agency in China directing people to put glue-stick X marks on certain stories in the special issue of *National Geographic*? Why were they trying to block people from viewing those stories? And why, of all things, people who read the magazine in English? What was it that we English readers should not see either? In any case, I found the clumsy attempt at censorship annoying and old school.

Of course, I wanted to read those sections of the magazine now more than ever. To my surprise, I was able to pull the pages (grudgingly) apart to see what I was not supposed to see, though some strips of paper tore off at the ends of key explanatory sentences I wanted to read. Yet the question for me after prying the pages apart was, *What in the world* was anyone doing censoring *those* things in particular? After discovering what the censors had tried to prevent me from seeing, I couldn't sustain feelings of anger. Instead, I was puzzled. The stakes seemed so minor.

After working for a few minutes to pull apart the first set of pages, I have to admit that I was disappointed. They contained a country map of China. I saw *nothing* on those pages that could in any way be deemed new or sensitive. The lines of the glue-stick X mark were unmistakable, and the map was badly damaged by my efforts to get access to what had been denied me, but had this been a mistake? Had the censor not been paying attention to what he or she was doing? The next thing I was not supposed to view was a short piece entitled "Mao Now." At least this had to do with a political figure. Yet it is hard to see why the few pop-culture images of Mao Zedong reproduced there, or the accompanying commentary, were deemed sensitive. One need only spend a few days in China to see equally irreverent images of one sort or another. This really did not seem like dangerous stuff.

The last two off-limits sections made a bit more sense. The two-page map of China depicting the country's ethnic minorities—where they live and how many of each there are—focuses on a subject that, because of the recent demonstrations in Tibet, may be deemed "sensitive." Still, it is hard to see why a map that simply illustrates China's ethnic diversity (which, one would think, is a good thing to make known) without any accompanying commentary should be considered offensive. Only the last glued pages made any sense to me; the short entry entitled "Cutting Off Dissent" deals with an obviously political and sensitive subject. There is delicious irony in the fact that my pages on the suppression of dissent and censorship contain a bold X mark and are difficult to read. It would be a good image to show in a lecture on censorship.

But all in all, pretty tame stuff. Was this censorship really worth the effort, and, if so, according to whom? Who actually glued the pages together? At what level was the decision to censor those pages made? Were those deciders the same people who are allowing more press openness now during the ongoing earthquake coverage? If so, they seem to have shifted direction very fast. If not, is the press opening the earthquake space on its own, with other muscle?

Would I have run into the same thing if I had instead bought the magazine at the new Beijing airport or the one in Canton? Fresh from viewing the open coverage of the earthquake on Chinese TV, I realized this is a moment of incredible possibility in China, one when greater press openness is emerging around a natural disaster but also one that feels like it could close down again at any moment. And if the next disaster should be human caused, perhaps in a way that implicates the political leadership itself, the frightened and rather arbitrary logic of the page gluers may once more prevail.

Finding Trust Online: Tigergate to the Sichuan Earthquakes ☆ Guobin Yang

On December 15, 2007, China Digital Times (CDT) posted a story about last year's "Tigergate incident." Titled "The Truth Is More Endangered Than Tigers in China," the story begins as follows:

"The 'South China Tiger' saga continues. Now known as 'Tigergate' among Chinese netizens, this event will no doubt be one of the top media/internet stories of 2007. On December 2nd, NetEase (one of China's leading news portals) published all 40 digital photos that farmer Zhou Zhenglong alleged he took of the tiger and also published six independent experts' evaluations of the authenticity of these photos. These six independent third party evaluations include no less than American Chinese criminologist Henry Lee, the China Photographers Association (CPA)'s digital photo authentification center, and China's top South China Tiger expert Hu Huijian. And all of their evaluations of the tiger photo reached the same conclusion: they're fake."

The story goes back to October 2007. At that time, the Shaanxi Forestry Bureau announced at a news conference the discovery of a South China tiger believed to be extinct in the wild. The proof of the discovery was a photograph taken by a peasant hunter called Zhou Zhenglong. The photograph was allegedly authenticated by a team of scientists and experts the local government had commissioned to appraise it. Yet as soon as the photograph was released on the Internet, China's inquisitive netizens challenged its authenticity. On November 16, someone posted the image of a traditional Chinese New Year tiger painting in an Internet forum, contending that Zhou's tiger was a photo of the tiger in the painting. Even as the evidence overwhelmingly showed that Zhou's photograph was a forgery, the Shaanxi Forestry Bureau remained evasive and refused to acknowledge the truth. Lasting for months, the online debates among frustrated netizens became a virtual quest for truth that was just not forthcoming. In September 2008, Zhou was sentenced to two and a half years in prison for fraud (there was a reward for a tiger spotting).

The "Tigergate" incident has symbolic significance. As the CDT posting puts it, it is "a reflection of the existing crisis of public trust in China society." It reflects citizens' yearning for trust.

Not only do people use the Internet in search of real-world trust, as the Tigergate case shows, but there are many acts of trust in cyberspace. This is not to say there is no dark matter on the Internet. Cyberspace is no more a pure land than other places. And yet, talk to any "Net friends" (*wangyou*), and they usually have a supply of stories about friendship, love, philanthropy, understanding, trust, and solidarity in virtual reality.

But let me turn to the 2008 Sichuan earthquakes. One striking thing about public responses to the earthquakes was the demonstration of public trust. According to a survey of 523 respondents conducted on June 1, 2008, by researchers from Qinghua University, the Internet was the most important channel of information after the earthquake, while television was second and newspapers third. The sample is admittedly small, but it is still revealing and thought provoking. If it is true that more people used the Internet than television for information, it indicates, among other things, a high degree of trust in information online.

Another example of such trust was the amount of donations people made online. In partnership with several other websites and Jet Li's One Foundation, Tianya.com began to solicit online donations for disaster relief on the day of the earthquake. Three days later, on May 15, it had already raised 24 million yuan (RMB). Most of this amount came from individual online donors who would have to trust the websites they use to make monetary donations.

Expressions of online trust interacted with and were matched by the outpourings of trust offline. Han Hai Sha, an environmental and educational nongovernmental organization (NGO) in Beijing, raised money, medicine, tents, and other materials and equipment for disaster relief within days of the earthquakes. Initially, however, activists in this small NGO were at a loss about how to transport these donations to the distant earthquake regions in Sichuan. They then thought of a friend in an Internet-based automobile friendship club (*che you hui*). This individual immediately posted messages in the websites of several such clubs. Within about ten minutes, Han Hai Sha had recruited ten netizens, who all volunteered to provide free transportation with their own automobiles at their own costs (which included expenses for gas, meals, and accommodation for a four- to five-day round-trip from Beijing to Chengdu).

These acts of trust among common citizens, online and offline, formed a contrast with a deep-seated distrust of government officials. Entertaining doubts about whether local government officials would put the donations to proper use, many people resorted to the Internet to push for transparency and accountability. In the middle of all the relief efforts, netizens revealed online, complete with digital photographs, "disaster-only" tents showing up in the streets in Chengdu when they should have belonged to the much more heavily hit earthquake regions. In response to such public demands, the Chinese government issued policy guidelines avowing severe punishment of corruption related to earthquake donations.

In China today, stories about the lack of trust are many and all too familiar: people have poor trust not just in government officials, businesses, and police but also in teachers, professors, scientists, and even physicians. There are fake foodstuffs, fake brand-name liquor, fake medicine, fake diplomas, and fake beauty products. Everything is fake. Nothing and nobody can be trusted. At least for some people, that seems to be China's harsh reality.

Why can there be trust in virtual reality when it is lacking in "real" reality? Why do people seek trust in cyberspace rather than in their communities? This puzzling phenomenon probably says more about the sorry condition of community than about the Internet. If the degree of trust is a good measure, its weakness indicates the weakness of community. If people go online in search of trust, does it mean that there is an alternative community online? Do online communities make up for the poverty of community in the "real" world? Are they signs of escape, or do they signal new practices of civic engagement? Contrasting citizens' quests for trust in the Tigergate incident and after the Sichuan earthquakes raises questions not only about how Chinese use and rely on the Internet but also, more fundamentally, about their feelings toward traditional communities.

Things We'd Rather You Not Say on the Web, or Anywhere Else ☆ David Bandurski

Following George Carlin's death in May 2008, China Beat *got to thinking about his "seven dirty words" and what those same "seven words" might be in China. We invited David Bandurski of the Hong Kong–based China Media Project, which monitors press trends in the People's Republic of China, to write a satirical piece in the style of Carlin, riffing on this idea of banned words in China.*

I love words. And I thank you in advance, dear citizens, for obeying mine. Words are dangerous and slippery things. Some people in the West will tell you that words are playthings and that we should all be free to do with them as we please. But I want to tell you that words are really all we have—and this is why the party has troubled itself to choose them so carefully on your behalf.

You will have heard, I suppose, that Article 35 of our nation's constitution guarantees that you enjoy "freedom of expression." You will no doubt agree, however, as a matter of moral principle, that responsible citizens must enjoy all things in moderation. No good can come of enjoying words too much—and this is why we have taken it upon ourselves to parcel out this freedom, so that all Chinese can enjoy words with more or less equal moderation.

Comrade Mao Zedong once said, "Power grows out of the barrel of a gun." But words too are powerful. It is not my intention to spook you, dear citizens, but we must all remember the way that too many words under the policy of "glasnost"—a Russian word whose direct translation is "chaos"—spelled the end of the Soviet Union.

We must not forget—and this begins with not remembering—how Zhao Ziyang said on May 6, 1989, in the midst of popular demonstrations, that propaganda leaders should "open things up just a bit." "There is no big danger in that," he said. His words were careless, and the end result was chaos. Nobody wants chaos. Just try to picture what it does to gross domestic product.

Comrade Zhao, you see, failed to understand the real power of words. He failed to understand that the party and the masses must not be too profligate with them if they are to "do the great work of socialism with Chinese characteristics." That is why the party had to step in afterward to reorder your words and ideas. We have our own word for this: "guidance of public opinion." Say it with me: "guidance of public opinion."

Good. Now, dear citizens, I think it is best to instruct you with a couple of examples of what I mean about words. This way you will understand how to use them with responsibility and care, correctly upholding—say it with me—"GUIDANCE of PUBLIC OPINION." Right. I hope these examples will help you remember how to forget the right things.

There are more than 40,000 characters in the Chinese language. Fortunately, basic literacy requires only about three thousand to four thousand of these words, which makes it much easier for us to keep an eye on the ones that matter. The most important thing is not the characters themselves but rather how they are put together. Words are like chemicals. You have to mix them carefully. I'm sure you would agree that's just good science.

Take, for example, the character for "people," *min*. When we place it behind the character for "person," *ren*, we get a very nice word that means generally "the people." We can use it in sentences like, "The party cannot do without the people, and the people cannot do without the party," in which the party and the people are more or less interchangeable.

On the other hand, if we take this harmless character *min* and place behind it the character for "host" or "master," *zhu*, the result, "democracy," is a dangerous discharge that upsets the harmony of our first sentence. One simple character rips the party and the people apart. We must not let words come between us, dear citizens.

This word, "democracy," is a perilous word that must be handled with great care. The only ones we can trust to use "democracy" safely are trained party scholars. They are able to neutralize the word by sealing it up in proper contexts. Phrases like "intraparty democracy" and "developing socialist democratic politics" are some of the more advanced ways the party has managed to quarantine this word and keep all of you safe. On the Web, we have more sophisticated technical means of protecting you—by blocking, for example, searches of words like "constitutional democracy."

We are constantly improving our technical and other means of fighting dangerous words so that your thoughts and ideas can be healthier. But we do need your help and cooperation. This is a "people's war" on vocabulary, and our enemies are spilling off the tongues of the West.

Still, if we use words like "democracy" at the discretion of the finer minds in the party, this can sometimes help promote international harmony. In my report to the seventeenth party congress last year, I used the word "democracy" in a safe context more than sixty times. Hearing the word so often, Western media got a bit overexcited. Their words for us were kind and harmonious.

"Harmony." Now that's a nice word. What should you say to help you fend off dirty words like "democracy"? That's right: "Harmony." Say it with me: "Harmony."

"Harmony" packs quite a punch for such a small word. It muffles socioeconomic problems of all kinds, most of which have arisen from the last decade of reforms.

Let's just say you're eaten up with words about how you were kicked off your farmland to make room for a big shopping mall that lined your local party secretary's pockets. The party deals proactively with such issues by stepping back and taking a bird's-eye view of your grievances. We call this the "scientific view of development." I don't want to get bogged down in details—the party prefers economy of words. But basically, we are working toward a "moderately well-off" and "harmonious society" where you can afford to buy Fendi at your neighborhood shopping mall.

Of course, a "harmonious society" can be achieved only by dint of hard work. No one can get anything done when faced with constant distractions. I urge you to keep your voice down and be "harmonious." I know that's easier said than done. And that is why the party lends a hand, "harmonizing" news, blogs, chat rooms, and any other places where words tend to cause trouble.

"Harmony" is one of my favorite words. It reminds us that the only way we can give proper and "scientific" attention to solutions is by drowning out the noise of nagging problems.

There are many words we'd rather you not say or enjoy publicly, especially as the Olympic Games draw nearer. But you need not worry yourself over this. The party has put numerous measures in place to ensure that you are free to make the right word choices. Sometimes, as your options are managed, you may feel at a loss for words—and really that is okay. After all, so long as your tongue is tied, we have no reason to bind your hands.

Chapter 13

Pop Culture in a Global Age

ROCKING BEIJING

Eric Setzekorn

Like almost every aspect of Beijing life in the past five years, the live music scene has undergone rapid but uneven development. Beijing has always prided itself on the gritty originality of its live music compared to the dominance of cover bands in Shanghai or the saccharine Canto-pop of Hong Kong. The recent opening of new, modern venues on both sides of the city has allowed dozens of new bands and a newly affluent urban youth to establish a flourishing but still shallow live music scene.

For live music, particularly rock and hip-hop music, the Olympics are bringing challenges such as new rules and regulations but could allow some bands to develop a global fan base that remains a central difficulty for Chinese groups. A less immediate and more difficult issue will be resolving the internal contradictions between Chinese rock and its relation to Chinese society. The elephant in the room of any discussion of China's music scene is how to rectify the antiauthoritarian values that infuse rock music and even more so punk and hip-hop with the boundaries of the Chinese political system. At present the young, often highly nationalistic youth seem to be pulling in the same direction as the government, which comes as a shock to many foreign visitors and seems to betray the core antiestablishment values of rock, punk, and hip-hop. However, the post-1989 cultural détente in which musicians stayed away from politics may be eroding.

Posted 7/23/2008 at 03:52:00 PM

The Olympics raised China's international profile in 2008, and, combined with the Tibetan riots and the Sichuan earthquake, China was front-page news around the world for the first two-thirds of the year. Interest in China spread to other areas as well, as publications ran an unprecedented number of reviews of China-focused books and books by Chinese authors. In 2008, Jiang Rong's best-selling novel Wolf Totem, *which won the inaugural Man Asian Literary Prize in Hong Kong in late 2007, was published in English translation to both glowing and censorious reviews (we have included examples of each in this chapter), while Mo Yan, author of* Red Sorghum *and* Life and Death Are Wearing Me Out, *was awarded the inaugural Newman Prize for Chinese literature (worth $10,000) at the University of Oklahoma.*

In 2003, Crouching Tiger, Hidden Dragon *became the highest-grossing foreign language film ever in the United States, and while nothing this year topped it, the movie paved the way for other crossover films. This year, the most successful "Chinese" films were, unlike* Crouching Tiger, *in English and included* The Forbidden Kingdom *and* Kung Fu Panda. *The latter was enormously popular in China, though it did provoke some controversy, as Haiyan Lee discusses in her piece, "Kung Fu Panda, Go Home!"*

Undoubtedly the biggest worldwide Chinese cultural impact in 2008 was the Olympic Games. As Timothy S. Oakes notes in his essay, many of the cultural questions that spun around the Olympics centered on debates of what was "real" and "fake." In recent years, China has been plagued by questions of "fakery," from its massive industry for knockoff designer goods to the practice of adding melamine (a chemical compound often used to make plastic) to pet food and milk powder, among other things, to inflate those products' readings for protein. The Olympics were, in this regard, no different. There were questions throughout the two weeks of the Games over the ages of some of the Chinese gymnasts (they were accused of being under the required age of fourteen years, though the International Olympic Committee eventually ruled that all were of age to compete), over several of the performances during the opening ceremonies (agencies reported that none of the children used to represent China's fifty-six minority groups were actually minorities), and over the fireworks that TV viewers saw during the ceremonies (some were prerecorded). As Oakes argues, fakery is no more (nor less) than a utopian desire, and what, after all, is the Olympics but an expression of a modern utopia where international fraternité—"One World, One Dream," indeed—could reign supreme?

Kung Fu Panda, Go Home! ☆ Haiyan Lee

It seems that boycott fatigue has finally hit the Chinese in a year that has lurched from one boycott to another—against such entities as a French supermarket chain, a Hollywood star, and an American cable channel. When the latest clarion call was issued by a performance artist named Zhao Bandi against *Kung Fu Panda*, he was greeted with jeers and mockery (*New York Times*, June 30, 2008). Zhao presented his case on a blog: Hollywood is morally corrupt for churning out loathsome personalities like Sharon Stone (who betrayed schadenfreude over the Sichuan earthquake as "karmic retribution" for Tibet) and Steven Spielberg (who quit his role as artistic adviser to the Olympics over Sudan). Therefore, it should not be allowed to profit, *in China* and so soon after the earthquake, from China's most iconic "national treasure"—the panda. And for Chinese to help line the pockets of the Hollywood reprobates would be tantamount to stripping valuables off the bodies of the quake victims.

The banner that Zhao strung up outside the State Administration of Radio, Film, and Television, telling *Kung Fu Panda* to go home (*Gongfu xiongmao gun hui qu!*), was taken down within twenty minutes by plainclothes police. The movie opened in multiple cities on June 20 as scheduled to huge, mirthful crowds. But Zhao's effort was not a complete failure: the release of the movie was delayed for one day in Sichuan—home of the panda reserve and site of the earthquake—over concerns about possible "misperceptions" and hurt feelings. For this minor victory, Zhao received a phone call from an irate Sichuanese who gave him a bank account number and demanded that a suitable sum be deposited into it. For what? To compensate for the psychological loss he allegedly sustained for being prevented from enjoying the movie simultaneously with his dear compatriots in the rest of the country!

Most of the detractors simply regarded Zhao as a clown and a hypocrite, asking tongue in cheek if he had come down with a case of "boycott disease" (*dizhibing*) or if he was jealous of Hollywood's high-tech virtuosity. Zhao has indeed made a name for himself ("the Pandaman," *xiongmao ren*) with his panda-themed performance art, most notably a goofy line of black-and-white and furry fashion gear. Apparently his being Chinese not only entitles him to playful (and gainful) appropriation of his national patrimony but also obligates him to guard it against profiteering interlopers.

Given how favorably predisposed the Chinese generally were to the movie, it seems that Dreamworks has hit the right note in saying that the movie is intended to be a love letter to the Chinese and a tribute to Chinese culture. Audiences across China have indeed been duly pleased (and tickled) by the movie's clever blend of made–in–Hong Kong kung fu lore, Chinatown chinoiserie, American teenage humor, and state-of-the-art animation technology. Commentators can't seem to get over the realization that a didactic story could also be so *fun*, unlike so many Chinese-made "main-melody" (*zhuxuanlü*) fares featuring humorless, grandstanding heroes. Of course, the tried-and-true technique of defamiliarization is key here: a wok may be just a wok in a Chinese movie, but in *Kung Fu Panda* it is also a fight prop and hence an ingredient of hilarity. Other everyday objects too tumble through a riotous chop-socky career: noodles, dumplings, chopsticks, and whatnot, cooking up a *panda*monium unlike anything the Chinese audiences are accustomed to—with perhaps the exception of Stephen Chow's manically droll *Kung Fu Hustle* and a few Jackie Chan movies.

The subversion and parodying of kung fu movie conventions doesn't stop with substituting woks and chopsticks for swords and nunchakus. Genre bending seems to come with the territory of global mass culture. If Zhao Bandi had spent some time pondering the losses and gains of commercialized cultural borrowing, including his own, he might come to see the movie not as a battered victim of cultural imperialism but as a celebration of middle-class values—hard work and having faith in yourself—and a dramatization of the middle-class predica-ment—to live a life of ordinary fulfillment (such as carrying on the family noodle soup business) or to pursue lofty ambitions (such as becoming the dragon war-rior and savior of the realm). These values and predicaments can hardly be stamped Chinese. They are rather the stuff of a bourgeois fairy tale in an amus-ingly exotic (or multicultural) getup designed to ensure the movie's global mar-ketability. Po the panda is the classic involuntary hero, a burly version of Spiderman. Martial arts (kung fu), like Spiderman's web or the Hulk's gamma rays, is the magical force that enables the virtuous to triumph over the wicked who wield it for nefarious ends.

Yet *Kung Fu Panda* does Americanize the kung fu genre far more radically than, say, Ang Lee's *Crouching Tiger, Hidden Dragon*. This it does by playing fast and loose with a crucial genre device. On the surface, both movies honor the idea that supreme martial arts skills can be codified in writing and that *the book*—the Holy Grail of kung fu—is usually hidden in some secret location or jealously guarded by an impartial agent. In *Crouching Tiger*, Jade Fox steals the secret manual from her master because he would not transmit esoteric Wudang techniques to a female disciple. She then uses it clandestinely to train her young aristocratic mistress Jen to fight. However, she does not know that Jen is stealth-ily studying the text of the manual, whereas she, being illiterate, can only make out the pictures. As a result, Jen blindsides Jade Fox when they are pitted against each other in a match. The assumption is that writing encodes higher cosmic martial truth than image. Those who can read attain greater occult powers than those who can only view. While this may sound hopelessly snooty in the age of YouTube, the basic idea still resonates in Chinese cultural spheres.

Variations of this idea can be found in most Chinese-language kung fu mov-ies. The literary and martial arts are taken to be two sides of the same cosmic coin, or the Way. Both are said to be inspired by the tracks and movements of birds and beasts. Hence, the same metaphors and protocols inform both the civil and the martial domains, invariably urging the harmony of heaven, earth, and man. Zhang Yimou rehearses this idea to a fare-thee-well in *Hero*. In that movie, the king becomes enlightened of the essence of swordsmanship by mediating on the majestically rendered calligraphic character for "sword" (*jian*). Such hyper-bole can strike an uninitiated viewer as all very "mystical and kung-fu-y" (Po's complaint against Master Shifu the red panda), if not downright silly. But it is of a piece with the revelatory conception of writing that also accords quasi-scriptural status to the handwritings of political leaders—even when the specimen in question is less than elegant—as testimony of their cosmic virtue and authority.[1]

Interestingly, *Crouching Tiger* almost went without the essential device of writing. James Schamus recalled that after his Taiwan-based script-writing partners perused his initial draft, they wanted to know where "the book" was (*New York Times*, November 5, 2000). Apparently not understanding the special status of writing in Chinese culture, he had done away with "all the bother about who has the book, who stole the book, who understood the book and why the book was variously hidden, coded, burned, memorized, etc." In the end, he was glad that his collaborators insisted on putting the book back in.

In *Kung Fu Panda*, the Holy Grail is the "dragon scroll" lodged securely in the mouth of a stone dragon on the high ceiling of the Jade Palace. It is destined, intones its guardian, Master Oogway the tortoise, for the eye of the true dragon warrior. And yet when Po finally sets eyes on it, he finds himself staring into a flimsy blank scroll with a reflective surface. The significance of the blank scroll eventually dawns on him when his goose father the noodle maker[2] confides to him that there is no such thing as the "secret ingredient of the secret recipe." "Things become special," he explains, "because people believe them to be special."

Thus, a homely American self-help maxim—dubbed "Hallmark-Fu" by a British reviewer (*Times Online*, July 5, 2008)—steals the thunder of Oriental mysticism. To be sure, the image of a wordless scroll is not entirely alien to Chinese audiences, and the idea that the ultimate truth is ineffable can be found in both Taoist and Zen Buddhist philosophy.[3] But given the movie's folksy-populist flavor, the blank scroll also evokes the ring as the forbidden symbol of power in the *Lord of the Rings* trilogy. In that case, the imperative to destroy the ring is connected to the idea that power in a democracy is in theory an "empty" place. Here, the secret that is supposed to empower whoever possesses it once and for all turns out to be a hoax, so to speak. The hero (Po) and the villain (Tai Lung the leopard) are forced to fall back on their moral and martial cultivation and have it out blow by blow. The true hero prevails because of the nobility of

---

1. See Richard Kraus's *China Beat* post on the quixotic effort to preserve Premier Wen Jiabao's chalk calligraphy left at an earthquake site.

2. Some Chinese viewers were baffled by the odd cross-species lineage from father to son and speculated that it might be a backhanded attempt on the part of Hollywood to assert seniority over Chinese culture by way of a disguised Donald Duck.

3. After this was posted, I was reminded by a couple of readers of the episode in the *Journey to the West* (a.k.a. *Monkey*) in which Tripitaka and his disciples are bestowed with bundles of blank scriptures at the end of their assiduous pilgrimage. However, their inability to appreciate such a supreme gift forces the Buddha to substitute "lesser" scriptures, with writing, which the motley crew happily carry back to China.

his purpose and because the people are on his side, not, in the last analysis, because he has *the book*.

Such is the coup pulled off by *Kung Fu Panda* against the genre to which it also pays earnest tribute. Audiences of course can enjoy the movie for whatever reasons, but at least part of the pleasure, I suspect, is coming from its cheeky deflation of the ponderous mood that sometimes weighs down the kung fu genre. If anyone should be upset about the movie, it should be the diehard kung fu aficionados. The movie has so upped the ante that future makers of kung fu movies will have to think twice before they whip out the obligatory book, however much it is rooted in Chinese cosmology. In this sense, *Kung Fu Panda* is a disarmingly cute and merry face of the global modernity that has made it impossible for anyone to lay claim to beloved cultural symbols as inviolable national patrimony.

In Defense of Jiang Rong's *Wolf Totem* ☆ Timothy B. Weston

I have a confession to make: I was moved by Jiang Rong's *Wolf Totem* and think it's an important novel and that it's well worth reading. The reason I say I feel a need to "confess" as opposed to just being able to state this is because postings on *China Beat*, as well as some of the reviews referenced in those postings, attack the book with a sharpness and thoroughgoingness that initially made me question my own taste and to think that I was politically incorrect for liking and being impressed by the novel as I read it. But after finishing Howard Goldblatt's translation of *Wolf Totem*—a book that we now know is the work of Lu Jiamin, using "Jiang Rong" as a pseudonym—my conviction remains unchanged that this is indeed a major work. Reactions to the novel have varied widely. Here, very briefly, I'd like to add one more voice of praise, for in my opinion it would be a pity if, swayed by the negative things they may have read about it, China experts (or other interested readers) were to decide that reading the novel isn't worth the effort.

Before saying more I want to make clear that I agree with many of the criticisms made of the book: it *is* didactic, *does* lack character development, and *is* too long. Moreover, to the extent that it advocates that Chinese adopt wolfish cunning and aggressiveness as national characteristics, it *does* open itself to the charge of being nationalistic, though personally I did not find this theme overly offensive. Fully mature and great literature it may not be, but I think it is courageous, imaginative, and a deserving winner of the inaugural Man Asian Literary Prize. No other novel, from any country, has given me so deep an appreciation for the vitally important and interconnected roles played by all creatures and species within the natural environment or of the fragile relationship between we human beings and the ecological setting in which we live. At a moment when awareness of our endangerment of the planet is rising to new levels, Jiang Rong has produced a profound lament about what it can mean when human beings and human societies carry on with little to no regard for the natural environment.

This message is of course universally relevant and highly timely. The fact that is has been articulated so passionately by a Chinese writer is remarkable, given the low level of environmental consciousness usually attributed to contemporary China. Here, then, we have a powerful Chinese contribution to the global discussion about our human-caused planetary environmental crisis. For me, this is a welcome development.

Also welcome, in my view, is Jiang Rong's willingness to merge his tale of environmental destruction with an open discussion of Han Chinese cultural and political imperialism. In *Wolf Totem* disregard for other cultures (in this case nomadic Mongolian culture) goes hand in hand with disregard for the natural environment; the same unthinking mind-set produces both. Having noted with sadness the scarcity of publicly expressed Chinese compassion for the feelings of Tibetans during the recent disturbances in Tibet and elsewhere, I find it refreshing to encounter Jiang Rong's concern over Han insensitivity to minority peoples.

While Jiang Rong is critical of Han Chinese ignorance and arrogance with regard to minority cultures and ways of life within China, *Wolf Totem* is not a simplistic good-guy-versus-bad-guy story, nor is it an overly determined good-ethnic-group-versus-bad-ethnic-group tale. Ethnicity is not treated in an essentialist fashion in this novel. Chen Zhen, the novel's protagonist, is a Han Chinese, as are several other important characters, and they develop a deep appreciation for the environment and the brutal and amoral ways of nature. Han Chinese are not irredeemable, in other words. Nor are Mongols portrayed as being wholly in touch with nature; among other things, in fact, the novel narrates fissures within Mongol society along generational, geographic, and ideological lines. As with the Chinese, some Mongols are shown to be sensitive to the environment, and some are not.

As environmental studies becomes an ever more important part of school curricula there's a growing need for books that speak to environmental issues in creative and compelling ways. While reading *Wolf Totem*, I kept thinking about how to use it in my teaching. Since I am a historian, I thought of pairing it with Mark Elvin's recent monumental historical study *The Retreat of the Elephants* or with Judith Shapiro's *Mao's War against Nature*. My sense is that Jiang Rong's literary exploration of environmental issues in China would work well with those more academic treatments.

There is of course also the question of why *Wolf Totem* has been so amazingly popular in China. I can imagine an entire class session devoted to that issue alone, for if, as one blurb on the cover of Goldblatt's translation states, the novel has in fact outsold any other book in Chinese history since Mao's *Little Red Book*, that is a truly astonishing fact. What does it tell us about Chinese society today? No doubt many things, not all of them positive (other reviewers are likely right that the macho tone of the novel is at least partially responsible for its extraordinary appeal in China). Nevertheless, at this time, when the price of decades of disregard for the natural environment is becoming painfully obvious to more and more Chinese, my hunch is that a great many of the millions of Chinese readers of *Wolf Totem* have been attracted to the message of environmental warning that is its central theme. Along the way, of course, they are treated to an unusually self-reflective discussion of Han Chinese relations with minority peoples who belong to the Chinese nation. One can hope that in this way, too, the novel is having a positive effect on those who have been reading it.

Wolf Totem: Romanticized Essentialization ☆ Nicole E. Barnes

Having proven his mettle as translator of Xiao Hong's angsty prose and Mo Yan's morbidly lascivious novels, famed translator Howard Goldblatt has now tried his hand at a certain piece of nostalgic drivel that leaked from the pen of Jiang Rong, the newly acclaimed novelist whose original work, *Wolf Totem* (*Lang Tuteng*), appeared in 2004 after more than thirty years of labor and immediately shot to the top of the bestseller lists, selling 2 million bookstore copies and countless more pirated copies. Although he hid his unorthodox ideas behind a pen name, Jiang Rong's endeavors earned him the very first Man Asian Literary Prize.

This semiautobiographical novel follows the young Chinese intellectual Chen Zhen in Inner Mongolia during the Cultural Revolution. Chen's drunken admiration for the steppe leads him to kidnap and raise a wolf cub. The novel essentializes ethnic identity as utterly contingent upon nature and identifies Mongols with the wolf (bold and brave) and Han Chinese with the sheep (meek and, well, sheepish). Despite its artless plot, *Lang Tuteng* appealed to millions of Chinese readers who found double happiness in its pages: romanticization of the Mongolian "wilderness" as the urbanites' playground and a symbolic reversal of the woes produced by internal colonization: wolves don't lose to sheep. The novel's closing scene underscores the limited capacity of this symbolic reversal, as Han immigration and resource exploitation turn the last of Inner Mongolia's majestic grasslands to desert and a foreboding sandstorm shrouds Beijing. The ecological disasters of internal colonization come home to roost on Beijingers' windowsills . . .

Despite Goldblatt's best intentions to enhance Western understanding of China by introducing a Chinese best-seller to an English readership, *Wolf Totem* is likely to appeal to an Orientalist audience. It was, for instance, hailed on Amazon.com as "an epic Chinese tale in the vein of *The Last Emperor*." We know where that leads. Now that China's eastern seaboard is packed to the gills with people, congested roads, and belching factories, it seems that we can all locate our nostalgia in Mongolia and Tibet (protests and their violent quashing aside, tourism in the Dalai Lama's homeland is on the rise). At least in this regard, urbanites the world over can be united.

Wei Cheng: From an Elite Novel to a Popular Metaphor ☆ Xia Shi

Wei Cheng (*Fortress Besieged*) has been hailed by some critics as "the most delightful and carefully wrought novel in modern Chinese literature" and "perhaps also its greatest."[4] Written by Qian Zhongshu in 1947, it is an acerbic comedy about the hapless hero Fang Hongjian's wanderings in middle-class society. Its 1979-translated English title is based on a French proverb: marriage is like a fortress besieged; those who are outside want to get in, and those who are inside want to get out. The British equivalent of this French saying draws a picture of a gilded birdcage with the birds outside wanting to get in and the birds inside wanting to fly out. Both these versions are mentioned by Qian's characters.

Since its initial publication, the novel's reception in China has swung from early criticism of the book as a product of elite culture to the 1980s and 1990s wide acclaim amid pop culture's frenzied consumption. Nowadays, *Wei Cheng* and Qian are household names. Its canonization process involved not merely "rediscovery" but "reinvention" in a surprisingly diverse number of ways. In 1990s China, "Wei Cheng" was a prominent popular word, ranked alongside "Karaoke," "stock market," "privacy," and "MBA." Nowadays, it has been incorporated into common people's daily speech. If you ask an urban Chinese of average education what "Wei Cheng" means, most of the time the answer will fall within the following four aspects:

First of all, "Wei Cheng" is used as a metaphor for marriage. It denotes the complexities of the institution of marriage. Jonathan Spence, in his foreword for the novel's English version, regards it as "one of the finest descriptions of the disintegration of a marriage ever penned in any language." When Fang Hongjian deplores marriage as a besieged fortress, Qian clearly conveys an antiromantic pessimism about marriage.

With an ever-increasing divorce rate in big cities, more and more Chinese

---

4. C. T. Hsia, *A History of Modern Chinese Fiction* (New Haven, CT: Yale University Press, 1961).

are catching Wei Cheng's connotation today, as the following typical daily life dialogue on marriage reveals:

FRIEND A: I am going to get married soon.

FRIEND B: (joking) Wanna enter "Wei Cheng," huh? Congratulations!

To be sure, ambivalence toward marriage is a universal mentality. However, it could be said that it was Qian who first created the Chinese equivalent of the French "fortress besieged" or the English "gilded birdcage." According to Jonathan Spence, the phrase "Wei Cheng" in Chinese "had been most prominently used by a Chinese poet back in 1842 to describe the city of Nanking when it was besieged by the British after their defeat of China in the first of the so-called 'opium wars.'" Thus, he infers, "shame and national humiliation would have been very much in people's thoughts." However, since Qian's usage, it has gained a new life, and it is this new meaning that contemporary Chinese are most familiar with.

Interestingly enough, the phrase "Wei Cheng" in Chinese not only conveys similar meanings to its French or English equivalent but also has unique national and cultural characteristics. If literally translated, it should be "surrounded cities." If you ask Chinese people what image they conjure when hearing this phrase, many will reply that they picture ancient Chinese architecture—walls in rectangular shape, with four gates, sometimes with four turrets. Even the textures of the bricks of the walls, they will sometimes vividly add, resemble those of the Great Wall. It is absolutely not a fortress or a birdcage or a modern city. Qian in his book never gives any specific descriptions on what this "Wei Cheng" looks like and thus left a space for individual imagination. In analyzing the varied meanings of Wei Cheng, however, it becomes clear that amazingly similar images can be deployed to represent a common human idea—that of marriage as an imprisonment, of sorts—despite vast national, cultural, and linguistic differences.

More broadly speaking, "Wei Cheng" can also be used to describe the dilemma of perpetual human dissatisfaction. By insisting that the human condition is doomed to dissatisfaction, Qian's attitude toward humanity is outside any particular context. In this sense, it is more often used in the phrase of "Wei Cheng Xianxiang" (the phenomenon of Wei Cheng). A Google search will reveal to you an amazing amount of "Wei Cheng Xianxiang" that are currently perplexing modern Chinese society in the fields of education, investment, retirement, and so on. For instance, online reports describe the current fever of college graduates taking the highly selective national examinations to vie for the limited posts of government employees. Here, the "Wei Cheng Xianxiang," the reporter points out, is between those who see stability and "invisible but potential" good income offered by government jobs and are thus eager to get in on them and those ambitious talents who are already in government jobs but soon became bored and thus wanted to quit.

The third aspect of the novel that has entered the Chinese idiomatic lexicon is associated with the fad of studying abroad and fake diplomas. In particular, the term "Carleton University," from which Qian's character Fang Hongjian purchased his fake PhD diploma, can refer to an illegitimate degree qualification or academic institution. Qian scorned the fake diploma as "Adam and Eve's fig leaf," which "could hide a person's shame and wrap up his disgrace." Since China's opening and reform, more and more Chinese have been choosing to study overseas so as to return years later with a "gilded" (*dujin*) layer. Correspondingly, many people soon realize that some of these returned students, like Fang Hongjian, have fake diplomas. As a result, we can see that public discourse on various media began to warn employers of those who were graduates of "Carleton University." However, it should be noted that Qian's satire was not merely limited to those fake degree holders. In his novel, even those characters with real PhD degrees were nothing but pretentious and arrogant intellectuals. In fact, in Spence's view, what Qian was aiming to satirize is the whole "baleful effects of the excessive adaptation of Western literary and aesthetic theories," which had "corroded the integrity of the Chinese." In other words, Qian expressed his doubts that China had to throw off the shackles of tradition and urgently modernize itself in order to be a strong, self-confident nation. He mocked the entire phenomenon of overseas studying as "modern *keju*" (Imperial Examination System), the alternative of "reflecting glory on one's ancestors" (*guang zong yao zu*). The following words from Wei Cheng have been widely regarded in China as the most classic satire of the mentality of those who blindly followed the fever of studying abroad:

> The studying abroad today is like passing examinations under the old Manchu system. . . . It's not for the broadening of knowledge that one goes abroad but to get rid of that inferiority complex. It's like having smallpox or measles, or in other words, it's essential to have them. . . . Once we've studied abroad, we've gotten the inferiority complex out of the system, and our souls become strengthened, and when we do come across such germs as Ph.D.'s or M.A.'s we've built up a resistance against them. . . . Since all other subjects . . . have already been Westernized, Chinese literature, the only native product, is still in need of a foreign trademark before it can hold its own.

It should be noted that Qian himself received a bachelor's degree in English literature from Oxford University in 1937. His thesis was "China in the English Literature of the Seventeenth and Eighteenth Century."

Last but not least, if you happened to be familiar with the more "vulgar" side of contemporary Chinese popular culture, unexpectedly, you will be amused to find that many *laobaixing* (commoners) like to use "Wei Cheng" to refer to playing mahjong. It is unclear why and when "Wei Cheng" became a mahjong nickname. Probably it is because playing mahjong is like building up "surrounded walls." It is interesting to notice that Qian mentioned mahjong in his novel. When he described bored Chinese students playing mahjong on the ship home from their overseas studies, Qian referred to it as "the Chinese national pastime," which was "said to be popular in America as well," and sarcastically remarked, "thus playing mahjong not only had a down-home flavor to it but was also in tune with world trends."

As early as the 1920s, if not earlier, mahjong was well known in China for its corrupting influence. In particular, it was often associated with the stereotypical image of the "parasitic and decadent" *taitais* (wives of upper- or middle-class men), as depicted in the beginning of Ang Lee's *Lust, Caution* or in the descriptions of novelist Eileen Chang (Zhang Ailing), whose works invoke popular nostalgia for 1930–1940s Shanghai. By using mahjong here, Qian expressed scorn that China's "bright future" was in the hands of these returning students, representatives of modern "civilization and progress," spending "their entire time gambling, except for eating and sleeping."

All of the above four aspects demonstrate the degrees to which *Wei Cheng* has permeated contemporary Chinese popular culture. In a sense, it could be argued that *Wei Cheng*'s "metamorphosis" from a novel to a phrase or idiom in Chinese daily lexicon provided a new arena for the expression and elaboration of social phenomenon and mentality in family life, work, and education.

Wei Cheng's later popularization was something that Qian could never have expected considering the various criticisms the book received after its initial publication in 1947. In spite of the accuracy of the novel's biting social commentary, it was derided by critics as "high-class reading," "out of this universe," and unconnected with ordinary people's devastating wartime living experiences and for being apolitical, "not embodying either leftist or anti-Japanese values." The majority of the population barely heard of it because of its limited circulation.

Half a century later, exhausted from various political struggles and movements, the Chinese masses have changed their tastes and reading expectations. Caught by its tone of futility, they began to enjoy its apolitical stance, honesty and humor, psychological insights, and the erudite display in its skillful manipulation of language. After its adaptation to a well-received TV show, mass media further led common people to find the rich relevance of this novel to their own lives in 1990s China, a society with a reflective orientation amid its everyday newness. Lacking even one lovable character or role model (including its four heroines), readers nonetheless believe that Qian gave them a sympathetic portrayal of real persons in whom they found a little bit of themselves.

Faking Heaven: It's All Done with Mirrors: Patty Chang's *Shangri-la* and the Utopian Will to Order in China ☆ Timothy S. Oakes

> How exquisitely human was the wish for permanent happiness, and how thin the human imagination became trying to achieve it. . . .

> How can they hold it together, he wondered, this hard-won heaven
> defined only by the absence of the unsaved, the unworthy, and the
> strange?
>
> —Toni Morrison, *Paradise*

Now that the 2008 Olympics have come and gone, Beijing can perhaps breathe
a sigh of relief that after two weeks of intensive scrutiny, the most embarrassing
thing the foreign media could come up with during the Games was that some of
the events in the spectacular opening ceremony were faked.[5] First, we learned
that nine-year old Lin Miaoke was not in fact singing a revised *Song of the Motherland* at all but was lip-synching the voice of the less photogenic Yang Peiyi.
Then we learned that some of the firework footprints leading up to the National
Stadium were Photoshopped ahead of time and never actually occurred. And
finally, we learned that the children dressed in nationality costumes were not
minority children at all but Han Chinese. A few newscasters and pundits did
their best to muster some shock (shock!) that the world had been hoodwinked
into believing China could really pull off the perfection we saw on our television
screens.[6]

We tend to smell in fakery like this the whiff of scandal. The fake carries
with it the stain of deception, of shame, even immorality. And yet, it turns out
that fakery is an important part of our ability to imagine perfection. This is not
because perfection is the opposite of fakery but because perfection *depends* upon
the fake. Only the real world is imperfect, blemished, and full of chaos and
unpredictability. The fake world of televised opening ceremonies, by contrast, is
dependable, predictable, and *orderly*. And while we may live in the messiness of
the real world, we *yearn to believe in* the more ordered and dependable replica
we see on television.

Of course, it also turned out that during the 2000 Olympics, Sydney faked
their opening ceremony too. The *Sydney Morning Herald* revealed only shortly
after the closing of the Beijing Olympics that the Sydney Symphony had mimed
its entire performance eight years ago. In fact, some of it wasn't even the Sydney
Symphony playing on the backing tape but their archrival, the Melbourne Symphony Orchestra. Such orchestral maneuvers, it seems, are routine for important
events where nothing can be left to chance. And so, China apparently has no
monopoly on faking it. Nevertheless, the situation in Beijing gave Ai Weiwei
occasion to lament in his August 18, 2008, column in *The Guardian* about how

---

5. Some *China Beat* readers pointed out that not permitting any protests to occur in
the official "protest zones" during the Olympic games was perhaps a more embarrassing
revelation than the faked opening ceremonies. However, it is arguable that the Beijing
government itself found the former any more embarrassing than the latter.

6. The faked ceremonies were the subject of many reports in the Western media during the Games; see also Geremie Barmé's *China Beat* post "Painting over Mao," an excerpt
from which is reprinted in the volume.

China may be able to fake its way to a perfect Olympics—to the "fake applause" of the media and the public—but "true happiness" can never be faked: "This nation is notorious for its ability to make or fake anything cheaply," he wrote. "'Made-in-China' goods now fill homes around the world. But our giant country has a small problem. We can't manufacture the happiness of our people." He added, "Real public contentment can't be pirated or copied."

Maybe so. But accusing China of faking itself into modernity is as old as, well, modernity itself. In the book *River Town*, Peter Hessler recounts a scandalized seventeenth-century Spanish priest named Domingo Navarrete, who described business methods in China thus: "The Chinese are very ingenious at imitation. They have imitated to perfection whatsoever they have seen brought out of Europe. In the Province of Canton they have counterfeited several things so exactly, that they sell them Inland for Goods brought out from Europe." While there's nothing novel in remarking on the ubiquity of China's knockoff economy, it may be worth reflecting on just what is so important about shoring up the boundary between the real and the fake, especially when using the yardstick of modernity to measure China's emergence as a world power.

To the extent that modernity can be conceived as a telos of progress toward an ever more perfect, rational, or ideal world, faking it is probably the best anyone can do. The reason for this, I think, lies within the idea of modernity itself. In *All That Is Solid Melts into Air*, Marshall Berman claimed that "to be modern is to find ourselves in an environment that promises us adventure, power, joy, growth, transformation of ourselves and the world—and, at the same time, that threatens to destroy everything we have, everything we know, everything we are." Modernity is paradoxical; it is both liberating and chaotic, creative and destructive. This has resulted in a host of projects throughout recent history—mostly directed by governments—to harness and control what Berman called the "juggernaut" of modernity, to point it toward an end point of some kind and protect us from its destructive side. This is the kind of rational or progressive modernity that states engage in, as James Scott has argued in *Seeing Like a State*. But it is folly to think that the juggernaut can really be controlled, that perfect order or rationality is achievable. And that is why this kind of modernity, the modernity that seeks only progress and liberation without any of the chaos, must be faked. The "paradise" of order and harmony that this view of modernity promises, like all utopias, cannot but be realized without dissolving the boundaries between the real and the fake, the sacred and profane, the original and the virtual.

So perhaps Ai Weiwei has it wrong. What if "true happiness" must *always* be complicit with fakery? What if something so lofty and pure as true happiness can never be realized except in some form of approximation or replication, where all the inevitable blemishes, mistakes, and unexpected turns of events can be controlled, deleted, and Photoshopped out? Judging from the comments posted on *The Guardian*'s website, many of Ai's readers bristled at the implication that true happiness could be found only in a "free and democratic" country like England. And that shouldn't be surprising. While the English are perhaps more enthusiastic than others at disowning happiness, the point is that true happiness is often something that is thought to be found far away, in other places or in other times. And should we actually ever experience true happiness here and now, it is likely to dissipate before we've had time to realize what hit us. From this way of looking at things, Ai Weiwei is simply following in the footsteps of generations of utopian thinkers who have imagined a paradise of perfect happiness lying just beyond the horizon, just out of reach, and just about anywhere but *here and now.*

So, for those of us who must live here in the present, where does that leave things? Toni Morrison's answer suggests that it leaves us only with a poorly imagined replica. Photoshopped fireworks and lip-synched songs. And that pretty accurately sums up the past few centuries of utopian thinking. Humanity has been collectively imagining a better world since the Fall of Eden, I suppose, and all we have to show for our efforts is Disneyland.

If, as Michael Sorkin has argued in *Variations on a Theme Park*, Disneyland marks the culmination of a century of utopian thinking as the "superannuated Shangri-la of the 1950s," then it fits well Morrison's belief that we're not up to the task of imagining paradise. Disneyland simply reflects a cleaner, more ordered (and fake!) version of our world back to us, from Main Street USA to Frontierland and Tomorrowland. At Disneyland we see the thinness of our imagination betrayed by the *order* we impose on paradise. Disneyland reveals a thin vision of perfection, of "true happiness" (call it what you will), that depends on the orderly blending of the real and the fake. As such, it provides the model for "faking it" that China is now seemingly taking to a new level. Like the Sydney Olympics, Disneyland, then, compels us to admit that there is nothing particularly *Chinese* about faking it.

But China's current enthusiasm for fakery is nevertheless disarming. In today's postreform consumer economy of leisure culture, there is little that *isn't* faked. It's almost too banal to mention how true this is of basic consumer goods from DVDs and liquor to iPhones and Rolexes. But that's just the beginning. China's cultural landscape is now littered with fake Eiffel Towers, fake Capitol buildings and White Houses, and fake English villages. There are towns, like Zhouzhuang, that are even fakes of themselves. And this is something that continues to scandalize the Western media. In an exposé titled "Faking It" and published several years ago in *The Observer*, Jasper Becker wrote of the "national scandal" of Zhouzhuang faking itself as an old town. In fact, Becker wrote, most of the town had been recently bulldozed, rebuilt, and repainted to *look* old. Not only were tourists being fooled into thinking they were visiting a real antique water town on the Yangzi Delta, but so too was UNESCO, whose World Heritage Committee awarded Zhouzhuang a tentative World Heritage listing in 1998.[7] For

7. For an example of tourists being "hoodwinked" by Zhouzhuang, see the travel blog post at http://chake.chinatefl.com/cc10f.html (accessed September 16, 2008). Here the

his part, the mayor of Zhouzhuang defended his preservation-by-bulldozer plan, arguing that his town could not thrive as an antique object "under a glass case."

If, like Becker, we are scandalized by this fakery, we must also admit that the high-stakes competition between localities in China's new economy of cultural capital *demands* the kind of creative blending seen in Zhouzhuang. In a recent review of Zhang Yimou's *Riding Alone for a Thousand Miles*, professors Chen Yao and Yang Guoying pondered the film's role in a debate that boiled over between Yunnan and Guizhou when the authenticity and origins of the *nuo* drama performed in the film came into question. Though the performance unmistakably came from Guizhou (and was even credited thus in the film itself), Zhang Yimou's decision to have it performed in the picturesque Yunnan tourist city of Lijiang emboldened many claims that it actually came from Yunnan. It wasn't long before tourists went looking for *nuo* in Lijiang. Chen and Yang concluded that economic success in today's China depends on localities—like Yunnan—"making an empty show of strength" (*shu zhang sheng shi*) with their cultural resources. That is, places should not be afraid to play with fakery. Indeed, they cannot afford not to.

Making the ultimate case for an "empty show of strength," however, was Lijiang's neighboring county, Zhongdian, whose bid to change its name to Shangri-la was approved by the State Council in 2001. This materialized in place the utopian and Orientalist imaginings of the English writer James Hilton in his 1933 novel *Lost Horizon*. The creation of Shangri-la in China has already been written about extensively.[8] But the common reaction among many Western observers has been similar to the whiff of scandal with which the faked Olympic ceremony was greeted: we tend to scoff at the commercial crassness of faking something that never really existed. Leave it to China, we might think, to fake (a European vision of) paradise. But this misses the point (*as if* Disneyland never existed!). Like the "scandal" of a fake Olympic ceremony or a fake Zhouzhuang, the fake paradise of Shangri-la is nothing more than an homage to modernity's insatiable appetite for order, efficiency, and rationality, all in the name of achieving that escape from the inevitable chaos that is always there, dogging our repose of harmony and tranquility.

But this is not the first time China has faked paradise. China's utopian archetype, Peach Blossom Spring, has inspired at least seven claims from various towns all believing they are the actual site of Tao Yuanming's classic prose poem. Indeed, Peach Blossom Spring inspired what is arguably China's first theme park,

---

author claims that "Zhou Zhuang, however, is a TRUE ancient canal town. Development stopped here about 500 years ago. The city has preserved the ancient village intact."

8. See, for example, Ben Hillman, "Paradise under Construction: Minorities, Myths and Modernity in Northwest Yunnan," *Asian Ethnicity* 4, no. 2 (June 2003): 175–88, and Gang Yue, "From Shambhala to Shangri-La: A Traveling Sign in the Era of Global Tourism," in *Cultural Studies in China*, ed. Y. Jin and D. Tao (Singapore: Times Media Academic Publishing, 2004), 165–83.

built in the late Qing dynasty in Hunan. In an otherwise forgettable travelogue of his search for the "real" Peach Blossom Spring—*Don Quixote in China: The Search for Peach Blossom Spring*—travel writer Dean Barrett visited the theme park version of Peach Blossom Spring and found a productive combination of the real and the fake:

> Chinese love clever tricks. And what better way to hide the *real* Peach Blossom Spring than by dressing it up and presenting it as a tourist attraction! The brilliance and daring of their plan is equal to anything Zhuge Liang ever thought of! Of course no one has ever found Peach Blossom Spring; precisely because the incredibly clever Chinese . . . have been hiding it *in plain sight* for God-knows-how-long! The residents of the real Peach Blossom Spring have become ticket takers, souvenir hawkers, noodle vendors, chair bearers and tea house waitresses, a Houdini-like sleight-of-hand so audacious it takes my breath away.

Tongue firmly in cheek, Barrett finds paradise hidden within a workaday world of the mundane tasks of building and servicing a tourist site. And this blending of the vulgar and sublime, of the profane and the sacred, lies at the heart of Patty Chang's production of *Shangri-la*, a work that includes the filming of several installations in Shangri-la itself as well as the display of a four-foot spinning glass "mountain." In *Shangri-la*, Chang works with the mundane labor that goes into building paradise, but she also plays with the arbitrary divide between the real and the fake, between the original and its replica, and between the sacred and the profane. This is a divide that Shangri-la compels us to question, being a perfect simulacrum itself, a replica of something that doesn't really exist. Shangri-la is, in other words, *both* fake (a fictional utopia in a novel) *and* real (a county in Yunnan, a town, a tourist site, a theme park). Patty Chang leaves us with the possibility that the representation, "the fake," is the only "real" version of paradise that we can hope to achieve.

There are various whimsical installations made and filmed on site in Shangri-la. Chang has a local bakery decorate a cake with a mountain of frosting and a little airplane fuselage crashed upon its slope. The scene of course recalls the airplane crash that brings Hilton's war refugees to Shangri-la in *Lost Horizon*. We see the cake through several stages of construction and then see it displayed in the bakery's glass case along with several other cakes. Much of the film focuses on the building of what seems to function as a decompression chamber in the shape of an airplane fuselage (which looks like a life-size version of the cake's airplane fuselage). Built within a Tibetan courtyard, Chang films Tibetan monks sitting inside the chamber with oxygen masks covering their faces. She also has some locals build a mountain range out of Styrofoam as well as a glass mountain made from plywood and hand-cut mirrors. The latter is then filmed sitting on the back of a battered blue pickup truck, as it is carted around the dusty construction zone that is Shangri-la. All around we see the real mountains surrounding the town, billboard advertisements depicting images of these mountains, and

Chang's own mirrored mountain, reflecting shattered images of all these things as it humbly traipses through town. As a whole, the installations seem to play with the thinness of our visions of paradise and the mundane materials (frosting, plywood, Styrofoam) with which these visions are made.

But there's also a clear *will to order* displayed in the film's scenes. One of the effects of the installations is to appreciate Shangri-la as a sort of encased display. The cake ends up on display behind glass; the monks are viewed in the decompression chamber through the chamber's small "porthole" windows. The most obvious instance, however, occurs at the film's beginning, where we see the sandaled feet of Tibetan monks climbing up a rocky mountain trail. As the camera pans back, however, we begin to see that the monks are hiking not up a real mountain but up a fake mountain inside the glass-covered atrium of Shangri-la's Paradise Hotel. The transparency of glass, along with the encased form of display, suggests an objectifying gaze that orders paradise (in this case, heavily coded as Tibet) into something knowable and, ultimately, subject to touristic commodification.

In this, Chang is referencing a much broader form of what a Foucauldian scholar might term power/knowledge: the nineteenth century's Great Exhibitions of imperial display that prefigured the World Expos and Disney theme parks of the twentieth century. Reaching their apogee perhaps in the Great Exhibition of 1851 with its monumental Crystal Palace, these imperial displays objectified the worlds of colony and empire, making them knowable for Europeans, all the while legitimizing imperialism in the name of science and modernity. There is something of this imperial gaze that Zhouzhuang's mayor finds in UNESCO's World Heritage efforts to put towns "under a glass case." Glass itself plays a special role in this story of power/knowledge, for its transparency not only facilitates an objectifying gaze but has tended to also suggest an *improvement* on the original. Cultural objects, for instance, might be better understood once they are isolated, explained, encased, and displayed behind glass in a museum than they would be in their unmediated local context. Similarly, as Timothy Mitchell has pointed out in *Colonizing Egypt*, the exhibitions' displays of colonial subjects were viewed by audiences as *better than the real thing* in their ability to isolate an imagined cultural essence, excising from the display all the chaos and imperfections of the real colonial world. And for this reason glass has long been associated with utopian thinking and visions of perfection and paradise.

"Utopian schemes have long been closely linked to a rhetoric of transparency, glass, and mirrors, a perpetually shiny vision of the future," says Russell Ferguson in the curator's notes to Patty Chang's exhibition. In 1914, Paul Scheerbart proposed glass as the basis for a new utopian architecture: "The surface of the earth would change greatly if brick architecture were everywhere displaced by glass architecture. . . . And we should then have on the Earth more exquisite things than the gardens of the Arabian Nights. Then we should have a paradise on Earth and would not need to gaze longingly at the paradise in the sky." And in an extension of this thinking, the fragility of glass also serves to convey the ephemeral quality of utopia. Robert Smithson, for instance, proposed a six-ton mound of broken glass to represent the lost continent of Atlantis in his 1970 installation *Map of Broken Glass (Atlantis)*.

Mirrors and glass also play a role in revealing—and breaking down—the arbitrary distinction between real and fake. The mirrored mountain is one way of expressing the juxtaposition of real and fake that one finds in Shangri-la. Perfection can be found only in a mirror, in a representation, in something that it isn't. And that representation requires careful construction. It requires a lot of work to build a paradise for tourists, where we are willing to suspend disbelief for awhile and enjoy the fake. Chang's mirrored mountain spins around in the exhibit hall throwing off shards of triangular reflections. It gives the walls of the room a shattered, broken feeling. Like Smithson's mound of broken glass representing the mythic lost continent of Atlantis or the Crystal Palace, which itself shattered and burned to the ground soon after it was built, utopias must always be shattered to be known at all. Perfect order can never hold before the real world inevitably intrudes, bringing "the unsaved, the unworthy, and the strange." Patty Chang's spinning mountain is deliberately flashy, gaudy. She calls it "a cross between a prayer wheel and a disco ball," challenging the division between the sacred and the profane, the blessed and the vulgar. Utopian visions have always had both this spiritual longing and crass profiteering—purification and hybridization, as Bruno Latour would call it—lost valleys where people live forever and Disneyland.

And it is this blending of pure and impure that Patty Chang's film leaves us with in a stunning final image: the blue pickup truck now carries not the mir-rored mountain as it lopes along the dusty streets of Shangri-la but a single mirror laid across its bed. Reflected in the mirror, we see a deep azure sky and puffy white clouds, while all around is dust, bricks, construction, and people going about their workaday lives. The scene reminds me of a similar image of sky and clouds that illustrates Sorkin's essay on Disneyland in *Variations on a Theme Park*. For Sorkin, that image of the heavens illustrates the only thing that *is not for sale* in Disneyland. And so, perhaps Chang offers a similar message: if you want paradise in Shangri-la, all you have to do is look up. The rest is just a poor imitation.

But I think there's more to Chang's mirrored blue sky than this. The camera, after all, is looking *not* up at the sky but *down* at a mirrored reflection of the sky. And by doing this, we catch glimpses of the messy streets of Shangri-la. It's as if we can't view the sublime except in its reflection. We need the mirror, the representation. We need the fake. Our imagination of paradise depends on it.

Lewis Mumford once wrote that there are two kinds of utopias: one of escape and one of reconstruction. The latter should be easily recognized in the socialist realist art of the Mao era. In the party's current version of this utopia, however, *order* is highly valued over the chaos of the Mao era. In fact, however, it is difficult to find a vision of utopia that does not imagine a highly ordered society of peace, harmony, and tranquility. This was, after all, Mao's vision too. It seems as true of utopias of escape (e.g., Peach Blossom Spring, Shangri-la) as of utopias of reconstruction (e.g., the Owenite community of New Harmony, Indiana). Orderliness is a virus of utopia that just won't go away.

China's current vision of a modern utopia similarly places a high value on order and harmony. If we are scandalized by the deliberate and repeated transgressions of the boundary between real and fake going on in China today, then we have only forgotten that keeping chaos at bay in the modern project has always been "done with mirrors" and that the utopian yearnings of any society have only ever trafficked in the arts of fakery. Patty Chang's *Shangri-la* reminds us of this with whimsy, subtlety, and, ultimately, grace and beauty.

Chapter 14

Reinvented Traditions

IT'S NOT JUST 8/8/08: A YEAR OF CHINESE ANNIVERSARIES
1008 C.E.: The Song Emperor, the Goddess of Mount Tai, and Transformations of Chinese Religion

Kenneth L. Pomeranz

In 1008, Song Zhenzong, the not-very-successful emperor (r. 998–1023), claimed that he had received a Heavenly Letter communicating instructions and approval from above. While many officials and literati expressed doubt about the legitimacy of this sacred text, the emperor announced that in gratitude for receiving it, he would journey to Mount Tai (a sacred mountain in Shandong province) and perform ancient ceremonies in which emperors reported to heaven on their accomplishments. These ceremonies were quite rare; they were supposed to be performed only when the realm was peaceful and prosperous, so to undertake them was to make a big (and contested) claim. It also turned out to be the last time these rituals were ever performed, unless you count the reenactments for tourists that began about ten years ago—but that's another story.

At any rate, while digging at the top of the mountain (probably to set up an altar), the emperor's men uncovered both a spring and a statue of a female figure. The statue was said to be that of a goddess of Mount Tai, and it was later claimed that this goddess had been known to the ancients but somehow forgotten. In fact, up to that point only a god of the mountain was worshipped: he was officially understood as a rather abstract nature spirit but also figured in the popular imagination as a sort of lord of the underworld.

Over the next few centuries, worship of this goddess spread gradually until she had almost completely eclipsed the god of the mountain and taken over (in the popular mind) his key functions, including regulating the length of human lives. Her main temple on the mountain received at least half a million pilgrims per year by the early 1600s and other shrines for her sprouted around the country. . . . Since the eighteenth century, her following has narrowed, but she remains very popular. . . . She is associated both with human fertility (she is one of the deities women go to if they have trouble conceiving or if they want to make sure their baby is a boy) and with prolonging the lives of elderly relatives. A previously unknown fifteenth-century temple to her was recently unearthed in the process of building the Olympic village in Beijing; a much larger temple that housed one of her most popular altars until the Revolution has recently reopened as a museum of popular religion. . . .

Posted 4/21/2008 at 02:06:00 PM

Attacks on Confucianism, Buddhism, Daoism, and folk practices as "backward"
began during the New Culture movement (1915–1923) and continued periodically
during the Nationalist era (1927–1949), but it was the Communists who claimed
in the 1950s and 1960s that they had finally snuffed out what they believed were
outdated and oppressive practices. But since China's reform and opening-up policies
began in 1978, in part because of waning belief in Maoism as a devotional creed,
interest in Confucianism has surged. While Confucianism is more a philosophical
system that provides guidelines for human relationships and moral action than a
religion, at least as that term is typically understood in the West, it was denounced
along with other schools of thought in Mao's day.

Its most famous proponent recently is a media studies professor at Beijing Nor-
mal University named Yu Dan, who is dismissed by many Chinese intellectuals as
a crude popularizer offering a watered-down version of philosophy (a kind of
Chicken Soup for the Chinese Soul) to the masses. Her book Yu Dan's Reflections
on "The Analects" *explores the way that Confucius's most famous work (actually*
written by his disciples) can help people today lead happy and fulfilling lives. The
book has routinely landed on best-seller lists in recent years, and its photogenic
author is a celebrity in China and often appears on television.

The reappearance of a traditional Chinese system of thought after so many
years gives lie to the Communist assertion that old ways of thinking had been eradi-
cated. On the other hand, these early twenty-first-century incarnations of Confu-
cianism don't look precisely like it did at the turn of the previous century. Yu Dan's
brand of Confucianism, for instance, is remarkable in its focus on personal fulfill-
ment—that has never been considered the central goal of Confucian thought, which
is much more focused on the responsibilities of the individual to his family and state
(in that order).

Conversations about where Chinese belief systems are headed must engage both
these issues—the desire to connect with the past but also the desire for belief systems
to address contemporary issues. As both Xujun Eberlein and Julia K. Murray explore
in this chapter, efforts to do this in China have bumped up against sticky questions
of what it means to be a modern Chinese person.

The Global Rebranding of Confucius ☆ Julia K. Murray

After years of being reviled in the People's Republic of China as the master-
mind of a feudal system that hobbled China's efforts to modernize, Confucius has come prominently back into favor as one of its most precious cultural
assets. Opening the 2008 Beijing Olympics, President and Communist Party
Chairman Hu Jintao welcomed the world with a famous line from the opening
chapter of the *Analects* of Confucius: "To have friends come from afar, is it not
a joy?" As he has done on many occasions since assuming power in 2003, Presi-

dent Hu went on to affirm the values of a peaceful and harmonious society, which he credits to the teachings of a man who lived from approximately 551 to 479 B.C.E. The Olympic torch even made a visit to Qufu, Shandong, the hometown of Confucius, where it was taken to the great hall of the Temple of Confucius by a man whom the Chinese media identified as a lineal descendant of the ancient sage. Clearly things have changed.

For anyone who is old enough to remember China's Cultural Revolution of 1966–1976, which attacked people and institutions associated with traditional values, the recent transformation of the arch-villain of feudalism into the revered theorist of a harmonious society is nothing short of mind-boggling. Confucius and his teachings formed an official canon for much of the long period of dynastic rule, making it an obvious target of Chairman Mao Zedong's campaign against the "Four Olds": old culture, old customs, old habits, and old ideas. During the early phase of the Cultural Revolution in 1966, Mao's Red Guards smashed temples and burned books all across China in their eagerness to obliterate any remaining veneration for China's Confucian heritage. At the magnificent temple in Qufu, founded over two thousand years ago, they destroyed large sculptural icons dating back to 1730 and toppled massive stone tablets on which emperors of successive ages had inscribed their praise of the sage. The marauders even dug up Confucius's grave in the cemetery nearby, intending to give his remains a thrashing. (The tomb was empty.)

In 1974, the "Criticize Confucius, Criticize Lin Biao" movement renewed the crusade to root out lingering vestiges of Confucius's insidious influence in China. Lin Biao, a People's Liberation Army general who once was Chairman Mao's designated successor, had died while trying to flee the country in 1971, allegedly after the failure of his plot to assassinate Mao. The posthumous discovery of quotations from the *Analects* in Lin's home linked Confucius with the fallen favorite and suggested deep origins for his infamous conduct.[1] Although this later attack on Confucius did not entail as much physical destruction as the 1966 rampages, the ancient sage got a reprieve only after Chairman Mao's death in 1976.

A process to rehabilitate Confucius and some aspects of traditional Chinese culture started quietly in the early 1980s. Major institutes for research on Confucius and Confucianism were established in China by the mid-1980s. In 1984, the government set up the China Confucius Foundation, whose mission was to advance the study of Confucius and Confucian philosophy as well as to promote international cultural exchange related to Chinese civilization. In the same year, Qufu hosted the first of what became an annual government-sponsored cultural festival celebrating the birthday of Confucius, which was observed on September

---

1. It is widely believed that Confucius was largely a symbolic target during the 1974 movement and that the attack was really aimed at Premier Zhou Enlai.

28 (as in Taiwan).[2] The highlight of the festival has been the performance of an increasingly elaborate ceremony, loosely based on a liturgy of sacrifice from the late imperial period. Although the costumes, music, and dances have been reconstructed from archival sources, some aspects of the traditional ritual have been discarded. For instance, painted facsimiles are substituted for real animals, which traditionally included a freshly killed sheep, ox, and pig (which are still used in the equivalent ceremony in the Taipei Confucius temple). In recent years, government officials, foreign diplomats, and descendants of Confucius residing overseas have come to Qufu to attend the sacrifice on his birthday, which has evolved into a grandly costumed and choreographed occasion.

The year 2008 saw the reintroduction of two additional celebrations long abandoned on the mainland. On April 6, a smaller-scale version of the September ritual was performed in the Qufu temple, apparently an attempt to revive an older tradition of semiannual sacrifices offered to Confucius in both spring and autumn. More significantly, a new public holiday was created for Qingming, the time-honored festival for sweeping family graves and presenting food and incense to deceased ancestors. This expression of quintessentially Confucian family values had been suspended on the mainland as a superstitious custom after 1949, but it continued to be observed by Chinese elsewhere. Traditionally celebrated on the fifteenth day after the spring equinox, Qingming fell on April 4 in 2008. A few days earlier, on March 30, self-identified descendants of Confucius from other countries held a memorial ceremony at the restored grave of Confucius, just outside of Qufu.

The annual September festivals in Qufu have also featured conferences highlighting the resurgence of academic study of Confucius and Confucianism. Major symposia were scheduled at five-year intervals to draw scholars from abroad as well. Like the reconstructed sacrificial ceremonies, these scholarly gatherings have become increasingly grand affairs, with high government or party officials on hand to open the proceedings. In 2007, it was announced that the World Confucian Conference in Qufu would become an annual event not only to advance scholarship but also "to provide a spiritual power for the modern world."[3] The 2008 convocation was a three-day affair organized by the national Ministry of Culture and the provincial government of Shandong, drawing participants from some twenty-two countries.[4]

---

2. During the centuries of imperial rule, the birthday of Confucius was not singled out as a date for regular celebration; rather, major sacrifices were offered to him twice a year, in the second months of spring and fall, respectively. His birthday began being annually observed in the early twentieth century as part of a movement to make Confucianism a religion and Confucius its founding figure, equivalent to Christ.

3. http://www.china.org.cn/culture/2007-09/28/content_1226252.htm (accessed September 28, 2008).

4. http://www.odtn.com/odtn/news/china/userobject1ai66320.html (accessed September 28, 2008).

Another aspect of the Confucian revival has been the restoration or complete reconstruction of buildings all across China that had once served as temples of Confucius but later were converted to other uses. Many temples of the late imperial period became schools in the early twentieth century, particularly following the demise of the civil service examination system in 1905. After 1949, the range of new functions for temple buildings became more diverse. Some were made into government offices or museums or even factories and animal stables. Although often detrimental to the buildings themselves, such uses caused little concern because Confucius was held in such low regard. Outright destruction came during the Cultural Revolution at the hands of the Red Guards, who completely demolished temples in some parts of China. Fortunately the Qufu temple survived. In 1984, its primary structures underwent extensive repairs, and new icons were sculpted to occupy the niches inside the main hall. With repairs to other buildings ongoing, the temple was opened for tourism. Ten years later, UNESCO conferred the World Heritage Site designation on the Qufu temple, together with the adjacent Kong Family Mansion and nearby Kong Cemetery. (Confucius and his male descendants bear the surname Kong.)

Besides representing a variety of efforts to reintroduce valued elements of China's heritage, these developments signaled the mainland government's change of policy toward the cultural legacy. Undoubtedly one motive was to encourage closer relations with Hong Kong and Taiwan, whose leaders had never repudiated Confucius or traditional Chinese culture. Honoring Confucius was a useful way to foster a greater sense of unity and commonality. Although most residents of Taiwan and Hong Kong had little interest in Confucius and considered him irrelevant to their daily lives, the social values loosely called "Confucian" were generally accepted there as a fundamental element of Chinese identity. In addition, small but prominent Confucian associations had continued to promote classical learning and maintained veneration rituals. In October 2007, the Confucian Academy of Hong Kong, the People's Government of Shandong Province, and the newspaper *Ta Kung Pao* collaborated in sponsoring celebrations that combined the observance of Confucius's birthday with the tenth anniversary of Hong Kong's return to the "motherland." Cultural exhibitions and an academic conference culminated in a huge public ceremony on October 7, 2007, held in Hong Kong stadium.

China's reembracing of Confucius and government-funded revivals of traditional ceremonies and structures are also intended to create a positive climate to attract overseas Chinese back to the motherland and foster closer relations with East Asian nations that share some form of Confucian heritage. The emphasis on Confucius as a common denominator or unifying element has nonetheless highlighted certain differences between the mainland and traditions practiced elsewhere. For instance, in the interests of gender equality, China does not follow the traditional practice of limiting participation in sacrificial ceremonies to males. Another example is the prominence of visual images of Confucius at newly refurbished temples on the mainland. After a major ritual reform in 1530, Confucian temples around the realm (except for Qufu's) were required to replace icons with tablets simply inscribed with the names of Confucius and his canonized followers. This aniconic practice has been continuously observed in Taiwan and South Korea. Although some restored temples in mainland China have installed just the inscribed tablets, they more often display anthropomorphic images of Confucius. These include large statues standing outside the main hall and smaller sculptures or even a two-dimensional picture hanging over the altar inside.

Confucius has also become the benign face of China's increasingly assertive participation in international affairs, and his name has been given to endeavors that sometimes have little connection with the ancient sage. Since 2004, a program under China's Ministry of Education has energetically promoted the study of Chinese language and culture by establishing "Confucius Institutes" in countries throughout the world. These organizations pair an educational institution in China with an interested foreign partner that houses the Confucius Institute. Teachers sent by the Chinese partner provide instruction in a set curriculum, training local instructors who in turn can teach in schools and community settings. Thus, Confucius Institutes spread a Chinese government–approved interpretation of China's heritage and encourage foreigners to understand and appreciate it. In addition to teaching Chinese language and culture, Confucius Institutes also serve as vehicles for advancing diplomatic relationships and business interests.

In December 2005, China persuaded UNESCO to establish a global literacy prize named for Confucius. The central government, Shandong provincial government, and Jining municipal government contributed funds for two awards to be made annually, starting in 2006.[5] The purpose of the Confucius Literacy Prize is to reward nongovernmental organizations that are working to promote literacy among disadvantaged people, such as rural adults and youths who are not in school, and particularly women and girls. The awards conferred to date— Morocco and India in 2006, Nigeria and the United States in 2007, South Africa and Ethiopia in 2008—have gone mostly to groups working in countries with which China would like to increase its influence. As the first international award named after a Chinese figure, the Confucius Literacy Prize also celebrates China's long tradition of valuing education. One commentator has called it the liberal arts' counterpart to the Nobel Prize.[6]

Coinciding with plans for the first award of the Confucius Literacy Prize, the China Confucius Foundation also pushed to standardize the visual representation of Confucius to make him a more effective symbol of Chinese civilization.

---

5. http://www.china.org.cn/english/China/150588.htm (accessed September 27, 2008).

6. Luo Chenglie, quoted in "Confucius Culture Festival Marked in Qufu," http://english.cri.cn/4026/2006/12/31/61@179987.htm# (accessed September 27, 2008).

Arguing that there were too many diverse portrayals worldwide, which could only be confusing to foreigners, the Foundation announced plans to develop an official portrait.[7] After several months of intensive research and consultation with scholars of Confucianism, historians, artists, and descendants of Confucius, the Foundation chose a picture known as the "Traveling Teacher" as the starting point for the new standard image. Attributed to the eighth-century Tang painter Wu Daozi, the composition was incised on a tablet in Qufu and was widely known from rubbings and photographs. In designing the new portrait, artists from the Shandong Academy of Art and Design modified the anachronistic clothing of the incised image to a style more appropriate for Confucius's lifetime based on evidence from recent archaeological finds.

An initial prototype for the standard portrait was cast and displayed in June 2006 at the Shandong International Cultural Industry Exposition in Jinan, the provincial capital. This preliminary version drew a number of comments and criticisms, including assertions that there was no need for a standard image of Confucius in the first place. Nonetheless, only minor changes were made to the model, and the final official version was unveiled in Qufu on September 23, 2006, just before the birthday celebrations. The 2.55-meter bronze figure depicted Confucius as an elderly man with a gentle expression on his broad features, standing with his hands before his chest and slightly crossed. After the ceremony, the statue was given to the Nishan Museum of Worldwide Portraits of Confucius, located near Qufu at Mount Ni, the alleged site of Confucius's birth.[8]

Significantly, this attempt to assert control over the portrayal of Confucius came a generation after a similar effort in Taiwan, where large public sculptures of him were first created in the mid-1970s. The Nationalist government promoted Confucius as an emblem of its commitment to preserve China's ancient heritage, in strong contrast with the radical iconoclasm of the Communist mainland. In 1974, at the height of the Cultural Revolution campaign to "Criticize Lin Biao, Criticize Confucius," the Taiwan Ministry of the Interior chose the same Wu Daozi "Traveling Teacher" image to disseminate as the official representation of Confucius. The picture was authenticated by none other than Kong Decheng (b. 1920), the most senior member of the seventy-seventh generation of Confucius's descendants, who remembered seeing the incised tablet as a youth in Qufu, before fleeing to Taiwan to escape the Communists. Over-life-size bronze statues faithfully copying the "Traveling Teacher" portrayal were cast in Taiwan and presented in 1974–1975 to sites of culture and learning around the world. Similar statues continued being put up around the Chinese diaspora worldwide during the 1980s, often with the sponsorship of a local Confucius society.

---

7. http://english.peopledaily.com.cn/200602/14/eng20060214_242680.html (accessed September 29, 2008).

8. http://www.design.gov.cn/show.php?id = 560793 (accessed September 29, 2008).

From the early 1990s onward, over-life-size statues of Confucius also began to proliferate on the mainland, particularly at the newly refurbished or rebuilt temples of Confucius. In Beijing, for example, two statues stand just a short distance apart in front of the restored National University and its associated Temple of Confucius, traditionally the place where the emperor himself offered sacrifice to the ancient sage. Statues of Confucius have also become a common sight in front of modern schools at all levels, from primary school to university. They inevitably recall the once-ubiquitous statues of Chairman Mao Zedong that formerly stood in public squares and on school campuses.

Initially, most of the statues of Confucius on the mainland were donated by Confucius Societies in Hong Kong, Taiwan, and Singapore. The China Confucius Foundation became increasingly concerned about the diverse appearances of the figures and made an initial attempt in 1999 to establish a standard image. To commemorate the 2,550th anniversary of Confucius's birth that year, the Foundation commissioned one thousand gold statuettes depicting Confucius in clothing that was archaeologically correct. But a larger standard image was needed to compete with the diverse public sculptures, leading to the 2006 effort.

In response to objections that it is impossible to produce a true portrait of Confucius so long after his lifetime, the secretary-general of the China Confucius Foundation stated that it was unimportant whether the portrayal really looked like Confucius, as long as it had the right qualities. If it was recognizable and consistent, it would be effective for "promoting Confucius around the globe."[9] This suggested to some critics that the China Confucius Foundation had a secret commercial intent in establishing the standard, the first step toward branding Confucius as a commercial trademark. However, Zhang also mentioned that Taiwan had previously issued its own standard image of Confucius, implying that the real "confusion" was about which regime controls his legacy. Thus, the 2006 "branding" of Confucius was not primarily for commercial motives but for political ones. Establishing an official portrait of Confucius is an assertion of authority over the heritage of Chinese civilization. The point of global branding is to enforce a uniform, official conception of the Chinese philosopher. As the director of Qufu's Confucius Research Institute put it, "Otherwise, foreigners will never know which one actually portrays the great man."[10]

After all the fuss died down, the Standard Portrait was judged to be too dull and serious to be useful for popularizing Confucius after all. Accordingly, in November 2007, the China Confucius Foundation announced an agreement with Shandong Radio & TV and Shenzhen Phoenix Star (a subsidiary of Hong Kong's Phoenix Satellite TV) to produce a cartoon series about the life of Confu-

---

9. http://english.people.com.cn/200609/26/eng20060926_306323.html (accessed September 30, 2008).

10. http://english.people.com.cn/200609/26/eng20060926_306323.html (accessed September 30, 2008).

cius and his teachings. Projected to cost U.S.$3.5 million, it will present one hundred episodes of thirteen minutes each. According to Wang Daqian, deputy secretary of the China Confucius Foundation, "The cartoon is one of the most effective ways to popularize the essence of Chinese culture to the overseas audience." The series will air in 2009, marking the 2,560th anniversary of Confucius's birth.

The year 2009 promises to be even more significant for state-supported projects related to Confucius. In addition to the cartoon series on his life, a feature-length film with a budget of U.S.$21.9 million is slated for release. Filming is scheduled to get under way in September 2008, and the movie has a female director, Hu Mei. Finally, 2009 should see the publication of the most ambitious update of the Kong genealogy ever undertaken, replacing the 1937 compilation, which included seventy-seven generations of Confucius's descendants. After thirteen years in preparation, the 2009 edition is expected to include some 3 million men and, for the first time ever, women. Another innovation is that it will also record overseas Chinese descendants who have verifiable documents. However, DNA tests will not suffice as proof of kinship with China's ancient sage. The Beijing Institute of Genomics at the Chinese Academy of Sciences offers a DNA test that it claims can identify descendants, but the genealogy project requires people to pinpoint their exact position on the immensely complicated family tree. Too bad if the Red Guards burned your documents!

China: Democracy or Confucianism? ☆ Xujun Eberlein

In October 2007, when the Chinese Communist Party (CCP) held its seventeenth congress, CNN reported the event with the headline "China Rules Out Copying Western Democracy." My first reaction to this headline was, *So what?* That spontaneous reaction might have been an unconscious consequence of my reading *Political Confucianism* by Jiang Qing, a contemporary Confucian in China. In this book, Jiang Qing draws a blueprint for China's political future based on Confucianism. It is the first such conception since the 1919 May Fourth movement that denounced the traditional Chinese ideology as a feudal relic and began the age-old country's modernization efforts.

It seems typical of American thinking to regard either a republic or a parliamentary democracy as absolutely the only right model for all countries. For a political system to succeed, however, it needs to be rooted in the particular country's cultural history. Throughout thousands of years, China has never lacked great thinkers, political or philosophical, which poses an interesting question: why does China need to adopt a Western model for its political system, be it Marxist communism or capitalist democracy?

But it is true that China hasn't had a great folk thinker like Confucius for quite some time. Especially in the Communist regime, there has been no soil for such a thinker to grow. This frozen ground seems to have begun thawing lately. Jiang Qing's Confucian unorthodox thoughts, at least, have not been subjected to suppression yet.

Among the contemporary Chinese scholars actively seeking solutions for their country's future, Jiang Qing is exceptional in that he investigated various philosophic schools and ideologies before embracing Confucianism. As a twenty-year-old soldier in the 1970s, with a mere middle school education, he had taken a stab at Marx's voluminous *Capital*. In 1980, an undergraduate student in Southwest Politics and Law College, he was the first in the country to criticize Chinese Communist practice as having abandoned the humanitarian essence of Marx's early works. His self-assigned, handwritten thesis "Return to Marx" spread apace in many universities and brought him years of political trouble.

In his early thirties, Jiang Qing's political predicament drove him first to existentialism and then Buddhism. After his visit to the Shaolin Temple in 1984, he shut himself up on Chongqing's Gele Mountain for four years to study Buddhist scriptures, eventually concluding that Buddhism solves the "life-and-death" issue on the individual level but provides inadequate guidance for national political problems. Later he would find that, unlike Buddhism, which teaches detachment from the dusty real world, Confucianism has a long tradition of involvement in political construction, and that would become the breakthrough point in Jiang Qing's theoretical exploration.

Jiang Qing had also turned to Christianity and translated several English books into Chinese, including James Reid's *Facing Life with Christ* and Louis Proal's *Political Crime*. He was deeply moved by Jesus' spirit and attempted several times to join a Christian church in Shenzhen. However, his attempts would not come to fruition as he felt "the entire Chinese culture dragging my leg."[11]

After all this exploration, only Confucianism makes him feel that he is at home and embracing his destiny. This is not because Confucius, some five hundred years older than Jesus, had seventy-two disciples while Jesus had only twelve; it is simply that cultural background has an indelible impact on one's ideological choice.

In 2001, forty-eight-year-old Jiang Qing quit his college teaching job and established a Confucian seminary in the remote mountains of Guizhou. For three seasons of the year, except winter, Jiang Qing dresses in the traditional long buttoned shirt, studies and teaches Confucianism in the mountains without electricity or a cell phone signal, and pushes a nationwide "children reading Confucian classics" movement.

Since 1989, Jiang Qing has published several scholarly books. *Political Confucianism*, available in Chinese only, was published, with partial sponsorship from the Harvard-Yenching Institute, in 2004 by SDX Joint Publishing in

---

11. Miwan, "Biography of Sensei Jiang Qing," unpublished manuscript in Chinese.

Beijing. It has not been banned, though I couldn't find it in China's bookstores during my visit last year. (The copy I read was lent to me by a friend.) On the other hand, Jiang Qing's plan to publish a collection of recent articles and speeches on political Confucianism was rejected this year because the book did not pass the publishing house's "political examination."

In his books and articles on *Political Confucianism*, Jiang Qing calls for a restoration of Confucianism as the state ideology, as it had been in many dynasties. Further, he outlines a Confucian political structure strongly distinct from both Soviet-style communism and Western-style democracy.

Democracy is westernized and imperfect in nature, Jiang Qing points out. If applied to China, a Western-style democratic system would have only one legitimacy—popular will, or civil legitimacy. Such unilegitimacy operates on the quantity of votes, regardless of the moral implications of decisions taken. Since human desire is selfish by nature, those decisions can be self-serving for a particular majority's interest. Because of this, Jiang Qing argues, civil legitimacy alone is not sufficient to build or keep a constructive social order.

The unilegitimacy criticism makes sense to me because Western countries, which have evolved the concepts of sufferance, law, tolerance, and community standards over hundreds of years, have a broad base for governance. China, on the other hand, does not have this same evolution. Western democracy simply dropped onto China is likely to face pitfalls parallel to those seen in Iraq. The foundation of majority rule alone is not sufficient to provide good governance.

In contrast, the Confucian state that Jiang proposes is trilegitimate: it carries numinous, historical, and civil legitimacy simultaneously. In particular, the governmental body consists of three mutually constraining institutions that represent religion (members chosen through community recommendation and Confucian examination), cultural tradition (members based on sovereign and sage lineage and by appointment), and popular will (members elected), respectively. Jiang Qing believes that such a structure would avoid many of the mistakes that appear inevitable under a unilegitimate system.

These ideas can be traced back to a Confucian concept: "The sovereign rules through the heaven, the earth, and the people." The Chinese had thousands of years of tradition with these elements in their political systems, and of all the great ancient cultures, China is unique in having survived with recognizable continuity.

Jiang Qing's idea of political Confucianism has found as many advocates as dissenters. Followers honor him as "the greatest contemporary Confucian," while dissenters accuse him of being a "benighted cultural conservative." Jiang Qing says he accepts both titles without the modifiers.

The website of *China Daily*, a government-run English newspaper, published an article on January 6, 2006, titled "Confucianism Will Never Be Religion [*sic*]." It concludes, "Religion as a state power, as Jiang advocates, should never be allowed, not in this country."

Chen Lai, China's top Confucianism scholar and professor of philosophy at Beijing University, welcomes the new departure in political Confucianism research conducted by Jiang Qing. In fact, he helped *Political Confucianism* become published. Still, he considers the suggestion that Confucianism become the state ideology, let alone a basis for government, impractical. In my chat with Chen Lai when he visited Harvard University last spring, he shook his head at the theology that does not separate state and church.

On the other hand, Daniel A. Bell, an Oxford-educated Canadian scholar and professor of philosophy at Tsinghua University in Beijing, deems that "it is not entirely fanciful to surmise that the Chinese Communist Party will be relabeled the Chinese Confucian Party in a few years time."

There is in fact a sign that China's current leaders have begun to encourage the revival of Confucianism. President Hu Jintao has alluded to Confucius's teaching in various speeches—a gesture toward the return to traditional values that was not seen in his predecessors. This tendency was again displayed in the CCP's seventeenth congress.

It is a welcome change, displaying a small degree of tolerance that has been lacking. But it is a far cry from the Confucian state proposed by Jiang Qing.

Last summer in Beijing, I had a conversation with Miwan, a disciple and friend of Jiang Qing's and a professor himself in a renowned Chinese university. When asked what he thought of the feasibility of Jiang Qing's ideal, Miwan said, "To a great thinker, feasibility does not have to be an immediate concern. Sensei Jiang is a great thinker." All of Jiang's disciples and followers reverently refer to him as "Jiang xiansheng"—*sensei Jiang*, whether in front of or behind him. This is a practice of the Confucian "respecting the teacher, valuing the *tao*" tradition, in sharp contrast to the behavior of today's irreverent young generation. To a Chinese history addict like me, the reappearance of this long-abandoned reverence for a teacher is heartwarming.

In an e-mail to me later, Miwan summarizes his association with Jiang Qing by using a classic phrase, "Though unreachable, my heart longs."

After Jiang Qing returned to his home in Shenzhen for winter last year, I e-mailed him, asking what he was busy on. He replied, "Reading all day long, nothing more." I asked what he thought of the potential for Confucianism to become the state ideology. "I'm not optimistic," he said, "I'm afraid it might have to wait for several decades."

Well, that is optimistic.

Chapter 15

China and the United States

CULTURE AND COLLAPSE

Pierre Fuller

The Chinese, British journalist turned pop historian Simon Winchester explained recently on the pages of the *New York Times*, long ago handed over science—and by extension earthquake-resistant engineering—to "the West," leaving "themselves to become mired, time and again, in the kind of tragic events that we are witnessing this week." The thrust of this piece was China's fall in the sixteenth century from mankind's technological pioneer to a "culture that turned its back on its remarkable and glittering history" and "became impoverished, backward and prey to the caprices of nature."

By asking why China has not kept pace with "America," this best-selling author forgets that Western advances are remarkably recent. San Francisco was reduced to a pancake in 1906. And I don't know what he means by today's "America" (trend-setting San Francisco? or the trailer-home communities across the country that fly like poker cards from every tornado?), but the University of California from which I am writing started retrofitting its buildings just in the past few decades. Winchester must then mean China is a few decades behind, but he makes it sound like centuries.

At what date did China become "impoverished" relative to Europe? By the standards of European welfare policies, eighteenth-century Qing China saw as high a standard of living and remarkably thorough disaster relief measures. The very engineering feats Winchester sees abandoned after the sixteenth century continued for centuries to carry grain north through vast river control works and canals from the lush paddies of the south, a flow of food that the state consistently diverted to drought-, flood-, or earthquake-stricken areas.

When determining that China fails to protect its people today, Winchester also confuses engineering know-how with the awesome sum of money required for its installation. The Politburo of the Chinese Communist Party is stocked with officials who were trained as engineers, but people want roofs over their heads today, not in a safer, richer tomorrow. Regardless, after the fiasco of the New Orleans levee system and the Minneapolis bridge collapse, how different does this look from Winchester's "America"? Maybe the problem here is one of perception. To us our problems are political or incidental: Bush's fault, money diverted to Iraq, a single inspector's negligence. But when people in Sichuan suffer, something is wrong with "China." Then it's a cultural problem.

Posted 5/30/2008 at 09:42:00 AM

There were a number of events that defined the U.S.–China relationship in 2008, from the protests on American campuses against the treatment of Tibetans to the outpouring of support for victims of the Sichuan earthquake to the scuffles and celebrations of the Olympic Games to the intertwined financial ills of the global economic system. But perhaps what characterized the relationship this year more than anything else was its consistency. In October, for instance, Beijing canceled a series of meetings with Washington over a proposed plan for the United States to sell arms to Taiwan. We have seen this before—in 2005, in 2004, and many years before that. Similarly, the food safety scandals of the autumn of 2008 were the most devastating so far in a series of product safety crises that originated in China, such as the pet food and toy recalls of 2007, an issue Amy Hanser raises in her piece, "Yellow Peril Consumerism."

This year, the U.S.–China relationship moved neither forward nor back (with the notable exception of continuing multilateral talks with North Korea). But the sense in the United States of China as a dangerous place increased dramatically, as Stephen Mihm notes in his essay, "A Nation of Outlaws." Consumers expressed increased concern about any China-made products, and stories of rising Chinese nationalism (a nationalism often fueled, or so the media reported, by anti-American sentiment) stoked fears of "China Rising."

In China, the sense was that Western powers continued to hold China to their own, unfair standards. In his essay in this chapter, David Porter characterizes this perspective as resulting in a narrative where "the Chinese fail to measure up, in each case." As the year rounded out, American critics could hardly continue to argue that case, as the American economy began to falter and dragged down with it credit markets and banks worldwide. If nothing else, the economic interconnections illustrated how closely linked are China and the United States—so closely linked that "their" problems are increasingly "our" problems, and, unfortunately for the growing population of Chinese investors, "our" problems are "theirs" as well.

Though the scale of interconnections between the United States and China may have increased, there is nothing new about either the relationship of these two economies or their particular shape. And though there is a tendency to view everything in China's rapidly growing and evolving economy as changing, as Kenneth Pomeranz describes in his piece in this chapter, the U.S.–China economic relationship remains stable in its instability. At this point in time, that seems like an apt description of China as a whole.

A Nation of Outlaws ☆ Stephen Mihm

Although this piece first appeared in the Boston Globe *on August 26, 2007, we feel that the continuing relevancy of the insights that American historian Stephen Mihm provides makes this well worth including in this volume.*

If recent headlines are any indication, China's rap sheet of capitalist crimes is growing as fast as its economy. Having exported poison pet food and toothpaste laced with antifreeze earlier this year, the world's emerging economic powerhouse has diversified into other, equally dubious product lines: scallops coated with putrefying bacteria, counterfeit diabetes tests, pirated Harry Potter books, and baby bibs coated with lead, to name but a few.

Politicians are belatedly putting China on notice. Representative Frank Wolf of Virginia delivered one of the more stinging counterattacks last month, warning that the United States "must be vigilant about protecting the values we hold dear" in the face of China's depredations.

His anger reflects the mounting disgust with how recklessly China plies its trade, apparently without regard for the things that make commerce not only dependable but possible: respect for intellectual property, food and drug purity, and basic product safety. With each tawdry revelation, China's brand of capitalism looks increasingly menacing and foreign to our own sensibilities.

That's a tempting way to see things but wrong. What's happening halfway around the world may be disturbing, even disgraceful, but it's hardly foreign. A century and a half ago, another fast-growing nation had a reputation for sacrificing standards to its pursuit of profit, and it was the United States.

As with China and Harry Potter, America was a hotbed of literary piracy; like China's poisonous pet-food makers, American factories turned out adulterated foods and willfully mislabeled products. Indeed, to see China today is to glimpse, in a distant mirror, the nineteenth-century American economy in all its corner-cutting, fraudulent glory.

China may be a very different country, but in many ways it is a younger version of us. The sooner we understand this, the sooner we can realize that China's fast-and-loose brand of commerce is not an expression of national character, much less a conspiracy to poison us and our pets, but a phase in the country's development. Call it adolescent capitalism, if you will: bursting with energy, exuberant, dynamic. Like any teenager, China's behavior is also maddening, irresponsible, and dangerous. But it is a phase, and understanding it that way gives us some much-needed perspective, as well as some tools for handling the problem. Indeed, if we want to understand how to deal with China, we could do worse than look to our own history as a guide.

A bit of empathy might even be in order. One hundred and fifty years ago, even America's closest trade partners were despairing about our cheating ways. Charles Dickens, who visited in 1842, was, like many Britons, stunned by the economic ambition of our nation's inhabitants and appalled by what they would do for the sake of profit. When he first stepped off the boat in Boston, he found the city's bookstores rife with pirated copies of his novels, along with those of his countrymen. Dickens would later deliver lectures decrying the practice and wrote home in outrage, "My blood so boiled as I thought of the monstrous injustice."

In the United States of the early nineteenth century, capitalism as we know it today was still very much in its infancy. Most people still lived on small farms, and despite the persistent myth that America was the land of laissez-faire, there were plenty of laws on the books aimed at keeping tight reins on the market economy. But as commerce became more complex and stretched over greater distances, this patchwork system of local and state-level regulations was gradually overwhelmed by a new generation of wheeler-dealer entrepreneurs.

Taking a page from the British, who had pioneered many ingenious methods of adulteration a generation or two earlier, American manufacturers, distributors, and vendors of food began tampering with their products en masse—bulking out supplies with cheap filler or using dangerous additives to mask spoilage or to give foodstuffs a more appealing color.

A committee of would-be reformers who met in Boston in 1859 launched one of the first studies of American food purity, and their findings make for less-than-appetizing reading: candy was found to contain arsenic and dyed with copper chloride, and conniving brewers mixed extracts of "nux vomica," a tree that yields strychnine, to simulate the bitter taste of hops. Pickles contained copper sulfate, and custard powders yielded traces of lead. Sugar was blended with plaster of Paris, as was flour. Milk had been watered down, then bulked up with chalk and sheep's brains. Hundred-pound bags of coffee labeled "Fine Old Java" turned out to consist of three-fifths dried peas, one-fifth chicory, and only one-fifth coffee.

Though there was the occasional clumsy attempt at domestic reform by mid-century—most famously in response to the practice of selling "swill milk" taken from diseased cows force-fed a diet of toxic refuse produced by liquor distilleries—little changed. And just as the worst sufferers of adulterated food in China today are the Chinese, so it was the Americans who suffered in the early nineteenth-century United States. But when America started exporting food more broadly after the Civil War, the practice started to catch up to us.

One of the first international scandals involved "oleo-margarine," a butter substitute originally made from an alchemical process involving beef fat, cattle stomach, and, for good measure, finely diced cow, hog, and ewe udders. This "greasy counterfeit," as one critic called it, was shipped to Europe as genuine butter, leading to a precipitous decline in butter exports by the mid-1880s. (Wily entrepreneurs, recognizing an opportunity, bought up genuine butter in Boston, affixed counterfeit labels of British butter manufacturers, and shipped them to England.) The same decade saw a similar though less unsettling problem as British authorities discovered that lard imported from the United States was often adulterated with cottonseed oil.

Even worse was the meatpacking industry, whose practices prompted a trade war with several European nations. The twentieth-century malfeasance of the industry is well known today: "deviled ham" made of beef fat, tripe, and veal by-products; sausages made from tubercular pork; and, if Upton Sinclair is to be believed, lard containing traces of the occasional human victim of workplace accidents. But the international arena was the scene of some of the first scandals, most notably in 1879, when Germany accused the United States of exporting pork contaminated with trichinae worms and cholera. That led several countries to boycott American pork. Similar scares over beef infected with a lung disease intensified these trade battles.

Food, of course, was only the beginning. In the literary realm, for most of the nineteenth century the United States remained an outlaw in the world of international copyright. The nation's publishers merrily pirated books without permission and without paying the authors or original publishers a dime. When Dickens published a scathing account of his visit, "American Notes for General Circulation," it was, appropriately enough, immediately pirated in the United States.

In one industry after another, nineteenth-century American producers churned out counterfeit products in remarkable quantities, slapping fake labels on locally made knockoffs of foreign ales, wines, gloves, and thread. As one expose at the time put it, "We have 'Paris hats' made in New York, 'London Gin' and 'London Porter' that never was in a ship's hold, 'Superfine French paper' made in Massachusetts."

Counterfeiters of patent medicines were especially notorious. This was a bit ironic, given that most of these remedies were pretty spurious already, but that didn't stop the practice. The most elaborate schemes involved importing empty bottles, filling them with bogus concoctions, and then affixing fake labels from well-respected European firms.

Americans also displayed a particular talent for counterfeiting currency. This was a time when individual banks, not the federal government, supplied the nation's paper money in a bewildering variety of so-called banknotes. Counterfeiters flourished to the point that in 1862 one British writer, after counting close to six thousand different species of counterfeit or fraudulent bills in circulation, could reasonably assure his readers that "in America, counterfeiting has long been practiced on a scale which to many will appear incredible."

What was it that made the nineteenth-century United States such a hotbed of bogus goods? And why is China's economic boom today, as *New York Times* writer Howard French clucked earlier this month, "minted in counterfeit"?

Piracy, fraud, and counterfeiting, whether of currency, commodities, or brand-name electronics, flourishes at a particular moment in a capitalist society: the regulatory interregnum that emerges in the wake of fast-paced capitalist change. This period is one in which technology has improved, often dramatically, and markets have burst their older boundaries. Yet the country still relies on obsolete ways of controlling commerce. Until there's something to replace them, counterfeiters and other flimflam operators flourish, pushing new means of making money to their logical, if unethical, conclusion.

Indeed, the ease with which counterfeiters and corner cutters operate in

China today can be attributed to many of the same failings that plagued the United States 150 years ago: a weak, outdated regulatory regime ill suited to handling the complexities of modern commerce; limited incentives for the state to police and eliminate fraud; and, perhaps most important of all, a blurring of the lines between legitimate and fraudulent means of making money.

All of these are typical of capitalism in its early, exuberant phase of development. The United States may have been the worst offender, but early industrial Britain had significant problems with food adulteration and counterfeiting, and Russia from the 1990s onward has been the scene of some of the worst capitalist excesses in recent memory. And in all likelihood, China's recklessness is just that: a phase that will eventually pass when the nation's regulatory institutions catch up with its economic ambition.

None of this is to suggest that we should exonerate China for shipping poisonous pet food and lead-impregnated toys or that we can count on China merely to follow in our footsteps. There are, obviously, enormous differences between modern China and the United States of 150 years ago. China is not a democracy; however angry its citizens may be, they have limited capacity to translate their rage into legislation aimed at putting the brakes on the economic free-for-all. And there's no equivalent of the muckraking American journalists who thrust these issues into the public spotlight. Just as bad, many of the worst excesses are being conducted under the auspices of the state.

But understanding the parallels does suggest a way to move forward. The rogue industries of the United States eventually responded to stiff international economic pressure. Beginning in the 1880s, the European meat boycotts spurred Congress to pass a raft of federal legislation aimed at imposing some inspection controls on the exports of meat. In response, European countries opened their doors to American meat again. And in 1891, Congress finally bowed to decades of angry lobbying and passed an international copyright law that protected foreign authors.

At a certain point, some of the push for change can come from within. As a capitalist system evolves, there can come a time when some players in the economy prefer to be held to more stringent standards, even ones that impose additional costs.

Partly, this happens when a country begins producing and exporting original goods that might appeal to counterfeiters elsewhere. The United States, for instance, strengthened its copyright laws to protect the growing number of American authors whose books sold overseas. If the Chinese movie business gains a significant international audience, it's safe to say that Hollywood will get a better reception next time it complains about knockoff DVDs of the latest Bruce Willis flick.

In the scandal-racked American food business, several industry leaders converted to the cause of regulation in no small part because there was money to be made: certain competitors would be put at a disadvantage, and the new federal laws would banish the inefficiencies of the older patchwork of state-level regulation.

But at a more fundamental level, producers began to realize that they could reap big profits from simple trust. By 1905, business leaders were testifying in Congress that the federal government could "do much toward preserving the reputation of US foods abroad"—in other words, they could make more money if potential trading partners believed the United States was finally cleaning up its act. And that's exactly what happened with the passage of the landmark Food and Drug Act the following year.

With each regulatory advance, the United States began gaining the trust of its own consumers, along with the rest of the world. In the process it went from being an upstart to the most powerful economy on the globe. China is far more than an upstart already, but as recent events suggest, it has a long way to go before it emerges, as the United States once did, from its own reckless youth.

Indeed, if the Chinese are truly following Deng Xiaoping's apocryphal maxim, "to get rich is glorious," then their own entrepreneurs and industries may eventually recognize that to get rich while bowing to international standards may be equally glorious—and even more profitable.

Democracy or Bust: Why Our Knowledge about What the Chinese Lack Is Really No Knowledge at All ☆ David L. Porter

A National Public Radio report in March 2008 on the opening of a new session of the National People's Congress in Beijing began with a disparaging comment to the effect that China is still a long way from democracy. As a statement of fact, this is no doubt both true and lamentable. As an attempt to convey useful knowledge to American listeners about China's current situation, however, it seems to me nearly useless. Like many such statements, it is based on an implicit comparison between the Chinese political system and Western-style democracy. And like many such implicit comparisons, it falls victim to a particularly seductive and misleading form of comparative fallacy.

Any time we set out to compare two things, we need to identify and describe the differences and similarities between their corresponding parts. There's no problem if we are comparing two equally familiar and equally distant objects by applying a neutral, objective standard of comparison. If I assert that granny apples have a green skin and sour flavor while Fuji apples have a golden skin and sweet flavor, I am unlikely to raise many hackles. If I claim that the average American's diet is relatively high in saturated fat and low in fiber, while the average Chinese diet is the reverse, I'm again on reasonably solid ground. As soon as we allow one of the two objects under study to represent, implicitly or explicitly, a normative standard of comparison, we're much more likely to produce skewed results. Imagine how a Washington apple would appear to a provincial Floridian who had encountered only navel oranges: as an abnormally hard orange with a dark smooth surface, lacking in internal sections and a readily peelable skin.

The vast majority of Western attempts to describe China, alas, have more than a little in common with our Floridian's account of an apple. We are inescapably products of our culture and so thoroughly identify with certain of its norms and values that we are strongly predisposed to take these elements as normative standards when attempting to identify or describe instances of cultural difference. We might well be entirely correct in the perception of difference. The trouble is that this predisposition warps the experience of difference so that all we finally see is the absence of qualities we take for granted in ourselves.

Consider, for a moment, some of the major themes that have dominated U.S. news coverage of China over the past year or two. Stories about poisoned toothpaste and lead paint–coated children's toys point out that China lacks effective oversight of product safety. Articles about the brown skies of Beijing and the algae-green lakes of Jiangsu make clear that the country lacks effective environmental regulation. And reports concerning the arrest and harassment of outspoken dissidents, lawyers, and journalists remind us, yet again, that the Chinese still lack freedom of speech and other basic political rights.

The common rhetorical thread running through all of these news stories is the notion of a Chinese lack or absence: the Chinese fail to measure up, in each case, to one normative Western standard or another. Once one becomes aware of this pattern, it turns up everywhere. The Chinese, we learn from reporters and commentators, lack intellectual property rights, worker protection laws, legal transparency, government accountability, journalistic freedom, and judicial independence. From twentieth-century historians, linguists, and comparative philosophers, we learn of deeper, structural deficiencies: the Chinese, in many recent accounts, lack a tradition of innovation, abstract reasoning, and hypothetical thought as well as taxonomic classification, a sense of public virtue, respect for personal freedom, declinable verbs, and so on. If you type the phrase "the Chinese lack" into Google, you can come up with 2,354 more examples. The Chinese would seem to be lacking in so many essential qualities, in fact, that it seems something of a wonder that they can sustain a functional society at all.

The problem with such formulations is not that they are factually "false," though some of them certainly are. It is true, after all, that Washington apples "lack" a readily peelable skin and internal sections, that declinable verbs are not a feature of the Chinese language, and that the discourse of individual rights has not been a dominant current in Chinese political thought over the past several centuries. The problem, rather, is that negative assertions make for utterly inadequate descriptions.

Imagine that I want to tell you about a creature I saw on a recent trip but that all I can remember about it is that it didn't have a trunk, tusks, floppy ears, teeth, legs, toenails, or deeply textured skin. You might surmise, correctly, that the creature I'd seen was not an elephant, but you'd be hard pressed to conjure up a satisfactory mental picture from my account. My account is an entirely true and accurate description of a whale, but it doesn't get us very far in understanding what a whale is. A knowledge of China consisting largely of a series of negations—no human rights, no free press, no environmental protection, no effective regulation, no public manners, no democracy—is really no knowledge at all.

What this kind of surrogate knowledge does provide, however, is a wonderfully flattering self-conception for those making the comparison. For if China lacks all these good things, the implication is that "we" possess them and presumably always have. What American, on reading yet another *New York Times* article on Chinese human rights violations, doesn't feel a certain pleasing rush of indignant self-righteousness? Perhaps Americans are justified in feeling pride in a constitution that succeeds in protecting most citizens' rights most of the time. To the extent, however, that we allow the "knowledge" of what China lacks to reinforce our appreciation for our own ways of doing things, we develop a compelling interest in seeking out and perpetuating such negative claims about China, which often, on closer examination, turn out to be useless and misleading. We run the very real risk of being led astray, in our well-intentioned pursuit of cross-cultural understanding, by the very conditions of that pursuit.

Follow the Money: A Tale of Two Economies ☆ Kenneth L. Pomeranz

At the beginning of 2008, it was already clear that the U.S.–China financial relationship was dangerously unbalanced—in particular, that there was no reason to expect China to keep lending the United States vast sums of money at low rates forever. By the fall, *Huobi zhanzheng*—a 2007 book warning that Western bankers would try to destroy China through currency machinations and encouraging a nationalistic Chinese response—had spent over a year atop Chinese best-seller lists, the U.S. savings rate and the U.S. dollar had tumbled further, and, above all, the American housing bubble had burst, revealing massive quantities of bad debt throughout the financial system and making it clear that the American market did not even offer safety to compensate for the low returns. Yet the "unsustainable" relationship continues, with very little change so far.

Here's what I wrote in late January, responding to a piece by James Fallows:

James Fallows has a piece in the February, 2008 *Atlantic* on what he calls "The $1.4 Trillion Question"—why China continues to accumulate $1 billion a day in relatively low-return American assets (mostly Treasury bills), why this can't go on forever, and what it could mean if this pattern of investment ends abruptly rather than slowly. On the whole, it's a good introduction, with some useful background on the people responsible for making the central government's investment decisions. (The point that one of the two key figures, unlike his counterparts almost anywhere else, has never invested for himself, or even bought a house, is a nice touch.) I think the article overdoes its emphasis on a lack of transparency in China—the way in which sub-prime mortgages were repackaged as "AAA" securities has made clear that the American financial markets China has been investing in aren't always that transparent, either—but that's a matter of tone and emphasis. What the article is missing, I think, are two important pieces of demographic and historical perspective, which help illustrate the pressures on the government. Fallows spends a fair amount of time on changes in China's mood that may be real but are hard to get a handle on—e.g. greater awareness among the population that their investments in the US are not earning much money (and some high profile ones have been outright losers, like the widely-publicized 2007 investment in the Blackstone Group) and that this is money that could be used to better things at home—and speculations about how much the government wants to, or can, continue resisting those popular desires in the interests of keeping inflation low, etc. I think the big story is more structural than that.

First the demography. Here the key point is one of the great under-played China stories: the rapid aging of the Chinese population. For roughly 30 years now, China has had compulsory birth control of various sorts, and (as most people reading this probably know) its birth rates declined at a rate that has very few historical parallels. So while the number of young people entering the work force every year has remained quite high until recently (China had so many births in the 1950s and 1960s that even with them having relatively few children per couple when they grew up, birth rates per 1,000 population stayed high into the late 1980s), the percentage of children in the population became quite low. Meanwhile, because Chinese death rates were very high before the Revolution, and stayed pretty high into the mid-1960s, there were also relatively few old people. So what economists call the "dependency ratio"—the ratio of people in the labor force to people whom workers need to support—has been extremely favorable for China over the last couple of decades. But that is now changing pretty quickly (thanks mostly to public health improvements under Mao) and China will soon have a fairly old population; by 2030, it will have as high a percentage of old people as countries like Italy and Germany today, whose pension problems, etc., you read about periodically.[1] A country with a higher ratio of dependents to workers—like a family in similar circumstances— simply cannot save at the same rate as a country with relatively few dependents, no matter what the government may want to do and how many provisions it has to siphon the dollars China's exports earn out of the economy and into a massive national savings account. And since China also has plenty of investment needs, as Fallows emphasizes—for schools, hospitals, sewers, you name it—it is

---

1. Some of the best work on this is by my University of California, Irvine, colleague Wang Feng and Andrew Mason at the University of Hawaii. Their paper in a newly published book, *China's Great Economic Transformation*, edited by Loren Brandt and Thomas Rawski, is well worth a look.

likely to start spending down its dollar hoard before too long, no matter what happens in U.S.-Chinese negotiations. It's true that both sides recognize the dangers of this happening too fast—leading to a run on the dollar and the collapse of China's biggest market—but the pressures for it to at least start happening soon are even stronger than Fallows lets on.

That brings us to the history. China, like Japan and Taiwan before it, differs from Europe and the US in having undergone very substantial industrialization before its countryside began to empty out. (Japan's rural population kept rising in absolute terms until World War II; China's until roughly 1998.) Thus they were quite industrial before they were heavily urban, in part because they had lots of industry in the countryside. (Think of China's Township and Village Enterprises.) Even today, China has a lower percentage of its population in cities than Britain had in 1840. There are all sorts of reasons for this—and anyone who becomes a loyal reader of my posts will eventually hear about them ad nauseam; but it is likely that in China, as in Japan, this will end with a period of extremely rapid urbanization. This rapid urbanization is now really getting underway (you ain't seen nothin' yet!), as rural industrial job creation slows to a crawl (as it now has) and the rural-urban income gap becomes so large that even with many barriers to migration remaining, many more people will pick up and leave. So far, China's urbanization rate pretty closely tracks Japan's, with a 50 year lag—and beginning in the mid-1950s, Japan went from about 35 percent urban to about 70 percent urban in less than 20 years. Most people think China is poised to do the same—which will require China's cities to grow by roughly the total population of the U.S. and Mexico combined by 2030.

And here's the rub. The Chinese government has worked very hard to avoid creating the kinds of slums that ring Mexico City, Manila, Cairo, etc. In fact, this has been one of the few real continuities in policy between pre- and post-1978, though the tools used to insure this—outright prohibition of migration, guaranteeing land allocations, encouragement of rural industry, phasing out land taxes, various local policies that deny rural migrants access to urban services, etc.—have been an ever-changing mix. To a great extent they've been successful in meeting this goal: certainly there are grim communities in Chinese cities, but the numbers of people lacking access to electricity hook-ups, running water (albeit of varying quality), etc., is quite low by "third world" standards. This matters, among other things, for social and political stability. Maintaining this record as urbanization accelerates will require huge amounts of investment.

Meanwhile, even though the number of new job-seekers entering the labor force each year is now declining, China can't really afford to see job creation slow down, because there is still a lot of labor to be absorbed. To go back to the Japan comparison, when Japan's phase of very rapid urbanization began in the 1950s, its unemployment rate was around 2 percent, so even though people newly arrived in the cities faced crowding and other ills, they all had jobs. Nobody knows for sure what China's urban unemployment rate is, but it is certainly far higher than 2 percent. So job growth has to keep going, and presumably, most of that growth has to be making things and providing services for people in China. And that means a lot of the money now abroad has to come home—no matter how much, or little, resentment grows over China subsidizing U.S. over-consumption, or American backlash against Chinese ownership of U.S. assets. Nonetheless, Fallows has the main point right—whether this happens smoothly or abruptly, and on what timetable, has enormous implications.

Writing in late September, with Wall Street in turmoil, Niall Ferguson took a much more structural and historical view—but vastly overstates the epochal significance of what he is seeing. And in his desire to blame the Chinese government and celebrate the unfettered market, he also largely misses the current political dynamics that Fallows caught nicely. In an article called "The End of Chimerica" posted online by *Stand Point* magazine, Ferguson begins by observing breakneck growth in Chongqing and by noting that state-directed investment decisions have a lot to do with it; he sees this as evidence of an essentially "Stalinist" economy, in contrast to what came before: "China's industrial take-off may have begun with foreign direct investment and an export drive aimed at Western markets. Today it has become domestically driven. . . . The state is in the driving seat."

What this ignores, most obviously, is that Chinese growth has always been a mosaic of regional processes based on very different models. Foreign direct investment did indeed drive growth in Guangdong. It was much less important in the Lower Yangtze, where a combination of private firms (in places like Wenzhou) and township and village enterprises are closely tied to local governments (though often later privatized) in southern Jiangsu and reformed but still state-owned enterprises play a central role in Shanghai. And in western China, the state has remained central all along: roughly two-thirds of all industry has remained state owned in several Western provinces, while the rates in many coastal provinces (with Shanghai a notable exception) have been under 20 percent for years. Just because a Western pundit visits Chongqing doesn't mean that the western provinces are now the quintessence of Chinese economic development, any more than an earlier tendency to overlook the interior meant that export-oriented private firms were the sole driver of growth in those years. China's exports of finished goods actually grew much faster in 1999–2007—at the same time that the domestic-oriented government investment in the interior noted by Ferguson was ramping up dramatically—than in any previous period.[2]

---

2. And, incidentally, while Ferguson is surely right that the costs of pollution and other negative side effects of Chinese growth are not being taken into account, there is not much evidence to support his assertion that this is the result of the continued role of state planning. Rapid industrialization, especially in its early stages, has been an ugly process in both state-dominated economies and private-dominated economies. Moreover, China's export sector, which is clearly driven by market demand rather than state-imposed quotas, may well be dirtier than its economy as a whole. A recent Carnegie Mellon study estimates that export production accounts for roughly one-third of China's greenhouse gas emissions, while *The Economist* estimates that exports account for only about 10 percent of *value added* in the Chinese economy.

It simply makes no sense to look at one piece of this highly varied mosaic, which happens to have the least symbiotic relationship with the West—in fact, little relationship at all, except through its demand for imported resources and its impact on the atmosphere—and conclude, as Ferguson does, that any mutually beneficial Chinese–U.S. relationship is "now merely a chimera" likely to soon devolve into direct imperial rivalry.

So what would a more balanced picture look like?

Well, first of all, that China and the United States are both very big—so even in a period of intense globalization, most of both economies will always be domestically oriented. One often reads figures that compare the total value of Chinese *trade* to gross domestic product (GDP) and get figures like 70 percent, but this reflects a difference in how we calculate GDP and how we calculate trade: the 10 percent figure, though it sounds low to me, is probably much closer to reality. For GDP we add up the value added by each firm; so if your local baker uses $7 worth of eggs, butter, and so on to produce $10 worth of cookies, the bakery's contribution to GDP is $3, even though its sales are $10. If we added up the sales for every firm, we'd be double-counting the value of the ingredients, which were already counted when they left the farm. But when we count imports and exports, we count the total value of stuff crossing the border in each direction: thus, if a Chinese firm imports $37 worth of high-tech components, assembles and puts a plastic case on them, and exports them for $40, there's $77 worth of trade counted, but the contribution to China's GDP is really only $3. And a lot of Chinese export production, especially in Guangdong, is very much like that. A complementary distortion occurs at the U.S. end: that $40 game cartridge arrives in Long Beach and gets counted as a $40 import from China, but much of its value may actually come from Malaysia, Taiwan, Japan, and so on. Our trade deficit is with *Asia*, not just China, which is one reason why revaluing the yuan won't change it dramatically.

Second, financially, nobody really knows for sure how much of China's "foreign direct investment" is truly foreign to begin with, even in a place like Guangdong. This is because there are favorable rules for treating foreign investment; thus, a lot of Chinese money goes to Hong Kong and gets invested in firms that then reinvest back on the mainland, where it gets "foreign" treatment. That's not to say China doesn't need the U.S. market—or that the reinvestment of much of China's trade surplus in U.S. assets hasn't helped keep America's debt-driven boom going—but "Chimerica" was always much more the limited overlap of two big circles (like on those Venn diagrams you learned in third grade) rather than a meaningful economic unit.

Third, remember the demographic facts above. Over the long haul, China's economy has to become more domestically oriented. The building of urban housing, schools, and the need to provide services for an aging population all mean that there has to be a gradual shift toward the home market. In the long run, certain niches in the global economy just aren't all that desirable: making shoes, socks, and so on for export is a hard business (not to mention a hard job for workers). Private-sector firms will also be increasingly motivated to look for opportunities at home if they want to increase their profit margins. On the one hand, soaring raw materials prices mean that profit margins are (at least for now) much higher in sectors like mining than in low-wage export manufacturing—and Chinese primary product producers are selling mostly to the voracious home market. On the other hand, the biggest profit margins in the making of consumer goods are in product design and marketing, not in actual manufacture. (It is better—or at least more lucrative—to be Apple than Foxconn, which makes many of Apple's machines, just as it is better to be Nike than one of its contractors.) So far at least, Chinese firms have been much more successful at moving into product design and marketing when they have focused on their home market than when they export—not all that surprising, given that they have much greater knowledge of the consumers there and do not generally face well-entrenched, heavily capitalized competitors. Becoming a major global *brand* is hard, even if you have great manufacturing and commercial prowess—Japan and Korea have done it, but for the most part Taiwanese firms still haven't. So you needn't be a government planner—much less a "Stalinist"—or be taken in by statistics exaggerating the size of China's foreign sector to think that there are lots of good reasons for its economic focus to shift inward quite a bit over time.

Of course, as long as the Chinese economy continues to grow rapidly, foreign trade can become a smaller percentage of the economy while still growing a lot in absolute terms. And, again, this is the long haul, and the long haul will not suddenly arrive tomorrow. Given China's continuing need to generate new jobs, foreign markets will continue to matter a lot, even if many of them provide only razor-thin profit margins. (The labor force will peak around 2015, but over 50 million new jobs will be needed between now and then; and even after 2015, the nonfarm labor force will keep growing for quite a while longer.) The regime clearly hopes that building infrastructure in the interior—which is what a lot of the state investment is—will help make places like Chongqing the export platforms of the next decade or two, as rising rents and living standards in Shanghai and Shenzhen make it harder for those places to compete with Vietnam and other new entrants into labor-intensive manufacturing. In short, more investment in the interior and in production for the home market doesn't mean that the U.S.–China economic relationship has to change soon and drastically or turn suddenly hostile.

Ferguson's final point is that China is increasing its economic and political presence in places that its raw materials come from, especially in Africa and Latin America; he sees this as empire building that may well lead to clashes with the United States. Increased tensions are certainly possible, and as somebody who tends to emphasize geographic and resource endowments more than most economic historians, I certainly wouldn't rule out access to raw materials as a flashpoint (though it is odd that Ferguson's list of places where things could get ugly does not include gas- and oil-rich central Asia, where the United States has vastly increased its presence not far from China's border). But again there's no particular reason to connect this with a Chinese turn away from markets, world trade, and the United States and toward the interior. China's export sector is, as we've seen, import intensive, including resource imports; and part of what the push into China's far west is about is in fact tapping more *domestic* sources of minerals, hydropower, and so on.

The "develop the West" program raises all sorts of problems—above all environmental problems and problems in Han–minority relations—but to think that it involves a strong and fateful turn away from the basic outlines of the U.S.–China relationship with the U.S. economy is itself a chimera. If a break comes *suddenly*, it is much more likely to result from changes on the Western side: a new protectionism or a financial crisis/recession so deep that it forces China's hand. In fact, as Fallows rightly noted, it's the Chinese central government—the same one that is indeed pushing crash development efforts in the interior—that is also resisting nationalist pressures (exemplified by the excitement over *Huobi zhanzheng*) to disinvest from the West and build even more, even faster, at home. The regime isn't doing this out of a deep desire to be nice to the United States—it's worried about inflation at home and about instability in world markets if it pushes too hard—but it's the effort that counts. For now, the U.S.–Chinese economic relationship remains unsustainable but oddly stable.

Yellow Peril Consumerism: China, North America, and an Era of Global Trade ☆ Amy Hanser

In 1885, the American journalist Bayard Taylor made the following statement: "The Chinese are, morally, the most debased people on the face of the earth . . . with a depravity so shocking and horrible, that their character cannot even be hinted. . . . Their touch is pollution." Comments such as Taylor's oft-quoted one, coupled with pervasively negative imagery and stereotypes about Chinese people, contributed to the passage of U.S., Australian, and Canadian immigration legislation designed to stem the tide of a Chinese "yellow peril": a much-feared flood of low-quality people who, it was believed, would endanger Western countries if allowed to enter them en masse.

Today, major journalists and major newspapers tend to steer clear of such explicitly racist rhetoric, but a contemporary equivalent of the negative imagery once used to characterize a faceless mass of potential Chinese immigrants has resurfaced recently in English-language media reports on China's exports. Readers of the *New York Times*, for example, regularly encounter articles that present China as a producer of food items that are "filthy and unfit to be eaten," tainted and toxic toys, substandard tires, and so on. Foreign reporting from within

China brings us stories of factories "churning out electronics" while "dumping mountains of waste" into the Chinese countryside. Even American drug use and abuse is "traced" to toxic Chinese origins, from which "chemicals flow unchecked" (e.g., *New York Times*, October 31, 2007). As a July 2007 article in the *New York Times* observed, "There was a time the words 'Made in China' immediately evoked 'shoddy.' Lately, many Americans are thinking 'danger.'"

The most recent scandal, as I write this in September 2008, involves powdered milk and other dairy products tainted with the chemical melamine. It promises to add yet another chapter to this evolving story of China as dangerous, toxic, contaminated, and unscrupulous. The parallels with nineteenth-century "yellow peril" imagery is not just superficial, for we saw then as we see now rhetoric that presents China as a place linked to the dirty, the untrustworthy, the contaminated, the contaminating. Whereas the old yellow peril discourse bolstered exclusionary immigration policies, today's "yellow peril consumerism" (as I dub it) acts to obscure the complex and sometimes disturbing aspects of global production by casting the problem as errant, immoral China. And whereas a century ago it was the flow of Chinese *people* that gave rise to yellow peril discourse, it is now the flow of *goods* (and money) that inspires fear.

What exactly was the original "yellow peril" idea? The first thing to note is that it was intricately intertwined with Western imperialism. Proponents of "yellow peril" arguments divided the world into racialized camps: on one side the "West" (Europe and white settler societies) and on the other a hostile, nonwhite world led by the "yellow hordes" of Asia. This ideology served to legitimate European empires through a discourse of racial difference and white superiority. The strong prejudices associated with the term "yellow peril" emerged in between the mid-1800s and early 1900s, the time when China's purportedly degenerate people were perceived as a global threat, none more so than in 1900, when the anti-Christian Boxers laid siege to the foreign legations of Beijing—an event that readers in Europe and North America followed closely via reports in newspapers and pictorial magazines.

Anti-Chinese sentiment was bolstered by negative media imagery of Chinese people (symbolized by the violent Boxers and later by fictional figures such as the diabolical Dr. Fu Manchu) and writings that used new and supposedly "scientific" ideas about racial difference and dirt and disease to assert that "essential" (and immutable) characteristics made Chinese people innately cunning, treacherous, uncivilized, dirty, and vicious. Between 1850 and 1882, when the Chinese Exclusion Act was passed in the United States, the idea that "Chinese filth and disease" endangered American society became widespread, a perspective fostered by missionary accounts of a China "rotten with disease" as well as by the medical profession, which actively portrayed the Chinese as a source of contagion, "decay," and even special germs.

At the local level, this larger, more abstract yellow peril discourse often took the form of extreme anxieties about racial proximity. Most notably, this led to the creation of Chinatowns. These emerged largely as the result of state interventions and provided spatial concentration and segregation of the city's Chinese population in disadvantaged city districts. But they quickly came to be seen as physical evidence of immutable racial characteristics and sites of contained contamination.

But perhaps above all, the threat to North American domesticity came in the form of "cheap" Chinese labor that threatened white working-class living standards. Ironically, in both the United States and Canada, it was the failure of Chinese workers as *consumers* that made them problematic workers and, by extension, an unsuitable addition to North American society. Historian Lawrence Glickman has shown that after the Civil War, American working-class advocates began to press for a "living wage" that was to serve as the basis for a democratic society made up of wage laborers, as opposed to the republican, independent producers of the past. Chinese people, it was believed, were satisfied with a lower standard of living that would, in turn, generally depress wages and thereby undermine the living wage, the "American" living standard that demanded it, and, by extension, American democracy. American Federation of Labor pamphleteer George Gunton, one of the people Glickman quotes, declared, "An American will starve or strike rather than accept Chinese wages [since] the American standard of living demands higher wages . . . [but the] Chinaman receives low wages because he will live in a low way."

A global economic system in which the free movement of people purportedly threatened American society and America's working class with "unfree" Chinese "coolie" labor led to calls for and ultimately produced internal segregation of Chinese people and barriers to further immigration. Ironically, in light of China–U.S. issues today, the specific issue that concerned organized labor then was cast in the language of trade and the *importation* of labor. Such arguments lent support to the passage of the Chinese Exclusion Act by the U.S. Congress in 1882, effectively banning Chinese immigration to the United States for the next sixty years.

Moving back to the present, we see the kinds of "fears of contagion" (to borrow an apt phrase Resnia Mawani uses in her work) that were once associated with Chinese bodies finding echoes in consumer-based "fears of contagion" that emphasize the danger of "China Made" goods entering the lives, homes, and even stomachs of Americans. A chronology of reporting on some recent issues reveals the production of a narrative about China that is steeped in yellow peril imagery.

In March 2007, a Canada-based manufacturer of pet foods, Menu Foods, initiated a recall of wet cat and dog food, reportedly as much as 60 million cans manufactured in U.S. plants. The food had been linked to the unexplained deaths of some ten animals. From the start a major clue seemed to be that the problem coincided with the company's switch to a new supplier of wheat gluten, a common addition to pet food.

Reports quickly began to appear in the media about the pet food recall and a growing hysteria among pet owners. On March 20, the *New York Times* described a Boston-area emergency room (for pets) that had been flooded by anxious pet owners. "'People are panic-stricken," a staff veterinarian was quoted as saying. "This is really scary to people, and I don't blame them." In the days that followed, newspaper headlines reported a growing official death toll: to fourteen and then sixteen. And it was revealed that the gluten had originated in China.

A week later, the U.S. Food and Drug Administration (FDA) announced that the recalled pet food had been contaminated with melamine, an industrial chemical used in fertilizers and some plastics. The chemical had also been found in wheat gluten samples from the Chinese supplier, though a link between the substance and pet deaths was still speculative.

Attention quickly shifted to China. On April 5, the FDA announced that it was testing all wheat gluten imports from that country. Days later, the *New York Times* sent a reporter to the Chinese company that was the alleged source of the tainted gluten. In his report, he mused that the gluten incident was "exposing some of the enormous challenges confronting the global marketplace as China becomes a worldwide supplier of agricultural products" and noted that China's own food markets were plagued by "fake milk powder for babies" while pointing out that, according to reports in the domestic media, rat poison–laced breakfast cereal had killed one person and sickened 202 others.

In the following weeks, the concern over tainted food products continued to grow. Another supplier of additives to pet food discovered melamine in yet another Chinese product, rice protein concentrate. The contaminated material was traced to feed given to livestock, including hogs raised in several states and, later, chickens raised in Indiana. Concern now turned to possible contamination of the human food supply. Testing of imported Chinese food products expanded to include ingredients, like cornmeal and corn gluten, more likely to end up in human food products, such as baby formulas, protein shakes, and energy bars. As the U.S. Congress geared up to hold previously scheduled hearings on the security of the nation's food supply and the FDA issued reassurances that the traces of melamine found in animal feed were not likely to pose a threat to humans, Chinese police detained the managers of the two companies identified as the sources of the melamine-tainted wheat gluten. As part of its effort to display to the world its resolve to strengthen enforcement of food safety laws, the Chinese government even sentenced Zheng Xiaoyu, the former director of China's State Food and Drug Administration, to death for accepting brides and approving fake medicines.

In the succeeding months, the tenor of reporting moved in two clear directions. The first emphasized the weakness of America's food borders and the failure to police those borders sufficiently in an increasingly globalizing world. President George W. Bush's former secretary of health and human services,

Tommy Thompson, cast this as a question of national security in a post-9/11 era: "For the life of me I cannot understand why the terrorists have not attacked our food supply because it is so easy to do," he told the *New York Times*. A former FDA official, William Hubbard, portrayed the situation as a problem of globalization, with American food manufacturers seeking out cheap ingredients from "less developed countries" that, Hubbard suggested, were gaming the system and turning the United States into a "dumping ground": "The word is out. . . . If you send a problem shipment to the United States it is going to get in and you won't get caught."

A second focus of reports centered on problems with China's brand of capitalism. Investigative reporting on the pet food scandal included exposure of a world of counterfeit goods and fake substitutes in China. The *New York Times* reported widespread and long-standing use of melamine in animal and fish feed in China, where it has served as a cheap substitute for vegetable proteins. Some of the examples of fraudulent products seemed calculated to titillate, such as soy sauce made from human hair. As one article in the newspaper asked of the "renegade businessmen" selling fake and counterfeit goods in China, "Just how far out of the Chinese mainstream are they?"

The answer, it seemed, was not far. *New York Times* reporter David Barboza went on to suggest that "cutting corners or producing fake goods is not just a legacy of China's initial rush toward the free market three decades ago but [is] still woven into the fabric of the nation's thriving industrial economy." The June 5 article reduced the reputation of the industrial area around the Chinese city of Wenzhou to a characterization of "first specializing in fake goods" copied from Proctor and Gamble, surely a surprise (and misrepresentation) to those more familiar with the region's long-standing production of a very wide range of consumer goods.

In May, the crisis of confidence in Chinese-made goods deepened with the seizure in Panama and several other countries of toothpaste that contained diethylene glycol, a cheap but toxic substitute for safer sweeteners. In June, "toxic toothpaste" had been found in a dollar store in Miami after tubes has been discovered all over the world, from Africa to Southeast Asia to South America. The *New York Times* also reported in June that the deaths of people in Haiti in 1996 and Panama in 2006 were connected to falsely labeled Chinese diethylene glycol used to produce cough syrup and other medicines.

Then, a recall of "Thomas the Tank Engine" toys coated with lead-tainted paint caused another furor, this time around toy safety. A series of other, major toy recalls followed in the summer months, as Mattel issued warnings about its China-made toys. The *New York Times* reported that "China manufactured every one of the 24 kinds of toys recalled for safety reasons in the United States so far" in 2007 and quoted concerned parents claiming that they would start scrutinizing the origins of their children's toys. One shocked parent was quoted as saying, "Lead paint in this day and age?"

Though it was acknowledged that China is the source of the vast majority of toys sold in North America—some 80 percent of the total—the new recall made it seem as if, in the words of one letter writer to the *New York Times,* "production of exported goods from China is seemingly driven by greed." While other letters pointed out the greed of U.S. companies (who outsource) and the dangers this lead paint posed to Chinese workers, this particular letter writer penned, "Let's not wait for hundreds or thousands of poisoned Americans (and pets) to force a revision of consumer safety laws governing imported products" (June 23, 2007). The threat to American well-being, it was suggested, demanded immediate and forceful action.

More problems followed: a recall of Chinese-made tires in June and then warnings about the quality of Chinese seafood, rejected as "filthy" (a formal designation in the evaluation of seafood). At this point, volleys were being traded between the United States and China, as the Xinhua news agency reported in late June that China began impounding food imports from the United States because of quality problems (identified as bacteria and mold). Nevertheless, there was no sign that China's exports to the United States were likely to slow: the *New York Times* reported in October that U.S. imports from China had grown by 27 percent in the first nine months of 2007, including growth in categories such as food and agricultural products. And by the end of 2007, imports of toys and related goods had risen by 24 percent over 2006.

By now, the parallels with an earlier era of yellow peril discourse should be clear: themes of contamination and pollution; unscrupulous, profit-oriented criminals; and threats to living standards span these two eras. More generally, reports on problems with consumer goods and food products shared pages with articles on China's increasingly polluted and degraded environment, what an October editorial in the *New York Times* referred to as the country's "unbreathable air and noxious rivers." This polluted air—in Beijing in particular—was the subject of concerned articles about the upcoming Summer Olympics, and the *Times* and other U.S. papers even carried articles about American athletes, fearful of tainted Chinese foods, planning to bring their own food to the Beijing Olympics—dubbed the "B.Y.O." or "Bring-Your-Own" Olympics.

But are these superficial parallels? After all, there are important truths in the media reporting described above. There are and have been long-standing problems with product quality and weak regulation of food and product safety in China, with sometimes lethal consequences for consumers. Even milk powder has been the subject of national-level scandals in the recent past; in 2004, at least twelve infants died and many more suffered developmental problems because of substandard milk powder. These problems have been going on for years—they have not, however, been deemed particularly newsworthy. The story of tainted cough syrup in Haiti and Panama reflects serious and committed reporting, and yet it seems to take on much greater significance only in the wake of poisoned American pets. Likewise, as Elizabeth Economy and other scholars have been stressing for years, China faces massive ecological challenges as a result of rapid and often environmentally destructive economic growth, but reporting on these issues uses heavily loaded language (e.g., China's "insatiable appetite" for raw materials) deeply evocative of an earlier discourse about China's perilous massiveness.

There are two levels to this narrative about contaminated Chinese-made products worth highlighting. First, there is the threat to North American domesticity that is posed by these tainted goods. Pets, children, and the physical well-being of Americans themselves seem under siege. Second, there is a curious critique of Chinese capitalism and its systematic failings. This critique simultaneously obscures the continuities and linkages across economic systems (especially North America's and China's) and produces an essentializing discourse about China and, by extension, Chinese people.

These narratives make use of older, "yellow peril" thematics, and in both eras, I'd argue, anxieties take on the form of racialized concerns about proximity and, perhaps, even intimacy. For example, today, much like the danger that North Americans believed Chinese immigrants and laborers posed in the late nineteenth and early twentieth centuries, Chinese goods in the early twenty-first century threaten to contaminate North American bodies in the most domestic and intimate of ways: through tainted food and toys and in the endangered bodies of beloved family pets and infants and small children. More important, China-made products furnish the material trappings of North American domesticity—an astonishing array of inexpensive, everyday items—that touch all spheres of private life. These items not only enter the home but also may gain entry to the body. The mouth—and things that enter the mouth—seem especially salient: toothpaste and food, for humans or otherwise, but also children's toys that are likely to be sucked or chewed by small children. This fear about consuming, bodily, Chinese goods was reflected in a move by grocery store chain Trader Joe's, which announced in February 2008 that it was removing "single-ingredient" Chinese products (like garlic, ginger, and spinach) from its shelves. "Our customers have voiced their concerns about products from this region and we have listened," the *Los Angeles Times* reported the company said in a formal statement. In relation to toys, in August, the Associated Press quoted Illinois Senator Dick Durbin as saying, "We can't wait any longer for China to crack down on its lax safety standards. This needs to stop now before more children and more families are put at risk."

The story of the presence of Chinese people, through consumption, in American daily life is largely obscured by a larger narrative about the failings of Chinese capitalism. There are, of course, deep contradictions in this "Chinese capitalism" narrative, and a close reading of the pet food incident reveals that the apparently sharp dividing line between legitimate North American capitalism and illicit Chinese capitalism was not necessarily so clear. There are some peculiar contradictions between elements of the stories that appeared in the pages of, for example, the *New York Times*. We learn, for example, that the North American pet food industry is mostly a large network of contractors, such that Menu Foods, a company unknown to the vast majority of people, dominates the North American pet food industry not through its own brands but rather as a contract supplier. By extension, Menu Foods has contracted out the supply of its ingredients, including the wheat gluten added to wet cat and dog foods to thicken gravy. The gluten was purchased from a distributor that procured it from a Chinese supplier. But in this extended chain of trade, distribution, and production, North American companies largely evade blame for what is seen to be a "Chinese" problem.

Similarly, reporting on the contamination of livestock feed in the United States reveals that hogs are routinely fed "salvaged pet food," which involves converting pet food that does not meet quality standards into livestock feed. A disturbing story about processed food and the industrial production of food in North America is overshadowed by the story of unscrupulous Chinese businesses and lack of state regulation and responsibility there. For example, in April 2007 the *New York Times* reported on Chinese eels "fed contraceptive pills to make them grow long and slim"—but at the same time U.S. cows are fed synthetic hormones to boost milk production. Similarly, a mid-May 2007 *New York Times* story on food safety in the United States disclosed that Alabama and Mississippi (major producers of catfish themselves) have banned the sale of Chinese catfish in their states after tests found illegal antibiotics in the fish—though U.S. domestically raised cattle are regularly fed antibiotics to combat the negative effects of overcrowding and industrial-scale farming. In fact, the U.S.-based Union of Concerned Scientists estimates that some 70 percent of all antibiotic use in the United States is devoted to meat and poultry production.

And again, a *New York Times* report in late May 2007 disclosed that a Canadian-owned U.S. manufacturer of feed binders appeared to have been knowingly using melamine in its products, which were shipped overseas to make shrimp feed and, in one case, used in the United States for the production of fish food. One of the company's executives seemed to suggest that the melamine was problematic only for use in the United States, given FDA regulations. The same article quoted Michael Doyle, the director of the Center for Food Safety at the University of Georgia, as saying that the incident "goes to show that we apparently have some bad actors out there [in the United States]." Similarly, another May 2007 article in the *New York Times* titled "Who's Watching What We Eat?" revealed that a U.S. producer of peanut butter contaminated with salmonella destroyed product before FDA inspectors could examine it and refused to provide access to company records without a written request—which was never made by the FDA. And yet, whereas the problem in China was cast as part of the "fabric" of its capitalist economy, in the United States similar problems seem to involve only bad individuals.

These contradictions are similarly present with the case of toy recalls. Whereas lead paint–related recalls clearly involved the use of unauthorized paint products, many other recalls, such as those involving dangerous small parts and powerful magnets, were clearly design-related flaws. In fact, as two business scholars, Paul Beamish and Hari Bapuji, have shown, the majority of toy recalls in the United States between 1988 and 2007 have been due to *design* flaws and not manufacturing flaws—over 75 percent. Not only this, but Beamish and Bapuji's data suggest that while there has been an increase in toy recalls in recent years, manufacturing-related recalls have risen faster for toys produced outside of China than for those produced within the country.

The pet food and toy recall controversies in particular reveal how the American consumer provides the moral mooring for U.S. economic hegemony. In a new global configuration of labor and consumption, it is the consumer as consumer that becomes the site of national interest to be defended. Whereas in an earlier era the "American standard" was represented by the everyman worker threatened by low-quality labor, today it is the everyperson (and everypet) consumer threatened by low-quality consumer goods. And as in the past, the flow from China is again cast as (to borrow the wording of David Goutor) "not just a question of quantity . . . but [also] of quality." In a context of gross trade imbalances between North America—especially the United States—and China, an imbalance driven in part by American consumerism, we find, somewhat oddly, that it is the consumer who is imperiled.

The fall 2008 milk scandal in China certainly raises questions about food safety standards and systematic problems with domestic food production in China. While the details remain obscure about how abuse of melamine to artificially boost "protein" levels in powered milk and other milk products could persist on such a large scale, the scope and degree of domestic public and international attention being drawn to the issue may result in real changes and real protections for Chinese consumers. At the same time, reporting on the milk issue—globally—falls very much into a "toxic China" genre, as story headlines speak of "toxic," "tainted," and "poisoned" milk; the scare also reinforces the fears of the contamination of intimate realms, as countries as unlikely to have Chinese milk powder on their shelves as France are assuring their populations that no babies will be harmed by illicit milk products.

One might even wonder how it is that the Chinese are consuming dairy products in such quantities anyway; consumption of milk has grown in China by a factor of fifteen since the 1960s, and this in a country where traditional cuisines contain little or no dairy. A complex nexus of ideas about health, nutrition, affluence, and modernity and, I would argue, even ideas about the beautifying capacity of milk linked to understandings of Western lifestyles and bodies has combined with government efforts to expand milk production and consumption (but not, apparently, product safety) to produce a rapid increase in milk consumption among Chinese urbanites. In other words, milk in China has ironically been tied to efforts to achieve the consumer lifestyles and physical good health associated with the American standard of living.

The historical pathways to what I have characterized as today's "yellow peril consumerism" are complex. Negative reporting on China has often characterized the country, in recent decades, as politically repressive and uncivilized. And to be sure, contemporary yellow peril discourse expresses anxieties about China's "rise." This too represents a historical continuity, as the immigration-rooted "yellow peril" fears also escalated at times when Asian powers were growing in prominence (as Japan did around 1900, for example).

I've tried here, though, to suggest a somewhat different reading of this negative portrayal of China. "Yellow peril consumerism" links a narrative of threatened health and safety in the domestic sphere to a broader one that identifies China's economy as illicit and unruly, its businesspeople as unscrupulous and greedy, and its products as polluted, tainted, contaminated—even filthy. Without seeking to make light of the serious issues related to consumer protections in China's economy, I have attempted to show the powerful parallels between an anti-Chinese rhetoric directed at Chinese immigrants to North America in the late nineteenth and early twentieth centuries and the discourse about China and especially its exports produced in twenty-first-century North American newspaper reports. The resulting "yellow peril consumerism" narrative obscures the interconnectedness of global production and also fails to address the underlying causes for why products are sourced in China and what the costs are to Chinese people, in terms of labor, resources extraction, and industrial pollution—the "China price," to borrow Alexandra Harney's term. Perhaps part of that price is the "insatiable appetite" of the American consumer?

Suggested Readings

Anderson, Kay. 1991. *Vancouver's Chinatown: Racial Discourse in Canada, 1875–1980.* Montreal: McGill-Queen's University Press.

Economy, Elizabeth C. 2004. *The River Runs Black: The Environmental Challenge to China's Future.* Ithaca, NY: Cornell University Press.

Glickman, Lawrence B. 1997. *A Living Wage: American Workers and the Making of Consumer Society.* Ithaca, NY: Cornell University Press.

Hooper, Beverly. 2000. "Consumer Voices: Asserting Rights in Post-Mao China." *China Information* 16:92–128.

Mawani, Renisa. 2003. "'The Island of the Unclean': Race, Colonialism, and 'Chinese Leprosy' in British Columbia, 1891–1924." *Law, Social Justice and Global Development* 1:2–21.

Miller, Stuart Creighton. 1969. *The Unwelcome Immigrant: The American Image of the Chinese, 1785–1882.* Berkeley: University of California Press.

Okihiro, Gary. 1994. *Margins and Mainstreams: Asians in American History and Culture.* Seattle: University of Washington Press.

Shah, Nayan. 2001. *Contagious Divides: Epidemics and Race in San Francisco's Chinatown.* Berkeley: University of California Press.

Conclusion

Postcard from December

A Year of What Significance?

Our title invokes Ray Huang's wonderfully named *1587: A Year of No Significance*. That book, as Kate Merkel-Hess's introduction to this volume reminds us, focuses on a year in which nothing spectacular happened—no invasions, rebellions, major assassinations, earthquakes, etc.—but which nonetheless seems to seal the fate of the Ming. We see that business as usual was exacerbating all the regime's problems, and there were no signs of forces that could change those ways of doing business in time to avert disaster. The paradox of 2008 seems to be exactly the opposite. It has been a year with many memorable events, including several that were deeply worrisome and one that cost tens of thousands of lives, and yet few people are predicting anything dire. On the contrary, polls suggest that China's citizens are more optimistic about their country's future and more positive about the higher levels of their political leadership than most people around the world, and both ordinary people and "experts" outside the country seem to take it for granted that China either is, or soon will be, a superpower (though one title labels it a "fragile superpower"). The situation brings to mind one of my other favorite academic titles: an essay by Mark Elvin on Chinese economic and environmental history called "Three Thousand Years of Unsustainable Development."

This might also suggest that some trends that did not crystallize in any single dramatic event—the ongoing accumulations of urbanites and Internet users, the continuing decline in state enterprise employment, or the ongoing depletion of north China water—may ultimately look more important than conflicts over the ages of Olympic gymnasts or even the safety of the milk supply. But that does not mean that 2008's big moments were just whitecaps carried along by inexorable tides below. While some of these events may only *reflect* larger processes of change, that is no small thing if they help make these patterns more intelligible, and others no doubt have *caused* change, too. And since, as Jonathan Spence's foreword notes, this is a book somewhat in the spirit of the Pompidou Center—a building with the pipes and wires plainly visible—we need not pretend that we are sure how the things we have commented on will appear when future commentators look back at them. Nonetheless, since the end of the year is a traditional time for summing up—and this chapter is the only one not sent to the press by November 2008—it seems a logical place both to update some stories and to assume the more traditional pose of a historian who confidently assembles day-to-day developments into less immediately visible but more meaningful patterns.

One important story that continued to December 31, more or less as we might have expected, is that of Taiwan–mainland relations, chronicled in our pages by Paul Katz (59–65). The late-October visit to Taiwan of Zhang Mingqing, vice chairman of the PRC's Association for Relations across the Taiwan Straits did not exactly go as planned—he was attacked by a crowd of DPP supporters when he visited a Confucian temple in Tainan—but the visit of Zhang's boss Chen Yunlin ten days later more or less did (though it also sparked protests; this time nonviolent). Some further steps toward rapprochement were taken, with agreements on direct flights (which actually began to operate in December), maritime shipping, and cooperation on food safety. (Zhang's visit to a Confucian temple, incidentally, fit nicely with Julia Murray's point (266) that by encouraging the current Confucian revival, the CCP is, among other things, building one possible base on which to build ideological reconciliation with Taiwan.) With the KMT back in power in Taiwan and economic interdependence growing steadily, it seems likely that political ties will also get closer over the next few years. What specific forms that may take, however, remains anybody's guess.

From Beijing's perspective, the second great "splittist" threat is in Tibet (with Xinjiang as number three), and here 2008 was a very tumultuous year. Late December brought more arrests—this time of fifty-nine Tibetans accused of "spreading rumors" and "stirring up ethnic hatreds," but the biggest Tibet politics news of late 2008 may have been what didn't happen. Meeting in late November, Tibetan exile representatives rejected proposals that they declare for independence, and instead proclaimed continued support for the Dalai Lama's "middle way." While this was not that surprising, neither was it automatic—various people have suggested that if Beijing does not reward more cautious exiles by making some concessions, younger and more radical elements will come to the fore. In that sense, the Dalai Lama's victory at the assembly was a victory for Beijing, too, though because Beijing still holds the Dalai Lama's supporters responsible for the March violence in Tibet (contrary to almost all the evidence), they cannot celebrate this publicly. As James Miles points out (38), part of what was striking about these Tibetan protests was that they were not monk-led; and as Pankaj Mishra notes (40), the targets were Han and Hui civilians rather than symbols of state power. While this choice of targets no doubt helped fuel the rage of netizens back in "China proper," it also probably reflected basic realities. The greatest threat to Tibetan culture can no longer be identified with any one state policy (e.g., closing of monasteries): instead it is represented by the influx of both settlers and tourists, the consumer culture they bring with them, and the economic transformation they are part of. (Another part of economic development—natural resource extraction—raises even bigger problems, to which we will turn later.)

Whether or not development efforts eventually create prosperity in Tibet, they will almost certainly create a world in which more and more Tibetans have many Han neighbors and pursue livelihoods (and material rewards) that fit awkwardly with Tibetan traditions. In that sense, while it is useful for Donald Lopez to describe Tibet as a mountainous Latvia (42–44)—a society relatively recently absorbed into an authoritarian multinational state and culturally more oriented toward a different set of neighbors—the analogy also has its limits. In many ways the Soviet Union and Western Europe shared a "modernist" view of the good society, despite their profound differences. The cultural disconnect in Tibet seems more profound. Nor does South Asia, undergoing rapid cultural change, offer the same sort of external anchor for Tibetan "traditionalists" that Western Europe offered to Latvian nationalists and liberals. And the PRC shows no signs of collapsing as the USSR did. So while some sense of Tibetan identity may well survive or even be strengthened—and may well be hostile to Beijing—it seems more and more likely that this will be accompanied by a very different sense of what being Tibetan means than that championed by the Dalai Lama; and in that sense, Pankaj Mishra's depressing analogy to the fate of many native American cultures (42) may well be apropos.

When we turn to booming east China, it is far easier to tell happy stories—and to highlight changes in day-to-day lifeways that blogs can capture exceptionally well. The greater challenge is in deciding what these individual stories add up to.

Western observers often fall into an "all or almost nothing" mode when describing the ways in which reform has expanded possibilities for China's citizens. Sometimes, in the rush to extol rising living standards and increased consumer choices, we forget the many ways in which there has been much less opening up—especially in politics—and the considerable loss of security. But it is also easy to fall into the opposite trap—writing as if, for those who cannot vote for their highest government leaders, all that market authoritarianism provides is a nearly worthless right to choose between Coke and Pepsi. (As David Porter points out (282–284) this latter position can be wonderfully self-flattering for Westerners; and the former is equally so, in different ways.) But after all, consumer choices can be ways of expressing oneself—and perhaps no less so when they express longing for things that are "fake," as Timothy Oakes suggests (251–259). People who dress, cut their hair, and so on to associate themselves with a particular "lifestyle" may often be choosing an advertiser's definition of who they should be, but having that definition to play off of, say, the one your parents have chosen for you still matters—particularly in the world of intense familial pressures conjured for us by Leslie Chang and Yan Yunxiang's articles (21–29,

33–35). It is no accident that many of the interesting public controversies we have chronicled—from arguments about the merits of music, books, and movies (240–248) to "NIMBY" protests by homeowners (15–21)—concern what we might think of as a penumbra of activities that occur where consumption meets community (and/or state).

And further beyond expanded consumer choice lie huge changes in other areas: the ability to choose whom one marries, and when and where one looks for partners. I have vivid memories of watching mid-1980s college seniors wait for job assignments—and hearing faculty playing matchmaker for students who had arrived at that point in life with little if any experience of dating. ("Say your favorite female student has been assigned to Harbin," one professor told me, "you call your trusted friends and find out if they have a nice male student assigned to Harbin . . .") And then there are the many choices that sit on the frontier between consumer choices and more fundamental ones: about where to live, what to read and listen to, and so on. All these choices are restricted in important ways, to be sure, but nobody who remembers China more than a few years ago can fail to see big differences. As Shi Xia's essay on the popularity of *Fortress Besieged* (248–251) makes clear, people may experience their expanded options as just so many different paths to disillusionment, but it is highly significant that the novel is no longer criticized as relevant only to a tiny elite. Even the rapid increase in divorces that helps make the novel relevant (up an estimated 20 percent last year—quadruple 1970 rates—but still only one-third of U.S. rates) has its good side, and is testimony both to changed social attitudes and to the (somewhat) greater ease of starting over now that the *danwei* does not define one's life nearly as much as it once did. In these ways, it is hard to overstate the broad impact of "reform."

When we move to more directly political matters, the limitations of Chinese life in 2008 are more obvious. Corruption is indeed rampant, though it appears in our book mostly indirectly, particularly as failure to regulate the safety of products and buildings. The milk scandal continues to unfold. The dairy industry announced mass payments to victims on December 27, which a number of lawyers and parents denounced as inadequate. (The proposed $300 per child for those "only" made ill—versus $29,000 each for the children who died—seemed to be particularly infuriating, perhaps because these children may discover further kidney problems later.) Dozens of lawsuits also have been filed. The criminal trials of seventeen industry principals began in late December, and the chairwoman of Sanlu (the firm at the center of the scandal) immediately pleaded guilty. Meanwhile, melamine continues to turn up in other food products (most recently, exported fish). Also, just before the end of the year, a Chinese government report estimated that 2.5 percent of all schools (including 20 percent of Yunnan primary schools) may be poorly built—just as a court in Sichuan was rejecting a lawsuit by parents whose children, killed in the Sichuan earthquake, may have been victims of these problems. (They have subsequently been offered

$8,823 per child.) And a page one *Los Angeles Times* article on December 29 painted an unusually grim picture of corruption seeping into almost every area of Chinese life, from school admissions to product and building safety to the land deals that have probably sparked the largest number of popular protests in China.

Yet it is also worth remembering that not every poorly built building or undercompensated victim of eminent domain represents deliberate malfeasance. As Pierre Fuller points out (276), people in China's rapidly growing cities need homes, schools, and so on, and not every problem that turns up in hurried construction necessarily represents a character flaw in the builder—much less in "the Chinese." Similarly, some cadres may sincerely intend to provide adequate jobs or payment streams to people displaced by new construction, only to see the venture go sour in China's rapidly shifting economy. Certainly there are any number of cases that leave little room for doubt—the payoffs that huge numbers of people report are required to get proper medical treatment, for instance—but there are also some exchanges of favors and/or cutting of corners that may well appear legitimate to the people involved; and these are the sorts of distinctions that often become clear only when reported by well-acclimated long-standing residents.

Repression turns up more often than corruption in our pages, and though my guess is that most Chinese would reverse the relative emphasis, there are clear connections between the two. Liu Xiaobo's arrest on December 8, presumably for signing the human rights manifesto Charter 2008, is but the latest high-profile example of the limits on political expression pointed to by Jeffrey Wasserstrom (210), Geremie Barmé (72, 76–78, 212–214), Jeremiah Jenne (220–223), and David Bandurski (235–237). As important as are people like Liu, whose protests explicitly target the central government and political/civil rights, the more typical victim of repression probably began by seeking redress for some instance of local corruption, and found to his or her cost that higher levels of officialdom either would not or could not intervene. Much of the political future probably rests on Beijing being able to keep enough people convinced that asking higher levels of government to clean up localities is a worthwhile endeavor, but sustaining such a belief will require both that such appeals become safer and that they succeed more often. Certainly, it is within Beijing's power to not retaliate against whistleblowers as often as it does, but I suspect many Chinese also understand better than some foreigners do that cleaning up corruption will require some genuinely new stratagems. While some Westerners have assumed that China has been able to make remarkably sharp policy turns without becoming unstable because an all-powerful central government makes the key decisions, people more familiar with the history of reform have noted that the regime has generally found ways to buy the cooperation of local and provincial power-holders rather than confronting them directly. (Arrangements that allowed local governments to retain most of the profits of industrialization during the 1980s, for instance, helped turn many cadres who had first been attracted to the party during the Cultural Revolution into unlikely entrepreneurs.) But it is not clear how a similar kind of indirection would provide enough incentives for local officials to greatly reduce corruption and accept accountability—even assuming that the central government can impose those same changes on itself.

So far, at least, those who doubted that hosting the Olympics would do much to liberalize China's politics seem to have been mostly right—which is very different from saying that denying Beijing the Games would have made things better. Indeed, the strong and genuinely popular nationalist reactions to disruptions of the torch relay (68–87) strongly suggest the opposite. Lijia Zhang's comment that "In the ecstatic cries [when Beijing was awarded the games] I heard Chinese people's longing for the recognition and respect from the world" (167) rings true to me. And much as we might like to tender that respect to "China" while withholding it from, say, its criminal justice system, there was never much chance for making that distinction clear through gestures aimed at the Beijing Games. As many incidents reported here and elsewhere make clear, there is a genuine and fervent mass nationalism in China. Beijing may sometimes manipulate that nationalism, but it does not need to create it and cannot consistently control it; which is all the more reason, as Jeff Wasserstrom and Kate Merkel-Hess point out (229), why it cannot afford to ignore these sentiments, even when they clash with other interests, such as maintaining calm relations with major trading partners. Meanwhile, the Olympic volunteerism noted in various ways by Susan Brownell (81–86,153–161), Daniel Beekman (192–199), and Mary Erbaugh (163–165) showed once again that nationalism and internationalism can sometimes be quite complementary; indeed, the desire to be full, self-confident, participants in a cosmopolitan modern world plays an important role in the Chinese variants of both. And for all the traumas of this past year, one suspects that most Chinese who care about such things will see 2008, on balance, as a sign that this long-sought full membership is within closer reach than ever.

But, as many of our contributors mentioned, this sense—and a more general sense that both personal and national fortunes are improving—depends on China's rapid economic growth continuing; and here, of course, the last part of the year brought dramatic and mostly unwelcome news. As ripples from the American-centered world financial crisis spread ever wider, Chinese firms that depend on export markets felt the pain. In Guangdong—the most export-oriented and therefore hardest-hit province—an estimated nine thousand factories have closed in recent months, with toy producers (already reeling from the safety scandals described by Stephen Mihm (277–282) and Amy Hanser (290–299) the hardest-hit. (One wonders how those who invested money early in 2008 to make sure they met American regulatory standards in the future feel now.) For the first time since the "Asian" financial crisis of 1997–1998, China's exports will contract this year; and nobody thinks that the world economy will bounce back from this meltdown as fast as at least some of the affected economies did that time. China's national government has estimated that some five million migrant workers are returning to the countryside earlier than planned because their jobs have disappeared; anecdotal reports from both sending and receiving areas suggest this is a low figure. And if this wasn't bad enough, many of these factories were months behind on their wages when they suddenly closed. While government officials scrambled to provide payments to at least some of the affected workers—and to defuse their protests—huge numbers of workers nonetheless have every reason to feel both desperate and betrayed. Higher up on the social scale, the largest group of college graduates in China's history is hitting the job market this year, just as hiring has plummeted; and as Leslie Chang and Yan Yunxiang make clear, those graduates—however privileged they may seem to peasants or factory workers—have made extraordinary sacrifices of their own (21–29, 33–35). Overall, according to one think-tank estimate, twenty-four million new job seekers will hit the market next year, pursuing about twelve million new jobs; another puts the likely job losses at a staggering forty million. For those observers who have speculated that any failure to deliver continued high growth could cost the CCP its remaining legitimacy, the moment of truth might seem to be coming.

But not so fast. Chinese society is also showing impressive signs of resilience amidst this disaster. First, it's worth noting that China's principal links to this mess are through trade, not finance: its customers are in trouble, but its own banks (which have plenty of troubles of their own, but different ones) don't have very many direct links to crumbling financial institutions. And (as Paul Krugman showed recently, http://www.princeton.edu/~pkrugman/finmult.pdf) trade multipliers are much smaller than financial ones. Second, the Chinese government has come up with a huge stimulus package—far larger, proportional to their economy, than anything yet on tap in Western economies—largely composed of infrastructure projects in the center and west of the country that they had hoped to launch sometime fairly soon anyway. What matters here isn't just that they have the cash on hand to do this—though that is certainly important—but also that this represents a shift in focus toward relying more on domestic demand, which people had long known the Chinese economy would have to make eventually. (See, for instance, my discussion, 284–290.) For Guangdong in particular, it also goes with another adjustment that has long been regarded as both inevitable and desirable: a shift toward the production of more sophisticated, higher value-added products and away from low-wage, low profit-margin products like plastic dolls, tube socks, and Christmas tree ornaments. And in the longer run, the shift toward an economy more focused on domestic demand should also mean a shift toward one in which services play a larger role: something that is vital to improving the quality of life (especially with a rapidly aging population), to creating more jobs that are at least somewhat sheltered from constant global competition and downward pressure on wages, and to allowing

China's economy to keep growing with somewhat less risk of environmental catastrophe than if it remains so heavily oriented toward manufacturing.

That's not to say, of course, that anybody wanted this shift to be suddenly accelerated this way—the export sector still provides loads of jobs, and it's hard to see how the capital-intensive building of airports, sewage-treatment plants, and so on can make up for their loss—much less to deny the horrible pain that the suddenness of this dislocation is bringing to millions of people. In fact, some of the worst pain is probably in places where Westerners generally don't see it—in remote villages where relatives depend on money sent home by migrants to the cities. That the meltdown happens to be coming at a moment when farm prices are relatively high may ease the pain in those villages a bit, but there is no getting around the basics. China has one of the largest gaps in the world between urban and rural incomes—worse yet if you leave out the many densely populated high-income regions in east China that are still classified as "rural," but where very few locals do much farming anymore. (Much of the agricultural labor in those areas is done by guest workers from poorer regions further inland.) Under the circumstances, even the small sums sent home by assembly line workers or peddlers in Shenzhen could be the crucial difference allowing a young couple to marry, or a sibling to stay in school, or an elderly parent some ease and dignity. Without any doubt, China's fragile safety net will be severely tested over the next year or two, and it is unlikely that it will fully meet the challenge. Though the state has made considerable efforts over the last five years or so to mitigate the most unequal results of economic competition, and to reduce risk of various sorts—creating new rural health cooperatives, making transfer payments to the rural elderly, creating various kinds of insurance arrangements—it is unclear how far these measures have actually gone, and even the most optimistic scholarly assessment I have read (in a paper delivered by the eminent political scientist Wang Shaoguang in November at the Beijing Forum, an event *China Beat* covered in blog posts) concedes that migrants are not well covered by most of these schemes. There is no question, then, that for tens of millions of Chinese, the fallout from the Wall Street meltdown is not only story number one for 2008 but is likely to dominate a grim 2009 as well. But still, my guess is that these painful stories will wind up being filed under "the human cost of continued development" rather than "the beginning of a breakdown" in economy, polity, or both.

The greatest looming dangers are probably ones that we have not covered extensively here: the many-faceted environmental crisis facing China and the world. The Olympics briefly focused attention on China's serious air pollution problems (see Alex Pasternack's essay, 187–192), and most people are probably at least vaguely aware of China's contribution to global warming .(By some measures, it passed the United States as the world's largest emitter of greenhouse gases, though of course it ranks much lower as a per-capita polluter, and as an overall contributor to the cumulative damage we have done to the atmosphere.)

But China's water woes are at least equally pressing, and it may be easier to see what effects they will have. Two little-noted news items from near the end of the year may illuminate that—after we review some background.

Water has always been a problem in China, and effective control of it has been associated with both personal heroism and legitimate sovereignty for as far back as our records go. The legendary sage-emperor Yu, for instance, supposedly showed his fitness to rule by taming floodwaters, and the success of flood control—especially on the Yellow River—has been taken as a sign of the state's vigor and concern for popular welfare ever since. But water scarcity is probably an even greater problem than excesses, especially in the modern period. Surface and near-surface water per capita in China today is roughly one-quarter of the global average, and worse yet, it is distributed very unevenly. The north and northwest, with over half the country's arable land, have about 7 percent of its surface water; the North China Plain, in particular, has 10–12 percent of the per-capita supply for the country as a whole, or less than 3 percent of the global average. China also has unusually violent seasonal fluctuations in water supply; both rainfall and river levels change much more over the course of the year than in either Europe or North America. (Fluctuations in India—likewise affected by both the monsoon and the annual Himalayan snow melt—are more similar.) While the most famous of China's roughly 85,000 dams are associated with hydropower (about which more in a minute), a great many exist mostly to store water during the peak flow of rivers for use at other times of year.

The People's Republic has made enormous efforts to address these problems—and achieved impressive short-term successes that are now extremely vulnerable. Irrigated acreage has more than tripled since 1950, with the vast majority of those gains coming in the north and northwest; this has turned the notorious "land of famine" of the 1850–1950 period into a crucial grain surplus area, and contributed mightily to improving per-capita food supplies for a national population that has more than doubled. Much of that, however, has come through the massive use of deep wells bringing up underground water far faster than it can be replaced; and a great deal of water is wasted, especially in agriculture, where costs to farmers are kept artificially low. (Chinese agriculture is not necessarily more wasteful in this regard than agriculture in many other places—and certainly the deviations from market prices are no worse than in the supposedly market-driven United States—but its limited supplies make waste a much more immediate problem.) Water tables are now dropping rapidly in much of North China, and water shortages are a frequent fact of life for most urban residents. (Beijing suffers fewer water shortages, but only because it can commandeer the water resources of a large surrounding rural area included in the municipality.) Various technologies that would reduce water waste exist, but most are expensive. More realistic pricing of irrigation water would help—but probably at the price of driving millions of marginal farmers to the wall, and greatly accelerating the already rapid rush of people to the cities. Consequently, adoption of both of these palliatives is likely to remain slow.

Instead, the state has chosen a massive three-pronged effort to move water from south to north China—by far the biggest construction project in history, if it is completed. Part of the eastern section began operating this year, and the central section is also underway (though the December 31 *Wall Street Journal* reported a delay due to environmental concerns). The big story in the long run, however is the western line, which will tap the enormous water resources of China's far southwest—Tibet alone has over 30 percent of China's fresh water supply, most of it coming from the annual runoff of some water from Himalayan glaciers. (This is an aspect of the Tibet question one rarely hears about, but rest assured that all the engineers in China's leadership, including Hu Jintao and Wen Jiabao, are very much aware of it. Tibetans, meanwhile, not only see a precious resource going elsewhere when their water is tapped: they regard many of the lakes and rivers to be dammed as sacred.) The engineering challenges in this mountainous region are enormous, but so are the potential rewards, both in water supply and in hydropower—the electricity water can generate is directly proportional to how far it falls into the turbines, and the Yangzi, for instance, completes 90 percent of its drop to the sea before it even enters China proper. The risks, as our two stories make clear, are social and political as well as environmental. But with greater technical and financial abilities than before, more pressing water and energy crises, and perhaps greater confidence in their ability to shrug off criticism, the government is now moving ahead rapidly on several projects connected to this scheme.

Call these two news stories the "double glacier shock." On December 9, *Asia Times Online* reported (http://atimes.com/atimes/China/JL09Ad01.html) that China was planning to go ahead with a major hydroelectric dam and water diversion scheme on the great bend of the Yarlong Tsangpo River in Tibet. The hydro project is planned to generate 40,000 megawatts—almost twice as much as Three Gorges. But the water that this dam would impound and turn northward currently flows south into Assam to form the Brahmaputra, which in turn joins the Ganges to form the world's largest river delta, supplying much of the water to a basin with over 300 million inhabitants. While South Asians have worried for some time that China might divert this river, the Chinese government had denied any such attentions, reportedly doing so again when Hu Jintao visited New Delhi in 2006. But when Indian Prime Minister Singh raised the issue again during his January 2008 visit to Beijing, the tone had changed, with Wen Jiabao supposedly replying that water scarcity is a threat to the "very survival of the Chinese nation" and providing no assurances. And so it is—not only for China, but for its neighbors. Most of Asia's major rivers—the Yellow, the Yangzi, the Mekong, Salween, Irrawaddy, Brahmaputra, Ganges, Sutlej, and Indus—draw on the glaciers of the Himalayas, and all of these except the Ganges have their source on the Chinese side of the border. Forty-seven percent of the world's people, from Karachi to Tianjin, draw on those rivers.

In short, the possible damage to China's neighbors from this approach to its water and energy needs is staggeringly large—and the potential to raise political tensions is commensurate. Previous water diversion projects affecting the source of the Mekong have already drawn protests from Vietnam (and from environmental groups), and a project on the Nu River (which becomes the Salween in Thailand and Burma) was suspended in 2004. But this project has vastly larger implications for both Chinese and foreigners. If, as some people think, the twenty-first century will be the century of conflicts over water, Tibet may well be ground zero.

Of course, China is hardly the only country that has ever appropriated water (not to mention other resources) that others see as theirs; I am writing in Southern California, made much more livable by denying Mexico the Colorado River water it is theoretically guaranteed by treaty. And there is also something to be said, environmentally, for anything that provides China with lots of electricity and isn't coal. Others will lose badly from projects like this, but for millions of Chinese, they *might* represent extremely welcome relief from very pressing problems.

But that's where the second glacier shock of 2008 comes in—news that this crucial water source is disappearing faster than anyone had previously realized. A report published in *Geophysical Research Letters* on November 22 noted that recent samples taken from Himalayan glaciers were missing two markers that are usually easy to find, reflecting open air nuclear tests in 1951–1952 and 1962–1963. The reason: the glacier apparently had lost *any* ice built up since the mid-1940s. This means it is not just losing ice from its edges but from all exposed surfaces, including the top center. And since the Inter-governmental Panel on Climate Change estimates that the Himalayan highlands will warm at about twice the average global rate over the next century, there is every reason to think the situation will get worse. One estimate has one-third of the Himalayan glaciers disappearing by 2050, and two-thirds by 2100. If that scenario is right, then even if all the engineering challenges of south–north water diversion can be solved, and even if China undertakes and gets away with taking water away from hundreds of millions of people in South and Southeast Asia, the resulting fix might not last very long.

Strangely, these stories have attracted very little press coverage. (There is, however, an excellent video at the Asia Society website: http://www.asiasociety.org/chinagreen/origins-of-rivers-omens-of-a-crisis/.) Perhaps they simply don't fit our normal expectations well enough. When we think "Tibet," we are more likely to think religion or politics than environment; when we think "melting ice," we are more likely to think polar ice caps than Tibet; and when we think "Chinese environmental problems" we tend to think of its most densely populated and industrialized regions. But if we someday look at 2008 in something like the way Ray Huang has looked at 1587—as a year in which the writing was on the wall, but people chose not to see it—these two stories, hiding in plain sight, might well be the reasons. And in that case, the writing would not be for China alone. One advantage of the relatively informal style of blog posts is that they make it easy to remember that the author does not write from a point of Olympian detachment; and environmental anxieties, perhaps more than any others, remind us of the global role in creating current Chinese ambitions, and the global stake in seeing them fulfilled without a catastrophic impact on others.

By laying special emphasis on the dark economic and environmental clouds that were evident in late 2008, I do not mean to suggest that these sorts of "material forces" are the "real" story, and the other issues surveyed in this book somehow less real. Seemingly inevitable outcomes based on "real" constraints have been averted many times before—and not only in the land of "Three Thousand Years of Unsustainable Development." Meanwhile, people continue their lives, and in the process remake the society that responds to crises. One thing that I hope emerges from our snapshots of this "year of great significance" is the remarkable energy evident in so many corners of Chinese society today—and the determination to make that energy add up to something. Perhaps this is where we should definitively part company with the historical allusion in our title. The late Ming was celebrated as a period of great economic and cultural creativity, but also widely condemned as an increasingly atomized and chaotic society. Part of what is haunting about the story told in *1587* in particular is that the book is full of people who, far from just thinking about themselves, were doing their best to serve society; but with the center paralyzed, people's individual attempts lacked the framework that they needed in order to do much good. But whatever else one may say about it, one can hardly doubt that China's central government today is vigorous, and intensely aware of the rapid change going on around it. The sheer range of improvisations on display in today's China—in everything from public policy to popular music to get rich quick schemes—makes it a fascinating place to watch; and the coexistence of seemingly crushing problems and impressive confidence in the future suggests that both insiders and outsiders have an awful lot left to figure out.

Kenneth L. Pomeranz

Appendix

China in 2008

A Chronology

January

12   The first of several high-profile, peaceful urban protests centered on local, quality-of-life issues takes place in Shanghai, where residents protested the extension of the high-speed maglev (magnetic levitation) train into their neighborhood.

25   The first of a series of devastating storms hit south China. Lasting until February 6, the storms crippled the national transportation system during the busiest travel time of the year (Chinese New Year). Millions suffered when their regions lost power and water.

February

7   Chinese New Year

March

10   Large protests in Lhasa to commemorate the Tibetan Uprising Day of 1959.

14   Riots in Lhasa, Tibet. Over the following days they spread to surrounding regions and provinces with large Tibetan populations.

24   The Olympic torch was lit in Athens and began its journey to Beijing, where it arrived on March 31.

April

7   The Olympic torch passed through Paris, where it met its most vehement protesters. The attempts to seize the torch from torchbearers there galvanized Chinese who felt insulted by the attacks. Some called for boycotts of Carrefour, a French superstore with numerous outlets in China.

May

12   Sichuan is struck by a 7.9-magnitude earthquake, with its epicenter at Wenchuan. In the following days, the death toll from the earthquake rose to almost 70,000, and it left almost 5 million homeless.

June

1   The government ban on plastic bags took effect on this day. In an effort to cut down on the 3 billion bags used daily, retailers had to charge for any plastic bags used and the ubiquitous carryall could not be carried on public transportation or in public areas. International organizations like Greenpeace hailed the move.

July

11   China (and Russia) vetoed a UN Security Council effort to impose sanctions on Robert Mugabe's government in Zimbabwe.

August

4   Sixteen Chinese border police were killed in an attack by suspected Uighur terrorists in western Xinjiang.

8   Opening Ceremony for the 2008 Beijing Summer Olympic Games. The Closing Ceremony was held on August 24.

September

10   News broke that Sanlu-Fonterra was recalling its infant milk formula after thousands of babies became sick and a few even died from ingesting the melamine-tainted product. Over the next month, melamine-tainted milk would be discovered in the products of numerous international and domestic companies everywhere from Japan to the Netherlands.

October

9   The Hong Kong stock market dropped 7.2 percent to its lowest point in three years, reflecting the weakening faith in worldwide markets as the U.S. credit crunch spread to Europe and Asia.

23   The European Parliament announced that it would award the Sakharov Prize for Freedom of Thought to human rights activist Hu Jia, currently imprisoned in Beijing. His wife, Zeng Jingyan, accepted the award via video from their monitored apartment.

November

3   Newspapers began to report a massive strike by taxi drivers in the southwestern city of Chongqing. Throughout November, taxi drivers in other locations also held short strikes, including Sanya (Hainan), Guangzhou, and Hong Kong. The government insisted it was a local matter, and actively worked to shape positive news coverage about local government officials' ability to manage the situation.

December

6   French president Nicholas Sarkozy met with the Dalai Lama at a Nobel Peace Prize meeting in Poland, sparking the ire of the Chinese government, who published an editorial in *People's Daily* accusing Sarkozy of damaging Sino-French relations.

10 On the sixtieth anniversary of the Universal Declaration of Human Rights, 303 Chinese dissidents submitted "Charter 2008," a call for political reforms modeled on Václav Havel's "Charter 77," which inspired political change in the Eastern Bloc in the late 1970s. In the weeks that followed, news of "Charter 2008" was suppressed on the mainland and many of the original signatories were detained, arrested, or disappeared. Meanwhile, thousands more signed their names to the Charter.

15 In a not-so-subtle rollback of Internet freedom, China again began to block websites that had been unblocked shortly before the Olympic Games in Beijing (though, in some cases, the blocks appear to have only lasted a week or so).

22 Though cross-strait tensions remained an issue in 2008, one big sign of an easing relationship between Taiwan and China came on December 23, when China sent two pandas to Taipei Zoo. Their names? Tuantuan and Yuanyuan, which, together as *tuanyuan*, means "reunion."

Acknowledgments

The editors would like to thank all of the contributors to *China Beat* as well as readers of the blog located in varied parts of the world—especially those who posted comments on the site during its first year in operation. We also want to express our deep gratitude to two individuals: Susan McEachern of Rowman & Littlefield, who went far beyond the call of duty in helping us both to envision this book and to see it through into production, and Miri Kim, who worked creatively and also tirelessly to ensure that we met daunting deadlines and more than earned the "with" credit she is given on the title page by virtue of her editorial advice and other input. We are grateful as well to the history department of the University of California, Irvine, which has provided us with an ideal working environment; filled as it is with faculty, graduate students, and staff members who are supportive of innovative projects; and, like us, see "outreach" activities and writing for nonacademics as worthy enterprises for scholars.

We also owe debts of gratitude to the many bloggers, website editors, and listserv directors who helped in various ways—reposting or linking to our pieces, telling their readers about us, and so on—to spread the word about *China Beat* after we launched it. We are doubtless leaving many people out, but those in this category deserving our thanks include Rick Shenkman (of the History News Network), Jennifer Schuessler (of the *New York Times*'s "Paper Cuts"), Andrew Leonard (of Salon.com's "How the World Works"), Joan Connell (of thenation.com), David Hayes (of openDemocracy.net), Jeremy Goldkorn (of Danwei.org), Rick Baum (of Chinapol), Richard Spencer (who blogs at telegraph.co.uk), Xiao Qiang (of the China Digital Times), Kenneth Tan (of Shanghaiist), David Flumenbaum (of the Huffington Post), Sky Canaves (of the *Wall Street Journal*'s "China Journal"), Pillarisetti Sudhir and Rob Townsend (of the American Historical Association's "AHA Today"), Marshal Zeringue (of the "Campaign for the American Reader"), Roland Soong (of "EastSouthWestNorth"), Rebecca MacKinnon (of "Rconversation"), Jana Remy (of "Making History Podcast: The Blog"), the editors of the *Far Eastern Economic Review*, Jeremiah Jenne (of "Jottings from the Granite Studio"), Karen Christensen (of Guanxiblogs.com), Andy Field (of H-Asia), T. Matthew Ciolek (of asia-www-monitor.blogspot.com), and contributors to the "Frog in the Well" blog.

Last but far from least, as this book contains a mixture of new writing and pieces that we have been given permission to reprint in full, excerpt, or run in expanded versions, we want to acknowledge the following people and organizations for allowing us to use previously published materials. Here, in a chapter-by-chapter listing, is relevant reprint information:

CHAPTER 1

"Coal Miner's Daughter." Kate Merkel-Hess from *China Beat*, September 28, 2008.

"NIMBY Comes to China." Used by permission from *thenation.com*, January 18, 2008. © thenation.com and Jeffrey Wasserstrom.

"Homeowners' Protests in Shanghai." Originally published in a slightly different form in *China Beat*, "Benjamin Read on Homeowners' Protests in Shanghai," February 2, 2008. © Angilee Shah. Used by permission of the author, Angilee Shah, and interviewee, Benjamin Read.

"Gilded Age, Gilded Cage." Reprinted from NationalGeographic.com, "China's Middle Class," May 2008. © Leslie T. Chang. Used by permission of the author.

"Little Emperors or Frail Pragmatists?" A longer version of this piece was published under the same name in *Current History* 105, no. 689 (September 2006): 255–62. Used by permission of the author and publisher.

CHAPTER 2

"Media Coverage of Tibet." Originally published in a slightly different form in *China Beat*, "James Miles on Media Coverage of Tibet," March 29, 2008. Used by permission of James Miles.

"At War with the Utopia of Modernity" was first published in the *Guardian* newspaper (guardian.co.uk), March 22, 2008. Used by permission of the author.

"How to Think about Tibet" was originally published in a slightly different form in *openDemocracy* (openDemocracy.net), March 31, 2008. Used by permission of the author and the publisher.

CHAPTER 3

"The Election in Taiwan." A longer version of this piece was published in *China Beat*, March 21, 2008. © Yong Chen. Used by permission of the author.

Paul Katz pieces: Excerpted from material originally published in *China Beat*: "What Shall We Do with the Dead Dictator?" January 28, 2008; "Trauma and Memory—228 in Taiwan Today," March 2, 2008; and "The Return of the Two Nationalisms," June 22, 2008. © Paul R. Katz. Used by permission of the author.

CHAPTER 4

"Follow the Bouncing Torch. "A longer version of this piece was published in *China Beat*, April 27, 2008. © Jeffrey N. Wasserstrom.

"Torching the Relay" was originally published in a slightly different form in *China Beat*, May 4, 2008. Used by permission of the author, with questions provided by Tom Swann and Tom Stayner of the *Woroni* newspaper (Australian National University). © Geremie R. Barmé.

"Chinese Protesters Extinguish Olympic Torch in Protest?" Reprinted from Danwei.org, May 8, 2008–May 10, 2008. Used by permission of the publisher.

"Why Were Chinese People So Angry about the Attempt to Seize the Torch in the International Torch Relay?" A longer version of this piece was published in *China Beat*, July 30, 2008. © Susan Brownell. Used by permission of the author.

CHAPTER 5

"Giving Long-Term Relief." A longer version of this piece was published in *China Beat*, May 23, 2008. © Yong Chen. Used by permission of the author.

"Rumor and the Sichuan Earthquake" was originally published in a slightly different form in *China Beat*, May 22, 2008. © S. A. Smith. Used by permission of the author.

"Earthquake and the Imperatives of Chinese Mourning" was originally published in a slightly different form in *China Beat*, June 12, 2008. © Donald S. Sutton. Used by permission of the author.

"Chinese Responses to Disaster" was originally published in a slightly different form in *China Beat*, May 19, 2008. © Kathryn Edgerton-Tarpley. Used by permission of the author.

"China and the Red Cross." A longer version of this piece was published in *China Beat*, "History of Chinese Red Cross," Parts I and II, May 18, 2008. © Carolyn Reeves. Used by permission of the author.

"After the Earthquake." Reprinted from the *New Yorker* (newyorker.com) with permission of the author (who retains reprint rights). © Peter Hessler.

"Letters from Sichuan II," was originally published in *China Beat*, May 20, 2008. © Peter Hessler.

CHAPTER 6

"A Better Life in New Shanghai?" was originally published in *China Beat*, November 3, 2008. © Maura Elizabeth Cunningham. Used by permission of the author.

"Disappearing Shanghai." Photographs and accompanying text used by permission of the author/photographer. © Howard W. French.

CHAPTER 7

"Revolutionary Anniversaries" is reprinted from *China Beat*, October 1, 2008. © Kate Merkel-Hess.

"Tiananmen's Shifting Legacy" is reprinted from openDemocracy.net, June 26, 2008. Used by permission of the author and the publisher.

"The Gate of Heavenly Peacemaking" was originally published in a slightly different form as "The Gate of Heavenly Pacification "in *China Beat*, June 18, 2008. © Pär K. Cassel. Used by permission of the author.

CHAPTER 8

"Vietnam's Youth Given a Rare Chance to Protest—against China" was originally published in a longer version in *China Beat*, May 6, 2008. © Caroline Finlay. Used by permission of the author.

Susan Brownell pieces: Excerpted from materials originally published in *China Beat*: "Could China Stop Taiwan from Coming to the Olympic Games?" June 14, 2008; "Which Previous Olympic Games Provides the Most Useful Historical Precedent for Understanding the 2008 Olympic Games?" May 3, 2008; "Why Can't the Chinese Authorities Allow a Little Space for Protests during the Olympics?" July 2, 2008; and "Are the Beijing Games Being Used as a Propaganda Campaign to Prop Up the Communist Party?" July 19, 2008. © Susan Brownell. Used by permission of the author.

"The Boycotts of '08 Revisited" by Jeffrey N. Wasserstrom was originally published in *Far Eastern Economic Review*, May 31, 2008 (www.feer.com/international-relations/2008/may/The-Boycotts-of-08-Revisited). Reprinted from the *Far Eastern Economic Review*. © 2008 Review Publishing Company Limited. All rights reserved.

"How to Talk to Strangers: Beijing's Advice" was originally published in a slightly different form in *China Beat*, August 12, 2008. © Mary S. Erbaugh. Used by permission of the author.

"Learning English, Learning Chinese" was originally published in a slightly different form in *China Beat*, August 14, 2008. © David L. Porter. Used by permission of the author.

"Hand Grenades and the Olympics" was first published in the *Observer* newspaper (observer.co.uk) as "Time to Stop Criticising China—We've Already Come So Far," August 3, 2008. Reprinted by permission of the author.

CHAPTER 9

"Painting over Mao" was originally published in a longer version in *China Beat*, August 12, 2008. © Geremie R. Barmé. Used by permission of the author.

"It's Right to Party, En Masse" was originally published in a slightly different form as "The Right to Party, En Masse" in *China Beat*, August 13, 2008. © Haiyan Lee. Used by permission of the author.

"Where Were China's Women on 8/8/08?" was originally published in *China Beat* as "What Happened to the Women?" August 10, 2008. © Nicole E. Barnes. Used by permission of the author.

"What Would Mao Think of the Games?" Used by permission from thenation.com, August 22, 2008). © thenation.com and Jeffrey Wasserstrom.

"The Olympics around the World" contains excerpts from the following materials originally published in *China Beat*: "Wishful Reporting in England," August 5, 2008 ©

Pierre Fuller; "Vancouver: Host to Winter 2010 Olympics," August 7, 2008 © David Luesink; "Nobody (?) Likes a Spoiler," August 1, 2008 © Miri Kim; "A View from Aotearoa–New Zealand," August 9, 2008 © Paola Voci; and "From the US to China, by Way of Israel," August 11, 2008 © Shakhar Rahav. Used by permission of the authors.

"From Lovers to Volunteers" was originally published in a longer version in *China Beat* as "From Lovers to Volunteers: Tian Han and the National Anthem," July 16, 2008. © Liang Luo. Used by permission of the author.

"Beijing's Olympic Weather" was originally published in a slightly different form in *China Beat* as "Beijing's Olympic Pollution Forecast: 'Haze' and Hot Air," August 6, 2008. © Alex Pasternack. Used by permission of the author.

CHAPTER 10

"After the Olympics, What?" originally appeared in a longer version in *China Beat*, July 10, 2008. © Nicolai Volland. Used by permission of the author.

"One Bed, Different Dreams," was originally published in a slightly different form in *Policy Innovations* (policyinnovations.org), August 28, 2008. Used by permission of the author, James Farrer, and the publisher.

"China's Olympic Run" was originally published in a longer version in *YaleGlobal Online* (yaleglobal.yale.edu) as "China's Olympic Run—Part II," August 29, 2008. Used by permission of the author, Pallavi Aiyar, and the publisher.

CHAPTER 11

"Early Critics of Deng Xiaoping—A 1978 Flashback" was originally published in *China Beat*, December 4, 2008. © Jeffrey N. Wasserstrom.

"Facing Up to Friendship" first appeared in the *Sydney Morning Herald* (smh.com.au) as "Rudd Rewrites the Rules of Engagement," April 12, 2008. © Geremie R. Barmé. Used by permission of the author.

"Preserving the Premier's Calligraphy at Beichuan Middle School" was originally published in a slightly different form in *China Beat*, June 17, 2008. © Richard C Kraus. Used by permission of the author.

"Boss Hu and the Press" was published in a slightly different form in *China Beat*, June 30, 2008. © Nicolai Volland. Used by permission of the author.

"Hua Guofeng: Remembering a Forgotten Leader" was originally published in a slightly different form in *China Beat* as "Where Have You Gone, Hua Guofeng?" August 24, 2008. © Jeremiah Jenne. Used by permission of the author.

CHAPTER 12

"Why Was Yao Ming Fined?" was originally published in a longer version in *China Beat*, February 6, 2008. © Susan Brownell. Used by permission of the author.

"The Chinese Press in the Spotlight" was originally published in a slightly different form in *China Beat*, May 31, 2008. © Timothy B. Weston. Used by permission of the author.

"Finding Trust Online" was originally published in a longer version in *China Beat*, June 26, 2008. © Guobin Yang. Used by permission of the author.

"Things We'd Rather You Not Say on the Web, or Anywhere Else" was originally published in a slightly different form in *China Beat*, July 17, 2008. © David L. Bandurski. Used by permission of the author.

CHAPTER 13

"Rocking Beijing" was originally published in a longer version in *China Beat*, July 23, 2008. © Eric Setzekorn. Used by permission of the author.

"*Kung Fu Panda*, Go Home!" was originally published in a slightly different form in *China Beat*, July 17, 2008. © Haiyan Lee. Used by permission of the author.

"In Defense of Jiang Rong's *Wolf Totem*" was originally published in a slightly different form in *China Beat* as "A Defense of Jiang Rong's *Wolf Totem*," July 25, 2008. © Timothy Weston. Used by permission of the author.

"*Wolf Totem*: Romanticized Essentialization" originally appeared in a longer version in *China Beat* as "Coming Distractions: *Wolf Totem*," March 24, 2008. © Nicole E. Barnes. Used by permission of the author.

"Wei Cheng: From an Elite Novel to a Popular Metaphor" was originally published in a slightly different form in *China Beat*, June 27, 2008. © Xia Shi. Used by permission of the author.

"Faking Heaven" was originally published in *China Beat* as "Faking Heaven: The Utopian Will to Order in China," September 4, 2008. © Timothy S. Oakes. Used by permission of the author.

CHAPTER 14

"It's Not Just 8/8/08" originally appeared in a longer version in *China Beat*, April 21, 2008. © Kenneth L. Pomeranz.

"China: Democracy or Confucianism?" was originally published in a slightly different form in *China Beat*, June 3, 2008. © Xujun Eberlein. Used by permission of the author.

CHAPTER 15

"Culture and Collapse" originally appeared in a longer version in *China Beat*, May 30, 2008. © Pierre Fuller. Used by permission of the author.

"A Nation of Outlaws" originally appeared in a longer version in the *Boston Globe* (boston.com/bostonglobe), August 26, 2007. Used by permission of the author, who retained all rights to the piece. © Stephen Mihm.

"Democracy or Bust" was originally published in a slightly different form in *China Beat*, March 6, 2008. © David L. Porter. Used by permission of the author.

"Follow the Money" originally appeared as a shorter version in *China Beat* as "Why China's Dollar Pile Has to Shrink (Relatively Soon)," January 19, 2008. © Kenneth L. Pomeranz.

About the Editors

Kate Merkel-Hess is a doctoral candidate in Chinese history at the University of California, Irvine. She is the founding editor of the *China Beat* and has blogged for the *Huffington Post*. She has also written for publications such as the *Times Literary Supplement* (London), the *Nation.com*, and the *Far Eastern Economic Review*.

Kenneth L. Pomeranz is Chancellor's Professor of History at the University of California, Irvine. He has published widely on a broad range of topics in Chinese history and world history, from economic issues to the environment to popular religion. His books include, as author, *The Great Divergence: China, Europe, and the Making of the World Economy* (2000) and, as coauthor, *The World That Trade Created* (2006).

Jeffrey N. Wasserstrom is professor of history at the University of California, Irvine, where he is also editor of the *Journal of Asian Studies*. A frequent contributor to newspapers, magazines, and online journals of opinion, he is the author, most recently, of *China's Brave New World—And Other Tales for Global Times* (2007) and *Global Shanghai, 1850–2010: A History in Fragments* (2008).

Miri Kim is a graduate student at the University of California, Irvine, specializing in East Asian and world history with a focus on modern China. She is also a contributor to *China Beat* and an editorial assistant at the *Journal of Asian Studies*.

n is associate professor of history at the University of California, Irvine.
author of *Chinese San Francisco, 1850–1943: A Transpacific Community*

lizabeth Cunningham** is a graduate student in Chinese history at the
y of California, Irvine.

erlein** is an award-winning writer and author of *Apologies Forthcoming*
er blog is at http://www.insideoutchina.com.

Edgerton-Tarpley is associate professor of history at San Diego State
y. She is the author of *Tears from Iron: Cultural Responses to Famine in
h-Century China* (2008).

rbaugh** is courtesy research associate in the center for Asian and Pacific
t the University of Oregon. Her publications include "China Expands
esy: Saying 'Hello' to Strangers" (2008).

rrer** is associate professor of sociology and director of the Institute of
tive Culture at Sophia University in Tokyo. He is the author of *Opening
1 Sex Culture and Market Reform in Shanghai* (2002).

Finlay is a freelance writer based in Southeast Asia. She is a regular
or to *Global Voices* and the Cambodia-based magazine *Southeastern*

W. French, who teaches at the Columbia University Graduate School
lism, was the Shanghai bureau chief of the *New York Times* from 2003
2008. He is the author of *A Continent for the Taking*, and his photo
"Disappearing Shanghai," has been shown in solo exhibitions on three
ts.

ller** is a doctoral candidate at the University of California, Irvine.

eenspan** is a Shanghai-based independent researcher and writer who
n the rise of Asia's giants. Her publications include *India and the IT
n: Networks of Global Culture* (2005) and articles about China contrib-
he *Globalist* and *YaleGlobal*. Her work can be viewed online at http://
inggiants.net.

nser** is assistant professor of sociology at the University of British
a. She is the author of *Service Encounters: Class, Gender, and the Market
Distinction in Urban China* (2008).

About the Contributors

Pallavi Aiyar is the Beijing-based China bureau chi
of *Smoke and Mirrors: An Experience of China* (20
across China for over five years and is the only Chir
correspondent to be based in the country throughou

David Bandurski is a freelance journalist and a s
Project, a research program of the Journalism & N
University of Hong Kong.

Geremie R. Barmé is professor of Chinese history
University, Canberra. He is the editor of *China Herita*
book is *The Forbidden City* (2008).

Nicole E. Barnes is a doctoral candidate in Chinese h
California, Irvine (UCI), and a contributor to *Choice*
to UCI, she worked for the University of Colorado's P
Asia.

Daniel Beekman was a Fulbright scholar to China from
September 2008. While in Beijing, he blogged about
2008 Olympic Games for the *Seattle Times*.

Susan Brownell is professor of anthropology at the Ur
Louis, who spent the 2007–2008 academic year in Chin
She is the author of *Training the Body for China* (199
What the Olympics Mean to China (2008).

Pär K. Cassel is assistant professor of history at the Univ
is writing a book with the working title of *Rule of Law*
Pluralism and Extraterritoriality in Nineteenth-Century Ea

Leslie T. Chang lived in China for a decade as a corres
Street Journal. She is the author of *Factory Girls: From Vill*
ing China (2008).

Yong C
He is th
(2000).

Maura
Univer

Xujun
(2008)

Kathr
Unive
Ninet

Mary
Studi
Its C

Jame
Com
Up:

Car
con
Glo

Ho
of I
thr
pro
co

Pi

A
fo
R
u
w

Peter Hessler has written about China for a range of publications, including the *New Yorker* and *National Geographic*. He is the author of *River Town: Two Years on the Yangtze* (2001) and *Oracle Bones: A Journey between China's Past and Present* (2006).

Jeremiah Jenne is a doctoral candidate in Chinese history at the University of California, Davis. He is also the author of the Chinese history blog at http://www.granitestudio.org.

Paul R. Katz is a research fellow at the Institute of Modern History, Academia Sinica. A specialist in the history of Chinese religion and society, his recent publications include *When Valleys Turned Blood Red: The Ta-pa-ni Incident in Colonial Taiwan* (2005) and the forthcoming *Divine Justice—Religion and the Development of Chinese Legal Culture*.

Richard C. Kraus is professor of political science at the University of Oregon. His most recent book is *The Party and the Arty in China: The New Politics of Culture* (2003).

Haiyan Lee is assistant professor of Chinese literature at Stanford University. She is the author of *Revolution of the Heart: A Genealogy of Love in China, 1900–1950* (2007).

Donald S. Lopez Jr. is the Arthur E. Link Distinguished University Professor of Buddhist and Tibetan Studies at the University of Michigan. His books include *Prisoners of Shangri-La: Tibetan Buddhism and the West* (1998) and *In the Forest of Faded Wisdom: 104 Poems by Gendun Chopel* (2009).

David Luesink is a doctoral candidate in Chinese history at the University of British Columbia, Vancouver.

Liang Luo is assistant professor of Chinese literature and culture at the University of Kentucky. Her recent publications include "Modern Girl, Modern Men, and the Politics of Androgyny in Modern China" (2008).

Charlene Makley is associate professor of anthropology at Reed College. She is the author of *The Violence of Liberation: Gender and Tibetan Buddhist Revival in Post-Mao China* (2007).

Stephen Mihm is assistant professor of history at the University of Georgia. He is the author of *A Nation of Counterfeiters: Capitalists, Con Men, and the Making of the United States* (2008) and writes frequently for the *New York Times*, the *Boston Globe*, and other general interest periodicals.

James Miles is the Beijing bureau chief of the *Economist*. He previously worked for the BBC, the *South China Morning Post*, and United Press International, and he is the author of *The Legacy of Tiananmen: China in Disarray* (1996).

Pankaj Mishra, the author of four books of fiction and nonfiction, writes political and literary essays for the *New York Review of Books*, the *Guardian*, and the *New York Times*.

Rana Mitter is professor of the history and politics of modern China at Oxford University. He is the author, most recently, of *A Bitter Revolution* (2004) and *Modern China: A Very Short Introduction* (2008), and he broadcasts regularly on BBC radio in the United Kingdom.

Julia K. Murray is professor of art history, East Asian studies, and religious studies at the University of Wisconsin. Her publications include *Mirror of Morality: Chinese Narrative Illustration and Confucian Ideology* (2007) and *Ma Hezhi and the Illustration of the Book of Odes* (1993).

Timothy S. Oakes teaches cultural geography at the University of Colorado at Boulder. He is the author of *Tourism and Modernity in China* (1998) and coeditor of several books, including, most recently, *The Cultural Geography Reader* (2008).

Alex Pasternack is a freelance writer on environmental and cultural issues. Based in Beijing and New York, he has written for magazines such as *Time* and newspapers such as the *Christian Science Monitor* and is a regular contributor to Treehugger.com and HuffingtonPost.com.

David L. Porter is associate professor of English and comparative literature and a faculty associate of the Center for Chinese Studies at the University of Michigan. He is the author of *Ideographia: The Chinese Cipher in Early Modern Europe* (2001) and *Monstrous Beauty: Chinese Taste in Eighteenth-Century England* (forthcoming) and the developer of the Chinese-language-learning software Clavis Sinica.

Shakhar Rahav is assistant professor of Asian studies at the University of Haifa. His recent research focuses on intellectuals in Wuhan during the May Fourth era.

Benjamin Read is assistant professor of politics at the University of California, Santa Cruz. He is the editor of *Local Organizations and Urban Governance in East and Southeast Asia: Straddling State and Society* (2009).

Caroline Reeves is assistant professor of history at Emmanuel College. Her writings on late imperial and republican China have appeared in venues such as the journal *Twentieth-Century China* and the edited volume *Interactions: Transregional Perspectives on World History* (2005).

Eric Setzekorn is a graduate student at the University of California, Irvine, specializing in military history.

Angilee Shah is a journalist and blogger based in California and around Asia and the former editor of *AsiaMedia*, an online press review published at the University of California, Los Angeles. Her work has been published in *Global Voices*, *Asian Geographic*, *Asia Pacific Arts*, and *Time Out Singapore*.

Xia Shi is a graduate student in Chinese history at the University of California, Irvine.

S. A. Smith, professor of history at the University of Essex, is currently teaching at the European University Institute in Florence. He is the author, most recently, of *Revolution and the People in Russia and China: A Comparative History* (2008).

Donald S. Sutton is professor of history at Carnegie Mellon University. His recent publications include, as coeditor, *Empire at the Margins*, which was published by the University of California Press in 2006.

Paola Voci is a senior lecturer at the University of Otago in New Zealand. She has contributed articles to venues such as *Modern Chinese Literature and Culture* and *Senses of Cinema* and is writing a book whose working title is *China on Video*.

Nicolai Volland is assistant professor in the department of Chinese studies of the National University of Singapore. His publications include "Translating the Socialist State: Cultural Exchange, National Identity, and the Socialist World in the Early PRC" (2008).

Timothy B. Weston is associate professor of history at the University of Colorado. His books include *The Power of Position: Beijing University, Intellectuals, and Chinese Political Culture: 1898–1929* (2004) and *China's Transformations: The Stories beyond the Headlines*, coedited with Lionel M. Jensen (2007).

Guobin Yang is associate professor in the department of Asian and Middle Eastern cultures in Barnard College and an affiliate of the Weatherhead East Asian

Institute of Columbia University. He is the author of *The Power of the Internet in China: Citizen Activism Online* (2009).

Lijia Zhang is a freelance writer based in Beijing who reports on Chinese society for various international publications. She is the author of *"Socialism Is Great!" A Worker's Memoir of the New China* (2008).